Penguin Books

The Read-Aloud Handbook

Before retiring from the lecture circuit in 2008, Jim Trelease spent thirty years addressing parents, teachers, and librarians on the subjects of children, literature, and the challenges of multimedia to print. A graduate of the University of Massachusetts, he was an award-winning artist and writer for the *Springfield Daily News* from 1963 to 1983.

Initially self-published in 1979, *The Read-Aloud Handbook* has had seven American editions as well as British, Australian, Japanese, Chinese, Indonesian, and Spanish editions. Mr. Trelease is also the editor of two popular read-aloud anthologies for Penguin: *Hey! Listen to This*, for grades K–4, and *Read All About It!* for preteens and teens. In 2010, Penguin Books named *The Read-Aloud Handbook* one of the seventy-five most important books it published in its seventy-five-year history.

The father of two grown children, Mr. Trelease lives in Enfield, Connecticut, with his wife, Susan. Although he occasionally scolds American fathers for obsessing too much about sports, recent years have found him involved in one of professional sports' most famous moments, when it was accidentally discovered that he had the only existing recording of the 1961 basketball game in which Wilt Chamberlain scored one hundred points. Visit his Web page (www.trelease-on-reading.com/wilt.html) for the story of how he came to make the recording and how Chamberlain's life intertwined with his own.

Jim Trelease's lectures are available on both DVD and CD. For information, go to www.trelease-on-reading.com.

It works with fathers, too.

The
Read-Aloud
Handbook

SEVENTH EDITION

Jim Trelease

Penguin Books

PENGUIN BOOKS
Published by the Penguin Group
Penguin Group (USA) Inc., 375 Hudson Street,
New York, New York 10014, USA

USA | Canada | UK | Ireland | Australia | New Zealand | India | South Africa | China
Penguin Books Ltd, Registered Offices: 80 Strand, London WC2R 0RL, England
For more information about the Penguin Group visit penguin.com

The Read-Aloud Handbook first published in Penguin Books 1982
First revised edition published 1985
Second revised edition (with the title *The New Read-Aloud Handbook*) published 1989
Third revised edition published 1995
Fourth revised edition published 2001
Fifth revised edition published 2006
This sixth revised edition published 2013

Portions of this book were originally published in pamphlet form.

"Disgraceful Interrogations" by Hector Tobar, *Los Angeles Times,* May 13, 2011. Copyright © 2011.
Los Angeles Times. Reprinted with permission.

Page 351 constitutes an extension of this copyright page.

LIBRARY OF CONGRESS CATALOGING-IN-PUBLICATION DATA
Trelease, Jim.
The read-aloud handbook / Jim Trelease.—Seventh edition.
pages cm.
Includes bibliographical references and index.
ISBN 978-0-14-312160-2 (pbk.)
1. Oral reading.   I. Title.
LB1573.5.T68 2013
372.45'2—dc23   2013002348

Printed in the United States of America
10

Set in Bembo • Designed by Elke Sigal

To my grandchildren, Connor, Tyler, Kiernan, Tess, and Addisyn—
the best audiences an old reader-aloud could hope to find.

And to Alvin R. Schmidt, a ninth-grade English teacher
in New Jersey who found the time a half century ago to write to the
parents of one of his students to tell them they had a talented child.
Neither he nor the vote of confidence has ever been forgotten.

We must take care that children's early encounters with reading are painless enough so they will cheerfully return to the experience now and forever. But if it's repeatedly painful, we will end up creating a school-time reader instead of a lifetime reader.

Acknowledgments

T HIS book could not have been written without the support and co-operation of many friends, associates, neighbors, children, teachers, and editors. I especially wish to acknowledge my everlasting gratitude to the late Mary A. Dryden, of Springfield, Massachusetts, who started it all by convincing me to visit her classroom forty-five years ago in the school that is now named in her honor.

I am also deeply indebted to my former editors and colleagues at the *Springfield Daily News* for their long standing support of staff involvement with the community's schoolchildren. It was this that provided the early impetus for my experiences in the classroom. At the same time, I am particularly grateful to my dear friend Jane Maroney, whose guiding hand shaped the initial concept of this book. I never had a better, smarter, or wittier editor.

It is impossible to express adequately the gratitude I feel toward the hundreds of individuals who, over the past three decades, took the time to share with me their personal experiences with reading and children, only a fraction of which I can use in each edition. For this edition, I am especially grateful to Melissa Olans Antinoff; Jim and Kristen Brozina; Tom Corbett; Bianca Cotton and her family; Kimberly Douglas; Henry Dutcher; Ellie Fernands; Jennie Fitzkee; Nancy Foote; Linda, Jim, and Erin Hassett; Skip Johnson; Stephen Krashen; Mary Kuntsal; Larry LaPrise; Cindy Lovell; Jade Malanson; Kathy Nozzolillo; Mike Oliver; Tom O'Neill Jr.; Jennifer, Marcia, and Mark Thomas; the Trelease-Keller-Reynolds clans of Massachusetts and Mississippi; Susan, Tad, Christopher, and David Williams; and Marty and Joan Wood.

In addition, I would like to thank my neighbor Shirley Uman, whose enthusiasm for my self-published edition back in 1979 was shared with a then-fledgling literary agent, Raphael Sagalyn, who carried it home to Penguin Books; Bee Cullinan for her early encouragement; my Penguin editors, Rebecca Hunt and Kathryn Court, for their faith and support through the book's three decades; and a lovely woman named Florence of Arlington, who wrote the fateful letter that Dear Abby published in 1983 that changed the Treleases' lives forever. And finally, I thank my wife, Susan, for her patience and sustenance during the long hours required for each revised edition, especially this one, which included one tornado recovery.

There are many education bloggers out there watchdogging the schoolhouse doors and alerting the rest of us when things go wrong, but none exceed the professionalism of Valerie Strauss, of the *Washington Post's The Answer Sheet* blog, and Maureen Downey, of the *Atlanta Journal-Constitution's Get Schooled* blog. They are the gold standard of education blogging.

This is the last edition of this handbook under my authorship. Henceforth I hope it will be in different hands. There isn't room to include all the people who helped steer me in the right direction over these seven editions, but I have posted online a retirement letter with a more complete listing (including the highs and lows from thirty years of lecture travels); it can be found at www.trelease-on-reading.com/trelease-retirement-letter.html.

Contents

Introduction

The central task of education is to implant a will and facility for learning; it should produce not learned but learning people. The truly human society is a learning society, where grandparents, parents, and children are students together.

—Eric Hoffer

IN the thirty years since the first edition of this book, much has changed in the world and in American education. And so, too, this book has evolved.

Back in 1982, when the first edition appeared, there was no Internet or e-mail, no cell phones, DVD players, iTunes, iPods, iPads, Amazon, e-books, Wi-Fi, Facebook, or Twitter. The closest thing to an instant message was a facial expression that exasperated mothers gave their children as a warning. Texting was something you did on a typewriter. The first CD player was just going on sale, Starbucks was just a coffee-bean shop in Seattle, and if you said "laptop" to people they'd have thought you were talking about a TV-dinner tray.

For all of those differences, there are some things that remain the same. In 1982, the U.S. economy was in its worst recession since the Great Depression, and the nation's business leaders were looking for someone or something to blame. Sound familiar? Since SAT scores had been in a twenty-year decline (because lots of average and below-average students, and not just the rich kids, were taking the test for the first time), the corporate executives blamed education as one of the culprits for the recession and demanded reforms and accountability at all levels—a more *businesslike* approach.[1] ("If our schools were more like Japanese schools, our economy would be more like theirs!")[2] This would open the door to nearly three decades of testing mania and school reforms.

At practically the same time, the cost of college began a 400 percent rise, outpacing the increases in medical care and median family income.[3]

By 2011, student loans would be larger than either the nation's credit card debt or the auto loan industry.[4]

Which brings us to the present time. With all the new technology in place and billions of dollars in testing accomplished, we made a one-point improvement in reading scores between 1971 and 2008 (chart below).

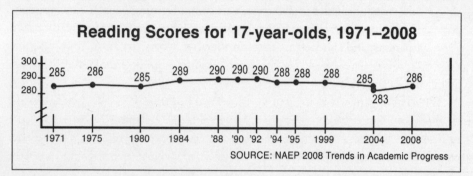

Reading scores for 17-year-olds, 1971–2008.

If you're even half-sane, you have to be asking yourself, "What in the world is wrong here?" I hope this book can answer that question, as well as what we can do about it, because surely there's a better way than what we've done in the past.

For all that is wrong in education, there are still some positives. With the hundreds of distractions imposed on American children in the past thirty years—two hundred cable channels; most children with TVs in their bedrooms (usually the lowest-scoring students); more than half of teens attached to cell phones most of the day; single parents raising one in four children; and a baby born every sixty seconds to a teen mother[5]—it's a wonder the scores actually rose by one point and didn't drop by ten or fifteen. If that is the case, then *something* must be working; this book will examine what really works. In fact, let's look now at one of those "some-things."

The Ideal (and Cheapest) Tutoring Plan

We start with the family of Susan and Tad Williams and their two sons, Christopher and David. Of the four hundred thousand students taking the ACT exam with Christopher back in 2002, only fifty-seven had perfect scores—he was the fifty-eighth. When word got out that this kid from Russell, Kentucky (population 3,645), had scored a perfect 36, the family was besieged with questions, the most common being "What prep course did he take? Kaplan? Princeton Review?" It turned out to be a course his parents enrolled him in as an infant, a free program, unlike some of the private plans that now cost up to $250 an hour.

In responding to inquiries about Christopher's prep courses, the Williamses simply told people—including the *New York Times*[6]—that he hadn't taken any, that he did no prep work. That, of course, wasn't completely true. His mother and father had been giving him and his younger brother free prep classes all through their childhoods, from infancy into adolescence: They read to them for thirty minutes a night, year after year, even after they learned how to read for themselves.

Theirs was a home brimming with books but no *TV Guide*, GameCube, or Hooked on Phonics. Even though Susan Williams was a fourth-generation teacher, she offered no home instruction in reading before the boys reached school age. She and Tad just read to them—sowed the sounds and syllables and endings and blendings of language into the love of books. Each boy easily learned to read—and loved reading, gobbling books up voraciously. Besides being a family bonding agent, reading aloud was used not as test prep as much as an "ensurance" policy—it ensured the boys would be ready for whatever came their way in school.

By 2011, David was a University of Louisville graduate working as an engineer and Christopher was pursuing his Ph.D. in biochemistry at Duke. Sometimes Christopher's early reading experiences surface even in the biochemistry department, like when he remarked to his lunch mates the day after a Duke basketball loss, "I guess there's no joy in Mudville today." None of the other grad students grasped the reference to Ernest Thayer's classic sports poem.[7]

The Williams family experience didn't surprise me at all, because I was already familiar with reading aloud as a prep course. Tom Parker recommends it all the time. He's the former admissions director for Williams College, now at Amherst College, two of the nation's prestigious small colleges. Parker tells anxious parents who ask about improving their child's SAT scores, "The best SAT preparation course in the world is to read to your children in bed when they're little. Eventually, if that's a wonderful experience for them, they'll start to read themselves."[8] Parker told me he's never met a student with high verbal SAT scores who wasn't a passionate reader, and nearly always they recall being read to. An ACT or SAT prep course can't package that passion, but parents like Susan and Tad Williams have done it and so can you. Even parents who are illiterate or semiliterate can do it—and we'll meet them later in the book, along with a father who read to his daughter, just for fun, for 3,218 nights in a row, never missing a night.

Never before in American history has so much been written about the subject of reading as in the past two decades. Never has so much money been spent to test children in any subject, and never have so many reading rules and regulations been imposed on schools by a succession of administrations—with little or no improvements to show for it.[9]

Strangely, the biggest impact seems to be on families that are the wealthiest and most educated. Where forty years ago children were spending their after-school hours at ballet classes, Scout meetings, or soccer practices, millennium moms and dads now have them enrolled in after-school tutoring. The suburban paranoia over state tests has ballooned the tutoring business into a $4 billion industry, and not just for school-age children. By 2005, Sylvan Learning was opening its 1,100 centers to four-year-olds, while Kumon was accepting two-year-olds. Where once these centers were mainly for remediation, half the enrollments now come from families looking to give their child an advantage—like the mother who told the *Wall Street Journal* she had enrolled her four-year-old because his scissors skills were not up to par. How about the parents (that's plural) who hire consultants to help their children make better eye contact and demonstrate "leadership qualities" with preschool directors while they're being considered for preschool admission?[10]

Just as they've hired life coaches for themselves, helicopter parents are hiring college counselors for their children, costing between $3,000 and $6,000. The counselors are supposed to ensure the "right" school choices are made, and that the paperwork is in order and on time.[11]

All of this provokes clinical psychologist Wendy Mogel to suggest these parents may someday be on the receiving end of a class action suit from their children "for stealing their childhoods."[12]

Not that parents are alone in their extreme behavior. They have more than enough company among school boards and high-ranking politicians who think if you "fix" the schools, you'll "fix" the kids. So, in Gadsden, Alabama, school officials eliminated kindergarten nap time in 2003 so the children would have more test-prep time.[13]

Two hours away in Atlanta, school officials figured that if you eliminate recess, the kids will study more. And just in case those shifty teachers try to sneak it in, Atlanta started building schools without playgrounds. "We are intent on improving academic performance," said the superintendent. "You don't do that by having kids hanging on the monkey bars."[14]

Several years later, when it was apparent the anti-recess strategy wasn't driving up the scores, a new Atlanta superintendent created what state investigators called "a culture of fear and a conspiracy of silence" in pursuit of higher scores. The scores rose and bonuses were awarded, but a subsequent state investigation led to the largest standardized testing scandal in America, with more than 170 educators involved in the cheating, including thirty-eight principals.[15]

The time and space for childhood play seem to be shrinking every day.

In a *New York Times* online essay about the disappearance of recess and play, David Bornstein compared today's test-oriented curriculum with Dickens's novel *Hard Times* and its aptly named schoolmaster, Thomas Gradgrind. "On average, American kids get only 26 minutes of recess per day, *including* lunchtime—and low income kids get less than that," Bornstein wrote.[16] (High-scoring Finland has fifteen minutes of recess for every forty-five-minute class, but more on Finland later.)

At the high school level, the new principal at one prestigious New England high school in Needham, Massachusetts, was so alarmed by the stress levels of his students, he formed a committee to develop coping strategies. The end result was mandatory yoga classes for seniors. He also dared to end the publication of the school's honor roll in the local newspaper and pushed to lighten the homework load. Both issues provoked parental ire and within a year he had accepted the principalship of the American School in London.[17] Nonetheless, four years later the yoga classes were still in place as part of faculty efforts to build student resiliency, homework was curtailed around holidays, and notice of honor roll achievement now comes in a letter to the parents from the principal instead of publicly via the local newspaper. Other select high schools have had to make lunch periods mandatory because so many students feel every period of the day must be filled with something that will reflect positively on their college application/résumé, and somehow lunch doesn't fit that bill.[18] Where once it was only institutions like the University of Chicago that could be tagged as places where "fun comes to die," now we can apply the label to elite high schools.

College admission officers and counselors are feeling the stress as well, but for different reasons. At Harvard, the nation's oldest university and recipient of the largest number of advanced placement students, a thirty-year veteran of the admissions office said today's students "seemed like dazed survivors of some bewildering lifelong boot camp" and warned that "unless things change, we're going to lose a lot of them." In our pursuit of higher and higher scores, he said, "the fabric of family life has just been destroyed."[19]

Surely there must be a way to raise a reader and a capable student without creating a stressed-out "dazed survivor." Of course, for every parent who is pressing children's stress buttons, there is the other extreme—the ones who think the job of education is the responsibility of teachers. These parents far outnumber the pushy ones, and they create another kind of problem. From this point on it might be helpful if I arrange the discussion according to the kinds of questions I receive from parents and educators. For example, from the parent who is the complete opposite of "helicoptering":

Are You Suggesting This Reading Stuff Is the Job of the Parent? I Thought It Was the School's Job.

This brings us to the "sponge factor," exemplified by a young lady named Bianca Cotton, whom I met in 2002 on the morning my grandson Tyler began kindergarten. Families were invited in for the first hour to help break the ice, and I was snapping some pictures of Tyler and a new friend when I became aware of an extended conversation going on behind me in the little housekeeping section of the kindergarten. Turning around, I found Bianca cooking up a make-believe meal on a make-believe stove while carrying on a make-believe conversation on a make-believe cordless phone. And, as you can see in the photo I snapped, she had all the body language down for talking on the phone and cooking at the same time.

Every child, kindergartner or otherwise, is like a sponge, soaking up the behavior of the people around them. If Bianca had never seen an adult

Bianca Cotton.

talking on the phone while cooking, she'd never have thought to grab a phone while "cooking" her first kindergarten meal.

If Bianca isn't proof enough for you, consider this: Since 1956, no newspaper, network, or news agency has a better record for predicting the outcomes in presidential elections than *Weekly Reader*, the late national classroom magazine. Every four years for a half century, a quarter million children voted in the *Weekly Reader* presidential poll, and in thirteen of the fourteen campaigns they were absolutely correct.[20] Like little sponges, they sat in their parents' living rooms, kitchens, and cars soaking up parental values, and then squeezed them out onto a *Weekly Reader* ballot.

It comes down to simple arithmetic: The child spends 900 hours a year in school and 7,800 hours outside school. Which teacher has the bigger influence? Where is more time available for change? Those two numbers—900 and 7,800—will appear over and over in this book.

Jay Mathews, the *Washington Post*'s longtime education columnist, looked back on all the student achievement stories he'd done in twenty-two years and observed: "I cannot think of a single instance in which the improvement in achievement was not tied, at least in part, to an increase in the amount of time students had to learn."[21] I've been saying the same thing for as many years. You either extend the school day (as have the successful KIPP charter schools)[22] or you tap into the 7,800 hours at home. Since the cost of lengthening the school day would be prohibitive in the places that need it most, the most realistic option is tapping the 7,800 hours at home.

Ronald F. Ferguson, a black scholar and Harvard lecturer, has long studied racial achievement gaps in public schools. Complicated as those issues are, Ferguson boils them down to one: "The real issue is historical differences in parenting. That is hard to talk about, but that is the root of the skill gap." According to Ferguson, black households traditionally see schooling as a job for teachers, while white families are more involved in schooling the child or paying for special services.[23]

Contrary to the current screed that blames teachers for just about everything wrong in schooling,[24] research shows that the seeds of reading and school success (or failure) are sown in the home, long before the child ever arrives at school. For example, twenty-one classes of kindergartners were examined to determine which children displayed either high or low interest in books.[25] Those students' home environments were then examined in detail (see the following table). The numbers reinforce the adage that the apple doesn't fall far from the tree. Therefore, if you want different apples, *change the tree.*

Kindergarten Children's Home/Behavior Inventory

Home Information	Children with High Interest in Books (%)	Children with Low Interest in Books (%)
Mother's leisure activities		
• Watches TV	39.3	63.2
• Reads	78.6	28.1
Mother reads newspapers	80.4	68.4
Mother reads novels	95.2	10.5
Father's leisure activities		
• Watches TV	35.1	48.2
• Reads	60.7	15.8
Father reads newspapers	91.1	84.2
Father reads novels	62.5	8.8
Number of books in home	80.6	31.7
Child owns library card	37.5	3.4
Child is taken to library	98.1	7.1
Child is read to daily	76.8	1.8

Based on Morrow, "Home and School Correlates of Early Interest in Literature," *Journal of Educational Research*, April 1983.

Research like this helps crystallize issues that are often politicized talk-show blather. But research can make for rather dry reading, so throughout the book I've also included the personal and anecdotal to bring the research alive.

By personal and anecdotal I mean people like Leonard Pitts Jr. and his mother. As he describes her, "She was not a learned woman, never finished high school. But then, it's hard to be learned when you grow up black in Depression-era Mississippi. Still, not being learned is not the same as not being smart." His mother "was a voracious consumer of books and newspapers, a woman filled with a thirst to know." With that in mind, picture this forty-six-year-old son, a writer, sitting down at his computer in 2004, typing the following words:

> My first reader was a welfare mother with a heart condition. She lived in a housing project near downtown Los Angeles. This is circa 1962 or '63 and technically, she wasn't my reader back then but my listener. I would follow her around as she ironed clothes or prepared a meal, reading aloud from my latest epic, which, like all my epics, was about a boy who was secretly a superhero, with super strength and the ability to fly.
>
> Surely there came a point when the poor woman secretly regretted having taught the bespectacled child his ABCs, but she never let on. Just nodded and exclaimed in all the right places and when the story was done, sent me off to clean up my room or wash my hands for dinner.[26]

Leonard Pitts Jr. was writing a thank-you note to his mother. Even though she had died sixteen years earlier, he wanted her to know how grateful he was. After all, you don't win the Pulitzer Prize for commentary just any day of the week. His thank-you note became his syndicated *Miami Herald* column for that day. Mrs. Pitts couldn't afford to spend her son's 7,800 hours driving him around to tutoring classes. Instead, she tutored him herself by listening, enthusing, and reading. She couldn't afford high-priced "eye contact" tutors, but she saved up to buy him a toy typewriter when he was eight and a used one when he was fourteen. Loose change? Just enough so her son could buy the latest Spider-Man and Fantastic Four comic books.[27]

What Mrs. Pitts and the Williamses did is one of the great trade secrets in American education. Ignoring that secret and focusing exclusively on testing is like telling people with cancer that they need to do something about their dandruff. Yet that is what government has been doing for decades with No Child Left Behind and Race to the Top.

What the Williams and Pitts families did wasn't expensive. It may not be easy for low-income families, but it's not impossible. For example, the most comprehensive study of American schoolchildren (22,000 students)[28] showed us that while children in poverty made up 52 percent of the bottom quarter when they entered kindergarten, 6 percent scored in the highest quarter—right up there with the richest children in America.

Of all students achieving advanced degrees each year, 9 percent come from poverty.[29] Those numbers demonstrate that it's not impossible for children to achieve at high or average levels if parents do the right things. But first someone must show and tell them the "right things" instead of telling them the fault lies with classroom teachers.[30]

Can We Really Change Families and Homes in America?

We did it once, why not again? Suppose we ran a national awareness campaign for what parents can, should, and must do in the home? And I don't mean a polite little campaign in which the First Lady runs around and visits child-care centers, saying, "Read to the kiddos!" I mean a real "in-your-face" crusade.

For the past fifty years, an incessant antismoking campaign has been waged in this country, a three-pronged attack that could be adopted in the battle for family literacy. In the case of tobacco, we (1) informed, (2) frightened, and (3) shamed people into changing their habits. Using all available media, we gave them statistics linking smoking to cancer and death, we offered deathbed confessions from smokers who were speaking through artificial voice boxes, and we erected billboards that insulted and shamed smokers with statements like "Kissing a smoker is like licking an ashtray."

Gradually, public opinion swayed public practice and public policy, forcing legislation and litigation that would affect most homes and every public space in America. After fifty years, fewer than 23 percent of Americans smoke, and hundreds of millions of lives and dollars have been affected or saved.

Following that model, we could change parental practices in this country—not in one year or one presidential administration, but over several decades. It would work, however, only if we followed that three-pronged attack, because different people are motivated to change for different reasons. One size does not fit all families. The campaign would give parents the statistics on children's reading that you'll find in this book (to inform). There also would be information on the damage that is done to children's and grandchildren's futures if families fail to do the right things for literacy (to scare). And finally, we'd have to shame some families into doing the right thing, as we did with smokers.

I'm not talking about public shame, but rather the private kind that comes with feeling guilty about what you're doing to your child. Didn't we do that with people who smoked in front of their children? Didn't we do it with drunk drivers? Didn't we do it with parents who didn't know where their children were at ten p.m.? Unfortunately, politicians have been reluctant to hold parents accountable because they're afraid of losing the parent vote (which is far larger than the teacher vote). It's long past time to change that kind of selfish thinking.

Here's a small example of the possibilities that exist for changing families and how little is done to reach them. For nearly three decades the federal government has harped on the need for school reform. But nobody was telling parents what *they* should be doing to help. So I tried an experiment. Taking some of the topics I've written and talked about, I condensed each one to a single-page trifold black-and-white brochure. Then I converted each one to a PDF file and uploaded them to my Web site, along with a few lines on my home page stating they could be freely downloaded and printed out for parents.[31] That was it. No advertisements, no promotions, no publishers' links. Just little brochures for nonprofit schools and libraries to give away to parents looking for help.

I was curious to see who, if anyone, would use them, so I put a note on the Web page asking users to send me a request for permission to use them—just a *request*. Over the next three years I received almost two thousand requests from schools, mostly in the United States, but also from nearly every continent. The e-mails came from large urban districts as well as little villages in the rural Southwest, from schools in the Middle East, from India, Korea, Japan, and the other day from Kazakhstan. Again and again, they said they had stumbled on the brochures by accident when they were surfing for something to help parents. Imagine what could be done if someone were *pushing* to reach parents, if someone were spending serious dollars and promoting it from the rooftops. Imagine what government could do with its reach and its millions if it thought parents and families were worth it. Imagine if we promoted parent education the way we promote the Super Bowl or *American Idol*.

Will This Book Help Me Teach My Child to Read?

This is not a book about teaching a child *how* to read; it's about teaching a child to *want* to read. There's an education adage that goes, "What we teach children to love and desire will always outweigh what we make them learn." The fact is some children learn to read sooner than others, while some learn better than others. There is a difference. For the parent who thinks that sooner is better, who has an eighteen-month-old child barking at flash cards, my response is: Sooner is *not* better. Are the dinner guests who arrive an hour early better guests than those who arrive on time?

However, I am concerned about the child who needlessly arrives late to reading and then struggles through years of pain with books. Not only will he miss out on large portions of what he needs to know in school; he'll connect reading with a pain that may stay with him for a lifetime. This book is about the things that families can do as "preventive mainte-nance" to insure against those pains. You've already read some examples, and you'll find more in the chapters ahead.

There should be no rush to have a child reading before age six or seven. That's developmentally the natural time. If a child *naturally* comes to reading sooner, fine. (See page 32 for the factors in such homes.) Finland refuses to teach children to read until age seven and it boasts the world's highest reading scores (more on this in chapter 1). This book is about raising children who fall in love with print and want to keep on reading long after they graduate; it's not about children who learn to read in order to perform for their parents or just to graduate.

How Is This Edition Different from Previous Ones?

Every time I do a revision, the text changes by about 40 percent, with new research and information, like the part about baby strollers in this edition. Does it make a difference in a child's language development which way the stroller is facing? You'll find out. And then there are the anecdotes I collected in my lecture travels, like the second-grade teacher whose stu-dents stole six hundred books from her classroom library—the very book series that some parents wanted banned from schools. I should also note that about half the people who buy this handbook are parents and the other half are teachers and librarians, along with aspiring teachers from dozens of universities. For the benefit of the students, many of the facts are docu-mented with footnotes, something one can use or ignore—your choice. But please know: The points I make are backed by research; they're not off-the-cuff remarks.

If this is your first edition, let me explain that this is really two books in one. The first half comprises the evidence in support of reading aloud and the practices that nurture lifetime readers; the second half is the "Treasury of Read-Alouds," a beginner's reference to recommended titles from pict-ure books to novels. The Treasury is intended to take the guesswork out of book choices for busy parents and teachers (many of whom were never read to in their own childhoods) who want to begin reading aloud but don't have the time to take a course in children's literature.

The subject of children's reading is broader than simply reading aloud, passionate as I am about that subject. That's why chapter 5 is devoted to sustained silent reading (SSR), reading aloud's silent partner. And just as most baseball players come from countries and states where they have more access and opportunities to play baseball, research shows that children who have access to more print (magazines, newspapers, and books) have better reading scores. That's the "print climate"; it's explored in chapter 6. And you can't address the subject of books these days without confronting new technology: Will e-books replace traditional books? Are e-gadgets (and all that texting) helping or hindering literacy? We'll even visit a school library that went all digital. And since children still spend a growing number of hours in front of television screens, chapter 8 will look at TV's impact on young brains.

How Did a Parent Instead of a Professor Come to Write This Book?

Some of my best friends are professors, and they would have done an excellent job at anything they worked on, but you'll have to ask them why they didn't write this book. Here's how *I* came to write it.

Back in the 1960s, I was a young father of two children, working as an artist and writer for the *Springfield Daily News* in Massachusetts. Each night I read to my daughter and son, unaware of any cognitive or emotional benefits that would come of it. I had no idea what it would do for their vocabulary, attention span, or interest in books. I read for one reason: because my father had read to me and it made me feel so good I never forgot it and wanted my children to taste it, too. (More on that in chapter 10.)

So there I was, reading to my children each night, when one day I found myself doing volunteer work in a classroom of sixth-graders (I'd been visiting classrooms on a weekly basis for several years, discussing my career as an artist and writer). After spending an hour with the class, I gathered my materials and prepared to leave, when I noticed a little novel on the shelf near the door. It was *The Bears' House*, by Marilyn Sachs, and it caught my eye because I'd just finished reading it to my daughter.

"Who's reading *The Bears' House*?" I asked the class. Several girls' hands went up. What followed was an unrehearsed lovefest about reading, talking with them about *The Bears' House* and other books I'd read to my children, and sharing secrets I knew about the authors. ("Did you know that when Robert McCloskey was illustrating *Make Way for Ducklings*, he had a dreadful time drawing those ducks? He finally brought six ducklings up to his apartment to get a closer look. In the end, because they kept moving around so much, do you know what he did? You may find this hard to believe, but I promise you it's true: In order to get them to hold still, he slowed them down by getting them drunk on wine!")

It was forty-five minutes before I could say good-bye. The teacher subsequently wrote to say that the children had begged and begged to go to the library to get the books I'd talked about. At the time, I wondered what it was that I had said that was so unusual. All I'd done was talk about my family's favorite books. I'd been giving these students book reports (just as Oprah would do twenty-five years later). As soon as I called it that, I realized what made it so special. It probably was the first time any of them had ever heard an adult give a book report. I'd piqued the children's interest by giving them a book "commercial." From then on, whenever I visited a classroom, I'd save some time at the end to talk about reading. I'd begin by asking, "What have you read lately? Anybody read any good books lately?"

To my dismay, I discovered they weren't reading much at all. But I slowly began to notice one difference. There were isolated classes in which the kids were reading—a lot! How is it, I puzzled, that these kids are so turned on to reading while the class across the hall (where I had visited the previous month) wasn't reading anything? Same principal, same neighborhood, same textbooks. What's up?

When I pursued it further I discovered the difference was standing in the front of the room: the teacher. In nearly every one of the turned-on classes, the teacher read to the class on a regular basis. Maybe there's something to this, more than just the feel-good stuff. In the libraries of the local teacher colleges I discovered research showing that reading aloud to children improves their reading, writing, speaking, listening—and, best of all, their attitudes about reading. There was one problem: The people who should have been reading the research weren't reading it. The teachers, supervisors, and principals didn't know it even existed.

I also found that most parents and teachers were unaware of good children's books. In the late 1970s, when I realized there was nothing generally available for parents on reading aloud, not even book lists (except those included in children's literature textbooks), I decided to compile my own—a modest self-published venture (costing me $650 for the first printing—the family vacation money for one summer). Some local bookstores took copies on consignment, and within three years the booklet had sold twenty thousand copies in thirty states and Canada. By 1982, Penguin Books had seen a copy and asked me to expand it into the first Penguin edition of the book you are reading now (seventh edition).

When adults read to children, they are also passing torches—literacy torches—from one generation to the next. In the growth of this book, we can easily see the torch metaphor. A few months after the first Penguin edition was published, someone gave a young graduate student a copy on the occasion of his becoming a new parent. He then gave a copy of it to an Arlington, Virginia, couple expecting a child and for whom he was doing part-time carpentry work. This Arlington mother, though, did more than just read it. She sent an unsolicited "book report" about it to a nationally syndicated advice columnist—a woman named Abigail Van Buren. And when her letter appeared in the "Dear Abby" column, along with Abby's response, on February 23, 1983, Penguin received orders almost overnight for 120,000 copies. Needless to say, February 23 is celebrated as Dear, Dear Abby Day in our house.[32]

How Do I Convince My Husband He Should Also Read to Our Children?

In the previous edition I had several pages in this spot that were devoted to the important role of fathers in developing boys as readers. When I wrote those pages, I thought we had a bit of a male reading problem. Not anymore. Now it's a *huge* problem, and from primary grades to college, they're asking: What's happened to the boys? As a result, this time I've devoted an entire chapter to the issue. So the strategy to get your partner involved with reading is to tell him he doesn't have to read the *whole* book—you just want him to read chapter 9 (and maybe a little of chapter 10). If those don't convince him he has to be more involved with his child's reading, his middle name is probably Clueless.

Is Reading Still Important in the Video Age?

Reading is the heart of education. The knowledge of almost every subject in school flows from reading. One must be able to read the word problem in math to understand it. If you cannot read the science or social studies chapter, how do you answer the questions at the end of the chapter?

Because reading is the lynchpin of education, one can say it's a safety belt for a long life. When RAND researchers examined all the possible causes of long life expectancy—race, gender, geography, education, marriage, diet, smoking, and even churchgoing—the biggest factor was education. Another researcher went back more than a hundred years to when states initiated compulsory education. She found that for every year of education, the individual lived an average of one and a half years longer.[33] When her research was applied to other countries, the same pattern appeared. Similarly, today's Alzheimer's researchers have found what they consider to be an immunizing effect from childhood reading and vocabulary buildup (see page 21).

All things considered, reading—not video—is the single most important social factor in American life. Here's a formula that may sound simplistic, but all its parts have been documented, and while not 100 percent universal, it holds true far more often than not.

1. The more you read, the more you know.[34]
2. The more you know, the smarter you grow.[35]
3. The smarter you grow, the longer you stay in school.[36]
4. The longer you stay in school, the more diplomas you earn and the longer you are employed—thus the more money you earn in a lifetime.[37]
5. The more diplomas you earn, the higher your children's grades are in school[38] and the longer you live.[39]

The opposite would also be true:

1. The less you read, the less you know.
2. The less you know, the sooner you drop out of school.[40]
3. The sooner you drop out, the sooner and longer you are poor[41] and the greater your chances of going to jail.[42]

The basis for that formula is firmly established, as poverty and illiteracy are related—they are the parents of desperation and imprisonment:

♦ Seventy to 82 percent of prison inmates are school dropouts.[43]
♦ Sixty percent of inmates are illiterate to semiliterate.[44]
♦ The more education, the greater likelihood of employment and less likelihood of imprisonment.[45]

Why are students failing and dropping out of school? Because they cannot read well enough to do the assigned work—which affects the entire report card. Change the reading scores and you change the graduation rate and then the prison population—which changes the social climate of America.

Considering Today's Economy and Rising Tuition Costs, Is College Worth the Money?

The economists at the Brookings Institution tackled that question and rephrased it to look like this: If you had $102,000 to spend on either a really good college education or to put into investments like stocks, bonds, gold, or housing, where would you get the best return on your dollar? Considering the average lifetime earnings of a college graduate and the investment market for the past sixty years, the long-term return would play out like the following chart.[46] Looks like an easy choice: College is double the return on anything else.

The Great Recession took its toll on everyone, but least hurt were those with the most education. Those with only a high school degree were twice as likely to be unemployed.[47]

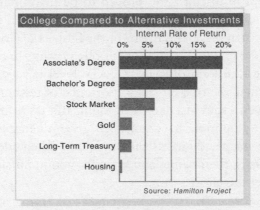

Of all investment possibilities, the single biggest return on the dollar comes from higher education.

So if college is the best investment of time and money for the student, and the best way to succeed at college is to be a proficient reader, then a parent's best financial investment is to spend the time and energy to raise a reader. If the child prefers not to attend college but is an avid reader, she will still make wiser decisions in her personal and business life, and certainly be a better-informed voter and juror—which benefits the entire community. Overall, raising readers is a win-win situation. We just have to care enough to do it.

Why Aren't National Testing and School Reform Working?

Since entire volumes have been written on the subject,[48] I'll restrict my thoughts to just a few paragraphs. The past three decades have been largely a huge money-grab by testing companies and their government pawns. If you need proof, look no further than the half-page summary of events done by *New York Times* education columnist Michael Winerip in 2011.[49] All he did was take the official statements of state education supervisors and politicians over the past decade, year by year, and compare them with the test results. City or state officials proudly would announce a new test format (created by the testing companies) that would turn the scores around. Voilà! Higher scores are announced for the new testing, followed months later by the same children's scores on national tests—oops! Scores drop. Over and again, predictions of instant cures proved to be inaccurate, deceitful, duplicitous, contradictory, and unworthy of trust. And this from one of the more progressive states—not Louisiana or the District of Columbia, but *New York*. God help the children with those public servants in charge.

Government education officials at every level have monopolized the airwaves with their rhetoric on the importance of testing, little of which was true or moved a soul to a deeper thought. But there are three singular voices that, in my opinion, have not been given due attention; each will provoke you to deeper thoughts on the issues. Their ideas are available online, so let me list their names and links for you to pursue on your own. You won't regret the effort.

1. Rick Roach is a former teacher (two master's degrees), counselor, coach, businessman, and member of the Orange County, Florida, school board since 1998. He took Florida's state-mandated tenth-grade proficiency exam himself and earned a "D" in math and reading. His conclusions about the test will give you pause.[50]

2. John Taylor is a former school superintendent in Lancaster, South Carolina, as well as a consultant to the state's department of education. In response to the national obsession with testing, he wrote an essay titled "No Dentist Left Behind," in which he likened teachers to dentists and test scores to cavities (www.trelease-on-reading.com/no-dentist.html).

3. David Root, a veteran principal at one of Ohio's "excellent" middle schools, wrote a letter of apology to his students and community at the end

of the 2008 school year. His misgivings will give you pause no matter where you stand on today's school issues (www.cleveland.com/brett/blog/index.ssf/2008/07/students_pass_state_test_but_a.html).

If we're waiting for government to save our reading souls, we've got a long wait. Ultimately it will come down to the individual student, parent, teacher, and librarian. So let's go visit them and see what they can do to help.

The
Read-Aloud
Handbook

Chapter 1

Why Read Aloud?

Education is not the filling of a bucket but the lighting of a fire.
—William Butler Yeats

ONE day back in the 1980s I visited the kindergarten room I had attended years earlier as a child at Connecticut Farms Elementary School, in Union, New Jersey. Gazing up at me were the faces of about fifteen children, each of them seated expectantly on their story rug. "How many of you want to learn to read this year?" I asked. Without a second's hesitation, every hand shot into the air, many accompanied by boasts like "I already know how!" Their excitement matched what every kindergarten teacher has told me: Every child begins school wanting to learn to read. In other words, we've got 100 percent enthusiasm and desire when they start school—the first chapter in their life.

In subsequent years, when the National Reading Report Card[1] surveyed students, they found very different attitudes and behavior as the students aged:

- Among fourth-graders, only 54 percent read something for pleasure every day.
- Among eighth-graders, only 30 percent read for pleasure daily.
- By twelfth grade, only 19 percent read anything for pleasure daily.
- The Kaiser Family Foundation's 2010 longitudinal study of children 8 to 18 years of age found 53 percent read no books in a given day, 65 percent read no magazines, and 77 percent no newspapers.[2]
- In a Bureau of Labor Statistics survey in 2010, young adults between ages 15 and 19 (the largest concentration of high school and college

students) reported spending only 12 minutes a day reading versus 2.23 hours watching television.[3]

Think about it: We have 100 percent interest in kindergarten but lose three-quarters of our potential lifetime readers by the time they're eighteen. Any business that kept losing that much of its customer base would be out of business. Admittedly there is a natural falloff during adolescence and early adulthood—these are the busiest social and emotional times of human life. But what if the early interest never returns? If schooling's objective is to create lifetime readers who continue to read and educate themselves after they graduate and then they fail to do so, that's a major indictment of the process.

Let's see how the childhood figures are reflected in adulthood these days. The National Endowment for the Arts surveyed adult reading habits for twenty-five years, and its most recent report coincided perfectly with the National Assessment of Educational Progress (NAEP) of pleasure reading among thirteen- and seventeen-year-olds. The number of adults who read literature was down 22 percent from its 1982 survey, in every age, gender, ethnic, and educational category. By 2002, only 46.7 percent had read any fiction in the previous year.[4] When expanded in a different survey to include newspapers or any kind of book or magazine, the figure rose to only 50 percent of adults.[5] In short, half of America is aliterate.

As I showed in the Introduction, reading scores improved by only one point for seventeen-year-olds and five points for thirteen-year-olds between 1971 and 2008.[6] That's thirty-seven years—half of it devoted to national and state curriculum reform. Couple those figures with mobile-multimedia usage soaring to more than seven and a half hours a day for students ages eight to eighteen, and one can see a perfect storm on the horizon, threatening to hinder reading even further,

But Aren't Kids Reading When They're Checking Facebook, Checking Tweets, or Online?

There is a school of thought that finds some hope in that theory.[7] I don't attend that school. Text messages are as close to reading as refrigerator magnets are—except the magnet messages are usually spelled better and have longer sentences. At last count, American teens are racking up 3,339 text messages a month (and rising), or six per waking hour.[8] If they're only absorbing 130 to 160 characters at a time, there's little opportunity to improve reading or thinking skills. Since most of the subject matter is gossip, clothes, music, and entertainment, there is not a lot of deep thinking taking place either, especially if your responses are "instant." As for online reading, studies indicate only 18 percent of a Web page is actually read by the visitor, with the average page view lasting ten seconds or less.[9] (More on this in chapter 7.)

It has always been true that a certain percent of students get through school without reading an entire book—in the old days and today. Now teachers worry the numbers are rising, including at the college level. The one refrain I hear from professors (including those teaching future teachers) is this: Only 25 to 30 percent of my students are avid readers, few have voluntarily read a novel in the past year, and they can't name a favorite author or a favorite childhood book.

One teacher at a top preparatory school explained how students pull it off: "They read the key parts of the text, or they go online, or they ask the kids who do the reading to tell them what happens, or they sit in class and listen to their teacher tell them what the reading is about and feed off that."[10] Having no affection for reading, they slip through the class by "gaming the system." Why no affection for reading? It was either never planted or driven out by seat work and test prep, leaving no room for a pleasure connection.

None of this means we're a nation of illiterates. We are not. The average American student can read. In fact, 60 percent of today's young people attempt advanced education, compared with 20 percent in 1940. In other words, they're "getting by."

It's when they haven't read much and then enroll in college classes that the void is exposed. Seventy-four percent of community college students never achieve a diploma and 43 percent of students of four-year public colleges never graduate.[11] Woody Allen may have been right when he said, "Showing up is eighty percent of life," but that doesn't include college diplomas. Those usually require more than just "showing up."

Why the diploma failure? Three-quarters of the incoming freshmen at New York State community colleges need remedial help in reading, writing, and/or math, putting a $33 million strain on the state's education budget.[12] Most of these are high school graduates. More important, these are students from working-class homes or lower, often among the first members of their families attempting college. Worth noting is that students who experience the least success in classrooms at any level usually come from homes and schools with the worst print climate—the fewest books, magazines, newspapers, etc.[13] It's difficult to get good at reading or even read much if there's nothing there to read. (More on this in chapter 6.)

So How Do We Fix the Reading Problem?

We start by looking at the recommendation of the 1983 Commission on Reading, funded by the U.S. Department of Education, which was alarmed by school scores. Since nearly everything in the curriculum rested upon reading, the consensus was that reading was at the heart of either the problem or the solution.

The commission spent two years poring through thousands of research projects conducted in the previous quarter century, and in 1985 issued its report, *Becoming a Nation of Readers*. Among its primary findings, two simple declarations rang loud and clear:

* "The single most important activity for building the knowledge required for eventual success in reading is reading aloud to children."[14]
* "It is a practice that should continue throughout the grades."[15] The commission found conclusive evidence to support reading aloud not only in the home but also in the classroom.

In their wording—"the single most important activity"—the experts were saying reading aloud was more important than work sheets, homework, book reports, and flash cards. One of the cheapest, simplest, and oldest tools of teaching was being promoted as a better tool than anything else in the home or classroom—and it's so simple you don't even need a high school diploma in order to do it.

And how exactly does a person become proficient at reading? It's a simple, two-part formula:

* The more you read, the better you get at it; the better you get at it, the more you like it; and the more you like it, the more you do it.
* The more you read, the more you know; and the more you know, the smarter you grow.[16]

The vast majority of students know how to read by fourth grade. In fact, by eighth grade, 24 percent are below basic level, 42 percent are at basic level, 25 percent are at proficient level, and only 3 percent are at advanced level.[17] To improve from basic to proficient and then advanced, one must practice by reading a lot. This is identical to riding a bicycle. The more you ride it, fall off, climb back on, and ride some more, the better you get at it. You learn to lean left when turning left, where to place your feet when coming to a stop, etc. This practice amounts to what Margaret Meek called "private lessons."[18]

Fourth grade is where they separate the strugglers from the readers.

The beginning of students' negative attitude toward reading appears to begin in fourth grade, when they must take the individual skills they have learned in the three previous years and apply them to whole paragraphs and pages. This juncture is famously called the Fourth Grade Slump, a phrase coined from the research of the late Jeanne Chall.[19] It's where school separates the readers from the strugglers and remedials.

But—and this is a very loud *but*—if the way they have learned or been exposed to basic reading skills is so boring and joyless they hate it, they will never read outside their classroom. Since the bulk of their time (7,800 hours a year) is spent outside school, these hours dictate whether they read often enough to become proficient or begin to fall behind. No reading outside school, low scores inside school.

Reading to these students, preferably from infancy but certainly as they got older, in school and out of school, is what the Commission on Reading was begging the nation to do—to sow the seeds of reading desire.

How Can Something as Simple as Reading to a Child Be So Effective?

As lumber is the primary support for building a house, words are the primary structure for learning. There are really only two efficient ways to get words into a person's brain: either by seeing them or by hearing them. Since it will be years before an infant uses his or her eyes for actual reading, the best source for vocabulary and brain building becomes the ear. What we send into that ear becomes the foundation for the child's "brain house."

Those meaningful sounds in the ear now will help the child make sense of the words coming in through the eye later when learning to read.

We read to children for all the same reasons we talk with children: to reassure, to entertain, to bond, to inform or explain, to arouse curiosity, and to inspire. But in reading aloud, we also:

+ build vocabulary
+ condition the child's brain to associate reading with pleasure
+ create background knowledge
+ provide a reading role model
+ plant the desire to read

One factor hidden in the decline of students' recreational reading is that it coincides with a decline in the amount of time adults read to them. By middle school, almost no one is reading aloud to students. If each read-aloud is a commercial for the pleasures of reading, then a decline in advertising would naturally be reflected in a decline in students' recreational reading.

There are two basic "reading facts of life" that are ignored in most education circles, yet without these two principles working in tandem, little else will work.

Reading Fact No. 1: Human beings are pleasure centered.
Reading Fact No. 2: Reading is an accrued skill.

Let's examine Fact No. 1. Human beings will voluntarily do over and over that which brings them pleasure. That is, we continually go to the restaurants we like, order the foods we like, listen to the radio stations that play the music we like, and visit the neighbors we like. Conversely, we avoid the foods, music, and neighbors we dislike. Far from being a theory, this is a physiological fact: We approach what causes pleasure, and we withdraw from what causes displeasure or pain.[20]

When we read to a child, we're sending a pleasure message to the child's brain. You could even call it a commercial, conditioning the child to associate books and print with pleasure. There are, however, displeasures associated with reading and school. The learning experience can be tedious or boring, threatening, and often without meaning—endless hours of work sheets, intensive phonics instruction, and unconnected test questions. If a child seldom experiences the pleasures of reading but increasingly meets its displeasures, then the natural reaction will be withdrawal.

And that brings us to Reading Fact No. 2. Reading is like riding a bicycle, driving a car, or sewing: In order to get better at it you must do it. And the more you read, the better you get at it. The past thirty years of reading research[21] confirms this simple formula, regardless of gender, race, nationality, or socioeconomic background. Students who read the most also read the best, achieve the most, and stay in school the longest. Conversely, those who don't read much cannot get better at it. Why don't students read more? Because of Reading Fact No. 1. The large number of displeasure messages they received throughout their school years coupled with the lack of pleasure messages in the home nullify any attraction books might have. They avoid print the same way a cat avoids a hot stovetop. There is ample proof for all these hypotheses in my answer to the next question.

Which Country Has the Best Readers?

One of the most comprehensive international reading studies was conducted by Warwick Elley for the International Association for the Evaluation of Educational Achievement (IEA) in 1990 and 1991. Involving thirty-two countries, it assessed 210,000 nine- and fourteen-year-olds.[22] Of all those children, which ones read best?

For nine-year-olds, the four top nations were: Finland (569), the United States (547), Sweden (539), and France (531). But the U.S. position dropped to a tie for eighth when fourteen-year-olds were evaluated.

This demonstrates that American children begin reading at a level that is among the best in the world, but since reading is an accrued skill and U.S. children appear to do less of it as they grow older, their scores decline when compared with countries where children read more as they mature. We also have a higher proportion of children in poverty, and their scores decline as they go through school (see page 88).[23] And while the racial gaps in education have narrowed in recent years, the achievement gap between rich and poor students has widened by an alarming 40 percent since the 1960s.[24] When Sarah Ransdell, a professor at Nova Southeastern, a Florida research university, studied the reading comprehension of 270,000 students at 259 schools in Broward County, Florida, she found poverty was the single largest common denominator among children who failed at reading.[25] As you will see, these are children who are spoken to the least, who are seldom read to, who see the least print in school or at home, and who therefore struggle the most with reading.

Do Finnish Children Start Reading Classes Sooner?

Just the opposite. Finland's high scores should give pause to those who think an earlier reading start ("hothousing") will produce better results. They're really not into Baby Einstein toys over there. There was only three months' difference in age between the first-place Finnish children and second-place American students, yet the Finnish children—who are introduced to formal reading instruction at age seven, two years later than American children—still managed to surpass them by age nine. Indeed, almost everything Finland does contradicts what some experts in America advocate: Most mothers work outside the home; most children are in child care by age one; school begins at age seven and then only for half days; children remain in the same school from age seven to age sixteen; there are no gifted programs; class size often reaches thirty; there are fifteen minutes of recess for every forty-five-minute class (Finnish students spend less time in class than any other developed nation); there is no national curriculum and no standardized testing until age sixteen; all meals are free, as is university education; and there is a high family literacy rate, with reading to children emphasized heavily and supported by a powerful public library system.[26]

Finally, Finnish families are heavy users of a mechanical device that serves as a reading tutor for their children. More on that in chapter 8. In the twenty years since Elley's study, the Finns have remained atop the international scoreboard for reading, math, and science as measured by the Organisation for Economic Co-operation and Development (OECD) every three years.[27] It's worth noting that one school system in the U.S. comes the closest to mimicking the Finnish environment for teacher assessments, student demographics, and testing regulations: U.S. military base schools—exempt from mandated testing and handily outscoring their public school counterparts who are awash in test mania.[28]

What Do the Best Readers Have in Common?

In Elley's study,[29] two of the factors that produced higher achievement (two others will be found later, in chapter 6) are:

* The frequency of teachers reading aloud to students.
* The frequency of sustained silent reading (SSR), or pleasure reading, in school. Children who had daily SSR scored much higher than those who had it only once a week.

Those two factors also represent the two reading facts we've just examined. Reading aloud is the catalyst for the child wanting to read on his own, but it also provides a foundation by nurturing the child's listening comprehension. In an international study of 150,000 fourth-graders, researchers found that students who were read to "often" at home scored thirty points higher than students who were read to "sometimes."[30] It stands to reason that the more often a child is read to, the more words are heard (bringing the child closer to comprehending more), and the more likely it is the child will associate reading with a daily pleasure experience.

Where Does Phonics Fit into All This?

There's more than enough research to validate the importance of phonics in children's reading. Children who understand the mechanics of reading—who know that words are made up of sounds and can break the sound code—have a great advantage, as the following chart demonstrates. The U.S. Department of Education's 1999 Early Childhood Longitudinal Study found that children who were read to at least three times a week had a significantly greater phonemic awareness when they entered kindergarten than did children who were read to less often, and that they were almost twice as likely to score in the top 25 percent in reading.[31]

Similarly, the higher the family's income (socioeconomic status, or SES), the more often the child was read to and the higher the child's literacy skills entering kindergarten.[32]

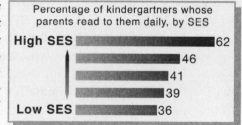

Percentage of kindergartners whose parents read to them daily, by SES

High SES 62
46
41
39
Low SES 36

Source: Based on Richard J. Coley, *An Uneven Start: Indicators of Inequality in School Readiness (Princeton, NJ: Policy Information Center, ETS, 2002).*

What phonics cannot do is motivate. Nobody has a favorite vowel or blend. Phonics is like teaching a boy how to wash his neck, an important skill for a growing boy. But teaching him how to scrub is no guarantee he'll have a clean neck, even if he knows how. The missing ingredient is motivation. If he knows how but doesn't want to wash his neck, it's going to stay dirty. But when that boy meets the right girl, he'll be motivated enough to have a clean neck. You need the combination of know-how and motivation.

If you ask doctors, coaches, even probation officers about the importance of motivation for the people they're dealing with, they all will tell you it's crucial. In a national survey of reading teachers on which education topic most interested them, motivation topped the list.[33] Nonetheless, little actual class time is spent in pursuit of motivation, unless you think test prep is motivating.

What motivates children and adults to read more is that (1) they like the experience, (2) they like the subject matter, and (3) they like and follow the lead of people who read a lot.

Is There Any Read-Aloud Proof in Research?

So many read-aloud claims had accumulated in a thirty-year period that researchers subjected thirty-three of them to a meta-analysis to see if the concept lived up to those claims.[34] Looking at the impact of frequent household reading on preschoolers, the analysis showed clear positive gains for phonemic awareness, language growth, and beginning reading skills. In addition, there was just as much of an impact for children of a lower socioeconomic status as there was for children with a higher SES, and the earlier or younger the reading began, the better the results. Research shows that even when children reach primary grades, repeated picture book reading of the same book (at least three times) increases vocabulary acquisition by 15 to 40 percent, and the learning is relatively permanent.[35] The international assessment of 150,000 fourth-graders in 2001 showed an average thirty-five-point advantage for students who were read to more often by parents.[36]

The OECD is a fifty-year-old cooperative among industrial nations aimed at helping member nations work through the modern growth challenges, including education. For more than a decade the organization has been testing hundreds of thousands of fifteen-year-olds in various school subjects and comparing scores among nations. Since 2006, the OECD has interviewed the parents of five thousand students who were part of the test-taking corps, asking them if they ever read to their children when they were in first grade and how often the reading took place. The responses, when compared with those children's reading scores on the Programme for International Student Assessment (PISA) exam, showed a powerful correlation: The more they were read to, the higher the scores at age fifteen, sometimes an advantage of as much as a half year's schooling. And the results were true regardless of family income.[37]

A few years after I'd lectured in a Northern California community, one of its residents sent me a copy of a letter to the editor in the local paper. Prompting the letter was an article about a fifth-grade teacher who had been named teacher of the year, including a quote from another teacher who marveled at the honoree's ability with voices as he read to his students. That apparently outraged a father in the district, who wrote, "I also am disturbed by his apparent taking of class time to read aloud to his students, capturing 'the voices of the characters and the attention of the students.' When did our schools become baby-sitting centers with story time? By the time my daughter is in the fifth grade, I hope she is able to read to herself. If [he] wants to re-create characters, he should join a local theater group."

Far from being "babysitting," reading aloud has a rich intellectual history. More than two thousand years ago Hebrew fathers were urged by the Talmud to take their children upon their laps and read to them. One thousand years later, in that manual of Christian monastic life called the *Rule of Saint Benedict*, chapter 38 specifies that meals be taken in silence, except for the spoken word of the monk designated to read aloud to the diners. Does anyone think this was "babysitting" the monks, the people who kept the lights on through the Dark Ages? I would also note that reading aloud "at table" is still practiced at least once a day among the Benedictines—sometimes spiritual readings, other times secular, but never textbooks. In one monk's words to me, "We have a fifteen-hundred-year-old love affair with books and manuscripts." As of this writing, the monks at Saint John's Abbey in Collegeville, Minnesota, are listening to *Marcel Breuer and a Committee of Twelve Plan a Church: A Monastic Memoir*, by Fr. Hilary Thimmesh. (The church in question is Saint John's very own, an edifice so magnificent the architect I. M. Pei once said it would be world famous if it were located in New York City.)[38]

Then there is the history of the reader-aloud in the labor force. One could even argue that this foreshadowed audiobooks. When the cigar industry blossomed in the mid-1800s, supposedly the best tobacco came from Cuba (though much of the industry later moved to the Tampa, Florida, area). These cigars were hand-rolled by workers who became artisans in the delicate craft, producing hundreds of perfectly rolled specimens daily. Artistic as it might have been, it was still repetitious labor done in stifling factories. To break the monotony, workers hit upon the idea of having someone read aloud to them while they worked, known in the trade as *la lectura*.

The reader (of which there were hundreds in the Tampa area alone) usually sat on an elevated platform or podium in the middle of the room

From his elevated platform, the reader-aloud informed and entertained cigar makers in Cuba and the United States.

Source. Cigar makers used with permission of Tampa-Hillsborough County Public Library System.

and read aloud for four hours, covering newspapers, classics, and even Shakespeare. (Somehow none of that sounds like babysitting to me.)

As labor became more organized in the United States, the readings kept workers informed of progressive ideas throughout the world as well as entertained. When factory owners realized the enlightening impact of the readings, they tried to stop them but met stiff resistance from the workers, each of whom was paying the readers as much as twenty-five cents per week out of pocket.

The daily readings added to the workers' intellect and general awareness while civilizing the atmosphere of the workplace. By the 1930s, however, with cigar sales slumping due to the Great Depression and unions growing restive with mechanization on the horizon, the owners declared that the reader-aloud had to go.[39] Protest strikes followed but to no avail, and eventually readers were replaced by the radio. But not in Cuba.

The Cuban novelist Miguel Barnet reports, "Today, all over Cuba, this tradition is alive and well. Readers are in all the factories, from Santiago to Havana to Pinar del Río. The readings have specific timetables and generally begin with the headlines of the day's newspapers. After reading the newspaper, the readers take a break and then begin reading the unfinished book from the day before. Most are women." Unlike the factories of yore, today's Cuban factory settings include modern lighting, air-conditioning, and microphones with amplifying systems. (Considerably better conditions than many contemporary American urban classrooms, I might add.)[40]

Considering the stifling boredom in the American classroom and the fact that many high schools look like factories, schools seem to me to be the perfect setting for reading aloud à la Cuba, especially when you couple the history of reading aloud with the academic benefits noted here. As for babysitting, any babysitter who could accomplish all of that would be a bargain.

You Mentioned "Background Knowledge"—What Is It?

The easiest way to understand background knowledge is to read the following two paragraphs and see if there is a difference in your understanding of each.

1. But Sabathia, who pitched three days earlier in Game 3, gave up a leadoff broken-bat double to Austin Jackson. He struck out the next two batters, then walked Miguel Cabrera intentionally with first base open.

2. Kallis and Rhodes put on 84 but, with the ball turning, Mark Waugh could not hit with impunity and his eight overs cost only 37. The runs still had to be scored at more than seven an over, with McGrath still to return and Warne having two overs left, when Rhodes pulled Reiffel to Beven at deep square leg.

You probably had an easier time grasping the first paragraph, a newspaper account of a baseball game in 2011. The second paragraph came from a newspaper story on the World Cricket Championship in 1999. Any confusion was because the less you know about a subject or the vocabulary associated with that subject, the slower you must read, the more difficult comprehension becomes, and the less you understand.[41] "Sounding out" the cricket paragraph phonetically wouldn't have helped much, would it?

Museum visits and travel help children acquire background knowledge that they will eventually need to understand what they are reading.

Background knowledge is one reason children who read the most bring the largest amount of information to the learning table and thus understand more of what the teacher or the textbook is teaching. Children whose families take them to museums and zoos, who visit historic sites, who travel abroad, or who camp in remote areas accumulate huge chunks of background knowledge without even studying. For the impoverished child lacking the travel portfolio of affluence, the best way to accumulate background knowledge is by either reading or being read to. (Yes, educational TV can help, but most at-risk children are not exposed to it often enough.)

The background knowledge of at-risk students took a further hit with No Child Left Behind, when 71 percent of districts narrowed their curriculum to math and reading, curtailing subjects like art, music, science, and languages.[42]

The lack of background knowledge surfaces very early in a child's school life. In the longitudinal kindergarten study, researchers found that more than 50 percent of children coming from the lowest education and income levels finished in the bottom quartile in background knowledge.[43] So once again poverty rears its ugly head as an obstacle to learning.

What Are the Skills a Child Needs for Kindergarten?

Let me make an analogy here. Inside a child's brain there is a huge reservoir called the Listening Vocabulary. You could say it's the child's very own Lake Pontchartrain, the famous estuary outside New Orleans that overflowed because of all the water brought by Hurricane Katrina. That extra water breached the levees and tragically flooded New Orleans. We want the same thing to happen but not in a tragic way—this time the levees will be breached inside the child's brain.

The first levee would be the Speaking Vocabulary. You pour enough words into the child's Listening Vocabulary and it will overflow and fill the Speaking Vocabulary pool—thus the child starts speaking the words he's heard. It's highly unlikely you'll ever say a word if you've never heard the word. More than a billion people speak Chinese—so why not the rest of us? Because we haven't heard enough Chinese words, especially in our childhoods. The next levee is the Reading Vocabulary.

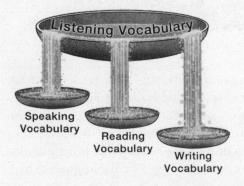

It's nearly impossible to understand a word in print if you've never said the word. And finally there's the Writing Vocabulary. If you've never said the word or read the word, how in the world will you be able to write it? All the language arts flow from the Listening Vocabulary—and that has to be filled by someone besides the child. Simple.

As you read to a child, you're pouring into the child's ears (and brain) all the sounds, syllables, endings, and blendings that will make up the words she will someday be asked to read and understand. And through stories you are filling in the background knowledge necessary to understand things that aren't in her neighborhood—like war or whales or locomotives.

The one prekindergarten skill that matters above all others, because it is the prime predictor of school success or failure, is the child's vocabulary upon entering school. Yes, the child goes to school to learn new words, but the words he already knows determine how much of what the teacher says will be understood. And since most instruction for the first four years of school is oral, the child who has the largest vocabulary will understand the most, while the child with the smallest vocabulary will grasp the least.

Once reading begins, personal vocabulary feeds (or frustrates) comprehension, since school grows increasingly complicated with each grade. That's why school-entry vocabulary tests predict so accurately.

How Is It That Some Kids Get a Head Start on Vocabulary?

Conversation is the prime garden in which vocabulary grows, but conversations vary greatly from home to home. The eye-opening findings of Drs. Betty Hart and Todd Risley at the University of Kansas, from their research on children's early lives, demonstrate the impact of this fact.

Published as *Meaningful Differences in the Everyday Experience of Young American Children*,[44] the research began in response to what Hart and Risley saw among the four-year-olds in the university lab school. With many children, the lines were already drawn: Some were far advanced and some far behind. When the children in the study were tested at age three and then again at nine, the differences held. What caused the differences so early? The researchers began by identifying forty-two normal families representing three socioeconomic groups: welfare, working class, and professional. Beginning when the children were seven months old, researchers visited the homes for one hour a month and continued their visits for two and a half years. During each visit, the researcher tape-recorded and transcribed by hand any conversations and actions taking place in front of the child.

Through 1,300 hours of visits, they accumulated 23 million bytes of information for the project database, categorizing every word (noun, verb, adjective, etc.) uttered in front of the child. The project held some surprises: Regardless of socioeconomic level, all forty-two families said and did the same things with their children. In other words, the basic instincts of good parenting are there for most people, rich or poor.

Then the researchers received the data printout and saw the "meaningful differences" among the forty-two families. When the daily number of words for each group of children is projected across four years, the four-year-old child from the professional family will have heard 45 million words, the working-class child 26 million, and the welfare child only 13 million. All three children will show up for kindergarten on the same day, but one will have heard 32 million fewer words. If legislators expect the teacher to get this child caught up, she'll have to speak ten words a second for nine hundred hours to reach the 32 million mark by year's end. I hope they have life support ready for her.

Those forty-two children would perform differently in class because their word totals created different brains. By the time the study group reached age three, the professionals' children had 1,100-word vocabularies to the welfare children's 525. Similarly, their IQs were 117 versus 79 by the time the study finished.

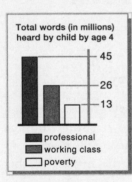

Total words (in millions) heard by child by age 4

- 45
- 26
- 13

■ professional
■ working class
☐ poverty

Source: Hart and Risley, *Meaningful Differences.*

Brain differences have nothing to do with how much parents love their children. They all love their children and want the best for them, but some parents have a better idea of what needs to be said and done to reach that "best." They know the child needs to hear words repeatedly in meaningful sentences and questions, and they know that plunking a two-year-old down in front of a television set for three hours at a time is more harmful than meaningful. Sociologists George Farkas and Kurt Beron studied the research on 6,800 children from ages three to twelve, and found that children from the lower SES were far more likely to arrive at school with smaller vocabularies (twelve to fourteen months behind), and they seldom made up the loss as they grew older.[45] (See the summer-loss chart on page 89.)

The message in this kind of research is unambiguous: It's not the toys in the house that make the difference in children's lives; it's the words in their heads. The least expensive thing we can give a child outside of a hug turns out to be the most valuable: words. You don't need a job, a checking account, or even a high school diploma to talk with a child. If I could select any piece of research that all parents would be exposed to, *Meaningful Differences* would be the one. And that's feasible. The authors took their 268-page book and condensed it into a six-page article for *American*

Educator, the journal of the American Federation of Teachers, which may be freely reproduced by schools.[46]

There is one inexpensive, commonsense move that parents could make that would impact their children's language skills (and maybe their emotional development as well), yet it goes largely unpublicized here in the U.S. First, consider how badly it would affect a conversation with someone if she wouldn't look at you while you were talking to her. Most conversations would slow to a crawl. Let's apply that principle of human behavior to children in strollers. Until the 1960s, nearly all strollers were engineered so the child was facing the parent. Now it's either way, but far more often facing away. Does it make a difference? Researchers found it makes a huge difference in how much conversation takes place between parent and child—twice as much when the child faces the parent. It was even more frequent when the child walked with or was carried by the parent.[47] Of

If the stroller were facing toward the parent, twice as much conversation (and learning) would be taking place. Maybe twice as much fun, too.

course, it's not going to help that much if the child is facing the parent and the parent is on the cell phone all the time.

Where Is the Better Vocabulary: Conversation or Reading?

Most conversation is plain and simple, whether it's between two adults or with children. It consists of the five thousand words we use all the time, called the Basic Lexicon. (Indeed, 83 percent of the words in normal conversation with a child come from the most commonly used thousand words, and it doesn't change much as the child ages.)[48] Then there are another five thousand words we use in conversation less often. Together,

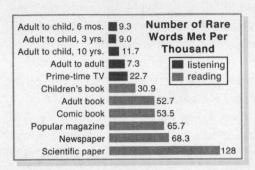

Regular family conversation takes care of basic vocabulary, but when you read to the child, you leap into the rare words that help most when it's time for school and formal learning. Simultaneously, you're familiarizing the child with print in a manner that brings him or her pleasure.

Source: Hayes and Ahrens, *Journal of Child Language.*

these ten thousand words are called the Common Lexicon. Beyond that ten thousand mark are the "rare words," and these play a critical role in reading as we grow older. The eventual strength of our vocabulary is determined not by the ten thousand common words but by how many rare words we understand.

If we don't use these rare words very often in conversation, where do we find them? The preceding chart shows that printed text contains the most rare words. Whereas an adult uses only nine rare words per thousand when talking with a three-year-old, there are three times as many in a children's book and more than seven times as many in a newspaper. As you can see from the chart, oral communication (including a TV script) is decidedly inferior to print for building vocabulary. As shown by the data for printed material, the number of rare words increases significantly. This poses serious problems for at-risk children who hear fewer words and encounter print less often at home. Such children face a gigantic word gap that impedes reading progress throughout school. And that gap can't possibly be breached in 120 hours of summer school[49] or through more phonics instruction.

How Can I Give My Kid Words If I Don't Have Them?

This is a question I've heard from parents who have learning disabilities or for whom English is a second language. While there are few easy answers in parenting, this one is easier than most. There is a public agency that comes to the rescue in such instances; in fact, it's been doing this job for more than a century. What the agency does is take all the nouns, verbs, and adjectives a person would ever need and bundle them into little packages for anyone to borrow—free. It asks only that you bring the packages back in a few weeks. I'm referring to the American free public library—the "people's university." And for those who can't read the words, they are now available on audiocassette and CD. Forty years ago you had to be blind to get a recorded book in America; now anyone can. More on this subject in chapter 8.

Has Anyone Ever Applied Reading Aloud and SSR to an At-Risk School?

Just as parents in low-income situations need to be reminded that their task is not insurmountable, so, too, do educators who work with children coming from those homes. Reading achievement and pleasure do not have to be mutually exclusive. During his ten years as principal of Boston's Solomon Lewenberg Middle School, Thomas P. O'Neill Jr. and his faculty proved it. The pride of Boston's junior high schools during the 1950s and early 1960s, Lewenberg subsequently suffered the ravages of urban decay, and by 1984, with the lowest academic record and Boston teachers calling it the "loony bin" instead of Lewenberg, the school was earmarked for closing. But first, Boston officials would give it one last chance.

The reins were handed to O'Neill, an upbeat, first-year principal and former high school English teacher whose experience there had taught him to "sell" the pleasures and importance of reading.

The first thing he did was abolish the school's intercom system. ("As a teacher I'd always sworn someday I'd rip the thing off the wall. Now I could do it legally.") He then set about establishing structure, routine, and discipline. "That's the easy part. What happens after is the important part—reading. It's the key element in the curriculum. IBM can teach our graduates to work the machine, but we have to teach them to read the manual." In O'Neill's first year, sustained silent reading (see chapter 5) was instituted for the nearly four hundred pupils and faculty for the last ten minutes of the day, during which everyone in the school read for pleasure. Each teacher (and administrator) was assigned a room—much to the consternation of some who felt those last ten minutes could be better used to clean up the shop or gym. "Prove to me on paper," O'Neill challenged them, "that you are busier than I am, and I'll give you the ten minutes to clean." He had no takers.

Within a year, critics became supporters and the school was relishing the quiet time that ended the day. The books that had been started during SSR were often still being read by students filing out to buses—in stark contrast to former dismissal scenes that bordered on chaos.

The next challenge was to ensure that each sixth-, seventh-, and eighth-grade student not only saw an adult reading each day but also heard one. Faculty members were assigned a classroom and the school day began with ten minutes of reading aloud, to complement the silent ending at the end of the day. Soon reading aloud began to inspire awareness, and new titles sprouted during SSR. In effect, the faculty was doing what the great art schools have always done: providing life models from which to draw.

In the first year, Lewenberg's scores were up; in the second year, not only did the scores climb but so, too, did student enrollment in response to the school's new reputation.

Three years later, in 1988, Lewenberg's 570 students had the highest reading scores in the city of Boston, there was a fifteen-page waiting list of children who wanted to attend, and O'Neill was portrayed by *Time* as a viable alternative to physical force in its cover story on Joe Clark, the bullhorn- and bat-toting principal from Paterson, New Jersey.[50]

Today, Tom O'Neill is retired, but the ripple effect of his work has reached shores that not even his great optimism would have anticipated. In the early 1990s, a junior high school civics teacher in Japan, Hiroshi Hayashi, read the Japanese edition of *The Read-Aloud Handbook*. Intrigued by the concept of SSR and Tom O'Neill's example, he immediately decided to apply it in his own school. (Contrary to what most Americans believe, not all Japanese public school students are single-minded over-achievers, and many are rebellious or reluctant readers—if they are readers at all.)[51] Although SSR was a foreign concept to Japanese secondary education, Hayashi saw quick results in his junior high school with just ten minutes at the start of the morning. Unwilling to keep his enthusiasm to himself, he spent the next two years sending forty thousand handwritten postcards to administrators in Japanese public schools, urging them to visit his school and adopt the concept. His personal crusade has won accolades from even the faculty skeptics: By 2006, more than 3,500 Japanese schools were using SSR to begin their school day.

Who Has the Time These Days?

People carry on these days as though the universal clock has somehow shrunk from twenty-four hours to eighteen. Granted there are a few people whose work schedules are truly beyond the norm—but they are few and far between. If there were a national time shortage, the malls would be empty, Netflix would be defunct, and the cable–TV companies would be bankrupt. Ultimately what it boils down to is Sister Patricia Joseph's cautionary words to me when I was sixteen. I was the designated class artist and she had asked me to draw something for her bulletin board over the weekend. I showed up empty-handed on Monday with the excuse that I hadn't had enough time. With a steely look, she said quietly, "That's all right, James. But please understand, even the busiest people find the time for the things they truly value."

Her thought was on target that day and it still is. If you understand what you've read so far and you truly value children and their futures, you will find the time. Like Sister said, it's all about the value system.

The Last Word on Reading Aloud, Vocabulary, and Old Brains

Of all the endorsements for reading aloud, the following is the most unusual and perhaps most sobering. Back in the mid-1990s, two men and a woman sat talking in an office of the University of Kentucky Medical Center. One man was an epidemiologist, the other man was a neurologist, and the woman was a psycholinguist. All were involved in what would become a celebrated Alzheimer's study. Two of them had been researching an order of nuns who had consented to regular mental examinations and brain autopsies upon death, and had turned all their personal records over to the researchers. The autopsies, when coupled with autobiographical essays written by the nuns when they were about twenty-two years old, showed a clear connection: Those with the densest sentences (the most ideas jam-packed into a sentence without breaking them into separate clauses) were far less likely either to develop Alzheimer's or to show its ravages. Simply put, the larger the vocabularies and the more complex the thinking processes in youth, the less chance of Alzheimer's damage later even if they develop the disease.

Could the rich vocabulary and crammed thinking process in one's youth be an early insurance policy against Alzheimer's? As the three discussed these issues, the neurologist, Bill Markesbery, father of two, asked Susan Kemper, the psycholinguist, "What does this mean for our children?"

In his absorbing book about the study, *Aging with Grace*, David Snowdon, the epidemiologist, describes what followed:[52]

> The question caught me off guard. But when I saw the look on his face, I realized that he was speaking as a father, not as a scientist. Bill

has three grown daughters, and it was clear he wanted to know whether he and his wife, Barbara, had done the right things as parents.

"Read to them," Susan answered. "It's that simple. It's the most important thing a parent can do with their children." Susan explained that idea density depends on at least two important learned skills: vocabulary and reading comprehension. "And the best way to increase vocabulary and reading comprehension is by starting early in life, by reading to your children," Susan declared. I could see the relief spread over Bill's face. "Barbara and I read to our kids every night," he said proudly.

. . . In the years since our study came out, I have been asked Markesbery's question many times. Parents ask me if they should play Mozart to their babies, or buy them expensive teaching toys, or prohibit television, or get them started early on the computer. I give them the same simple answer Susan Kemper gave to Markesbery: "Read to your children."

Chapter 2

When to Begin (and End) Read-Aloud

What we learn in childhood is carved in stone.
What we learn as adults is carved in ice.
                                        —David Kherdian, poet

HOW old must a child be before you start reading to him?" That is the question I am most often asked by parents. The next is: "When is the child too old to be read to?"

In answer to the first question, I ask one of my own: "When did you start talking to the child? Did you wait until he was six months old?"

"We started talking to him the day he was born," parents respond.

"And what language did your child speak the day he was born? English? Japanese? Italian?" They're about to say English when it dawns on them the child didn't speak any language yet.

"Wonderful!" I say. "There you were, holding that newborn infant in your arms, whispering, 'We love you, Tess. Daddy and I think you are the most beautiful baby in the world.' You were speaking multisyllable words and complex sentences in a foreign language to a child who didn't understand one word you were saying! And you never felt crazy or thought twice about doing it. But most people can't imagine reading to the child. And that's sad. If a child is old enough to talk to, she's old enough to read to. It's the same language."

Obviously, from birth to six months of age we are concerned less with understanding than with conditioning the child to your voice and the sight of books. Dr. T. Berry Brazelton, when he was chief of the child development unit of Boston Children's Hospital Medical Center, observed that new parents' most critical task during these early stages is learning how to calm the child, how to bring him under control, so he can begin to look around and listen when you pass on information.[1] Much the same task confronts the classroom teacher facing a new class each September— gaining control.

Is "In Utero Learning" a Myth?

We've long known the human voice is one of the most powerful tools a parent has for calming a child. And what many previously suspected is now firmly established in research indicating that the voice's influence starts even earlier than birth. University of North Carolina psychologist Anthony DeCasper and colleagues explored the effects of reading to children in utero, thinking that infants might be able to recognize something they had heard prenatally.

DeCasper asked thirty-three pregnant women to recite a specific paragraph of a children's story three times a day for the last six weeks of pregnancy. Three different paragraphs were used among the thirty-three women, but each woman used just one passage for the entire recitation period. Fifty-two hours after birth, the newborns were given an artificial nipple and earphones through which they could hear a woman (not the mother) reciting all three paragraphs. By measuring each child's sucking rate, researchers concluded the infants preferred the passages their mothers had recited during the third trimester.[2]

"The babies' reactions to the stories had been influenced by earlier exposure," DeCasper concluded. "That constitutes learning in a very general way." In a similar experiment involving reading to fetuses during the two and a half months before birth, DeCasper found the child's heartbeat increased with a new story and decreased with a familiar one.[3]

*She's already picked
up an accent.*

Researchers recently examined a thousand recorded cries from thirty French newborns and thirty German newborns. French and German languages have very distinct patterns of intonation, quite different from each other. And what did all the cries demonstrate? The babies cried in the melodic "accents" of their parents, mimicking the patterns they had been listening to during the last trimester in the womb.[4]

All of these experiments establish that a child becomes familiar with certain sounds while in utero and associates them with comfort and security. The baby is being conditioned—his first class in learning. Not only should this encourage us to read to the fetus during that last trimester, but imagine how much more can be accomplished when a newborn can see and touch the book, understand the words, and feel the reader.

What About Reading Aloud
to Children with Special Needs?

In *Cushla and Her Books*, author Dorothy Butler described how Cushla Yeoman's parents began reading aloud to her when she was four months of age. By nine months the child was able to respond to the sight of certain books and convey to her parents that these were her favorites. By age five she had taught herself to read.[5]

What makes Cushla's story so dramatic is that she was born with chromosome damage that caused deformities of the spleen, kidney, and mouth cavity. It also produced muscle spasms—which prevented her from sleeping for more than two hours a night or holding anything in her hand until she was three years old—and hazy vision beyond her fingertips.

Until she was three, the doctors diagnosed Cushla as "mentally and physically retarded" and recommended that she be institutionalized. Her parents, after seeing her early responses to books, refused; instead, they put her on a dose of fourteen read-aloud books a day. By age five, Cushla was found by psychologists to be well above average in intelligence and a socially well-adjusted child.

The story of Cushla and her family has appeared in each edition of *The Read-Aloud Handbook*, and each time it has been my hope that it would inspire an unknown reader someplace. One day I received a letter from Marcia Thomas, then of Memphis, Tennessee:

Our daughter Jennifer was born in September 1984. One of the first gifts we received was a copy of *The Read-Aloud Handbook*. We read the introductory chapters and were very impressed by the story of Cushla and her family. We decided to put our daughter on a "diet" of at least ten books a day. She had to stay in the hospital for seven weeks as a result of a heart defect and corrective surgery. However, we began reading to her while she was still in intensive care; and when we couldn't be there, we left story tapes and asked the nurses to play them for her.

For the past seven years we have read to Jennifer at every opportunity. She is now in the first grade and is one of the best readers in her class. She consistently makes 100 on reading tests and has a very impressive vocabulary. She can usually be found in the reading loft at school during free time, and at home she loves to sit with my husband or me and read a book.

What makes our story so remarkable is that Jennifer was born with Down syndrome. At two months of age, we were told Jennifer most likely was blind, deaf, and severely retarded. When she was tested at age four, her IQ was 111.

Jennifer Thomas graduated from her Concord, Massachusetts, high school, passed her state MCAS test, and was a member of the National Honor Society. I was honored to have been an invited guest at her graduation party. A talented artist, Jennifer competed in the juried VSA competition in 2003 for artists between the ages of sixteen and twenty-five who live in the United States and have a disability. Her piece was one of the fifteen chosen to tour the United States. In 2005, she enrolled in the Threshold Program at Lesley University in Cambridge, Massachusetts, and graduated in 2008. Today she has her own condo in Cambridge, is still an avid reader, has two dictionaries on her desk that she consults frequently, and is an ardent fan of Wikipedia.

If the Yeomans and the Thomases can accomplish all they did with their children, imagine how much can be realized by average families if they begin reading to their children early and in earnest.

What Could You Expect If You Started Reading to a Child on Day One?

Erin had no idea what a lucky girl she was when Linda Kelly-Hassett and her husband, Jim, brought her home from the hospital that Thanksgiving Day in 1988—but she soon found out. A few years later, I found out, too, when Erin's mom shared with me her journal of reading experiences. Since I didn't keep such a document with my own children, and since

Linda began even earlier than I did (ignorant parent that I was back in those days), I think her words speak louder than anything I might write in this space. Linda had been an elementary school teacher for twenty-two years when Erin was born and a devoted reader-aloud to her students. Everything she did in class, and recommended to the parents of her students, she applied to Erin. Not every parent has the time to do all that Linda did, but if they did even half as much, all children's futures would be brighter. In the following essay by Linda, note the unforced and gradual manner in which books were introduced to Erin and the way in which they were tied to everyday events.

Erin's first book, on her first day of life, was *Love You Forever* by Robert Munsch. My husband videotaped me reading it. He was unfamiliar with the story and was moved to tears as we rocked "back and forth, back and forth." That video went to relatives and friends, helping to bring Erin into their lives in a special way, and it also went to my former class of third-graders—planting a seed for the next generation.

Erin's first four months saw mostly soft chunky books, board books, and firmer-paged, lift-the-flap books. These were not only read but tasted and enjoyed. When she was four months old she began to enjoy time in her Johnny Jump Up, often spending forty-five minutes at a time, two or three times a day, jumping happily to poems, songs, and pop-up books. Over and over we read poems from *Read-Aloud Rhymes for the Very Young* by Jack Prelutsky and sang along with the Wee Sing tapes.

The enjoyment of Johnny Jump Up diminished around eight months when crawling and seeking her own entertainment took over. She loved tearing paper at this time, so we put out lots of magazines, but only very durable books. At reading time we stayed with the same kind of book until she was around ten months. At this stage, I became so eager to read storybooks to her that I decided to read these to her while she was in her highchair (so she couldn't tear the pages). It worked beautifully and provided some surprises.

For starters, we never had any food battles because I was too busy reading to let myself become overly concerned with her food intake. As I read, she ate her finger foods while I spooned in some baby fruit and veggies. Mealtime was fun, positive, and usually ended with her pointing to the bookshelf and requesting another "Boo(k)." This practice set a precedent that followed through the years. I continued to read to her at breakfast and lunchtime. When she had friends over, we always had a story or two at snack time. Using big books from my teaching days was a special treat.

Several memorable events happened during this period of early reading. My husband was transferred to the East Coast and got home every other weekend. Between Erin's tenth and fifteenth months, we were pretty much by ourselves when eating, so mealtime reading grew in length. It was nothing for her to actively listen to stories from twenty to forty minutes after a meal. A note in my journal for February 4, 1990, reads: "9 books after breakfast; 10 books and 4 poems after lunch; 7 books after dinner." This was not an unusual day's reading.

Ten days later, February 14, 1990, I wrote this entry: "After breakfast, Erin asked for a book. Since we were moving at the end of the month, I read her *Good-Bye House* by Frank Asch. She kept asking for another book as soon as I finished one. I ended up reading seventy-five minutes, covering twenty-five books. At fourteen months of age, she had sustained interest in the stories—actively listening, pointing, saying words, and making sounds."

I want to note that all these books were familiar to Erin. She did not immediately take to a new book. I would introduce it to her over a period of days. The first day we would look at the cover and "talk" about it. On the second day, I would then proceed to read the first page or so. I would read a few more pages each additional day until about the fifth or sixth day, when the book would be familiar enough for me to read it in its entirety.

Shortly after our move to Pennsylvania, I was reading her *The Very Hungry Caterpillar* by Eric Carle—as I had been doing for the last six months. This time, during the reading of the second sentence ("One Sunday morning the warm sun came up and—pop!—out of the egg came a tiny and very hungry caterpillar"), while I was still forming my mouth to say "pop," Erin said the word "pop!" and with perfect inflection. She was seventeen months that day and it was the start of her inserting words into familiar stories. What an addition to an already pleasant experience.

Beyond the love of reading nurtured by these parent-child experiences, Erin's verbal skills were growing. She spoke in complete sentences at twenty-one months and had a vocabulary of a thousand words by twenty-four months—all achieved without flash cards or "drill-and-skill." Erin's father wasn't excluded from the readings, and the two had a collection of books she labeled "Daddy Books" that became a personal cache.

With all of this reading, Erin's attention span and interests grew by leaps and bounds. By four years of age, she was listening to hundred-page novels along with her picture books. When it came time for Erin to attend school, her mom decided to use her own years of professional teaching experience and homeschool Erin. Homeschooling wasn't a political or religious issue with the Hassetts; they felt that their only child should receive the best they could possibly give her—a veteran twenty-two-year teacher called Mom. Furthermore, with the head start she had received at home, much of her first years in formal school would have been redundant and probably would have bored her to tears. In the ensuing years, Linda and Erin would be involved in weekly cooperative ventures with other community homeschoolers, and by age twelve, Erin began taking band and physical education at the local middle school for five hours a week.

Aware of the bonding that occurs during read-aloud as well as the difference between a child's listening level and reading level (more on that later), the Hassetts continued to read to Erin. For a list of all the novels heard by Erin from ages four to twelve, see my Web site (www.trelease-on-reading .com/erinlist.html).

Erin's progress in learning to read is a story in itself. After expressing a desire at age five to know her letters and sounds, she quickly mastered them but balked at formal reading. Listening to Mom and Dad reading novels was still a daily experience, but when her mother began to press her about reading herself in first grade, Erin declared, "I don't want to read those dumb books, those baby books [primers and easy-readers]. I'm not going to read until I can do chapter books."

Her mother backed off—to a degree. There was a local Head Start program of four- and five-year-olds that Linda and Erin had begun visiting as volunteers once a week, and one of the activities was reading to the children. Since the children quickly began to look up to Erin, she hedged on her determination and agreed to read some "big books" like Eric Carle's *The Very Hungry Caterpillar* to these classes. Obviously, Erin had learned how to read.

In the summer between first and second grade, the Hassetts were visiting friends who had a daughter three years older than Erin. Though the two girls went to bed at the same time, Erin was a night owl and not at all tired. When she was told she could read in bed, the older girl gave her some chapter books she had outgrown. The next morning, Erin came down to breakfast, handed her mother a novel, and said, "I read that last night." Thinking she meant she had glanced through it, Linda said that was nice and didn't think more about it. When it happened with a second novel the following morning, Linda asked her to read aloud a chapter. Erin did, with perfect inflection, and didn't miss a word.

Through the years, thanks to that initial letter from her mom, I've lunched and dined with Erin, even interviewed her in front of seminar audiences. She is poised, enthusiastic, articulate, talented, and one of the most extraordinary young ladies I've ever known. Far from being a bookworm, she loves swimming, softball, and music. Before Erin began college at Oklahoma City University, the Hassetts' choice for a final book together was *The Adventures of Tom Sawyer*, book number 694 since their first chapter book when Erin was four years old. That total didn't hurt a bit in her achieving either National Merit Scholar in high school or a perfect 800 Verbal on the SAT. College life didn't diminish her academic skills either— she graduated summa cum laude with the top GPA in her college class.

Erin Hassett today.

What If My Child Prefers to Read on Her Own?

One of the goals in all of this is to inspire children to read on their own. But reading alone and reading aloud are not mutually exclusive. We can do both—and should. (See chapter 5 for more on reading aloud's silent partner.)

To be honest, not all older children are responsive listeners, although the vast majority are once they're acclimated to it. Some, especially the more precocious readers, grow impatient with the read-aloud pace (which is slower than silent reading) and prefer to read on their own. Such was the case with Kathy Brozina, who told her father, Jim, a school librarian who incorporated read-aloud into his every school day, that she'd take it from there now that she was in fourth grade. Abruptly his read-alouds were over—with Kathy. There was, however, a much younger sibling, Kristen, and their readings continued.

When the fateful fourth-grade year arrived, Jim, remembering his older daughter's earlier response, made a suggestion to Kristen: How about if we try to read for a hundred straight bedtimes? When that goal was reached, Kristen suggested they try for a streak of a thousand straight nights. On it stretched, through sickness and health, a divorce, and even an auto accident. From picture books to classics, nothing stood in the way of what they called the Streak. While the father-daughter bond grew stronger, dates were interrupted or delayed for readings, as were play rehearsals and even prom night.

But nothing lasts forever, and the Streak finally came to an end when another streak intervened: four straight years of college. In a college dormitory's stairwell on Kristen's first day on campus, they read one last chapter—it was night number 3,218 in a row.

During his thirty-eight years in education, Jim Brozina once worked for an elementary school principal who told him he was wasting valuable instructional time reading to his students. Are you kidding? After 3,218 consecutive readings to Kristen, with no work sheets or vocabulary quizzes attached, what did she have to show for her father's efforts—beyond the affection, bonding, and shared experiences? You could start with a four-year college record that was all A's and one B, as well as winning two national writing contests. And one more thing—a nationally published literary memoir called *The Reading Promise: My Father and the Books We Shared*,[6] written under her pen name, Alice Ozma, one year out of college. How's that for "wasting valuable instructional time"?

Can You Recommend Something That Will Teach My Child to Read Before Kindergarten?

We have instant pudding, instant photos, instant coffee—but there are no instant adults. Yet some parents are in a hurry to make their children old before their time. Finland, on the other hand, has the highest reading scores in the world despite the fact that its laws forbid the formal teaching of reading until the child is seven years of age.[7] In fact, in Warwick Elley's thirty-two-country study of more than two hundred thousand readers, three other countries in the top ten don't begin formal reading instruction until age seven.[8]

Dr. T. Berry Brazelton has noted that an interest in your child's intellectual growth is important, but you can expect negative consequences if that interest takes the form of an obsession with teaching your child to read. "I've had children in my practice," Brazelton explained to NPR, "who were reading from a dictionary at the age of three and one-half or four, and had learned to read and type successfully by age four. But those kids went through a very tough time later on. They went through first grade successfully, but second grade they really bombed out on. And I have a feeling that they've been pushed so hard from outside to learn to read early, that the cost of it didn't show up until later."[9]

Experts like Brazelton and David Elkind[10] aren't saying that early reading is intrinsically bad; rather, they feel the early reader should arrive at the skill naturally, on his own, without a structured time each day when the mother or father sits down with him and teaches letters, sounds, and syllables. The "natural way" is the way Scout learned in Harper Lee's *To Kill a Mockingbird*—by sitting on the lap of a parent and listening as the parent's finger moves over the pages, until gradually, in the child's own good time, a connection is made between the sound of a certain word and the appearance of certain letters on the page, like the connections made by Erin Hassett, all without stress.

There are, however, children who come to reading prematurely, who arrive at the kindergarten door already knowing how to read without having been formally taught. These children are called early fluent readers, and they're more than worth our attention. During the past fifty years, intensive studies have been done of such children.[11] The majority of them were never formally taught to read at home, nor did they use any commercial reading programs.

The research, as well as studies done of pupils who respond to initial classroom instruction without difficulty, indicates four factors are present in the home environment of nearly every early reader:

1. The child is read to on a regular basis. This is the factor most often cited among early readers. In Dolores Durkin's 1966 study, all of the early readers had been read to regularly. In addition, the parents were avid readers and led by example. The reading included not only books but package labels, street and truck signs, billboards, and so on. International research forty years later with fourth-graders and their families in thirty-five countries mirrored this with the highest-scoring students.[12]

2. A wide variety of printed material—books, magazines, newspapers, comics—is available in the home. Nearly thirty years after Durkin's study, NAEP studies reported that the more printed materials found in a child's home, the higher the student's writing, reading, and math skills,[13] and

chapter 6 here is devoted largely to the influence of the print climate, both at home and in school.

3. Paper and pencil are readily available for the child. Durkin explained: "Almost without exception, the starting point of curiosity about written language was an interest in scribbling and drawing. From this developed an interest in copying objects and letters of the alphabet."

4. The people in the child's home stimulate the child's interest in reading and writing by answering endless questions, praising the child's efforts at reading and writing, taking the child to the library frequently, buying books, writing stories that the child dictates, and displaying his paperwork in a prominent place in the home. This also is supported by the aforementioned study of 150,000 fourth-graders and their families in thirty-five countries,[14] as well as by the anecdote about the role of Leonard Pitts's mother in his winning a Pulitzer Prize (Introduction, page xviii).

I want to emphasize that these four factors were present in the home of nearly every child who was an early reader. None of these factors was expensive or involved much more than interest on the part of the parent.

How Is My Child's Reading Going to Get Better If *I'm* Doing the Reading?

Listening comprehension feeds reading comprehension. Sounds complicated, right? So let's make it simple. We'll use the most frequently used word in the English language: *the*. I often asked my lecture audiences if there was anyone present who thought this little three-letter word was a difficult word to understand, and out of three hundred people I'd get about five who raised their hands—amid snickers from the rest.

I then asked those who didn't raise their hands to "pretend I am a Russian exchange student living in your home. It's also important to know there is no equivalent word in Russian for *the*, as we use it." Indeed, many languages—Chinese, Japanese, Korean, Persian, Polish, Punjabi, Croatian, and Vietnamese—don't have such articles.

"Now, as the Russian exchange student, I've been living in your home and listening to you and your family for three weeks when one day I come to you and say, 'Don't understand word you use over, over. What means word *the*'?"

How would you begin to explain the meaning of the word to this person? Everyone in the audience would laugh in embarrassment. Explaining this simple word is very difficult, yet most of us knew how to use it by the time we showed up for kindergarten.

How did you learn it? One morning when you were three years old, did your mother take you into the kitchen, sit you down at the table with a little workbook, and say, "*The* is a definite article. It comes before nouns. Now take your green crayon and underline all the definite articles on this page"? Of course not.

We learned the meaning of this tiny but complex word by hearing it. In fact, we heard it three ways:

1. Over and over and over (immersion);
2. From superheroes—Mom, Dad, brother, and sister (role models);
3. In a meaningful context—the cookie, the crayons, and the potty.

Whenever an adult reads to a child, three important things are happening simultaneously and painlessly: (1) a pleasure connection is being made between child and book, (2) both parent and child are learning something from the book they're sharing (double learning), and (3) the adult is pouring sounds and syllables called words into the child's ear (see page 14 and the Listening Vocabulary).

The research on oral comprehension versus reading comprehension certifies this concept and offers a sobering note about children who enter school with small vocabularies. Where you might expect school to narrow the gap between children with small oral vocabularies and those with larger ones, the reverse is true; the gap between these vocabularies widens instead of narrows.[15]

The reason is twofold: (1) Since children in the early grades are reading only the words most of them already know ("decodable text"), neither the slow nor the advanced child is meeting many new words in class; and (2) therefore the students' only exposure to new or advanced language would have to be from parents, peers, and teachers. While there's a shortage of new words in school, at home the advantaged child is more likely to be read to from advanced books, to be exposed to educational television, and to be engaged in meaningful conversation for longer periods of time. The child with the smaller vocabulary ends up hearing the same routine words at home.

To make matters worse, the advantaged child is more apt to be in a school that recognizes the advantages of reading aloud and will hear even more new words. In Nell Duke's study of ten urban and ten suburban first-grade classes, seven out of the ten suburban classes were read chapter books, while only two of the ten urban classes experienced chapter books.[16] The children with the smallest vocabularies were exposed to the fewest words and the least complex sentences; thus the gap widens. Another factor is "summer slump," explained on page 88.

Narrowing the achievement gap, a noble objective in government's No Child Left Behind and Race to the Top, depends entirely on bridging the vocabulary gap. The most efficient way to do that is to tap into the 7,800 hours the child spends at home. Imagine the impact if even half the parents of at-risk children were reading to them from library books beginning at infancy (or listening to recorded books if family literacy is a problem). A second way, though not as efficient, would be for the classroom teacher to read aloud from richer literature—at least richer than the decodable text—in class. Children's books, even good picture books, are much richer than ordinary home or classroom conversation, as the chart indicates on page 18.

How Can I Expand My Child's Attention Span?

The best tool for expanding attention span is one-on-one time with the child; it is by far the most effective teaching/bonding arrangement ever invented. In studying methods to reverse language problems among disadvantaged children, Harvard psychologist Jerome Kagan found intensified one-on-one attention to be especially effective.[17] His studies indicate the advantages of reading to children and of listening attentively to their responses to the reading, but they also point to the desirability of reading to each of your children separately, if possible.

I recognize this approach poses an extra problem for working mothers and fathers with more than one child. But somewhere in that seven-day

One-on-one time is a key factor in how soon a child learns the purpose of books.

week there must be time for your child to discover the specialness of you, one-on-one, even if it's only once or twice a week.

One-on-one time between adult and child—be it reading or talking or playing—is essential to teaching the concept of books or puppies or flowers or water. Once the concept of something has been learned, the foundation has been laid for the next accomplishment: attention span. Without a concept of what is happening and why, a child cannot pay attention to it for any appreciable amount of time.

Here, for example, are two concepts entirely within the grasp of a three-year-old:

♦ The telephone can be used to make and receive calls.
♦ Books contain stories that give me pleasure if I listen and watch.

Nearly thirty years ago, my friend and neighbor Ellie Fernands, today a retired elementary school principal, returned to teaching after a ten-year hiatus. Since her former experience was in junior high, this new job—preschool—was almost extraterrestrial. I recall Ellie telling me of her experiences on the first day of school with those two concepts: the telephone and books. She said, "All morning the three-year-olds used the toy telephone in class to make pretend calls to their mothers for reassurances that they'd be picked up and brought home. They dialed make-believe numbers, talked for long periods of time, and even used telephone etiquette." Understanding the concept of the telephone, these children were able to use and enjoy it for a considerable length of time. Their telephone attention span was excellent. (See page xvi for the story of Bianca Cotton's phone comprehension.)

Now compare that with story time in Ellie's class that day. "Thirty seconds after the story began, two of the children stood up and moved away from the circle, obviously bored. More children quickly joined them. Within two minutes, half the children had abandoned the story." (Ellie later learned that one of the two children who listened through the entire story was a child who had been read to from day one. We both later discovered he—Michael Nozzolillo—had been pictured in the very first edition of this book; his parents were lifelong friends of mine.)

The difference between the attention spans for phone and book is based on the concept that each child brought to the subject. When a child has little or no experience with books, it is impossible for him to have a concept of them and the pleasure they afford. No experience means no attention span.[18]

Is There Something I Could Buy That Would Help My Child Read Better?

Since parents often think there are quick fixes they can buy, some kind of kit or phonics game to help a child do better at school, I began asking my associates years ago, "What did you have in your home as a child that helped you become a reader? Things your folks had to buy." Besides the library card they all named, which is free, their responses form what I call the Three B's, an inexpensive "reading kit" that nearly all parents can afford:

The first B is books: Ownership of a book is important, with the child's name inscribed inside, a book that doesn't have to be returned to the library or even shared with siblings. Chapter 6 here shows the clear connection between book ownership (or access) and reading achievement.

The second B is book basket (or magazine rack), placed where it can be used most often: There is probably more reading done in the bathrooms of America than in all the libraries and classrooms combined. Put a book basket in there, stocked with books, magazines, and newspapers.

A book basket offers easy, immediate access to print.

Put another book basket on or near the kitchen table. Take a hint from all those newspaper coin boxes standing in front of fast-food restaurants; they're not for decoration. If you sit in your car in the parking lot and watch who uses those coin boxes, invariably it's the person who's eating alone. I'm convinced most human beings want or need to read when they're eating alone. And with more and more children eating at least one daily meal alone, the kitchen is a prime spot for recreational reading. If there's a book on the table, they'll read it—unless, of course, you're foolish enough to have a television in your kitchen, as do more than 60 percent of parents in America.[19] Morrow's study of twenty-one classes of kindergartners showed that children with the most interest in reading came from homes where books and print were spread throughout the house, not just in one or two places.[20]

The third B is bed lamp: Does your child have a bed lamp or reading light? If not, and you wish to raise a reader, the first order of business is to go out and buy one. Install it, and say to your child: "We think you're old enough now to stay up later at night and read in bed like Mom and Dad. So we bought this little lamp and we're going to leave it on an extra fifteen minutes [or longer, depending on the age of the child] if you want to read in bed. On the other hand, if you don't want to read—that's okay, too. We'll just turn off the light at the same old time." Most children will do anything in order to stay up later—even read.

At What Age Should I Stop Reading to My Child?

Almost as big a mistake as not reading to children at all is stopping too soon. The 1983 Commission on Reading stated that reading aloud is "a practice that should continue throughout the grades."[21] In this recommendation the commission was really asking us to model the extremely successful marketing strategy of McDonald's. The fast-food chain has been in business for more than a half century and has never cut its advertising budget. Every year McDonald's spends more money on advertising than it did the previous year, which comes to more than $5.4 million per day. Its marketing people never think, "Everyone has heard our message. They should be coming to us on their own, instead of our spending all this money on advertising."

Every time we read aloud to a child or class, we're giving a commercial for the pleasures of reading. But, unlike McDonald's, we often cut our advertising each year instead of increasing it. The older the child, the less she is read to—in the home and in the classroom. A thirty-year survey of graduate students confirms how seldom they were read to in middle and upper grades.[22]

Parents (and sometimes teachers) say, "He's in the top fourth-grade reading group—why should I read to him? Isn't that why we're sending him to school, so he'll learn how to read by himself?" There are many mistaken assumptions in that question.

Let's say the student is reading on a fourth-grade level. Wonderful. But what level is the child listening on? Most people have no idea that one is higher than the other, until they stop and think about it. Here's an easy way to visualize it: For seven years, the most popular show on American television was *The Cosby Show,* enjoyed by tens of millions each week—including first-graders. Even in reruns it's still one of the most watched shows all over the world. On what reading level would you estimate the script to have been written? When a Cosby script was subjected to the Harris-Jacobson Wide Range Readability Formula, it came out to approximately a fourth-grade level (3.7).[23]

Few, if any, of the first-graders watching the show would be able to read its script. But most could understand it if it was read to them—that is, recited by the actors. According to experts, it is a reasonable assertion that reading and listening skills begin to converge at about eighth grade.[24] Until then, kids usually listen on a higher level than they read on. Therefore, children can hear and understand stories that are more complicated and more interesting than what they could read on their own—which has to be one of God's greatest blessings for first-graders. The last thing you want first-graders thinking is that what they're reading in first grade is as good as books are going to get! First-graders can enjoy books written on a fourth-grade level, and fifth-graders can enjoy books written on a seventh-grade reading level. (This is, of course, contingent upon the social level of the books' subject matter; some seventh-grade material is above the fifth-grader's social experience and might be off-putting. Page 167 details the nun who read a novel to my first-grade class of ninety-four pupils.)

Now that I've established the idea that there is a significant difference between listening level and reading level, you can better understand why one should continue to read aloud to children as they grow older, as the Hassetts did with Erin. Beyond the emotional bond that is established between parent and child (or teacher and class), you're feeding those higher vocabulary words through the ear; eventually they'll reach the brain and register in the child-reader's eyes.

That's the argument for continuing the reading to a higher level. Now let's divert to a lower level. If you've got a beginning reader in your home or classroom—five-, six-, or seven-year-old—and you're still reading to the child, wonderful! Keep it up. But if you're still reading those Dr. Seuss controlled-vocabulary books to the child—like *The Cat in the Hat* or *Hop on Pop*—you're insulting the six-year-old's brain cells nightly!

With either book, you have a volume of 225 words and a six-year-old with a six-thousand-word vocabulary. The child has understood and been using all 225 of those words since she was four years old. If this is what you're still reading to the child every night, there's something wrong with the child if she's not lying in bed at night thinking, "One of us here is brain-dead!"

At age six, you're a beginning reader. As such, you've got a limited number of words you can decode by sight or sound. But you're not a beginning listener. You've been listening for six years; you're a veteran listener! Dr. Seuss deliberately wrote the controlled-vocabulary books to be read by children to themselves. And just to make sure people understood this was a book to be read *by* the child and not *to* the child, the covers of the controlled-vocabulary books like *The Cat in the Hat* and *Hop on Pop* contain a logo with the words "I Can Read It All by Myself."[25] The "myself" refers to the child, not the parent!

In chapter 3, I explore what you could be reading instead of controlled-vocabulary books, including some chapter books that kindergarten and preschool teachers have used successfully in their classes.

Would Reading Aloud to Them Help Children with Grammar?

Grammar is more caught than taught, and the way you catch it is the same way you catch the flu: You're exposed to it. By hearing the language spoken correctly, you begin to imitate the pattern—both in what you say and in what you write. The easiest test of whether something is grammatically correct or not is to say it out loud. If, in response, you find yourself saying, "That doesn't sound right," there's a good chance it's not correct. The only way of telling if it sounds right or wrong is if you've read it or heard it said correctly. Therefore, those who seldom read and/or live with people who speak incorrect English have little chance of ever mastering grammar.

In a nation that is becoming a more and more service-oriented economy, oral communication is an essential skill in the workplace. The richer the words you hear, the richer will be the words you give back—in speech or in writing. Reading aloud to all students—ESL or native born—beginning as early in their lives as possible and continuing through the grades will expose them to a rich, organized, and interesting language model as an alternative to the tongue-tied language of their peers.

Discounting sign language and body language, there are two main forms of language: spoken and written. While they are intimately related to each other, they are not twins. As I showed in the chart on page 18, written words are far more structured than spoken words. Conversation is imprecise, often ungrammatical, and less organized than print. Therefore, children who enjoy conversations with adults and hear stories are exposed to richer language than is the child who experiences only conversation (or e-mails) with peers.

In listening to stories being read aloud, you're learning a second language—the standard English of books, the classroom, and most of the workplace. Most of us process at least two spoken languages—home language and standard language.

This gift of standard English cannot be overemphasized. I say that not because I am a native speaker of English, but for purely practical reasons. Standard English is the primary tongue of the classroom and the business world. The most recent Internet survey showed English language Web pages made up 56.4 percent of all pages, with German a distant second with 7.7 percent.

Today's student needs home English for the neighborhood and standard English for the marketplace, and hearing it is an easy and contagious manner in which to meet it in large doses.

How Do We Improve the Basics Like Writing and Spelling?

By reading, reading, and reading. Vocabulary and spelling are not learned best by looking up words in the dictionary. You learn the meanings and spellings in the same way teachers learn the names of students and parents learn the names of neighbors: by seeing them again and again, and making the connection between the face and the name.

Nearly everyone spells by visual memory, not by rules. (There is ample research to indicate that people who have the best recall of graphic or geometric symbols are also the best spellers. This, say the scientists, may have more to do with your memory genetics than with anything else.)[26] Most people, when they doubt the correctness of what they have just spelled, write the word out several different ways and choose the one that looks correct. (That city in Pennsylvania—is it spelled Pittsberg or Pittsburgh? How about humor, humer, or hughmer? Does that celebrity have a large eigo, eago, or ego? Which ones look right?) The more a child looks at published words in sentences and paragraphs, the greater the chances he will recognize when the word is spelled correctly or incorrectly. Conversely, the less you read, the fewer words you meet and the less certain you are of both meaning and spelling.[27]

As for writing, there is the traditional approach, what you might call the "Vince Lombardi school" of writing. That is, you write, write, write until you bleed it across the paper and the curriculum. You get better at writing the way you get better at tackling! Do it over and over. The trouble with this approach is that it is not supported by research. Students who write the most are not the best writers.[28] Indeed, for all the testing and portfolio collections and the raising of writing standards over the past twenty years, the NAEP assessments show little significant change in national writing scores, especially in the Proficient category.[29]

Now, before anyone suffers apoplexy, I'm not suggesting we do away with writing in school. I'm just suggesting—strongly—that we back off a bit, that we might be doing too much writing in some places. Good writers are like baseball players. Baseball players have to play regularly, but they spend most of their time either in the field or in the dugout, watching others run, hit, catch, and throw. Good writers do the same—they write, but they read even more, watching how other people throw words around to catch meaning. The more you read, the better you write—and the NAEP's Writing Report Card proves it.[30] The highest-scoring student writers were not those who wrote the most each day, but rather the students who read the most recreationally, had the most printed materials in their homes, and did regular essay writing in class.

Writing and baseball have much in common.

What is flawed in our current writing curriculum is our failure to grasp the simple observation that Jacques Barzun once made—that writing and speaking are "copycat" experiences: "Words get in through the ear or eye and come out at the tongue or the end of a pencil."[31]

We say what we hear and we write what we see. My relatives in Georgia and New Jersey speak the same English language but not the same way, because they grew up hearing it spoken differently. What goes in the ear comes out the mouth. If you ask children in Wisconsin and Alaska to draw cows, you'll get different-looking cows, because cows are tough to draw if you haven't seen them, and the kids in Alaska haven't seen that many—so their cows look like dogs.

The same principle holds for writing. It's tough to write compound, complex, or good old simple sentences if you haven't seen them that often. And when do you see them most often? When you read—you see them over and over and over.

Here is a crucial fact to consider in the reading and writing connection: Visual receptors in the brain outnumber auditory receptors 30:1.[32] In other words, the chances of a word (or sentence) being retained in our memory bank are thirty times greater if we see it instead of just hear it. If our experience with language consists largely of television dialogue and conversation, we will never be able to write coherent sentences until we see a lot more of them. If we wait until we're in middle management and worrying about our writing skills, it might even be too late. Learning to write well at age thirty-five is a lot like learning to Rollerblade or speak a foreign language at age thirty-five: It's not as easy as it would have been at age seven. Vocabulary and coherent sentences can't be downloaded onto paper unless they've first been uploaded to the head—by reading.

Is It Ever Too Late to Start Reading to a Child?

They're never too old—but it's not as easy with older children as it is when they're two or six years old.

Because she has a captive audience, the classroom teacher holds a distinct advantage over the parent who suddenly wants to begin reading to a thirteen-year-old. Regardless of how well intentioned the parent may be, reading aloud to an adolescent at home can be difficult. During this period of social and emotional development, teenagers' out-of-school time is largely spent coping with body changes, sex drive, vocational anxieties, and the need to form an identity apart from that of their families. These kinds of concerns and their attendant schedules don't leave much time for Mom's and Dad's reading aloud, although the example of Jim Brozina and his daughter Kristen is a beacon of hope (page 30).

But the situation is not hopeless if you pick your spots. Don't suggest that your daughter listen to a story when she's sitting down to watch her favorite television show or fuming after a fight with her boyfriend. Along with timing, consider the length of what you read. Keep it short—unless you see an interest in more.

When the child is in early adolescence, from ages twelve to fourteen, try sharing a small part of a book, a page or two, when you see she is at loose ends—and downplay any motivational or educational aspects connected with the reading. When Jamie and Elizabeth were teens, I was always reading excerpts to them from whatever I was reading myself—be it fiction or nonfiction. Late one evening I was reading Ferrol Sams's *Run with the Horsemen*, a wonderful Southern adult novel by a Georgia physician. When

I came to a scene in which a boy has two outrageously funny incidents with a mule in a field and a rooster in an outhouse, I thought, "Oh, Jamie will love these!"

So in the morning, I caught up with him. "Hey, Jamie—listen to this!" Edging to the door, he said, "Sorry, Dad, but I gotta run. I'm supposed to meet the guys."

"I know, but it'll just take a minute—I promise." Rolling his eyes, he reluctantly sat and I began to read it aloud. And, as I expected, he loved it. Several hours later he was back with his buddies in tow, asking me to read it to them, too.

Because so many parents and teachers seem at loose ends over what to read to this age group, I created an anthology of fifty read-aloud selections for pre-teens and teens called *Read All About It!* It contains a broad cross section of fiction and nonfiction, short stories and chapters from novels (which will whet the child's appetite for the rest of the book), newspaper columns, and biographical sketches of each author. I'll bet you think all those yellow ribbon bumper stickers ("Support our troops") began with Tony Orlando and Dawn's rendition of "Tie a Yellow Ribbon." Wrong. Check out Pete Hamill's "The Yellow Handkerchief" column in *Read All About It!*

How Does This Fit with the Calls for Higher National Standards?

As a nation, we want to be sure to raise all the standards. Since 1983's *A Nation at Risk* report, CEOs and politicians have emphasized only one standard: IQ. And as the demands for higher scores are pressed on superintendents, principals, and teachers, the curriculum narrows to only what will be on the standardized test.[33] Since the tests include only IQ subjects, there remains little or no time for HQ subjects—the "heart quotient." Who has time for the teachable moment when the class hamster dies and you've got test prep to cover? Who bothers to discuss the ethical thing to do if there are no ethics questions on the state standards exam?

As Clifton Fadiman once observed, "There is no shortage of smart people. We've got lots of those. The real shortage is in better people." And you make better people by educating children's brains and hearts. Daniel Goleman's enormously successful *Emotional Intelligence*[34] is perhaps the most eloquent argument in support of that.

Consider the following headlines, all of them involving people of high IQ, graduates of our finest colleges and universities, many with degrees as high as Ph.D.:

- 19 Wall St. Firms Broke SEC Laws 51 Times in 15 Years
- Leader of Big Mortgage Lender Guilty of $2.9 Billion Fraud
- 4th Recent Illinois Governor En Route to Jail
- Test-Cheating Scandal Envelops Atlanta Schools, Including Principals
- Bristol-Myers Pays $300 Million in Fraud Penalties
- Walmart Hushed Up $24 Million Bribery Case
- Insurers Say Doctors Filed $1 Billion in False Fees
- World's Biggest Insurance Broker to Pay $850M for Fraud
- Major Drugmaker Agrees to Pay Record $3 Billion for Fraud
- Catholic Church's Costs Pass $1 Billion in Child Abuse Cases
- Microsoft to Pay $1.1B for Overcharging Customers
- Long Island Teens Paid $3G for Others to Take Their SATs[35]

Those scandals weren't caused by a lack of algebraic skills, nor were they the result of former remedial students being in charge. Many of the people behind those scandals were the gifted and talented guys, the ones from the head of the class. They also fit a carefully researched psychological profile: The higher the person's social class, the lower (on average) is their index for compassion and ethical behavior.[36] To ignore students' emotional and social education (as the state standards and exit exams do) is to invite a plethora of such headlines and behaviors. If all we're doing in school is teaching students how to answer the calls they'll someday get on their smartphones, then the curriculum is half-worthless.

So how do we educate the heart? There are really only two ways: life experience and stories about life experience, which is called literature. Great preachers and teachers—Aesop, Socrates, Confucius, Moses, and Jesus—have traditionally used stories to get their lesson plans across, educating both the mind and the heart.

But when school scores either dropped or failed to rise, administrators and politicians seized on nonfiction as a salvation tool. Since most standardized test questions didn't involve subjective thinking or personal values, they reasoned, let's narrow the reading curriculum to nonfiction.

That thinking is flawed on several counts: Neither education research nor brain science supports it. Literature is considered an important medium because it brings us closest to the human heart. And of the two forms of literature (fiction and nonfiction), the one that brings us closest to the meaning of life is fiction. That's one reason most of the recommendations for read-alouds at the back of this book are fiction. It's also worth noting that in the OECD study of 250,000 teens in thirty-two nations,[37] students who read the widest variety of material, but the most fiction, had the highest literacy scores.

Additionally, recent brain science tells us fiction engages a larger portion of the brain.[38] More than nonfiction, fiction forces us to concentrate in order to find meaning, and therefore deepens our engagement and helps comprehension. Furthermore, good fiction is often built on a carefully researched infrastructure of fact—take, for instance, *Missy Violet and Me* by Barbara Hathaway; *The Rifle* by Gary Paulsen; *Caddie Woodlawn* by Carol Ryrie Brink; *The Call of the Wild* by Jack London; *City of Orphans* by Avi; and *Finding Buck McHenry* by Alfred Slote. None of those can be read without the reader coming away with a wider understanding of another time and place (background knowledge).

None of this is to diminish good nonfiction. You'll find an abundance of nonfiction picture books in the Treasury here, and most of them carry the hallmark that distinguishes memorable reading: a darn good story. On the other hand, traditional textbooks or even an encyclopedia don't do much to awaken a sense of empathy or demonstrate social skills in the way that, say, Kathryn Erskine's novel *Mockingbird* does, using the first-person narrative of a ten-year-old girl with Asperger's syndrome. Because the book enables us to see the world through the child's eyes, we're that much closer to understanding the otherwise incomprehensible soul of autism. Since souls don't show up on X-rays or CAT scans, nonfiction seldom works on souls. But fiction does. (See page 267 in the Treasury for a full description of *Mockingbird*.)

One final word on behalf of fiction: The great American novelist Robert Penn Warren once observed that one of the reasons we read fiction is to discover clues as to how our own stories are going to turn out. A kind of heads-up, if you will. The politician reading *All the King's Men*, for example, is forewarned of the pitfalls ahead. I thought of Warren's quote the day I read about a corporate jet returning to Houston from a company conference. One of the executives aboard was leisurely reading a novel when the CEO chanced by and wondered aloud how he could waste his free time reading novels. If the employee had been reading Dickens's *Hard Times*, Fitzgerald's *The Great Gatsby*, or even Tom Wolfe's *The Bonfire of the Vanities*, he might have been able to reply, "Just checking to see what's ahead of us." I wonder if that CEO—Ken Lay of Enron—would have understood what he was talking about.

Chapter 3

The Stages of Read-Aloud

Few children learn to love books by themselves. Someone has to lure them into the wonderful world of the written word; someone has to show them the way.

—Orville Prescott,
A Father Reads to His Children

UNTIL a child is four months old, it doesn't matter a great deal what you read as long as you are reading. Doing so lets the child become accustomed to the rhythmic sound of your reading voice and to associate it with a peaceful, secure time of day. Mother Goose, of course, is always appropriate, but my neighbor read aloud Kipling when she was nursing her daughter, who eventually went on to both Princeton and Harvard. Did Kipling have anything to do with that? Not much, compared to her mother's reading to her day in and day out.

Over the past decade and a half, a heated debate has raged over the importance of the infant years in a person's brain development. Although psychologists and neuroscientists have argued in public conferences, newsmagazines, and professional journals, the jury remains out on exactly how critical the first three years of life really are. Do the doors of opportunity really slam shut after age three, or are there second, third, or fourth chances later on?

I personally tend to compromise between the two extremes: Learning (and life) is easier if the first three years are enriched, but later opportunities can be rewarding if there is an ideal learning environment and if—a big *if*—the brain's architecture has not been damaged by emotional or physical distress. Anyone wishing to pursue the debate will find it fully explored in *The Scientist in the Crib: Minds, Brains, and How Children Learn* by Gopnik, Meltzoff, and Kuhl and *The Myth of the First Three Years* by John T. Bruer.

A less time-consuming option now available for those pursuing child-brain issues is the Internet, one of the places you'll find the work of Dr. Jack Shonkoff, director of the Center on the Developing Child at Harvard University. Shonkoff is one of the nation's leading authorities on children's brain development and has the ability to make complicated ideas understandable to ordinary parents and teachers. Supported by extensive brain research, he is adamant that early childhood education should not be just about education, but also about playing and exploring and nurturing emotional development—in short, the whole child.

Under Shonkoff's direction, the Center on the Developing Child offers a half dozen short videos online, ranging from two minutes to seven minutes.[1] A crucial point made by the center is that childhood trauma, such as malnutrition or emotional deprivation (both of which go hand in hand with addicted or alcoholic parents), often causes structural damage to the young brain. This damage, especially if it occurs between birth and age three, cannot be repaired later in special education and remedial classes.[2] The center believes a good part of our present remediation could be prevented with proper early childhood care and heightened awareness of "toxic stress" in early childhood.[3]

Also firmly established by the research is that measurable long-term storage of sound and word patterns begins as early as eight months of age. Children hearing the most language will have the best chance of having the best language skills.[4]

Let me reiterate an earlier statement: None of this is intended to create a super-baby. The focus should be on nurturing whatever abilities are already there, creating an intimate bond between parent and child, and building a happy bridge between child and books that can be crossed whenever the child is developmentally ready as a reader.

Which Books Are Best for Infants?

Your book selections for the first year should be ones that stimulate your child's sight and hearing—colorful pictures and exciting sounds upon which the child can focus easily. One of the reasons for Mother Goose's success is that she echoes the first sound a child falls in love with—the rhythmic, rhyming beat-beat-beat of a mother's heart.

Mother Goose and Dr. Seuss not only rhyme in name and text; they also must have sensed what researchers would later prove. According to learning specialists at the National Institute of Child Health and Human

Development in Bethesda, Maryland, the ability to find words that rhyme appears to be an important one in children. Indeed, kindergartners who struggle to find words that rhyme with *cat* are prime candidates for later reading problems. Moreover, considering the many rhyming chants found in children's games (such as jump-rope rhymes) and popular children's books like Seuss's *The Foot Book* and Mem Fox's *Ten Little Fingers and Ten Little Toes*, it's obvious that children find pleasure in words that rhyme. But why? Researchers say it is for the same reason adults subconsciously enjoy looking at stripes and plaids or listening to musical harmony—they help to arrange a chaotic world.

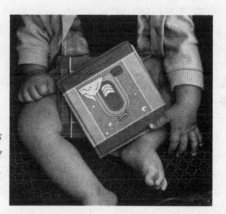

The early months should build happy bridges to books.

With that in mind, a prime recommendation is that parents frequently read aloud books and stories that rhyme. You can find a list of such titles on pages 187.

The impact of rhyme can be traced as early as the womb. For one study, women in the last trimester of pregnancy repeatedly read aloud Dr. Seuss's *The Cat in the Hat*; then, fifty-two hours after birth, monitored infants were able to distinguish Seuss's rhyming verse from a book without rhymes.[5]

We don't turn to Mother Goose for the plot. We turn to her because she takes all those sounds, syllables, endings, and blendings and mixes them in with the rhythm and rhyme of language for us to feed to a child who already takes delight in rocking back and forth in his crib, repeating a single syllable over and over: "Ba, ba, ba, ba, ba . . ." There are many collections of Mother Goose, but my two present favorites are *The Neighborhood Mother Goose* by Nina Crews and *Tomie dePaola's Mother Goose*. If you're musically inclined, Crews has a marvelous collection of favorite childhood singsongs (like "Wheels on the Bus") from the classroom, bedroom, and playground in *The Neighborhood Sing-Along*, including colorful photos of children playing. Fitting right in with these books is the aforementioned *Ten Little Fingers and Ten Little Toes*, also available as a board book.

Many parents find that singing or reciting these rhymes during the appropriate activity further reinforces the relationship between rhyme and activity in the child's mind. Compact discs and tapes of these rhymes are available at your library and local bookstore, and you can download them from the iTunes Store.

Books for this age group don't usually stay in print for very long, and unless they're in board book format, they don't "live" long among the rambunctious very young. One series of books seems to defy that norm: the "gosling" series, which began with *Gossie* (page 191) back in 2002 and is still in print (hardcover, board book, and Kindle). Small in size (six inches) and plot, it uses the little gosling's barnyard adventures to reflect the curiosity and life of babies and toddlers, including lost clothes, favorite toys, sharing, and avoiding naps.

Also keep in mind the physical bonding that occurs during the time you are holding the child and reading. To make sure you never convey the message that the book is more important than the child, maintain skin-to-skin contact as often as possible, patting, touching, and hugging the child while you read.[6] Linked with the normal parent-infant dialogue, this reinforces a feeling of being well loved.

What Is Normal Behavior of the Infant or Toddler During Readings?

Recent interest in early learning has spurred investigations into how infants and their parents react in read-aloud situations, though any reading parent can tell you a child's interest in and response to books varies a great deal from child to child, or day to day. But if you are a new parent, any seeming lack of interest can be discouraging. Here is a forecast so you'll not be discouraged or think your child is hopeless.

+ At four months of age, since he has limited mobility, a child has little or no choice but to listen and observe, thus making a passive and noncombative audience for the parent, who is probably thinking, "This is easy!"
+ Your arms should encircle the child in such a way as to suggest support and bonding, but not imprisonment, allowing the child to view the pages if you're reading a picture book.

- By six months, however, the child is more interested in grabbing the book to suck on it than listening (which he's also doing). Bypass the problem by giving him a teething toy or other distraction.
- At eight months, he may prefer turning pages to steady listening. Allow him ample opportunity to explore this activity, but don't give up the book entirely.
- At twelve months, the child's involvement grows to turning pages for you, pointing to objects you name on the page, even making noises for animals on cue.
- By fifteen months and the onset of walking, his restlessness blossoms fully, and your reading times must be chosen so as not to frustrate his immediate interests.

In nearly all these studies,[7] attention spans during infant reading time averaged only three minutes, though several daily readings often brought the total as high as thirty minutes a day. There are some one-year-olds who will listen to stories for that long in one sitting, but they are more the exception than the rule.

As babies mature, good parent-readers profit from earlier experiences. They don't force the reading times; they direct attention by pointing to something on the page, and they learn to vary their voices between whispers and excited tones. They also learn that attention spans are not built overnight—they are built minute by minute, page by page, day by day.

Once the child starts to respond to the sight of books and your voice, begin a book dialogue—talking the book instead of just reading it. Reading aloud with a young child shouldn't be a solitary, passive experience. As much as possible you want the child to interact with you and the book. You elicit the interaction by the questions or comments you interject in the reading, as you'll see in a moment. What you want in the reading is the same thing you want when you talk with a child—give-and-take, or, as one educator put it, "Play Ping-Pong, not darts." When you simply throw words or orders at a child, you're playing verbal darts. Here is a sample dialogue between a mother and her twenty-month-old during a reading of *Blueberries for Sal* by Robert McCloskey. Note that the parent doesn't stay tied to the exact text, which is underlined here.

Parent: Little Bear's mother turned around to see what on earth could make a noise like kuplunk! And there, right in front of her, was—Sal!
Child: Saa.

Parent: Right, Sal. And <u>mother bear</u> was very surprised to see Sal and not <u>Little Bear</u> behind her. Look at the surprised look on her face. Sal looks a little surprised, too, don't you think?

Child: Yeh.

Parent: Yes. "<u>Garumpf!</u>" <u>she cried. This is not my child!</u> Where is Little Bear? And mother bear ran off to find him. Where do you think Little Bear is?

Child: D-no.

Parent: You don't know? Well, let's turn the page—you can turn it—and maybe we'll find him *there*.

In this simple exchange, a number of important things are being accomplished with language.

1. Parent and child are sharing the pleasures of a book together, a story that unfolds gradually at their pace (not a video's pace) on pages that have illustrations that are stationary enough for the child to study or scrutinize closely.
2. The mother uses both her own words and the words in the book. How closely you follow the exact text is determined by the age of the child and the attention span.
3. The dialogue is interactive—that is, the parent interjects simple questions that elicit responses.
4. When the child answers, the parent affirms the response ("Right") and/or corrects it (pronouncing "Sal," "yes," and "don't know" correctly).

What Comes After Mother Goose?

During the toddler stage, an important parental role is to serve as a welcoming committee—welcoming the child to your world. Think of yourself as the host of a huge party, with your child as the guest of honor. Naturally, you want to introduce her to all the invited guests to make her feel at home. As the child grows older a huge number of things become objects of fascination: holes, cars, snow, birds, bugs, stars, trucks, dogs, rain, planes, cats, storms, babies, mommies, and daddies. This stage is called "labeling the environment."

Picture books are perfect teaching vehicles at this stage. Point to the various items illustrated in the book, call them by name, ask the child to say the name with you, and praise any responses. Two books are excellent for this purpose: *The Everything Book* by Denise Fleming and *First 100 Words* by Roger Priddy. The latter is a collection of photographs of one hundred common items, while *The Everything Book* contains a smaller number of images, including animals, shapes, colors, rhymes, finger games, food, faces, letters, traffic, and toys.

The very best picture book at this stage may be the one you make, using photographs taken in your home and of your family. Desktop printing has made this kind of publishing easy for families. Take photos of your child's day and environment, add some captions, print them out on your home printer, laminate the pages, punch a couple of holes, and you've got a homemade family book. (Note to "pushy" parents: Try to refrain from including work sheets and quiz pages at the back of the book.)

Why Do They Want the Same Book Read Over and Over? And What's with All the Questions?

Just as you didn't learn the names of everyone in your neighborhood or parish overnight, children also need repeated readings in order to learn. Thus, although reading a different book every day may keep the adult from being bored, it prevents the child from getting the reinforcement he needs for learning. Prior to age two, repeated readings of fewer books are better than a huge collection read infrequently.

Those of us who have seen a movie more than once fully realize how many subtleties escaped us the first time. This is even more the case with children and books. Because they're learning a complex language at the adult's speaking pace, there often are misunderstandings that can be sorted out only through repeated readings. I fondly recall the New York City teacher who told me that as a child he called *The Night Before Christmas* "the book about the man who got sick." Why? Until his grandmother finally explained it to him, he had misunderstood the phrase "Tore open the shutters and *threw up* the sash."

Parents sometimes are irritated by a child's incessant questions: "My child interrupts the book so often for questions, it ruins the story." First, you need to define the kinds of questions. Are they silly? Are they the result of curiosity or extraneous to the story? Is the child sincerely trying to learn something or just postponing bedtime? You can solve the latter problem if you make a regular habit of talking about the story when you finish instead of simply closing the book, kissing the child good night, and turning off the light.

In the case of intelligent questions, try to respond immediately if the child's question involves background knowledge ("Why did Mr.

MacGregor put Peter's father in a pie, Mom? Why couldn't he just hop out?"), and thus help the child better understand the story. Extraneous questions can be handled by saying, "Good question! Let's come back to that when we're done." And be sure to live up to that promise. Ultimately, one must acknowledge that questions are a child's primary learning tool. Don't destroy natural curiosity by ignoring it.

As boring as repeated readings may be for the adult, they can accomplish very important things within a child. To begin with, he will learn language by hearing it over and over—this is called immersion. Hearing the same story over and over is definitely a part of that immersion process.

For as long as possible, your read-aloud efforts should be balanced by outside experiences. Barring cases of bedridden children, it is not enough simply to read to the child. The background knowledge I noted earlier applies to life experience as well. The words in the book are just the beginning. What you as a parent or teacher do after the reading can turn a mini-lesson into a sizable learning experience. For example, *Corduroy* by Don Freeman is a much-loved children's book about a little girl and a department store teddy bear. The story alone is heartwarming, but the name Corduroy could also be used as a springboard to a discussion and comparison of other common fabrics like denim, wool, cotton, canvas, and felt. And it works in reverse as well: When you find a caterpillar outside, read Eric Carle's *The Very Hungry Caterpillar* inside the house or classroom. (See page 28 for ways Linda Kelly Hassett expanded books with Erin.)

What About Vocabulary Words the Child or Class Might Not Know?

While it's not necessary to turn every book into a lesson, there are some reading styles that are shown to be more effective than others. For example, Warwick Elley had teachers of six classes of eight-year-olds read picture books to the students using different styles. Certain target words were identified to teachers beforehand, and students were given a pretest into which those words were subtly inserted.[8]

Group A classes heard the book with the teacher giving brief explanations of unknown words, either using synonyms for the word or pointing to a picture on the page of, for example, a "roadster." This was the "reading with explanation" style. In a period of seven days, the class heard the story three times.

Group B classes heard the same book three times in the same period but without explanations of the target words ("no explanation" style).

Additionally, there was a control group of children who did not hear the story at all. Using pretests, posttests, and three-month delayed posttests, Elley found the "with explanation" classes had a 39.9 percent vocabulary gain while the "no explanation" classes gained 14.8 percent, and the control group (hearing none of the books) gained less than 2 percent. Students scoring low on the pretest showed posttest gains as large as their higher-scoring classmates.[9]

In looking at readings of various books and the difference in results (some more modest than others), researchers noted that books that hold children's attention will garner larger learning benefits, especially books that include "novelty, humor, conflict, and suspense." In other words, the more interesting the book, the keener the child's attention and the more learning results.

How Can Illiterate or Semiliterate Parents Read to Children?

Forty-five years ago, this would have been an insurmountable problem, but not now. One kind of book and a piece of technology help to save the day. The books are wordless and predictable books (or easy-readers) and the technology is the CD player.

Thirty thousand years ago, in a step toward writing, our ancestors used cave drawings to tell stories without words. Wordless books follow that tradition. These books convey a story without using words; pictures (interpreted orally by the reader) tell the whole story. The parent who can't read (or can't read English) has little difficulty in looking at the pictures and talking the book to the child.[10] The popularity of this genre has decreased in recent years, but there are still dozens of wordless books in print or in your free public library, from the simple (like *Deep in the Forest* by Brinton Turkle) to the complex (*The Silver Pony* by Lynd Ward or *Tuesday* by David Wiesner). There is a beginner's list on page 175.

Forty-five years ago, a person had to be blind to obtain a book on tape in America. Now thousands of titles are available for parents or anyone wishing to listen, learn, and enjoy a good book, all at the public library. Illiterate or semiliterate parents can listen to these recorded books along with the child and, hearing them often enough, will begin to memorize them. The illiterate parent and child can sit together and listen to a book, even follow along on the page. They're sharing time and a common story. Is someone else's voice better than the parent's? No, but it's a whole lot better than no story at all from the parent who struggles with literacy or language. Taking the time to listen beside the child, instead of watching TV or talking on the phone, sends a message to the child about the importance the parent places on books. For parents or teachers of older children, see page 153 in chapter 8 for further discussion of children's recorded books.

If We Have Only a Small Amount of Time for Read-Aloud, How Do We Incorporate Discussion?

Discussion after the story is of critical importance, but it doesn't have to last forever. Students from classrooms where there were more book discussions tend to score higher in national reading assessments[11] and read more outside school.[12] Look at the more than fifty books Oprah's Book Club put on the *New York Times* best-seller list. How many would have made the list if there had been only advertisements for the books on her show instead of discussions? Ever hear of a state test being responsible for making a book into a best seller? For many people (though not all), reading needs to be a social experience, giving them the chance to share their feelings about the book and its characters: "What I don't get is how she could have made that decision after what happened in her own childhood. How could she?" If there really is a shortage of time, steal it from other subjects that are not as essential as reading, which includes pretty much everything else.

What Kind of Read-Alouds Should We Expect in Preschool?

Preschools and child care come in all sizes and shapes, from excellent to dreadful. I highly recommend you spend an entire day at a school or site before you enroll your child. If the program does not include read-alouds, I would have a serious discussion before making a decision. For example, here's an e-mail sent to me by a rightly concerned parent:

Dear Mr. Trelease,
   I am happy to report that my son (let's call him Jason), who has recently turned two, loves nothing better than to snuggle up, either with a beloved adult, or alone with a "buddy" (stuffed animal), and peruse his books. Last night he surprised his dad and me when, during story time, he jumped in and recited several long passages from his current favorite, Robert McCloskey's *Make Way for Ducklings*. Though

we often stop toward the end of a sentence for Jason to finish off, we had no idea he had memorized whole paragraphs, parrot-perfect inflection and all. What a hoot!

Recently Jason began part time at a reputable early-childhood program in our community. I spent Jason's first day there with him, from 9:30 am until 4 pm, with nap-time excluded. This was meant to give me a chance to get to know the teachers, the other children, and how Jason would be spending his day. To my surprise, not one book was opened all day. Not one.

I asked one of the teachers in this well-staffed room if they ever read. She said, "Sometimes—during circle time we'll read a book—sometimes."

I believe I might have audibly gasped and asked, "Just one?" The response had something to do with the weather and new teachers and did not really seem like an answer to me. I left feeling disappointed and, frankly, confused. Why on earth would you not read to toddlers as a central part of their day?

A very good question to be posed to the staff. As further proof of how disconnected that particular staff might be, see Jennie Fitzkee's preschool class later in this chapter.

Is There a Natural Transition from Picture Book to Novel?

Thanks to our primal need to find out what happens next, read-aloud is a particularly effective tool in stretching children's attention spans. Just keep in mind that endurance in readers, like runners, is not built overnight; start slowly and build gradually. Begin with short picture books, then move to longer ones that can be spread over several days, then to short novels (already broken into convenient chapters), and finally to full-length novels (longer than one hundred pages).

The amount of text on a page is a good way to gauge how much the child's attention span is being stretched. When my grandson Tyler was two years old, he regularly heard books with just a few sentences on a page, but by three and a half he was listening to books that had three times as much text. The transition from short to longer should be done gradually over many different books. While you don't want to drown the child in words, you do want to unconsciously entice him away from a complete dependence on illustrations for comprehension and into more words.

If I had a primary class (or child) that had never been read to (like the ones who spent all of kindergarten filling in blanks and circling letters), I'd start the year with: the repetition of *Tikki Tikki Tembo* by Arlene Mosel, the poignancy of *The Biggest Bear* by Lynd Ward, the mystery of *The Island of the Skog* by Steven Kellogg, *Snip Snap! What's That?* by Mara Bergman, which elicits loud class responses to the plot, and the suspense of Paul Zelinsky's retelling of *Rumpelstiltskin*.

Then I'd do a week of picture books from the Treasury at the back of this book, including *Chewie Louie* by Howie Schneider (humor), *The Secret Shortcut* by Mark Teague (excuses), *I Am So Strong* by Mario Ramos (boasting versus humility), *The Great Fuzz Frenzy* by Janet Stevens and Susan Stevens Crummel (copycatting), and *Lost and Found: Three Dog Stories* by Jim La-Marche (determination), with each very short story read at a different hour of the day, stretching the one book through the day.

Next would be Red Riding Hood Week, focusing on different versions of that famous red-hooded pilgrim—starting with Trina Schart Hyman's *Little Red Riding Hood* and followed by books chosen from the titles listed with it in the Treasury.

Then I'd schedule several "author weeks," each focusing exclusively on one author's books. I'd start with Kevin Henkes, who uses his mouse tales to read the pulse of childhood so touchingly (see the list of his books accompanying *Lilly's Purple Plastic Purse* in the Treasury). As their attention grew, I'd have a Bill Peet Week, choosing a week's worth of reading listed with *The Whingdingdilly* in the Treasury. On the day I read *Kermit the Hermit* (about a stingy hermit crab), I'd introduce it with "Hector the Collector" from Shel Silverstein's poetry collection *Where the Sidewalk Ends*. From then on I would sprinkle poetry throughout the day: waiting for the bell in the morning, between classes, etc.

(Mentioning Bill Peet reminds me to offer a thought here about old versus new book choices: Our culture tends to disproportionately honor the new—new books, music, movies, hairstyles, etc. The danger in that is we'll stop paying attention to the older books, children then grow up not knowing them, those books don't get worn out and need replacing with new copies, and eventually the publisher lets the books go out of print. Keep the great old books alive by including them in your readings.)

Next I'd move on to a picture book series, with each volume treated as a chapter in an ongoing book—like Bernard Waber's seven-book Lyle the Crocodile series, which begins with *The House on East 88th Street*. (See its Treasury listing for titles in the series.)

Once you've built a child's or class's attention span, it's an easy jump to chapter books—either long picture books or short novels of sixty to one hundred pages. These are books that don't have to end with Monday but can be stretched into Tuesday and Wednesday, breaking them into your own "chapters." Preschoolers can enjoy picture books that are divided into chapters, like *Wagon Wheels* by Barbara Brenner and *The Josefina Story Quilt* by Eleanor Coerr. Then I'd do a collection of stories in one volume about one family. One of the best is *All About Alfie* by Shirley Hughes, a collection of four stories about a spirited preschooler and his family. Nobody has a better handle on young families than Shirley Hughes. Be sure to include her latest, *Don't Want to Go!* and *Bobbo Goes to School.*

As for actual short novels, my immediate nominees would be *Look Out, Jeremy Bean!* by Alice Schertle and *Two Times the Fun* by Beverly Cleary, then moving to *My Father's Dragon* by Ruth Stiles Gannett, Johanna Hurwitz's *Rip-Roaring Russell* (see the Treasury's short novel listings for the other books in the Russell series), and then *James and the Giant Peach* by Roald Dahl, now a half century old and achieving classic status.

At What Age Can You Begin Chapter Books?

Let me give you an idea of how widespread the misunderstanding is about the difference between listening to and reading levels, as well as the magic that can occur when they are understood. About twenty years ago I was doing an all-day seminar in a blue-collar community on the Jersey shore. At lunch, a young teacher named Melissa Olans Antinoff introduced herself and said, "You'd love my kindergarten class!" She explained that she read one hundred picture books a year to the class, but also read ten to twelve chapter books. The socioeconomic level of the class had 60 percent of the children on free lunch, and Antinoff was in only her fourth year of teaching.

When the seminar resumed after lunch, I asked how many kindergarten teachers were in the room and learned there were eight. Further investigation showed that Antinoff was the only one who read chapter books to her class. Which of those eight classes will be better prepared for first grade: the ones that heard 150 four-minute picture books, or the one that heard a hundred picture books along with a dozen novels? Which class will have the longer attention spans at the end of the year and larger vocabularies, and exercise more complex thinking?

Sadly, the children most in need of such doses of extended listening—at-risk students—hear the least. Nell Duke's study of ten low- and ten high-socioeconomic first grades showed seven of the advantaged classes were read to from chapter books while only two of the low-SES classes heard chapter books.[13]

A few years later Melissa Antinoff, the daughter of two teachers, began teaching fourth grade in a different town and continued reading aloud to her students. She shared this anecdote with me:

"Bobby" hated to read when fourth grade started. In fact, in the beginning he didn't want to sit still when I read aloud. He'd wiggle, poke people, want to sit at his desk, etc. I began the year with Louis Sachar's *There's a Boy in the Girls' Bathroom*. Eventually, by the end of September, he not only sat still, he moved so that he was sitting in front of me when I was reading, and then, around the beginning of November, he began asking to read ahead in the novel when there was free time.

I was amazed. This is a boy who, at the beginning of the year, was in the lowest reading group (I hate that term, but I'm not sure what else to use) and had great difficulty answering any questions about what he had read. I rarely used the basal readers this year and we read a ton of novels. By October, Bobby was the first one in his reading group to raise his hand to answer a question. In fact, I moved him up to one of my middle groups at the start of the second marking period. What excited me the most was that Bobby began reading on his own—every chance he could. (My general rule is that, if a student finishes any work in any subject early, he or she should read.)

By the time parent conferences came around, Bobby was reading three books—three! When I asked him why he didn't just read one book at a time, he told me he liked them all and couldn't decide which one to start, so he was reading all three. It got so that I had to specifically walk up to him and get his attention back to what we were doing, he was so engrossed in the books.

All of this came up at his conference. Bobby had come with his mother and was participating in the discussions concerning his progress for the first marking period. He was describing one of the books he was reading, and his mother was marveling at her son. I asked Bobby why he seemed to dislike anything to do with reading in September and three months later couldn't get enough of books.

He replied, "Well, at first I was really bored, especially when you read aloud, because I had to pretend to pay attention. But when you read, you made it sound so interesting, and I liked Bradley (the main character in *There's a Boy in the Girls' Bathroom*), and I wanted to see if it was as good if I read it myself, so I started reading about Bradley. It was. So I tried a book you weren't reading and liked it."[14]

Melissa is presently out of the classroom until her children are both in school. Nonetheless, she's proved the read-aloud concept works in school and out. Her son, who's in kindergarten, learned to read at age five and a half and now insists on closed-captioning for his favorite TV programs. His painless slide into reading was certainly aided by hearing hundreds of picture books and novels like Beverly Cleary's Ramona books, lots of Roald Dahl, and *The Tale of Despereaux* by Kate DiCamillo.

Could You Read Chapter Books at the Preschool Level?

Ask that question of Jennie Fitzkee and you'll get "Oh, yes!" as a quick response. Jennie's been teaching preschool for thirty years, all but one at the nonprofit Groton Community School, in Groton, Massachusetts (population 10,000). An upscale bedroom community of Boston with a median family income of $136,000, Groton has one of the region's lowest poverty rates (1 percent). Parents in such places tend to be highly educated, competitive, busy, and pretty sure of themselves. And although Groton parents may be living just down the road from two legendary New England prep schools (Groton School and Lawrence Academy), they really don't know it all, at least when it comes to raising children. For most of them, it's their first experience with the process—and that's where experienced early childhood teachers like Jennie Fitzkee are so valuable. As the school's director, Linda Kosinski, points out: "It's all about parent education, parent education, parent education"—helping parents help their children.

Jennie teaches parents in two ways: through their children and through her newsletters sent home, which offer childhood insights garnered through her classroom activities, heavily focused on books—multiple picture books each day and thirty minutes of a chapter book daily. Thirty minutes of a novel with fifteen children ages three to four? I had to see it for myself, so I spent the day in the "aqua room" observing Jennie and her teaching team with the children. By the way, she's been reading novels to preschoolers for more than fifteen years.

That morning, after the children heard *Goldilocks and the Three Bears*, they dictated their own version of the story, something that included voting on the best way for the bears to wake up Goldilocks (dancing) and what to do if she wouldn't wake up (call 911). Then it was time to act out the story, arranging their sit-upon mats as substitute bear beds (two mats for baby bear, four for mama bear, and five for papa bear), then over to a table where there were three different-size bowls with teddy bears and a single golden-haired doll, and finally on to the kitchen area to mix flour and water as porridge. No one tried to eat any of it, maybe because they were having such a good time "squooshing and mooshing" it through their fingers.

Later Jennie read *The Magic Porridge Pot* by Paul Galdone to three children nestling around her, pausing to underline the words "Stop, little pot, stop!" and then enticing them to join in that response throughout the story. When she later read *The Story of Little Babaji* (Bannerman and Marcellino) she paused occasionally to ask little questions that never interrupted the flow of the story (at the picture of Mamaji working at her sewing machine, "What is that?"; the meaning of "trousers," "bazaar," and "feeling grand").

Lunchtime in class still centered on story, but of a different kind: true stories from Jennie's personal life, of which there is an extensive repertoire, including adventures like the Gorilla story, the Peanut Man story, the Birthday story, and the Bat and the Tennis Racket story. The class votes for which story they want on a given day (with votes carefully counted aloud), and each true story begins with the words "It happened like this." The children told me that make-believe stories begin with "Once upon a time." After lunch, the room's curtains are drawn and the lights dimmed for rest or nap time, each child curling up on his or her floor mat, blanket in hand.

At one p.m. Jennie Fitzkee begins the most ambitious part of the day: reading aloud for thirty minutes from a chapter book (novel). On the day I visited, Jennie sat in her rocking chair and read from *The Story of Doctor Dolittle* by Hugh Lofting, written in 1920 and weighing in at 156 pages. Since it was a Monday, she recounted the plot from Friday's chapter, soliciting the names of characters from the children. "And what was the name of the parrot who taught Doctor Dolittle how to speak with the animals?" "Polynesia!" was the *Jeopardy*-quick response from a pair of four-year-olds at her feet. As she reads and encounters unusual terms, she either clarifies the term or asks the class: "What is 'less and less'?"

" 'The man walked away saying rude things.' What does that mean?" Occasionally she'll stop and exclaim, "Oh—here's an important part." When Dolittle needed an anchor for his boat trip to Africa, a class discussion ensued about anchors, their purpose, and what they look like.

"My class is a mixed-age

group, so often the younger ones do fall asleep. The older ones are then engaged in the books. But, as the year goes on, those children who slept through many parts of the books in the fall are really listening in the spring," she explains.

During the half hour's reading, questions and answers were exchanged in a spirit of conversation, without a hint of testing or right/wrong answers. The exchanges were language and experience rich, each book gently opening doors and windows to the world outside. Jennie Fitzkee doesn't read abridged editions and never skips a word. Incidentally, there wasn't a work sheet in sight.

A two-minute drive from Jennie's classroom, over at Lawrence Academy ($50,000 tuition), Laura Moore has dimmed the lights in her senior English classroom, and also is reading aloud to her students, having discovered some years ago that it is the single best way to implant the love of literature in those teens who have either lost it or never had it.[15]

At What Age Do You Stop the Picture Books?

Although I understand the impatience to get on with the business of growing up, I wince whenever I hear that question. A good story is a good story, whether it has pictures or not. All those pictures in museums don't have a lot of words under them but they still move us, right?

I know preschool teachers who read Judith Viorst's *Alexander and the Terrible, Horrible, No Good, Very Bad Day* to their classes, and I know a high school English teacher who read it to his sophomores twice a year— first in September and again, by popular demand, in June. A picture book should be on the reading list at every grade level.

Many U.S. high school students were not read to regularly in middle grades and do little or no recreational reading on their own. I remember talking with a remedial class of ninth-graders in California one day. Of the twenty-one students, not one had ever heard of the Pied Piper, none had heard of the Wright brothers, and only two had heard of David and Goliath. Their mainstream cultural references were a bit shallow and ripe for planting.

Some recommendations to win over those who think older students won't respond to picture books include:

+ *Johnny on the Spot* by Edward Sorel. (Johnny and his adult neighbor accidentally invent a radio that broadcasts events one day in advance; the conflict arises when Johnny is sworn to secrecy and forbidden to interfere with the future—even if he knows a calamity is about to occur.)

- *The Man Who Walked Between the Towers* by Mordicai Gerstein. (Winner of the 2003 Caldecott Medal, this is the true story of the young Frenchman who strung a tightrope between the two unfinished towers of the World Trade Center in 1974 and walked between them for two hours during morning rush hour. The story focuses on that event and not on the 9/11 tragedy twenty-seven years later, although there is a fleeting reference to the fact that the towers are no more.)
- *An Orange for Frankie* by Patricia Polacco. (A great story that happens to have pictures to go with it. In this tale from the author's family history, we have a family of nine on Christmas Eve, a father missing in a snowstorm, a boxcar of hungry and freezing hobos, one missing sweater, and a lost Christmas orange—all of it neatly tied into a happy holiday ending. This is as good as holiday stories get!)
- *The Story of Ruby Bridges* by Robert Coles. (Teens who think they're overstressed might take some comfort from this true story from the pen of a Pulitzer Prize–winning research psychiatrist, relating the school days of six-year-old Ruby Bridges, one of four black children selected by a federal judge to integrate the New Orleans public schools in 1960.)

Are There Pitfalls to Avoid in Choosing Long Novels?

The difference between short and full-length novels (I use approximately one hundred pages as a demarcation point) is sometimes found in the amount of description, the shorter ones having less detail, the longer ones requiring more imagination on the part of the reader-listener. Children whose imaginations have been atrophying in front of a television for years are not comfortable with long descriptive passages. But the more you read to them, the less trouble they have in constructing mental images. Indeed, research shows us that listening to stories stimulates the imagination significantly more than television or film.[16]

In approaching longer books, remember that all books are not meant to be read aloud; indeed, some books aren't even worth reading to yourself, never mind boring a family or class with them. Some books are written in a convoluted or elliptical style that can be read silently but not aloud.

One of the best rules on the difference between listening to text and reading text was defined by the great Canadian novelist Robertson Davies in the preface to a volume of his speeches. He asked readers to remember they were reading speeches, not essays: "What is meant to be heard is necessarily more direct in expression, and perhaps more boldly coloured, than what is meant for the reader."[17] This is a fact missed by many speakers, preachers, and professors who write their speeches as if the audience were going to read them instead of listen to them. Be sure to take Davies's advice into consideration when choosing your longer read-alouds.

Also be alert to the subject matter of the novels. With longer books, it's imperative for the adult to preview the text before reading it aloud. The length of such books allows them to treat subject matter that can be very sensitive, far more so than a picture book could. As the reader, you should first familiarize yourself with the subject and the author's approach. Ask yourself as you read it through: "Can my child or class handle not only the vocabulary and the complexity of this story, but its emotions as well? Is there anything here that will do more harm than good to my child or class? Anything that might embarrass someone?"

Along with enabling you to avoid that kind of damaging situation, reading the book ahead of time will allow you to read it the second time to the class or child with more confidence, accenting important passages, leaving out dull ones (I mark these lightly in pencil in the margins), and providing sound effects to dramatize the story line (I'm always ready to knock on a table or wall where the story calls for a knock at the door).

What Makes a Good Read-Aloud?

The overwhelming criteria for selecting the read-alouds in the Treasury list at the back of this book: *plot*, the wind beneath the story's wings. Does anything happen that we care about? Do we want to turn the page to see what happens next? How long does it take to get things moving? Are we begging for more when the final page is read? Conversely, the author who spends a whole page in a novel describing the butterfly on the pinewood plank on a spring morning by the lake may be a fine poet but the end product is not going to hold an audience for long unless the butterfly soon turns into a dangerous . . .

There is also an intangible that certifies most of the books in the Treasury listing here: The story stays with the reader and listener for days afterward. Many books, like movies or songs, are forgotten almost immediately. But the great ones—you can still taste them years later, even remember the exact spot where you met them. You can't always put your finger on why they linger with you, but they do.

If plot is so important, where does that leave nonfiction? They're usually not great read-alouds, unless the audience is especially interested in the subject. This means if you have a child who is very keen on a subject (the Civil War or Derek Jeter), he or she will usually be ripe for a read-aloud on that subject—but a whole class might not be. On the other hand, there are excellent picture books that incorporate plot into nonfiction, often focusing on singular events in a person's life. See the lists in the Treasury that are labeled (nonfiction) or check out these Treasury titles and the books listed with them as related books: *My Brother Martin* by Christine King Farris; *Nurse, Soldier, Spy* by Marissa Moss; *Odd Boy Out: Young Albert Einstein* by Don Brown; *POP! The Invention of Bubble Gum* by Meghan McCarthy; *Thank You, Sarah: The Woman Who Saved Thanksgiving* by Laurie Halse Anderson; and *The Kid Who Invented the Popsicle* by Don Wulffson. They are entertaining, informative, and, unlike textbooks, never dull.

Needless to say, plot is not going to be a factor for infants and young toddlers. For them the ideal read-aloud floats on its sounds—good rhythm and rhyme, lots of repetition, sounds that are silly or dramatic or exciting, and lots of splashy color, along with plenty of the familiar.

For a child age two and a half to three, the idea of plot begins to creep in, but nothing too complicated: the lost puppy or the consequences of a little naughtiness. Good examples are *You Can Do It, Sam* by Amy Hest and Martin Waddell's *The Super Hungry Dinosaur*. Language is still exciting and repetitious, but with a little more narrative. *Whistle for Willie* by Ezra Jack Keats is one example, because it has enough of a story to keep the very young interested and pleased when, in the end, the boy is able to master the art of whistling, something that can be demonstrated to the child listener. Considering how much competition there is for a child's attention as he or she grows older, plot is increasingly important as a magnet for that attention.

The challenge arrives as the child approaches eight or nine years of age and the literature takes on a more realistic tone. The plots begin to center on social and emotional issues, many of them growing more severe as the books creep into what is called "young adult" literature: divorce, incest, child abuse, death, substance abuse, and violence. None of those are new issues to literature—Dickens handled them all.

In choosing books that explore such issues, however, we must ensure they do so at an appropriate developmental level. What a thirteen-year-old can handle in a story may not be appropriate for a nine-year-old. There is a great advantage to having certain serious issues shared between an adult and a child or teachers and students, because the adult can then serve as a guide through the pain of the book's events.

As children grow older, we must also make the distinction between books that are emotionally appropriate for hearing and those for reading. The subject matter of some books may be too personal to be shared out

loud, especially in a classroom. It would have to be a highly unusual cir-
cumstance for me to read aloud to a class of teenagers a book that had
incest as its central focus. What you might read one-on-one with a
daughter or son could come across very differently in a classroom.

When It's Obvious You've Made a Poor Choice of a Book, Is It Okay to Abandon It, or Parts of It, and Move On?

I know very learned people who are adamant that if you start a book, you
finish it. In my mind, these are people who need either a second job or a
larger family. Instead, I side with those who will give a book several
chapters before setting it aside. (Better yet, rather than drag the child
through the boredom, read the first couple of chapters to yourself before
choosing it as a read-aloud.)

My support in this approach comes from Nancy Pearl, former executive director of the Washington Center for the Book, who conceived the
One City, One Book movement that swept many American cities and
towns. In *Book Lust*, Pearl offers advice to adults that can apply to both
reading to children and children's own reading. She calls it the Rule of 50:
If you're fifty or younger, give every book about fifty pages. If you're over
fifty, then subtract your age from one hundred and give it that many pages.[18]
Simply put, there's a limit to how much mental punishment anyone should
have to endure from an author.

As for the long descriptive passages, I follow the Charles Dickens policy:
When reading aloud, bowdlerize the text where needed. When the great
author was reading aloud his texts to audiences, he used abbreviated versions, excising his own long descriptive passages. I always read ahead, and
when I find long passages that slow things down, I put a small check mark
in the margin and skip that section when I read aloud.

Do Children Have to Follow Along in a Book as You Read Aloud?

While it's not always necessary, it can be extremely helpful with certain
students. Here's how.

Karl "Skip" Johnson, the principal at El Crystal Elementary in San
Bruno, California, can't take all the credit for his brainstorm. He pretty
much stumbled on it. As we pick up his story, Johnson had been principal there for fourteen years, one of the many stops he'd made in a

three-decade career that ran up and down the West Coast, teaching second through twelfth grades, and then in administration. His first love in education had always been reading, so it figures that subject would be linked to his brainstorm. In fact, it was his love of reading that brought him into teaching in the first place. The high school counselor asked him what he loved the most and Skip answered "reading." So the counselor recommended a career in education, an easy choice in those days.

So now it was 2004, his district was using a standard textbook approach to reading supplemented by one of the computerized reading incentive programs (theirs was Reading Counts), and No Child Left Behind was turning up the pressure to get everyone scoring at the same reading level. It wasn't going to be easy. (The computerized reading incentive programs usually offer prizes and grade points for the number of books read, according to their difficulty. More on this on page 92 in chapter 5.)

San Bruno is a small community that runs blue-collar to affluent, and it geographically bounds the west edge of the San Francisco airport. Johnson's 250-student body is 40 percent Caucasian and 40 percent Latino, and the remaining 20 percent is a United Nations mix. What preoccupied Johnson and his faculty was the challenge of lifting the kids who came from homes where English was not the primary language—English Language Learners (ELL). They wanted to read what the other students were reading and pass the Reading Counts test afterward, but they couldn't understand it or pass the test.

As Johnson and his teachers saw it, there was a language gap—these students hadn't heard enough of the words and expressions that make up everyday English conversation and its idioms, expressions like: Gets on my nerves. Hopping mad. Cute as a button. So what? Hits the spot. Sweating bullets. On the double. Give me a break. He's a real card. Feel at home.

If only there were a way to enrich their language during their home hours. Johnson knew firsthand how nurturing the home could be for early reading experiences. Back when he was in elementary school, he loved to read so much his mother used to reward him with days off from school just to stay home and read all day. That, however, wasn't going to happen today in a world where both parents were working outside the home.

It was 2004 when someone gave Johnson a $50 iTunes gift card and he thought, "I already have enough music on my iPod to last a lifetime, so what am I going to spend this on?" And that's when he saw the audiobook category in the iTunes Store, which included children's titles. Maybe he'd download a few and discuss them with the kids in school after he listened to them. But before that happened, another idea intruded, an idea that would help bridge the gap between home and school, as well as the gap between proficient readers and the strugglers.

The brainstorm became known as eCAP (El Crystal Audiobook Project) and added up to sixty iPod kits (from grant money), along with six hundred audiobooks. When a teacher identifies a non-proficient reader, she sits down with the student and they construct a fifteen-book playlist from the school's master list and load it into an iPod. The kit that accompanies it includes the book's text, a charger, headphones, and any necessary instructions. Best of all, it stays with the student—in school and out—for the entire school year, with more books loaded as needed. The student listens to the book on the iPod while following along in the text with his eyes. The reader's voice and inflection, in turn, serves as a vocabulary and reading coach, especially during critical hours away from the classroom. Afterward, the Reading Counts quiz measures how well the student comprehended what was read. (Note: The school makes a serious effort not to go overboard with Reading Counts competition.)

El Crystal teachers use a textbook for instruction, continue to read aloud to their K–6 classes, and then adopt an Oprah Winfrey role in literature circles, in which independent reading is shared among the children. How well is the program working? El Crystal's students are sixty points higher than the state's Academic Performance Index, and annually read one million words more than their closest district rivals. While an average student gains 100 lexile points in a school year, most of the eCAP students double that number.[19] The lexile score measures the vocabulary level at which a student can read; the higher the student's lexile score, the more difficult the books he or she will be able to comprehend. (For more on audiobooks, see chapter 8.)

Shouldn't There Be a Test to See If the Class Is Truly Learning from Read-Aloud?

By all means, there should be a test—and there *is* one. Only you don't *give* it. It's the test of time, the real measure of anything we teach. What do they remember ten, twenty, thirty years from now? Of all the lessons taught, what lasted?

Kimberly Douglas, of Hillsboro, Ohio, had the satisfaction of learning the answer to that question. Back in 1989 she was in her second year of teaching when she picked up an early edition of this handbook and began reading to her classes. I'll let her pick up the story in her e-mail to me:

I am now an administrator who works with first year teachers. In planning for an upcoming meeting and presentation on building relationships with students, I Facebook-messaged seventy-one of my former students, asking them to share their memories of being a sixth-grader in my classroom. I told them it didn't matter if they remembered how to divide fractions or knew the chemical symbol for copper, I wanted to know what they truly remembered. The response has been overwhelming. They've remembered some pretty incredible things, but the common theme among all of their memories is the books we read together. We've discussed titles and authors and how they've read those same books to their own children. Keep in mind, these "kids" range in age from 26-37, and they've remembered: *Gentle Ben; Bridge to Terabithia; From the Mixed-up Files of Mrs. Basil E. Frankweiler; Hatchet; Where the Red Fern Grows;* and many others. Several of them have also commented that they wish their children's teachers would read to them the way I did all those years ago.[20]

I would say both Kimberly and her students passed the test handsomely. As Kimberly's e-mail attests, the reader-aloud is planting seeds she hopes will bear fruit with the students' future children. It might even be motivating enough to get students to class on time or at least more regularly. Consider the experience of Nancy Foote, of Higley, Arizona, former recipient of the Presidential Award for Excellence in Mathematics and Science Teaching, a National Board Certified teacher (less than 3 percent of teachers achieve this honored status), and a devotee of reading aloud and its impact on reluctant teens. As she explains it:

I was a teacher for almost 20 years in traditional schools. For several years, I taught at an alternative high school. Many of my students were convicted felons who were on probation. Some of my students were on house arrest, allowed to leave home only to go to school. Many had drug addictions that they were fighting. They were wonderful kids who had bigger problems than I could ever imagine.

We had a relatively long passing between classes, amounting to five minutes. Our campus was rather small, so there was no reason for kids to come late to class. Yet day after day they arrived late—sometimes just a minute or two, other times much longer. I wanted to find a way to motivate them to get to class on time. I thought about the book *Frindle* by Andrew Clements, a book I had heard you talk about in your workshops. I wasn't sure if these kids would like the book—they were tough kids—but decided to give it a try.

Exactly three minutes before the tardy bell rang, I would begin reading aloud from the book. Once the tardy bell rang, I continued reading until I finished the chapter. At first, I felt sort of foolish. I was reading to a totally empty classroom! That was OK because I loved the story and Nick is one of my favorite characters. Within a few days, the kids started getting to class early so that they could hear about Nick. Within one week, I no longer had problems with tardy students. Once we finished *Frindle*, we moved on to *Loser* by Jerry Spinelli and then Clements's *Things Not Seen*.

Not only did reading aloud get my students to class on time, attendance improved. Whenever someone came back to school after being absent, they wanted to hear what they missed. Some would borrow the book and read it themselves, but most wanted to come in at lunch so I could read it to them. (These were not young children—they ranged in age from 13 to 19.) They couldn't wait to hear what happened next. They were eager to find out what our next story would be.

Near the end of the year, one of my students, a tall, gangly young man, came in to see me. He was 19 years old and fighting a crystal meth addiction. He was trying to raise his young son, since the baby's mother abandoned him in favor of drugs. He had an uphill battle, as did his infant son. In spite of his challenges, he made it to school most days, and kept off drugs. He thanked me for being a great teacher and helping him. He told me that my reading to them was wonderful and he really enjoyed it. He also told me that no one had ever read aloud to him—I was the first. And he promised he would read aloud to his son.[21]

The seeds that are planted for the love of reading may not always bear immediate fruit, but if we are patient enough there will be rewards. Cindy Lovell tells her own story from a striking vantage point in life:

My 4th grade teacher used to choose a chapter from a book, put it in context, read it to us, pause and explain or ask a question or two, and then say, "There! That's just one chapter. If you liked it, here's the book!" Needless to say he baited many hooks, and that's where I met *Tom Sawyer*. I didn't know Mark Twain was a famous author or that he had written many other books until my first week in junior high school. I stopped in the library to ask if they had any books by this author Mark Twain. The librarian grinned and gave me a Twain collection of short stories they were about to discard. Fast-forward to my junior year of high school. I was bored with school and dropped out (much like my hero, Twain, and his boy, Huck), even though I had always wanted to be a teacher. I went to work, married, had two children, had my own business, and still read for pure pleasure during every free second. One day at the age of 35 I had an epiphany. Two years and 9 months later I had a college degree and began teaching, eventually earning a PhD. Now I tell my students that "PhD" stands for Post High school Dropout. I took a nontraditional path and was successful only because of my love of reading.

> —Cindy Lovell
> Executive Director
> Mark Twain Boyhood Home & Museum
> Hannibal, Missouri

Considering Cindy's current employer, there's more than a grain of truth in the adage "What goes around comes around," something a certain Pittsburgh native would attest to as well. He was only six years old when his family read him *Ben and Me* by Robert Lawson, a historical novel about a whimsical mouse's observations on history while living in Ben Franklin's fur hat. It was just the right dose of history at just the right time for little David McCullough, who would never lose his love for that book or for all things historical, becoming one of the nation's leading historians.[22]

Chapter 4

The Dos and Don'ts of Read-Aloud

The first and conceivably the most important instructor in composition is the teacher, parent, or older sibling who reads aloud to the small child.

—Clifton Fadiman,
*Empty Pages: A Search for Writing
Competence in School and Society*

Dos

♦ Begin reading to children as soon as possible. The younger you start them, the easier and better it is.

♦ Use Mother Goose rhymes and songs to stimulate an infant's language and listening. Begin with simple black-and-white illustrations, and then boldly colored picture books to arouse children's curiosity and visual sense.

♦ With infants through toddlers, it is critically important to include in your readings those books that contain repetitions; as they mature, add predictable and rhyming books.

♦ During repeat readings of a predictable book, occasionally stop at one of the key words or phrases and allow the listener to provide the word.

♦ Read as often as you and the child (or students) have time for.

♦ Set aside at least one consistent time each day for a story.

♦ Remember: The art of listening is an acquired one. It must be taught and cultivated gradually—it doesn't happen overnight.

♦ Start with picture books that have only a few sentences on the page, then gradually move to books with more and more text and fewer pictures, and build to chapter books and novels.

- Vary the length and subject matter of your readings, fiction and non-fiction.
- To encourage involvement, invite the child to turn pages for you when it is time.
- Before you begin to read, always say the name of the book, the author, and the illustrator—no matter how many times you have read the book.
- The first time you read a book, discuss the illustration on the cover. Ask, "What do you think this is going to be about?"
- As you read, keep listeners involved by occasionally asking, "What do you think is going to happen next?"
- Follow through with your reading. If you start a book, it is your responsibility to continue it, unless it turns out to be a bad book. Don't leave the child or students hanging for three or four days between chapters and expect interest to be sustained.
- Occasionally read above children's intellectual levels and challenge their minds.
- Picture books can be read easily to a family of children widely separated in age. Novels, however, pose a challenge. If there are more than two years (and thus social and emotional differences) between the children, each child would benefit greatly if you read to him or her individually. This requires more effort on the part of the parents, but it will reap rewards in direct proportion to the effort expended. You will reinforce the specialness of each child.
- Avoid long descriptive passages until the child's imagination and attention span are capable of handling them. There is nothing wrong with shortening or eliminating them. Prereading helps to locate such passages, and they can then be marked with pencil in the margin.
- If the chapters are long or if you don't have enough time each day to finish an entire chapter, find a suspenseful spot at which to stop. Leave the audience hanging; they'll be counting the minutes until the next reading.
- Allow your listeners a few minutes to settle down and adjust their bodies and minds to the story. If it's a novel, begin by asking what happened when you left off yesterday. Mood is an important factor in listening. An authoritarian "Now stop that and settle down! Sit up straight. Pay attention" doesn't create a receptive atmosphere.
- If you are reading a picture book, make sure the children can see the pictures easily. In school, with the children in a semicircle around you, seat yourself just slightly above them so that the children in the back row can see the pictures above the heads of the others.

+ Because other students in a classroom can be a distraction, consider dimming the lights during read-aloud time.
+ In reading a novel, position yourself where both you and the children are comfortable. In the classroom, whether you are sitting on the edge of your desk or standing, your head should be above the heads of your listeners for your voice to carry to the far side of the room. Do not read or stand in front of brightly lit windows. Backlighting strains the eyes of your audience.
+ Remember that everyone enjoys a good picture book, even a teenager.
+ Allow time for class and home discussion after reading a story. Thoughts, hopes, fears, and discoveries are aroused by a book. Allow them to surface, and help the child to deal with them through verbal, written, or artistic expression if he or she is so inclined. Do not turn discussions into quizzes or insist upon prying story interpretations from the child.
+ Remember that reading aloud comes naturally to very few people. To do it successfully and with ease, you must practice.
+ Use plenty of expression when reading. If possible, change your tone of voice to fit the dialogue.
+ Adjust your pace to fit the story. During a suspenseful part, slow down and lower your voice. A lowered voice in the right place moves listeners to the edge of their chairs.
+ The most common mistake in reading aloud—whether the reader is a seven-year-old or a forty-year-old—is reading too fast. Read slowly enough for the child to build mental pictures of what he just heard you read. Slow down enough for the children to see the pictures in the book without feeling hurried. Reading quickly allows no time for the reader to use vocal expression.
+ Preview the book by reading it to yourself ahead of time. Such advance reading allows you to spot material you may wish to shorten, eliminate, or elaborate on.
+ Bring the author to life, as well as the book. Google the author's name to find a personal Web page, and always read the information on your book's dust jacket. Either before or during the reading, tell your audience something about the author. This lets them know that books are written by people, not by machines.
+ Be a good "coach." When you come to a part of the story that the audience might not sense is important, pause and then whisper, "Mmmmmm. That could be important."
+ Add a third dimension to the book whenever possible. For example, have a bowl of blueberries ready to be eaten during or after the reading

of Robert McCloskey's *Blueberries for Sal*; bring a harmonica and a lemon to class before reading McCloskey's *Lentil*.

♦ Every once in a while, when a child asks a question involving the text, make a point of looking up the answer in a reference book with him or her. This greatly expands a child's knowledge base and nurtures library skills.

♦ Follow the suggestion of Dr. Caroline Bauer and post a reminder sign by your door: "Don't Forget Your Flood Book." Analogous to emergency rations in case of natural disasters, "flood" books should be taken along in the car or even stored like spares in the trunk. A few chapters from these books can be squeezed into traffic jams on the way to the beach or long waits at the doctor's office.

♦ Create a wall chart or back-of-the-bedroom-door book chart so the child or class can see how much has been read; images of caterpillars, snakes, worms, and trains work well for this purpose, with each section representing a book. Similarly, post a world or U.S. wall map, on which small stickers can be attached to locations where your books have been set.

♦ When children are old enough to distinguish between library books and their own, start reading with a pencil in hand. When you and the child encounter a passage worth remembering, put a small mark— maybe a star—in the margin. Readers should interact with books, and one way is to acknowledge beautiful writing.

♦ Encourage relatives living far away to record stories on audiocassettes that can be mailed to the child.

♦ Reluctant readers or unusually active children frequently find it difficult to just sit and listen. Paper, crayons, and pencils allow them to keep their hands busy while listening. (You doodle while talking on the telephone, don't you?)

♦ Always have a supply of books for the babysitter to share with the child, and make it understood that reading aloud comes with the job and is preferable to the TV.

+ Fathers should make an extra effort to read to their children. Because the vast majority of primary school teachers are women, young boys often associate reading with women and schoolwork. And just as unfortunately, too many fathers would rather be seen playing catch in the driveway with their sons than taking them to the library. It is not by chance that male school scores have taken a dramatic downturn in the past four decades. A father's early involvement with books and reading can do much to elevate books to at least the same status as sports in a boy's estimation.

+ Arrange for time each day, in the classroom or in the home, for the child to read by herself (even if "read" only means turning pages and looking at the pictures). All your read-aloud motivation goes for naught if time is not available to put that motivation into practice.

+ Lead (or is it "Read"?) by example. Make sure your children see you reading for pleasure other than at read-aloud time. Share with them your enthusiasm for whatever you are reading. If you're reading an e-book, it's important to let the child know you're reading a book, not checking your e-mail or Facebook.

+ When children wish to read to you, it is better for the book to be too easy than too hard, just as a beginner's bicycle is better too small rather than too big.

+ Encourage older children to read to younger ones, but make this a part-time, not a full-time, substitution for you. Remember: The adult is the ultimate role model.

+ Regulate the amount of time children spend in front of the television. Research shows that after about ten TV hours a week, a child's school scores begin to drop. Excessive television viewing is habit forming and damaging to a child's development.

+ When children are watching television, closed-captioning should be activated along with sound. For older children who know how to read but are lazy about it, keep the captioning on and turn the volume down.

Don'ts

+ Don't read stories that you don't enjoy yourself. Your dislike will show in the reading, and that defeats your purpose.

+ Don't continue reading a book once it is obvious that it was a poor choice. Admit the mistake and choose another. Make sure, however, that you've given the book a fair chance to get rolling; some, like *Tuck Everlasting*, start slower than others. (You can avoid the problem by prereading at least part of the book yourself.)

*Don't tie every
book to the class.*

- If you are a teacher, don't feel you have to tie every book to class work. Don't confine the broad spectrum of literature to the narrow limits of the curriculum.
- Don't overwhelm your listener. Consider the intellectual, social, and emotional level of your audience in making a read-aloud selection. Never read above a child's emotional level.
- Don't select a book that many of the children already have heard or seen on television. Once a novel's plot is known, much of their interest is lost. You can, however, read a book and view the video afterward. That's a good way for children to see how much more can be portrayed in print than on film.
- In choosing novels for reading aloud, avoid books that are heavy with dialogue; they are difficult for reading aloud and listening. All those indented paragraphs and quotations make for easy silent reading—the reader sees the quotations marks and knows it is a new voice, a different person speaking, but the listener doesn't. And if the writer fails to include a notation at the end of the dialogue, such as "said Mrs. Murphy," the audience has no idea who said what.
- Don't be fooled by awards. Just because a book won an award doesn't guarantee that it will make a good read-aloud. In most cases, a book award is given for the quality of the writing, not for its read-aloud qualities.
- Don't start reading if you are not going to have enough time to do it justice. Having to stop after one or two pages only serves to frustrate, rather than stimulate, the child's interest in reading.
- Don't get too comfortable while reading. A reclining or slouching position is most apt to bring on drowsiness.
- Don't be unnerved by questions during the reading, particularly from very young children in your own family. If the question is obviously not for the purpose of distracting or postponing bedtime, answer it

patiently. There is no time limit for reading a book, but there is a time limit on a child's inquisitiveness. Foster that curiosity with patient answers, and then resume your reading. Classroom questions, however, need to be held until the end. With twenty children all deciding to ask questions to impress the teacher, you might never reach the end of the book.

• Don't impose interpretations of a story upon your audience. A story can be just plain enjoyable, no reason necessary, and still give you plenty to talk about. The highest literacy gains occur with children who have access to discussions following a story.

• Don't confuse quantity with quality. Reading to your child for ten minutes, with your full attention and enthusiasm, may very well last longer in the child's mind than two hours of solitary television viewing.

• Don't use the book as a threat ("If you don't pick up your room, no story tonight!"). As soon as your child or class sees that you've turned the book into a weapon, they'll change their attitude about books from positive to negative.

• Don't try to compete with television. If you say, "Which do you want, a story or TV?" they will usually choose the latter. That is like saying to a nine-year-old, "Which do you want, vegetables or a doughnut?" Since you are the adult, you choose. "The television goes off at eight thirty in this house. If you want a story before bed, that's fine. If not, that's fine, too. But no television after eight thirty." But don't let books appear to be responsible for depriving the children of viewing time.

Chapter 5

Sustained Silent Reading: Reading Aloud's Natural Partner

An unread story is not a story; it is little black marks on wood pulp.
—Ursula Le Guin

AMONG the many purposes of reading aloud, a primary one is to motivate the child to read independently for pleasure. In academic terms, such reading is called SSR—sustained silent reading. Take a book, a newspaper, a magazine, and enjoy it! No interruptions for questions, assessments, or reports; just read for pleasure. The concept operates under a variety of pseudonyms, including DEAR (drop everything and read), DIRT (daily individual reading time), SQUIRT (sustained quiet uninterrupted reading time), and FVR (free voluntary reading).

This chapter will be devoted to SSR in school as well as at home. I'll also examine a variety of topics associated with silent reading: reading incentive programs (like Accelerated Reader and Reading Counts), teachers' reading habits, junk reading, and "summer setback."

Because we adults have done this thing called reading for so much of our lives, we take many of its facets for granted. Children do not, as evidenced by the story told to me by Lee Sullivan Hill, of Clarendon Hills, Illinois. One day her young son Colin came upon her reading silently to herself and asked, "What are you doing?"

"Reading," she answered.

"Then why aren't you making any noise?"

So she explained how people read to themselves as well as to others, like when she reads to him. Hearing that, the light dawned for Colin. "So that's what Daddy does!" he exclaimed, recalling when he had seen his father reading silently to himself—in fact, practicing SSR. Until it is explained, silent reading is sometimes a mystery to young children.

Apparently, SSR is also a mystery to some school administrators. Here is the exact wording from an evaluation a principal completed of an eighth-grade language arts teacher who had included a forty-minute SSR period in her students' weekly schedule (as prescribed by the school improvement plan): "I see a great deal of free reading taking place in your classroom. I realize the students are working on assigned reading, however I feel that much of the reading taking place in the classroom could take place out of the class. This would allow you more time to interact with the students. Decisions as to how class time is used must be sound if our students are going to be successful later on."

Here's how would I respond to that principal:

1. SSR works as well as any other method, and the research proves it (see page 82).
2. It's almost impossible to interact with students about literature they haven't read—so they're reading it.
3. The students who are the least likely to read outside school are the ones who either hate reading and/or come from homes where there is the least space and quiet for solitary reading; my classroom is a clinic where such reading ills can be cured.
4. There is a natural falloff in recreational reading during adolescence due to the hormonal and social conflict inflicted on their twenty-four-hour day; this is most often reflected in how badly they use their out-of-school time, so I'm providing structured time for reading.
5. My classroom may be the only place where some of them ever see other people reading silently to themselves, and it might be the only place they ever see an adult reading for pleasure and not just for work. My classroom is a laboratory for positive role modeling.

My final word to the principal would be to read the Tom O'Neill anecdote on page 19.

Didn't the National Reading Panel (NRP) Condemn SSR or Independent Reading?

"Condemn" is a little harsh, but the panel didn't exactly give an unqualified endorsement of it, and that bumped the practice from some districts afraid of losing federal funds. In a nutshell, here's the scoop on the NRP versus SSR. (Don't confuse the National Reading Panel of 2000 with the 1985 Commission on Reading—they are two very different animals but probably had the same goals.)

The National Reading Panel's 2000 report noted that there wasn't sufficient scientific evidence to support SSR's use in school, especially if it is being used as the only method of instruction.[1] I know of no one in their right mind who is advocating that SSR be the *only* way to teach reading. Certainly there needs to be instruction, but you also need the opportunity to put it into practice. How can anyone imagine students could get better at reading without reading and reading *a lot*?

The NRP study subgroup deemed only fourteen short-term studies worthy of their disputed[2] "medical-scientific" standards and found insufficient evidence among them to support SSR, even though SSR students performed the same as ten of the control groups and surpassed the control groups in the four remaining studies. There was not one negative SSR performance in their fourteen "scientific" studies, but this was not convincing enough for the NRP.

Which brings us to Stephen Krashen, the leading proponent of inclusion of independent reading in the classroom schedule. (If you are contemplating SSR for your school or class and haven't read his *The Power of Reading*, do so immediately. It should be the bible of SSR.) This professor emeritus from the University of Southern California has thoroughly refuted the NRP's claims, as have a host of other qualified reading authorities.[3] Krashen examined not fourteen short-term SSR studies, as the NRP did, but a total of fifty-three studies, long ones and short ones. Overwhelmingly the results favor SSR, especially in the yearlong studies. The only three negative results for SSR were in short-term studies, compared with twenty-five positive results. If that were a baseball or football score (25–3), could it be more decisive?

SSR is based upon a single simple principle: Reading is a skill—and the more you use it, the better you get at it. Conversely, the less you use it, the more difficult it is.[4]

In 2002, the Organisation for Economic Co-operation and Development (OECD), which for decades has helped its thirty-four member governments monitor school achievement worldwide, issued a report[5] in which it examined the reading literacy of 250,000 fifteen-year-olds in thirty-two countries. In every country, those who read the most read the best regardless of income level (see chart on page 9). A decade earlier, a similar study by the International Association for the Evaluation of Educational Achievement (IEA) compared the reading skills of 210,000 students from thirty-two different countries; it found the highest scores (regardless of income level) among children who:[6]

♦ were read to by their teachers daily;
♦ read the most pages for pleasure daily.

Moreover, the frequency of SSR had a marked impact on scores: Children who had it daily scored much higher than those who had it only once a week. The National Assessment of Educational Progress (NAEP) assessments found an identical pattern for the nearly thirty-five years the NAEP has been testing hundreds of thousands of U.S. students.[7] The evidence for reading aloud to children and for SSR is overwhelming—yet most children are neither read to nor experience SSR in the course of a school day.

As an Adult I Don't *Hate* to Read but I Don't Do It Very Much. Maybe Kids Are the Same Way. Why?

It's a fact: Some people, including highly educated ones, read very little, and some (with or without higher education) read a great deal. So it's not always a literacy problem. As it turns out, one could say it's a math problem. And that brings us to Wilbur Schramm.[8]

Schramm (1907–1987) was a former journalist, professional baseball player, Harvard graduate, O. Henry Award winner, symphony flutist, and the founding father of mass communication as a science. Talk about a guy who could do it all! During World War II, besides working on some of President Roosevelt's fireside chats, he worked for the Office of War Information as its education director and became intrigued by the impact of propaganda on people's thinking and behavior. Although the term *propaganda* traditionally left a sour taste with Americans, Schramm saw it as just another form of mass communication, like news and advertising on the radio, something that could be manipulated to achieve a certain result. By the end of the war, with newspaper and radio audiences reaching their zeniths and television hovering on the horizon, Schramm saw a new day dawning for the scientific study of how we communicate. He eventually founded communication science programs at both the University of Illinois and Stanford. Indeed, he was so far ahead of his time that when his first doctoral students arrived at Illinois, there were no textbooks—no one had ever written a book on the subject of mass communication.

And here is where Schramm comes to our rescue with the question of why we read more or less. One of his studies examined why some people read certain items in a newspaper or magazine and not other items. In explaining that, he developed a formula called the Fraction of Selection, and when applied to the general field of recreational reading, it explains many root problems.

First, a quick math review. In the equation on the left (below), the quotient is arrived at by dividing the dividend by the divisor. If you increase the dividend you increase the quotient. Conversely, increasing the divisor will decrease the quotient. Thus, to increase the quotient one must either increase the dividend or decrease the divisor. Got it? Good, let's move on.

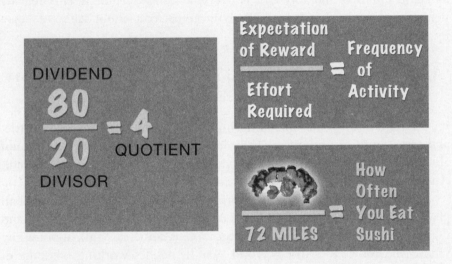

In Schramm's Fraction of Selection (above right), the dividend consists of all the rewards we expect to receive from doing something. The divisor is whatever effort or difficulty we have to endure to get the reward. And the quotient is the frequency—that is, how often we end up doing the action that gives us the reward. For example, if you love sushi but the nearest sushi restaurant is a seventy-two-mile drive, chances are you don't eat there frequently. But if it's twenty minutes away, you'll eat there a lot more often. That's how the Fraction of Selection works. Rewards divided by Difficulties equals Frequency.

Now let's apply this to reading. We'll start with the dividend—the rewards that some people might expect from reading. Pleasure is right at the top, but it includes various subcategories. For example, some people enjoy reading anything they can escape into; others find satisfaction in gathering information; some expect pleasure from the grades or diplomas they'll earn from the reading, the prestige they'll have with peers in class, book club members they socialize with, or a boss or teacher they want to impress; and for some it's the pleasure that comes with higher pay scales associated with diplomas they earned with the reading. Different people expect different rewards—or *no* rewards—from reading. But anyone who reads expects to get something out of it—or he or she won't do it.

Now for the divisor, or the difficulties or effort required for reading. Distractions are a major problem for some—TV, DVDs, their cell phone, video games, e-mails, the computer, or just the chaos in the home or school. For others there's a lack of print—no newspapers, magazines, or books to read (this is most true in poverty situations). For some folks it's a lack of time—working too many hours, raising kids, rushing to too many games or to the mall, or too much homework. For some people it's a case of not being able to read easily because they're plagued by learning disabilities; other people are surrounded by family or peers with negative attitudes toward school and reading; and finally, there can be a lack of quiet space—too much noise at home or too many tests and demands in the classroom.

All of these factors are going to determine how often a competent reader actually reads. Where you maintain strong reward factors and lower the number of difficulties, you will see a higher frequency of reading. And the higher that number is for students, the higher will be their chances of success in school. Those who read the most read the best.

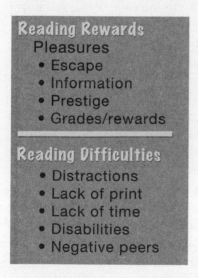

Reading Rewards
Pleasures
• Escape
• Information
• Prestige
• Grades/rewards

Reading Difficulties
• Distractions
• Lack of print
• Lack of time
• Disabilities
• Negative peers

Here's an example of an entire nation that practiced SSR successfully for four decades and then ran into a snag. As a reading model, Japan has been unrivaled in the world. Its citizens consume enormous amounts of print, and lead the world in newspaper readership (64 percent of Japanese adults read a daily newspaper, compared with 23 percent in the United States).[9] Few outsiders, however, understand the reason behind the Japanese numbers: time. They get the same twenty-four hours everyone else gets, but they get them in different doses.

Japan's highway tolls have long been among the highest in the world. A typical U.S. toll of $14 would be $47 in Japan, unless there's a bridge to cross, and then it jumps to $97. The result is that almost everyone in Japan takes public transportation to work, commutes that often average an hour each way.[10] This allows for 120 uninterrupted daily minutes of either reading or napping. All that time and all that reading put Japan over the top in book, magazine, and newspaper consumption—that is, until the mid-1990s.

That's when Japanese readership began to drop, and it continues to drop.[11] The cause was the arrival of what they call the "thumb tribe"—commuters with computer games, e-mail, cell phones, and laptops. In short, *distractions*.

As in Schramm's Fraction of Selection, the more distractions confronting a nation, family, or class, the less reading is accomplished. If you really want to get more reading done, then take control of the distractions: needless trips to the mall, phone calls, multiple televisions, DVD players, e-mails, computer games—each calling for immediate attention or multitasking. The thumb tribe is flourishing in America as well—see chapter 7.

When Does SSR Become Effective?

The benefits vary with the individual, but in its simplest form SSR allows a person to read long enough and far enough that the act of reading becomes automatic. If one must stop to concentrate on each word, sounding it out and searching for meaning, then fluency is lost along with meaning. Reading this way is also fatiguing. Being able to do it automatically is the goal.[12] To achieve this, the Commission on Reading (in *Becoming a Nation of Readers*) recommended two hours a week of independent reading. Where do you find that time? The commission recommended less time be spent on skill sheets and workbooks.[13]

On the secondary level, SSR may not cause an immediate or short-term change in student skills (no quick fix), but it can result in positive changes in attitude toward the library, voluntary reading, assigned reading, and the importance of reading. This affects the amount students read and thus their facility with the process.[14] A striking example of this is Lewenberg Middle School, discussed in chapter 1 on page 19.

Younger readers, however, show significant improvement in both attitude and skills with SSR. "Poor readers," points out Richard Allington,[15] a leading researcher and former president of the International Reading Association, "when given ten minutes a day to read, initially will achieve five hundred words and quickly increase that amount in the same period as proficiency grows."[16]

By the third grade, SSR can be the student's most important vocabulary builder, more so than basal textbooks or even daily oral language.

The Commission on Reading noted: "Basal readers and textbooks do not offer the same richness of vocabulary, sentence structure, or literary form as do trade books. . . . A diet consisting only of basal stories probably will not prepare children well to deal with real literature."[17] Indeed, about half of the three thousand most commonly used words are not even included in K–6 basals.[18] As shown in the chart on page 18, printed material introduces rare words three to six times more than conversation does.

While on the subject of struggling readers, let me point out that research scientists in 2009 at Carnegie Mellon University demonstrated that struggling young readers receiving one hundred hours of reading remediation instruction had significantly rewired their brain networks in the process. Earlier scans of the children indicated a low amount of white matter connecting different parts of the brain. After remediation, the white matter increased to normal, giving the students increased reading ability,[19] not unlike going from dial-up Internet service to DSL.

After reading the research, I e-mailed one of its lead scientists, Dr. Timothy Keller, to ask if improvement in the brain's white matter could be accomplished with strong doses of recreational or independent reading. I received an immediate and enthusiastic response that included the following observations endorsing the positives in SSR:

> Although we don't have direct evidence for this, I do believe that the critical determinant of the increase in the organization of white matter that we found is the amount of time spent engaged in reading behavior, both within and outside the classroom. We did not measure the amount of time spent reading, but parents of children in the treatment program did anecdotally report that their children read more for pleasure at home during and following the program, and this increased reading behavior may have substantially contributed to the changes we found, above and beyond the specific practice they received in the classroom. It seems possible that there is a "boot-strapping" effect that occurs once a child who is struggling with phonological decoding skills receives explicit instruction and becomes more proficient, allowing them and encouraging them to engage in more reading behavior. We speculate in the paper that the change is due to increased myelin that is promoted by activity in reading-relevant circuits, suggesting that the key is to activate these circuits, and whether this activation is the result of time spent engaged in specific exercises or in reading for pleasure may not matter to the axons. . . . I would predict that our measure of white

matter integrity in reading-relevant circuits would be significantly correlated with time spent reading if both were measured in a large population of children.[20]

What Would Cause SSR to Fail?

Two of the early experts on SSR, Robert and Marlene McCracken,[21] reported that most instances in which SSR fails are due to:

• teachers (or aides) who are supervising instead of reading;
• classrooms that lack enough SSR reading materials.

The McCrackens cite the teacher as a critical role model in SSR, reporting widespread imitation of the teacher's reading habits by students. Students in one class noticed the teacher interrupting her reading to look up words in the dictionary and began doing the same. When a junior high teacher began to read the newspaper each day, the class began doing the same. But if the teacher spends the SSR period doing paperwork or policing the room, the role modeling effect is lost.

What About Summer School Reading Programs?

Further proof of SSR's benefits is found in the research on "summer setback." Many parents, especially those whose children are having difficulty with school, see summertime as a vacation from school and take it literally: "Everyone needs a vacation, for goodness' sake. He needs to get away from school and relax. Next year will be a new start." That attitude can be extremely detrimental, especially to a poor reader, because the better readers don't take the summer off and thus the gap widens.

There is an axiom in education that goes, "You get dumber in the summer." A two-year study of three thousand students in Atlanta attempted to see if it was true. They found that everyone—top students and poor students—learns more slowly in the summer. Some, though, do worse than slow down; they actually go into reverse, as you can see in the following figure.[22]

Top students' scores rise slightly between the end of one school year and the beginning of the next. Conversely, the bottom 25 percent (largely urban poor) lose most of what they gained the previous school year. Average students (the middle 50 percent) make no gains during the summer but lose nothing either—except in the widening gap between themselves and the top students. Projected across the first four years of school, the "rich-poor" reading gap that was present at the start of kindergarten has actually widened.

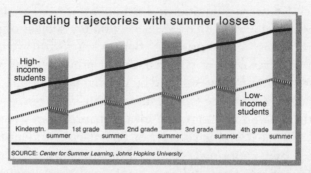

Based on findings by the National Center for Summer Learning, Johns Hopkins University.

Many factors cause the loss. The affluent child's summer includes a family of readers who model that behavior and offer quiet spaces conducive to reading; a home that is print-rich with books, magazines, and newspapers; visits to the mall with stops at the bookstore or library; a family vacation or summer camp out of town in which new people, places, and experiences extend background knowledge and offer new vocabulary; and a high probability that educational or informational TV and radio will be seen and heard.

Conversely, the at-risk child's summer includes a home without books, magazines, or newspapers, and without adults who read avidly; no car by which to leave a dangerous neighborhood; no bookstores or convenient library; a daily routine in which the child seldom encounters new people, new experiences, or new vocabulary, thus there is no growth in background knowledge; and little likelihood that educational or informational TV or radio will be seen or heard.

How can you prevent the traditional summer reading gap? Research gives little support to traditional summer school but a great deal to summer reading—reading *to* the child and reading *by* the child. Jimmy Kim's study of 1,600 sixth-graders in eighteen schools showed that the reading of four to six books during the summer was enough to alleviate summer loss. He further noted that when schools required either a report or essay to be written about a book read during the summer or that parents verify the student had read one summer book, this greatly increased the chances of its being read.[23]

Most libraries have summer reading incentive programs, so make sure your child is enrolled and participates. And take your child on field trips—even if you just visit local places like a fire station, the museum, or the zoo—and talk and listen. One of the most original suggestions I've heard comes from Paul E. Barton, senior associate in the Policy Evaluation and Research Center at Educational Testing Service (ETS), and someone who has researched and written extensively on the subject of poverty and schooling from preschool to prisons.[24] Barton knows full well the scarcity of books in the lives of poor children, and it provoked him to tell *USA Today* that at-risk communities should be making bookmobiles or traveling libraries "as ubiquitous as the Good Humor man."[25]

Would that "Good Humor man" idea, equating books with Popsicles, really work? What if you gave each of 852 at-risk students twelve free books of their own choosing at the beginning of summer? If you did this for three straight summers and then contrasted those students' reading scores with comparable at-risk students who didn't receive the twelve books each summer, would there be a difference? See page 110.

Will SSR Work in the Home as Well?

The same SSR principles apply in the home as in the classroom. Indeed, considering that by the end of eighth grade, a child has spent only nine thousand hours in school compared with ninety-five thousand outside school, it behooves parents to involve themselves in home SSR before they challenge a teacher, "Why isn't Jesse doing better in reading this year?"

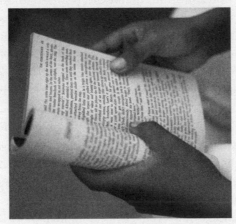

Since out-of-school hours far outnumber in-school hours, the ultimate goal is to motivate the student to read more at home.

If the classroom teacher is pivotal, so, too, is the parent; don't tell your child to go read for fifteen minutes while you watch television. You can, of course, tailor SSR to fit your family. For children who are not used to reading for more than brief periods of time, it is important at first to limit

SSR to ten or fifteen minutes. Later, when they are used to reading in this manner and are more involved in books, the period can be extended—often at the child's request. As in the classroom, it is important to have a variety of available material—magazines, newspapers, novels, picture books. A weekly trip to the library can do much to fill this need. Three decades of NAEP research along with a thirty-two-nation study of teens showed that the more kinds of reading material in a home, the higher the child's reading scores in school (see figure on page 96).[26] I should also note that the Three B's (books, book baskets, and bed lamps) I mentioned earlier are invaluable to the success of family SSR.

The time selected for family SSR is also important. Involve everyone in the decision, if possible. Bedtime seems to be the most popular time, perhaps because the child does not have to give up any activity for it except sleeping—and most children gladly surrender that. But some children are too tired to read with engagement, so you need to take that into account as well.

Won't Requiring Children to Read Eventually Turn Them Off?

When I was doing a parent program, I would ask: "How many of you have ever forced a child to do something—like pick up his room or brush his teeth?" The question received a positive response from 90 percent of the audience.

I would continue, "We can all concede that it's easier for everyone involved if the child can be *enticed* instead of forced into doing those things, but sometimes we haven't the time, choice, or patience. Now let's take it further: How many of you think you should ever force a child to read?" Far fewer hands go up.

The reason parents avoid forcing reading is fear that the child will grow to hate reading and eventually stop. How true is that? Take ten-year-olds who are forced to brush their teeth or change their underwear—do they stop doing those things when they grow up? No. So why do we think forcing children to read will kill the love of reading?

Of course, the better word to use here is *require*, as opposed to *force*. Nearly all children are required to attend school, and all adults are required to observe the speed limit, but few end up hating it because of the requirement. The way to take the sting out of the "requirement" is to make it so appealing and delicious that it becomes a pleasure—and that's where reading aloud comes into play.

In chapter 8, I share the story of Sonya Carson, a single parent who required her two sons to obtain library cards and read two books a week. Today one is an engineer and the other is a preeminent pediatric brain surgeon. Dr. Michael DeBakey, the man who invented the mobile army surgical hospital (MASH) and became one of the world's leading heart specialists, was required to read a book a week as a child. Where nothing is asked, usually nothing is received. In offices where punctuality is not required, people seldom arrive on time. So how to require reading and keep it pleasure oriented? First, remember that pleasure is more often caught than taught (that means read aloud to them). Next:

+ Make sure you, the adult role model, are seen reading daily. It works even better if you read at the same time as the child.
+ For young children, looking at the pictures in books and turning pages qualifies as "reading."
+ Allow children to choose the books they wish to read to themselves, even if they don't meet your high standards.
+ Set some time parameters, short at first and longer as children get older and read more.
+ Newspapers and magazines should count toward reading time.

The self-selection, self-interest factor is important here. Let children read what interests *them*. Unfortunately, school summer reading lists require them to read what interests the *faculty*.

If this idea of a reading requirement still puts you off, think about this: If you require a child to pick up her room or brush her teeth but don't require her to read, then it could be said that you think household and personal hygiene are more important than the child's brain cells.

What About Those Computerized "Reading Incentive" Programs?

Thirty years ago, when *The Read-Aloud Handbook* was first published, the idea of computerized reading incentive/reading management programs would have sounded like futurism. Today it is one of the hotly debated concepts among educators and parents: Should children read for intrinsic rewards (the pleasure of the book) or should they be enticed to read for extrinsic rewards—prizes (or grades)?

Advantage Learning Systems' Accelerated Reader and Scholastic's Reading Counts, the two industry leaders, work this way: The school library contains a core collection of popular and traditional children's books, each rated by difficulty (the harder and thicker the book, the more points it has). Accompanying the books is a computer program that poses questions after the student has read each book. Passing the computer quiz earns points for the student reader, which can be redeemed for prizes like school T-shirts, privileges, or items donated by local businesses. Both programs strongly endorse SSR as an integral part of their program and require substantial library collections. Both Accelerated Reader and Reading Counts have expanded their scope beyond incentives to include substantial student management and assessment tools.

Before going forward with this subject, I must note in full disclosure that I have been a paid speaker at three Accelerated Reader national conventions. I spoke on the subjects of reading aloud, SSR, and home/school communication problems, topics I have addressed at conventions for major education associations over a three-decade period.

I have written and spoken both favorably and negatively about these computerized programs, but in recent years I've grown increasingly uneasy with the way they are being used by school districts. Too often now I see them being abused in ways similar to the way some places abuse a sport, turning it from recreation into a form of religion.

An increasing number of dedicated educators and librarians also are alarmed by the way computerized reading programs are being used. The original design was a kind of "carrot on a stick"—using points and prizes to lure reluctant readers to read more. For a while the big complaint from critics was about these points or incentives. I didn't have a problem with that as long as the rewards didn't get out of hand (and some have). As for rewards, I think Schramm's Fraction of Selection research discussed earlier in this chapter established that nobody reads without expecting some kind of pleasure reward from the process.

The real problem, as I see it, arrived when districts bought the programs with the idea that they would absolutely lift reading scores. "Listen," declared the school board member, "if we're spending fifty grand on this program that's supposed to raise scores, then how can we allow it to be optional? You know the kids who'll never opt for it, the ones with the low scores, will drag everyone else's scores down. No, it's gotta be mandatory participation." And to cement it into place, the district makes the point system 25 percent of the child's grade for a marking period. They just took the carrot off the stick, leaving just the stick—a new grading weapon.

Here is a scenario that has been painted by more than a few irate librarians (school and public) in affluent districts that are using the computerized programs:

The parent comes into the library looking desperately for a "seven-point book."

"What kind of book does your son like to read?" asks the librarian.

The parent replies impatiently, "Doesn't matter. He needs seven more points to make his quota for the marking period, which ends this week. Give me anything with seven points."

In cases like that, we're back to same ol' same ol': "I need a book for a book report. It's due on Friday, so it can't have too many pages."

As for the research supporting the computerized programs, that's hotly contested with no long-term studies with adequate control groups. True, the students read more, but is that because the district has poured all that money into school libraries and added SSR to the daily schedule? Where's the long-term research to compare twenty-five "computerized" classes with twenty-five classes that have rich school and classroom libraries and daily SSR in the schedule? So far, it's not there.[27]

Believe it or not, high reading scores have been achieved in communities without computerized incentive programs, places where there are first-class school and classroom libraries, where the teachers motivate children by reading aloud to them, give book talks, and include SSR time as an essential part of the daily curriculum. James K Zaharis Elementary School in Mesa, Arizona, under principal Mike Oliver, is just such a place. And the money that would have gone to the computer programs went instead to building a larger library collection. Unfortunately, such schools are rare. Where the scores are low, often the teachers' knowledge of children's literature is also low, the library collection is meager to dreadful, and drill-and-skill supplants SSR time. (Consider the blight of empty bookshelves in urban and rural schools noted in chapter 6.)

Are There Any Other Negatives Associated with These Computerized Programs?

Here are some serious negatives to guard against:[28]

+ Some teachers and librarians have stopped reading children's and young adult books because the computer will ask the questions instead.
+ Class discussion of books decreases because a discussion would give away test answers, and all that matters is the electronic score.

- Students narrow their book selection to only those included in the program (points).
- In areas where the points have been made part of either the grade or classroom competition, some students attempt books far beyond their level and end up frustrated. (For an example of how to use such programs correctly, see page 69.)

Before committing precious dollars to such a program, a district should decide its purpose: Is the program there to motivate children to read more or to create another grading platform?

Susan Straight is no lightweight critic. With six novels to her credit (including a finalist for the National Book Award), along with an Edgar Award (given to mystery writers) and inclusion in the 2003 *Best American Short Stories*, this literature professor and mother of three carries some ballast in her literary criticism. In 2009 she took on Accelerated Reader. Her argument was not with its good intentions but with how it is implemented and its point system (which often comes down to "thicker is better"). She wrote:

> Librarians and teachers report that students will almost always refuse to read a book not on the Accelerated Reader list, because they won't receive points. They base their reading choices not on something they think looks interesting, but by how many points they will get. The passion and serendipity of choosing a book at the library based on the subject or the cover or the first page is nearly gone, as well as the excitement of reading a book simply for pleasure. This is not all the fault of Renaissance Learning [AR], which I believe is trying to help schools encourage students to read. Defenders of the program say the problem isn't with Accelerated Reader itself, but with how it is often implemented, with the emphasis on point-gathering above all else. But when I looked at Renaissance Learning's Web site again this summer, I noticed the tag line under the company name: "Advanced Technology for Data-Driven Schools." That constant drive for data is all too typical in the age of No Child Left Behind helping to replace a freely discovered love of language and story with a more rigid way of reading.[29]

Straight and her daughter winced at the rating given to *To Kill a Mockingbird*: 15 points. She couldn't help but gulp at the rating for *Harry Potter and the Order of the Phoenix*: 44 points. And then there was *Gossip Girl*, 8 points, with this AR description: "Enter the world of *Gossip Girl* and watch the girls drown in luxury while indulging in their favorite sports—jealousy, betrayal and late-night bar-hopping." If you were keeping score, the evaluations would look like this: *Harry Potter* is three times better than *Mockingbird*, and *Mockingbird* is only twice as good as *Gossip Girl*. Is there something wrong with the rating system here? How about the value system?

My Daughter Is Very Much into Magazines. Do They Count?

I'm sorry to be the one to tell you this, but your daughter is engaged. But it's not in the way you're thinking. *Engagement* is one of the hot terms in reading research these days. Reading engagement includes asking: How deeply involved is the student in reading? How often does the student read? For how long? Which kinds of text are read—books? magazines? newspapers? comics? How much pleasure (if any) does the student find in it, or is it always done as work? Taken collectively, these offer a very accurate gauge of how engaged the student is in reading. It's the "want to" factor in reading, unmeasured by standardized testing but a giant impetus for voluntarily reading in the 7,800 annual hours outside school. The psychological term for this is *flow*, and the athletic term is *zone*—when individuals are so immersed in what they're doing they forget the time and seem to be floating in space.[30]

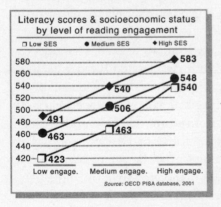

As engagement levels increase, so, too, do reading scores, even for students at the lowest income levels.

Based on the report *Reading for Change: Performance and Engagement Across Countries, Results from Pisa 2000*, Organisation for Economic Co-operation and Development (OECD).

The OECD published a 2002 study of fifteen-year-olds in thirty-two countries, measuring the effect of student engagement on reading literacy: The higher the engagement, the higher the scores; the lower the engagement, the lower the scores.[31] What parts of the engagement formula were important? The best readers read from the widest variety of texts and read longest from the deepest material—books, which require (and nurture) longer attention spans. Those who read less fiction but lots of comic books, newspapers, and magazines didn't finish at the top but were a close second. Thus all kinds of reading count (fiction being highest), as long as it is done often. The greater the variety of print in the home, the higher the student score (and vice versa). A larger number of books also led to higher scores and to more reading diversity and greater interest.

As seen in the preceding chart, students from lower-income families tended to have lower scores, but when they were highly engaged (motivated) readers, they scored higher than students from the highest income levels who were poorly engaged, and very close to the most engaged middle income students. Thus, high reading engagement is capable of vaulting the lowest-SES student to significantly higher scores and overcoming family culture. Motivation (which pushes frequency) is therefore a critical factor in elevating the at-risk readers.

How Can Reading a Newspaper or Magazine Make You Smarter?

Back in the 1980s, Dr. Max Cowan, a world-renowned neurobiologist, was invited to speak with some congressional aides about the structure of the brain. Figuring most of them had never seen an actual brain, he grabbed a postmortem specimen, wrapped it in plastic, and headed off to Capitol Hill. However, when security opened his briefcase and came across the brain, there was considerable alarm. When Cowan patiently explained that it was just a brain, the guards asked warily, "What are you going to do with it?"

Cowan found the opportunity too good to pass up. "It's like this," he explained. "My colleagues here come from sophisticated places like Boston and New York. I come from the Midwest. . . . I feel I need all the help I can get, so I always carry a spare."[32]

Beyond the humor of that situation, an extra brain would certainly give a person an advantage, especially if you could handpick the brain. Imagine how helpful it would be in taking a test. If only there were a way to carry a spare brain, not too large, mind you, about the size of a— paperback book! And that's exactly what a book (or a magazine or news paper) amounts to: a spare brain. The reader is walking around with the brain of the author stuffed into a back pocket or a purse. With that arrangement, you're no longer limited to just your own experiences. Every time you read, you're tapping into the author's experiences, and tomorrow it's a different author, a different brain. It's the reader's advantage.

My mother was fond of the adage "Tell me who your friends are and I'll tell you who you are." She used it to caution her four sons against associating with people who might lead us into trouble. But it also works in a positive way. I have a retired librarian friend, Jan Lieberman, who, when I'm in her company, leaves me exhaustingly stimulated about books and theater and food and music and libraries. We're all products of the people we "hang around with," and if we make room in our lives for people who are smarter than we are, we make ourselves better.

The easiest self-improvement is through reading. On average, I spend one hour a day reading the *New York Times*, along with a wide variety of blogs and magazine articles. In so doing, I'm hanging around with some of the most knowledgeable people in journalism. These reporters, in turn, are hanging around with some of the most knowledgeable people in their respective circles, and I'm allowed to eavesdrop on their conversations—about politics and war and sports and theater and movies and books. I should add that associating with this crowd is also humbling; every day I'm reminded how little I know about a great many things. It also means there's more to learn and more incentive to read!

How Do I Stop Them from Reading "Junk" During SSR?

Someone once said you couldn't really appreciate the great center fielder Willie Mays until you saw the rest of the league's center fielders. That prescription applies to reading as well. You can't appreciate a great book until you've met enough junk.

There's an aspect of junk that fits into SSR—what Krashen calls "lite" reading. Series books often fit this category because they're accessible, having both simple sentence structure and simple plots. With that in mind, Krashen and graduate student Kyung-Sook Cho decided to try series books with adults for whom English is a second language (ESL).[33] They selected four immigrant women, three Korean and one Hispanic, whose ages were thirty, twenty-three, thirty-five, and twenty-one. Their average residency in the United States was 6.5 years. The oldest of the four was a thirty-five-year-old Korean who had majored in English in college and had taught it for three years in a high school. None of them, however, felt confident enough with English to speak it unless it was required, and most did little or no recreational reading in English.

Wishing to combine the women's low reading levels with interesting text, the researchers chose the grade-two-level books in the Sweet Valley High series, called Sweet Valley Kids (seventy pages each). After being given some background information about the series and characters, the women were simply asked to read the books during their free time for several months. Occasional discussions took place between one of the researchers and the women, to answer any questions they might have, but for the most part they were comprehending what they read.

The response was just as anticipated. "All four women became enthusiastic readers. Mi-ae reported she read eight Sweet Valley Kids books during one month; Su-jin read eighteen volumes in two months; Jin-hee (the English major) read twenty-three in a little less than a month; and Alma (Hispanic) read ten volumes over a two-week period. Two of the women read as many words per month as would a native born student."

All became very fond of the series. "This is the first experience in which I wanted to read a book in English continuously," said one woman. The one who had taught English in high school said, "I read the Sweet Valley series with interest and without the headache that I got when reading *Time* magazine in Korea. Most interestingly, I enjoyed reading the psychological descriptions of each character." She went on to read thirty Kids volumes, along with seven of the Twins series and eight of the Sweet Valley High books. All of the women reported an involvement with the characters in the books that served to bring them back for more.

All displayed greater proficiency not only in their reading but in speaking English as well. And all demonstrated increased vocabulary development.

Krashen and Cho noted: "Our brief study with these four women also supports the value of 'narrow' reading—reading texts in only one genre or by only one author—for promoting literacy development. Narrow reading allows the reader to take full advantage of the knowledge gained in previously read text."

This study is one of many that demonstrate the powerful role that recreational "lite" reading—series books and comic books—plays in developing good and lifetime readers. Is it classic literature? Of course not. Does it have a better chance of creating fluent readers than the classics would? Definitely. Can it eventually lead to the classics? Yes, and certainly sooner than would *The Red Badge of Courage*.

My Son Loves Comic Books—Is That Good or Bad?

Comic books are a frequent childhood choice of people who grow up to become very fluent readers.[34] The reasons for their popularity and success are the same as for series books. And anyone questioning their success in creating readers should consider this: In the IEA assessment of more than two hundred thousand children from thirty-two countries, Finnish children achieved the highest reading scores. And what is the most common choice for recreational reading among Finnish nine-year-olds? Fifty-nine percent read a comic almost every day.[35]

I am not recommending comic books as a steady diet for reading aloud, except as an introduction to the comic format. Young children must be shown how a comic "works": the sequence of the panels; how to tell when a character is thinking and when he is speaking; the meaning of stars, question marks, and exclamation points.

In recent years, with the arrival of manga, along with the graphic novel, comic books have experienced a revival and revolution, one that sometimes includes heavy strains of sex and violence. (Need I say this is not specific to comics? Books and film have similar situations.) So the days of giving a child the money for a comic book and sending him or her off to the corner convenience store are a thing of the past. As with television, videos, and books, responsible adults must stay aware and awake. On the basis of my personal experiences and the research available, I would go so far as to say if you have a child who is struggling with reading, connect him or her with comics.

As a child, I had the largest comic book collection in my neighborhood, as did Stephen Krashen, Cynthia Rylant, John Updike, and Ray Bradbury. And there is this reflection from a Nobel Peace Prize winner, South Africa's Bishop Desmond Tutu: "My father was the headmaster of a Methodist primary school. Like most fathers in those days, he was very patriarchal, very concerned that we did well in school. But one of the things I am very grateful to him for is that, contrary to conventional educational principles, he allowed me to read comics. I think that is how I developed my love for English and for reading."[36]

If you're looking to challenge a child's mind and vocabulary with comics, then I suggest *The Adventures of Tintin*. When you've been in print for nearly eighty years, translated into eighty languages, sold three hundred million copies, and been made into movies by Peter Jackson and Stephen Spielberg, you must be special. When the Pulitzer-winning historian Arthur Schlesinger Jr. listed his favorite read-aloud choices for his family, Hergé's *Tintin* ranked between *Huckleberry Finn* and the Greek myths.[37] Nice company.

Two years were spent researching and drawing the seven hundred detailed illustrations in each issue. But *Tintin* must be read in order to be understood—and that is the key for parents and teachers. Each issue contains eight thousand words. The beautiful part of it is that children are unaware they are reading eight thousand words. (See *Tintin in Tibet*, in the picture book section of the Treasury.)

If Adults Are Supposed to Be Role Models, How Much Should Teachers Read?

Throughout this book I've offered research showing the impact of parent role models on children's reading habits. Though they have less impact than parents, teachers should be reading role models as well—especially for children whose parents cannot or will not do the job. The trouble, however, is that most teachers are seldom seen reading for pleasure. Reading for work, from the text, from lesson plans, yes. But sitting back and savoring a book for its own sake or talking about a book they read last night? Seldom.

Research about teachers shows that in schools where their administrators talk about books and professional journals, the teachers read more on their own.[38] So why wouldn't the same be true for students if their instructional leaders talked more about books? In other words, the teacher stands before the class and daily gives mini–book talks based on the classroom library.

The fly in this ointment is that book talks work only when the person talking has actually read the book. And the harsh reality here is most teachers don't read much.

That's not a speculative comment but one based on both research and personal experience. One study of 224 teachers pursuing graduate degrees showed they read few or no professional journals that included research.[39] (Suppose your doctor read only *Prevention* magazine?) More than half said they had read only one or two professional books in the previous year, and an additional 20 percent said they had read nothing in the past six months or one year. What did they read beyond professional material?

- Twenty-two percent read a newspaper only once a week.
- Seventy-five percent were only "light" book readers—one or two a year.
- Twenty-five percent were "heavy" readers (three to four books a month). This means that teachers don't read any more often than adults in the general population.[40] In a 1998 national survey of 666 high school teachers, almost half reported not reading a single professional journal or magazine.[41]

How Can We Tell If SSR Readers Have Actually Read the Book?

Congressional hearings are a whole lot more reliable than congressional writings. It's much harder to fake it orally than in writing. Have a conversation about a book. "Tell me about this book. What's it about? Why did you choose it in the first place? What genre of literature would you say it fits into? Who was your favorite character? Why? Did the character change during the story?" And each of the responses could lead to other queries that easily determine if the book actually was read. But more important, it gives the child a chance to turn a solitary experience (reading) into a social one. More on that in a minute.

I'm suggesting here that the child enters a school or library and meets a clone of America's number one reading teacher: Oprah Winfrey. For more than a decade Oprah inspired more people to read more pages in more good books than anyone in American history. If that's not a reading teacher, what is? So if children walk into a classroom or library that has an Oprah clone in it, they're far more likely to be inspired to start reading the particular author or book she talked about. Now the kid is reading, and reading a lot—outside school, where he has the most time; on the bus, in bed, on the toilet, and at the breakfast table. And through all those pages, he's accumulating the vocabulary words he might not be hearing at home or from family. That is a gigantic gift for the at-risk child.

In order for that to happen, however, the teacher or librarian has to be an avid reader like Oprah. At this juncture in my teacher seminars, I would walk over to a teacher, pick up her bottle of water, and say, "You and I could share this bottle today, we could share a cell phone, even a pen, and you can't catch a cold from me today. Because I don't have a cold. In the same way, if a teacher or librarian doesn't have the love of reading, the class can't catch it from her. And half the teachers don't have the love— which is a big problem for half the kids in the country, especially the ones coming from homes where the parents don't have it either."

When someone becomes a teacher, she's like the matchmaker in *Fiddler on the Roof.* All year long she's trying to entice students to go out on dates with authors—that is, to pick up this book or that book and spend twenty minutes with the author, someone they've never met. The better she knows her students and authors or books, the more successful will be the "matchmaking." But the teacher (or librarian) who doesn't read much will fail for sure.[42] For more on this subject, see Mary Kuntsal's library discussion program in Goleta, California, which I discuss later in this chapter.

How Did Oprah Do It So Successfully?

Oprah and her producers were smart enough at the very beginning not to use the word *class*. They knew very well the connotations carried by that word with many in their audience: requirements, demands, and tests. So they used the word *club*, which suggests belonging, membership, and invitation.

Having selected a book, Oprah walked out to her audience of twenty-two million people and talked about the book she'd selected. She talked animatedly, passionately, and sincerely. No writing, no tests, no dumb dioramas to make, just good old-fashioned enthusiasm.

Above everything else, that is the key to Oprah's Book Club success—she recognized what too many educators have forgotten: We're an oral species. We define ourselves first and foremost orally. When we see a good movie, a good ball game, a great concert—the first thing we want to do afterward is talk about it. After my wife and I see a good movie, do you think we rush out to the car, pull napkins out of the glove compartment, and write down the main idea? "Honey, what do you think was the theme?"

What can we apply from this to our work with children? Well, let's eliminate not all but much of the writing they're required to do whenever they read. ("The more we read, the more we gotta write, so let's read less and we can work less.") We adults don't labor when we read, so why are we forcing children to? It hasn't created a nation of writers or readers.

On the other hand, look what Oprah created: When she began her book club there were 250,000 discussion groups nationally. Today there are more than 500,000 such groups,[43] nearly all of them female, I regret to say (see chapter 9). Whether you're contemplating a book discussion club for a family or class, my favorite guide is *Deconstructing Penguins* by Lawrence and Nancy Goldstone, a manual on how to "dig a tunnel" into the heart and soul of a book. As the authors note, "You don't need an advanced degree in English literature or forty hours a week of free time to effectively discuss a book with your child. This isn't *Crime and Punishment*, it's *Charlotte's Web*."

Librarians and Parents as "Oprahs"

By every measure, suburban schools outscore urban schools, and rich kids outscore the less affluent, largely due to the advantages that higher-educated parents offer their children throughout their childhoods. One such example of these advantages is the Montessori Center School of Goleta, California, situated in a university community (University of California, Santa Barbara), with an enrollment of more than three hundred students, ranging from age two to sixth grade. The reading culture of the school is inspired by Mary Kuntsal, a librarian for thirty-five years, nineteen at the Center School.

The school's reading philosophy is aimed at overcoming the outside culture, where it's not always cool to be smart, and to get the students to think deeply. Mary summarizes her approach this way:

> For 4th thru 6th graders, the Library runs a Reading Passport program in which we track their independent (mostly fiction) chapter book reading. We strongly encourage them to try different genres, etc., but there's a lot of free choice. One goal is for them to learn to select books they will enjoy reading.
>
> The most unique aspect to making all of that work is a cadre of trained parent volunteers (five) who help by holding weekly discussions (five to fifteen minutes each) with individual students about each book they've read. No book reports, no Accelerated Reader quizzes. Just one-on-one discussions aimed at getting children to reflect on their reading at a deeper level than multiple choice questions, but in a more enjoyable format than a formal book report.
>
> When they start the Passport program in fourth grade there is a lot of straightforward comprehension of the plot line, but by sixth grade the discussions are quite amazing and insightful. Most years the average is about twenty-five chapter books per student, not including any assigned reading in their classroom subjects.
>
> At the end of the year we have the Reading Passport Celebration where, among other things, graduating sixth-graders choose a book that made some kind of special connection with them, and they write and read aloud a short essay for the ceremony. I specifically require that it not be a book report per se, but that it tell about their own personal relationship with the book. It's amazing to hear what individuals choose and why—from "I have a brother with Tourette's so I connected to *Al Capone Does My Shirts*" to "My grandparents were interned during WWII so I chose *Weedflower*." This year we had a burly sixth-grade hockey player who wrote that *The Breadwinner* had opened his eyes to how fortunate he was, that his biggest worry had always been the defensive players on the opposing hockey team, not the Taliban. His essay so inspired a father in the audience

that he volunteered to facilitate one of the two parent-child book clubs we have.[44]

What happens at the Montessori Center School are the life-changing learning experiences we should be working to include in the lives of every American child, rich or poor, instead of blaming the teachers when scores aren't high enough. One way to help those left behind is to give them the same school experiences of those who get ahead. Instead, we give them more test prep and they think that's what reading is all about—and grow to hate it.

Chapter 6

The Print Climate in the Home, School, and Library

Few forms of theft are quite as damaging to inner-city children
as the denial of a well-endowed school library.

—Jonathan Kozol

DID you ever notice the similarity between reading scores and rodeo scores?

For the sake of discussion, let's say the nation's leaders suddenly decided that rodeo was the most important subject in our schools' curriculum. (This is not as far-fetched as you might think: If the price of gas keeps rising, some people are going to be looking very differently at horses.) There would suddenly be new courses created around horsemanship, saddles and equipment would have to be ordered, riding coaches credentialed, and mandatory riding and roping instruction begun in rodeo lab classes. All of this would culminate in mandatory grade-level rodeos (including "exit rodeos" for the high school seniors) to ensure that "no rider was left behind," and everyone would be "racing to the top corral."

And sure as the sun sinks in the West, in this scenario there would be states that excelled and those that failed. In fact, to show this idea isn't all that wacky, set your browser for the Professional Rodeo Cowboys Association and look at any of their standings. You'll find the high scorers all come from states like Utah, Texas, Nebraska, Oregon, and Colorado, rich with ranches, horses, and cattle. Already we could easily predict which states would be on the "failing schools" list for rodeo—places that have the fewest horses, like New Jersey, Illinois, Delaware, and Maine. It's tough to get good at rodeo if you're missing a horse, right?

The same role played by horses in the rodeo world is played by print in the reading world. Like Texas or Oregon with rodeo, there are places in America where they annually have the highest reading scores. And in the same country, under the same government, there are homes, schools, and communities that scarcely have seen a new book in decades. And newspapers seldom hit their doorstep.

It's difficult to get good at reading if you're short of print. Government programs like No Child Left Behind and Race to the Top ensure that children who are behind in reading are entitled to after-school tutoring and extra help with phonics. Nice. But giving phonics lessons to kids who don't have any print in their lives is like giving oars to people who don't have a boat—you don't get very far.

Let me repeat here a portion of the table/chart from the Introduction, the part that characterizes the print climate in the homes of two kinds of kindergartners: those with high interest in print and those with low interest.[1]

Home Information	High Interest in Books (%)	Low Interest in Books (%)
Number of books in home	80.6 books	31.7 books
Child owns library card	37.5	3.4
Child is taken to library	98.1	7.1
Child is read to daily	76.8	1.8

Before I go any further, allow me to state that the gap in the American print climate—home or school—is entirely fixable. Price is not a problem. If we can rebuild Afghanistan and Iraq at a cost of $800-plus billion,[2] we can easily fix all the urban schools and public libraries in America. All we have to do is believe that it's worth it. If we had to, we could build a strong case that it would come under Homeland Security: Today's desperate fifteen-year-old semiliterate in urban America is tomorrow's unemployed homegrown terrorist.

The past two decades of research by respected researchers like Neuman,[3] Duke,[4] Krashen,[5] McQuillan,[6] Allington,[7] and Lance[8] powerfully connect access to print with higher reading scores and, conversely, lack of access with lower scores. It's a shame the education experts haven't figured this out, even when one of the researchers (Neuman) was an assistant secretary of education in Washington.

Books in the Home and Average Science Scores, Grade 12

Reported Number of Books at Home	Average Science Score
More than 100	161
26–100	147
11–25	132
0–10	122

Source: U.S. Department of Education, National Center for Education Statistics.

The National Assessment of Educational Progress (NAEP) has been measuring student performance in most major subjects since 1972. It has also been surveying students on the number of books in their homes, then drawing correlations to their scores in reading, math, science, civics, history, and writing. In every test subject, the more books in the home, the higher the score, often by as much as forty points. In fact, the prevalence of books often compensates for differences in parental education.[9] International studies have drawn the same conclusions,[10] and Elley's 1992 study of 210,000 students found the larger the school and classroom libraries, the higher the students' reading scores.[11]

More than thirteen states have produced research connecting a stronger library program to higher student scores, including Baughman's research on the Massachusetts MCAS exam, which showed a higher number of books per pupil and a full-time librarian meant an eleven-point advantage, and that a higher percentage of the student body visiting the library per week accounted for a twelve-point advantage.[12]

My favorite example of the impact of the book climate on entire school districts is the one involving three California communities, twenty and forty miles apart on the map but worlds apart in other ways. Stephen Krashen and colleagues at USC did a print inventory of homes, classrooms, and libraries in the three communities—Beverly Hills, Watts, and Compton.[13] In Beverly Hills, 93 percent of its high school students go to college, while relatively few go to college from Watts and Compton. In 1999, Compton's state-appointed administrator reported that barely one in ten students was performing at grade level. One look at the following chart clearly shows the print desert surrounding urban children, versus the print "rain forest" surrounding others.

Average Print Climate in Three California Communities

	Books in Home	Books in Class	Books in School Library	Books in Public Library
Beverly Hills	199	392	60,000	200,600
Watts	4.5	54	23,000	110,000
Compton	2.7	47	16,000	90,000

Krashen's evidence[14] was presented to a state commission revising California's language-arts curriculum in the 1990s after the state tied for last in the nation in reading. With the state holding one of the nation's largest child-poverty populations, and lowest support for school and public libraries, California politicians responded with $195 million for more phonics instruction.[15] How effective was that? Last in the nation in 1996, even with the increased phonics funding, by 2011 it had risen to forty-six out of fifty-two states and jurisdictions—District of Columbia taking sole dominion over last place. By the reckoning of its own Department of Education, California's ratio of school librarian to student ranks fifty-first in the nation, with 1 librarian for every 5,124 students, more than five times the national average of 1 to 916.[16] Even the state's adult prison system does better, with 1 librarian to 4,283 inmates.[17]

Since school is meant to make up for home deficits, you would expect at-risk children to meet good classroom libraries—or some semblance of No Child Left Without a Good Library. Instead, Nell Duke found the same home deficits in the school when she spent a year studying twenty first-grade classrooms—ten suburban and ten urban—in Massachusetts. Despite having teachers with an average eighteen years' experience, the urban students were more restricted in how often they could use the classroom library, the library selections were older and of a poorer grade, their class reading time was spent on less complex text, they spent more time copying and taking dictation, their teachers read to them less often and from simpler texts, and the books-per-pupil ratio was half that of the high-SES classrooms.[18] Additionally, seven of the advantaged classes were read to from chapter books, while only two of the low-SES classes heard chapter books.

In the previous chapter I mentioned Paul E. Barton of the Educational Testing Service and his statement that at-risk communities should be making bookmobiles or traveling libraries "as ubiquitous as the Good

Humor man."[19] Here is a three-year research project that proved Barton's concept to be on target: Provide the books and they will read them—*and the scores will rise.*

Aware of the negative impact of "summer setback,"[20] the low scores of poverty children, and how little access these children have to print outside of school, Richard Allington, Anne McGill-Franzen, and research colleagues identified 852 early-primary student participants at seventeen high-poverty schools. They would be compared with 478 similar students in a control group, and the study would be conducted over three consecutive summers.[21]

During the spring semester, the experimental students were allowed to select books at a school book fair, twelve paperbacks that would not be given to them until the beginning of each summer vacation but would be theirs to keep. (The control group had no book fair and received no free books for the summer.) The books placed in the fair, selected in advance by the researchers, were on early-primary levels and aimed at meeting the students' interests in pop culture (movie, sports stars), series books, minority characters, and science/social studies subjects in the curriculum. (The last two categories were the least popular.)

End result after three years: The experimental group had significantly higher reading achievement (compared with the control group), directly attributed to more frequent reading because of easy access over three straight summers. Interestingly, the most disadvantaged students had the highest gains of all students in the study. Among the factors driving the students' success were (1) access to books, (2) personal ownership of the books, and (3) self-selection of the books. While the reading gains were not large, the researchers found the gains were equal to or greater than those made by either a comprehensive school reform or summer school; the experiment was also less expensive and less extensive than school reform or summer school.

How much would a three-year book program like that cost for 852 students? Less than $120,000. And where do we find that kind of money on a national scale? Well, if you took just one week's expense for the Iraq war ($2 billion), you could run this program in 16,000 schools. That would be absolutely workable, if we truly wanted it.

How Many Books Should Be in the Home Library?

The mere presence of books can often be enough. Not two hundred of them or even fifty, but a dozen to call your own, with enough pages to occupy a child's imagination on winter nights or rainy days. (My own relationship with one particular book I bought in kindergarten is detailed on page 165.)

I think of the impact a handful of books made on one lad and then the impact he made on so many afterward. He was ten at the time, and he and his sister were considered a bit uncivilized, though he'd had a year's worth of schooling and had learned to read. His school didn't have enough books for each child, and his family owned no books until his stepmother arrived with a small collection. Although illiterate herself, she knew the power contained in print and impressed that immediately but kindly on the boy. She became his best friend, and eventually he became president of the United States.

The stack of books—what one writer later described as the equivalent of today's iPad—included *Aesop's Fables*, *Robinson Crusoe*, *Pilgrim's Progress*, and *Sinbad the Sailor*. These weren't Little Golden Book versions; these were the real thing, and included text like:

> My father left me a considerable estate, the best part of which I spent in riotous living during my youth; but I perceived my error, and reflected that riches were perishable, and quickly consumed by such ill managers as myself. I further considered that by my irregular way of living I had wretchedly misspent my time which is the most valuable thing in the world.—from *Sinbad the Sailor*

What the little stack of books and Sarah Bush Lincoln did for a boy named Abraham was ignite the love of reading in him (something the regimented year in "blab school" failed to accomplish; I bet the schoolmaster would have loved all of today's testing) and open a world beyond the forty-family hamlet of Little Pigeon Creek, Indiana. As he "read everything he could get his hands on," it dawned on him there could be more to life than tilling and harvesting a field.[22] And that changed America forever.

Print in the home is a proven life changer worldwide. Using data from seventy thousand families in twenty-seven nations, accumulated over multiple decades, researchers showed more books in the home led to a higher grade-level completion rate.[23] The higher the number of books in the home library (0, 25, 75, 500), the greater were the chances of the student completing ninth grade, high school, or university, even after adjusting for parents' income, education, and occupation.

It stands to reason that if we're not giving children time to read recreationally in school (because they're too busy doing test prep), then the reading must be done at home if they're going to become competent readers. The obstacles to home reading are (1) at-risk homes contain the least amount of print, and (2) libraries in at-risk neighborhoods are open the fewest hours and are the first ones cut or closed if there's a budget shortfall. This makes it imperative for communities to do everything in their power to cultivate a rich print environment in at-risk families, as noted with the Allington McGill-Franzen study earlier in this chapter.[24]

Does the Disappearance of Newspapers in the Home Have an Impact?

Newspapers and magazines are the home's "soft" library. For a century they were commonplace enough to be taken for granted. But behind the scenes they were conditioning children to print. All those articles and headlines coupled with so many reading role models spending so much time waving print flags called newspapers and magazines—they were literacy torches passed from parent to child.

The daily newspaper and weekly magazines are presently on life support, the slowest-growing industry in the U.S. From the largest cities to the smallest hamlets, newspaper circulation has been dropping since the 1980s, when it was at 62.8 million papers, sinking to 47 million in 2011.[25]

A Pew Research survey in 2010 found only 31 percent of Americans had obtained news from a newspaper the previous day, as opposed to 56 percent in 1991.[26] Weekly and monthly magazine circulations are dropping as well. *Reader's Digest*, once the world's most popular American magazine, has sunk from 23 million to 5 million. Staffers at print magazines like *Time* permanently have their bags packed. (Even the 110-year-old classroom staple *Weekly Reader* saw its demise in 2012.)[27]

These are the publications by which whole generations in America were assimilated into the world of reading, and now they have all but evaporated. David Carr of the *New York Times* painted a vivid portrait of the print chasm in today's family, recalling how he grew up in a home where his father and brother jousted for the newspaper (the Minneapolis *Star Tribune*) over breakfast. Watching them imbibing the scores and headlines with breakfast, Carr thought:

> This is what it means to be a grown-up. You eat your food standing up, and you read the newspaper. So I did the same thing when I turned 13. I still do.
>
> Last Wednesday morning at my house, one of my daughters back from college was staying at a friend's house in the city, no doubt getting alerts on her cellphone for new postings to her Facebook page. Her sister got up, skipped breakfast and checked the mail for her NetFlix movies. My wife left early before the papers even arrived to commute to her job in the city while listening to the iPod she got for Christmas.
>
> True enough, my 10-year-old gave me five minutes over a bowl of Cheerios, but then she went into the dining room and opened the laptop to surf the Disney Channel on broadband, leaving me standing in the kitchen with my four newspapers. A few of those included news about the sale of *The Star Tribune*, a newspaper that found itself in reduced circumstances and sold at a reduced price to a private equity group.
>
> I looked around me and realized I didn't really need to read the papers to know why.[28]

True, many newspapers are available for reading online, but that's done out of children's sight line, not with a paper waving in their faces. Furthermore, most young parents can't be bothered anymore. Reading a newspaper is so—so yesterday! Nobody reads all that stuff anymore. We get the news from RSS feeds, blogs, e-tablet alerts, Google, and, of course, from our 729 friends on Facebook. That's the new way, Daddy.

Reading, when it's done today, doesn't go very deep, and it's so private it's invisible. The trouble is, how do you pass invisible torches? How do you pose as an invisible role model?

If Libraries Are So Important, Why Are They the First to Get Cut in Hard Times?

It has become the norm to cut library services whenever a community or state runs low on funds. The fact that it's been there for so long, taken for granted, and is free—that leads some people to see it as worthless, a faceless victim. It even happens with school libraries (see page 115).

As the Great Recession tightened its squeeze in 2010, Los Angeles's seventy-three public libraries shut their doors on Mondays, as did hundreds of others across the nation. A city of immigrants, brimming with poverty, containing some of the lowest school scores in the nation, and L.A.'s county fathers close the library.

As the travel writer Pico Iyer observed at the time of the Los Angeles closings, "To save money by reducing library services and resources is like trying to save a bleeding man by cutting out his heart."

An extraordinary public library rescue effort occurred in 2012 in Troy, Michigan, a city of 80,000 (eleventh largest in the state) and one of Detroit's attractive suburbs—just the place to be lulled into believing the library will always be there.

With a median household income of $85,000 (nearly double the state average), Troy met the Great Recession with a resolve that it wasn't going to go the way of Detroit. When state support declined by 20 percent, the city told the Troy Public Library (243,000 books) that it didn't have the funds to keep it alive any longer. The library sought support through a tax increase of 0.7 percent, but voters turned it down twice, led by strong support from local Tea Party forces. Finally a last-gasp third vote was planned for August 2—just when many families would be away on vacation. If they lost on this vote, the library would be closed and its contents sold.

What to do? In mid-June library supporters, with $3,500 in hand, sought help from the famous Leo Burnett advertising agency, which had a regional headquarters right there in Troy. The agency reasoned that if the same 19 percent of voters turned out for the next election, the results would be the same. How to convince the rest of Troy to turn out, the ones who took the library for granted? Previous votes had focused on the tax increase, but the real issue was the life of the library. A vote to close the library would really be a vote to betray—*burn*, if you will—the books. Now *that* would start a different kind of conversation, wouldn't it?

The agency and library supporters formed a fake community action group called Safeguarding American Families (SAFe) and, posing as opponents of the tax increase, flooded Troy with announcements in social media, along with lawn signs, each with the message: "Vote to close Troy library Aug. 2nd, book burning party Aug. 5th." They even placed an ad for clowns and ice-cream vendors for the burning party.[29]

Suddenly the debate was no longer just about money but the very life of the library. Library users of all ages were awakened, even secretly taking down SAFe's signs at night. (SAFe replaced them with more signs.)

The debate and resulting furor made state, national, and international news and, finally, two weeks before the election, SAFe revealed itself as a faux opponent. By then, however, the patrons and voters were awake enough to double previous voter turnout (38 percent) and give the library a landslide victory. The advertising agency, in turn, won both national and international awards for the campaign.

If one were to look at the public library as strictly a tax issue, it still comes out as a community plus. Let's consider the library in my little town of forty-five thousand people (eleven thousand families). Strictly from a money-saving point of view, the town library works better than any bank in town: four to one! Yup, that's the return on the tax dollar. Here's how it works: If you take all the items the library circulates each year (books, movies, audios, magazines, newspapers), questions answered, programs attended, and licensed databases used, and compare them with what it would cost taxpayers to commercially pay for those items, it's a four-dollar savings for every tax dollar spent.[30] Even Bernie Madoff wasn't promising that kind of return. Yet cities and states cut the library first.

Saving money by cutting school librarians has been a favorite tool in California whenever it hits a budget crisis, but the Great Recession added new dimensions to the state's daffiness. Before their positions were eliminated, the librarians were interrogated in a Kafkaesque basement courtroom in hopes of tripping them into proving their incompetence. I cannot think of a more demeaning and egregious effort to drive good people out of their profession.

Here's a partial account of the scene, as described by veteran reporter Hector Tobar of the *Los Angeles Times*:[31]

If state education cuts are drastic, the librarians' only chance of keeping a paycheck is to prove they're qualified to be switched to classroom teaching. So LAUSD attorneys grill them.

In a basement downtown, the librarians are being interrogated.

On most days, they work in middle schools and high schools operated by the Los Angeles Unified School District, fielding student queries about American history and Greek mythology, and retrieving copies of vampire novels.

But this week, you'll find them in a makeshift LAUSD courtroom set up on the bare concrete floor of a building on East 9th Street. Several sit in plastic chairs, watching from an improvised gallery as their fellow librarians are questioned.

A court reporter takes down testimony. A judge grants or denies objections from attorneys. Armed police officers hover nearby. On the witness stand, one librarian at a time is summoned to explain why she—the vast majority are women—should be allowed to keep her job.

The librarians are guilty of nothing except earning salaries the district feels the need to cut. But as they're cross-examined by determined LAUSD attorneys, they're continually put on the defensive.

"When was the last time you taught a course for which your librarian credential was not required?" an LAUSD attorney asked Laura Graff, the librarian at Sun Valley High School, at a court session on Monday.

"I'm not sure what you're asking," Graff said. "I teach all subjects, all day. In the library."

"Do you take attendance?" the attorney insisted. "Do you issue grades?"

I've seen a lot of strange things in two decades as a reporter, but nothing quite as disgraceful and weird as this inquisition the LAUSD is inflicting upon more than 80 school librarians.

What Do You Do About the Bad Grammar in Books like the Junie B. Jones Series, to Say Nothing of Her Misbehavior?

Once people finally agreed there was in fact nothing satanic in the Harry Potter books, little Junie B. became the censors' whipping boy (Captain Underpants having faded like so much underwear). With more than $25 million in sales, what's with naughty Junie B.?

First of all, in my subjective opinion, author Barbara Park is the single funniest person to ever write for children. Once, while reading her to my grandson, I fell out of the bed laughing. Beyond the humor, the magnetism of Junie B. is that she personifies perfectly and humorously so many of our repressed thoughts and fears as children. If her occasional misbehavior went unaddressed, she'd be a bad example. But that's not the case. She receives her just rewards and punishments, serving as a morality tale for young readers but without sermons.

Her lapses in grammar and diction ("pasketti") go uncorrected, but so did the vernacular in *The Adventures of Tom Sawyer* and that didn't turn the nation into thick-tongued illiterates. Remember President George W. Bush's struggles with "nuculur" (nuclear)? And he had degrees from Yale and Harvard. Relax. The Junie B. Jones books are creative fiction, not grammar or spelling books, and let's all thank God for that. What we have in these books is what has always been missing from textbooks— something you'd like to "hang around with" after school.

Nothing epitomizes that situation better than this anecdote from 2006. I was working with the faculty at an elementary school in downtown Los Angeles, a school filled with children coming from migrant, immigrant, and often poverty-stricken families. In my talk with the faculty I brought up the Junie B. books, and afterward a second-grade teacher approached me and said, "I was so glad to hear you mention the Junie B. books."

"You're a fan?" I asked.

"Oh, yes," she replied, "and so are my students. Big fans. They've stolen six hundred copies from my classroom in five years." She went on to explain that she kept replacing them, at her own expense, and reasoned that if they loved Junie so much they wanted to bring her home with them, then she would somehow feed that hunger.

Please note: Those second-graders were not stealing their textbooks. Just Junie B. There's a lesson there, and it's hidden only to the witless who want to ban her. On July 26, 2007, the *New York Times* devoted almost a half page to the ongoing debate in the affluent suburbs about Junie

B.'s antics and whether she should be banned from classrooms and bed-rooms.[32]

If you're looking for the next step up from Junie B., someone with a softer edge but no less unique and irrepressible, then check out Lois Lowry's *Gooney Bird Greene*, listed with the novels in the Treasury here.

The issues pertinent to book censoring are more fully explored on my Web site at www.trelease-on-reading.com/censor_entry.html.

How Do I Make My School Library More Successful on a Limited Budget?

You can start by taking a hard look at your local grocery store. As noted in a *New York Times Magazine* feature,[33] there used to be only one rule for supermarkets: Put the milk at one end of the store and bread at the other—to get people to walk through the entire store. That rule still applies: The more they see, the more they buy. Shopper surveys and the Universal Product Code scanner offer other insights, including some we might apply to libraries:

* Only 31 percent of grocery patrons bring a shopping list (more than half of adult library patrons arrive without a book in mind; even more so for children).
* Two-thirds of purchases are unplanned (very similar to book choices).
* Products placed at the optimum level (15 degrees below eye level) sell 8 percent better (which means you should clear or weed spaces at eye level for displaying books).

Few grocery customers know that food companies pay more than $9 billion for shelf space ("slotting fees"), accounting for one-half of stores' annual profits. In simple terms, they're renting shelf space. Paying that kind of money, the manufacturer makes sure its product is displayed on the shelf to its best advantage—that is, face out. This visibility is so connected to sales, the low-paying companies receive the worst seats in the house—the top and bottom shelves.[34]

The reason companies want each product face out is simple: It's the cover that most often influences our choices—the picture of the cookie, cereal, cake, magazine, and a newspaper's front page. The lesson here is to display the cover as often as possible.

The power of face-out works even at the lowest levels of literacy. When researchers observed a kindergarten classroom library for one week, 90 percent of the books that children chose had been shelved with the covers facing out.[35] Publishers know the cover sells the book, so not only do they work extra hard designing the right cover; many pay a book chain as much as $750 a month per book to have the cover showing.[36] When publishers recently began jazzing up their "classic" titles with flashy colors and modern jackets, mimicking the Twilight and Hunger Games series, the sales response was immediate. *Wuthering Heights*, for example, sold 125,000 copies in three years after a cover makeover.[37]

Where Do I Get the Library Shelf Space for Face-Out Books?

I'm not talking about positioning every book face out. Bookstores don't do it, but the ones they really want to move—the new arrivals, the best sellers—always go face out.

Nonetheless, classroom teachers have even less room than libraries for this approach. In response to the space challenge, a few years ago a teacher (whose name I wish I had jotted down) told me how she'd solved the problem by installing rain gutters in the dead spaces throughout her classroom: the space between the chalk ledge and the floor, the two-foot space between the closet and the chalkboard. Then another teacher sent me photographs of the rain gutters she'd installed.

The rain gutters they were talking about were purchased at the local hardware store for about three dollars per ten-foot strip, made of enameled, reinforced plastic. They were easily cut to any size and were supported by plastic brackets that could be screwed into almost any wall, including concrete blocks. (To read about how one principal and his schools used the rain gutter shelving idea, go to www.trelease-on-reading.com/oliver .html.)

Rain gutters aren't going to solve a school's or community's reading problems. They're merely a piece of a marketing strategy for books. But without marketing, few products get off the ground, no matter how good their design.

Why Are Children So Enchanted by Series Books? Shouldn't They Be Reading the Classics?

Many of the classics were not written for children. They were so popular among the adult elite that they became the gold standard and therefore were foisted upon children. Reading the classics too soon as a child can do more to turn you off reading than on to reading. Remember: The goal is to create a lifetime reader, not a future English teacher.

I am reminded of the rebellious teenager who was sent off to the Groton School (think Roosevelts and Auchinclosses) back in the fifties and eventually provoked a letter home to his parents that included this observation by the headmaster:

> He is still a boy who lacks intellectual discipline. He reads a lot, but he reads superficially, and I hope very much that next year he will greatly increase his capacity to get the real substance out of a superior book. Incidentally I hope that before long he will reach a stage of maturity beyond his present strong appetite for comic books.[38]

If you're a frustrated English teacher (or parent) and have such students in your care, please know that the sixteen-year-old in question here, Jonathan Yardley, may have grown up with little fondness in his heart for Groton but maintained enough affection for reading and literature to win a 1981 Pulitzer Prize for his book reviews in the *Washington Post*. (Twenty-five years later his reporter son, Jim, would add a second Pulitzer Prize to the family heritage.)

Children easily gravitate to junk—it's like they have built-in junk magnets. Our job is to lead them eventually to the better books by reading aloud to them. That allows them to compare junk with what they're hearing from you, offering a frame of reference in making reading choices. Most classics can and should come later, when you're truly ready for them. I shudder at the thought of Upton Sinclair's *The Jungle* being force-fed to high-schoolers, but what a great book when I was forty-five—the audience he originally wrote it for.

I prefer Professor Mark Van Doren's description of a classic as a definition: any book that continues to sell. After a half century, that opens the field wide enough to include *James and the Giant Peach* and *Charlotte's Web*.

The "series books" question is best answered with the research of Dr. Catherine Sheldrick Ross.[39] Ross found series to be the uncontested favorite of young readers for the past one hundred years, but acknowledges they have long been objects of scorn among the cultural gatekeepers—teachers and librarians. They were either too sensational or there was too much fiction, once regarded as bad for children in a *fact*-ual world.

What alarmed the adults even more was the "addictive" nature of series like Nancy Drew, the Hardy Boys, the Bobbsey twins, the Rover Boys, Tom Swift, and the Outdoor Girls. The young readers wouldn't read just one—they wanted another and another. Few of the adults, however, were bothering to think what good readers children were becoming in the process.

Doing great good and little harm, series books have been the uncontested favorite of children for a century.

Elitists were so certain Nancy Drew would corrupt girls' minds, H. W. Wilson Company, the largest U.S. manufacturer of library supplies, refused to print Nancy Drew index cards for the card catalog.

The important thing about series books is they make a pleasure connection with the child. As I noted in chapter 1, humans seldom do something over and over unless it brings repeated pleasure. Pleasure is the "glue" that holds us to a particular activity.

How much damage these mindless adventure stories might do was hotly debated back then, but not by young Jacques, who was fresh off the boat from France in 1920 and soaking up every Frank Merriwell sports novel he could find. Nor was he ashamed years later to admit the profoundly positive influence the books played in his reading development and acclimation to America, except by then he was well on his way to becoming America's best-known humanities scholar—Jacques Barzun (who, when turning ninety-six in 2000, celebrated by producing a best seller on the history of world culture).[40] On page 98, we saw Krashen's research on the effectiveness of using series books like Sweet Valley High with ESL students.

And finally, Ross points to the large chunks of reading done by the series reader as examples of what Margaret Meek called "private lessons." That is, these daily readings teach the child the rules about skimming and inferring, about where one must slow down to decipher the clues, about the importance of chapter titles or of character and setting.[41] The adage "the more you read, the better you get at it" is not only true; it should also be the slogan of series books.

The most conclusive evidence of series books' ability to produce better readers can be found in the thirty years of surveys done by Professor G. Robert Carlsen. Each semester he asked his graduate students to write their "reading autobiographies," recollections of their early years with reading—what they loved and what they hated. As he reported in *Voices of Readers: How We Come to Love Books*,[42] the majority of those students had strong relationships with series books in their early years. Did it stunt their intellectual growth? Well, if they made it all the way to graduate school, apparently not.

So if your child or student is reading a series book, whether it's about wimpy kids, vampires, or a wizard named Harry, count your blessings and feed the habit. Your child is not on the road to jail. He's on the road to becoming a terrific reader who in his own good time will be ready for classics.

With the Internet and e-Books, Who Needs a Library?

What a contrast between today's library worries and those of twenty years ago. Back then, the controversy was whether or not to allow beverages and snacks in the library, the way those dreadful mega-bookstores were doing. Today, when there are more books available on the iPhone than from the New York Public Library,[43] the question is whether libraries will be entirely replaced by the Internet and e-books.

While no one can predict the digital future with even 75 percent certainty, there are things I would bet the mortgage on. Libraries are going to change. They will be smaller in size, scope, and budget. Simultaneously the librarian's role will change by necessity into "data hound, guide, sherpa, and teacher."[44]

And finally, the book will change, as it has for thousands of years. In the

*The textbooks of 75 years ago have undergone a
sudden and thorough makeover.*

first quarter of 2012, for the first time ever, more e-books were sold in the
U.S. than hardcover books.[45] The writing may not be on the wall, but it is
on the receipts. Just as it took a decade for television sets to reach every
American home, it will take at least that long for the e-book to envelop libraries. After all, there was no previous version of TV to supplant. It'll be a
while before we can replace five hundred years of print—unless you want
to declare the world started with Google. As of 2012, less than 3 percent of
the average public library's collection consisted of e-books.

Having made those predictions, let's look at some qualifying e-book
issues. (We'll look at the challenges of learning from a *screen* in the next
chapter.)

What About e-Books for the Very Young?

I believe cars and aspirin are good things—but not in the hands of the
very young. The same goes for e-books. Educated parents, who now do
much of their own reading with digital devices, seem to have the same
feelings as I do about e-books. They've drawn a forbidding line when it
comes to their young children: all paper, no digital—for now. In 2011
only 5 percent of children's books were e-books.[46]

That may change, however, if publishers put enough sound and video
into the e-books, converting them from books to products. The danger
for the e-book as product is that it will fall prey to the temptations that
twisted television. If that happens with children's e-books, subtlety or

thinking will be lost in a maze of sounds and colors. And while there should be room for a certain amount of commercial junk in what we read, if children's publishing is run by corporate bottom-liners (a growing threat), a large number of books will be "gimmicked" and the e-book will become another television.[47] (Junior's in the backseat with the iPad, tapping away at letters and numbers to produce a cacophony of noises that salve the parent's guilt about being on the phone instead of having a conversation with the four-year-old.)

Young hands and minds need to explore the world in front of them. In order for them to do that, the world needs to stand still long enough to be examined, for the child to turn the page and then examine the picture without it moving or making noises. The very young cannot accumulate essential knowledge and detail from a speeding train. (The combination of e-books and young learners is further explored in chapter 7.)

E-books and older children is another issue, one that is especially pressing on school and public libraries. Growing up in a digital world, these are children who often use smartphones by age seven or earlier. Many are expecting their next novel to be on a handheld screen. Whether their minds will learn as easily from the screen page as the paper page is open to debate (see chapter 7).

Just as it took more than a dozen years in the early 1900s for the motion picture industry to work out all the copyrights and permissions to stabilize that industry, similar battles are being fought today between publishers, manufacturers (of Nooks, Kindles, iPads, etc.), and libraries. The battle of the moment is over how many times a library can loan an e-book before buying new rights (digital rights management—DRM), but given the pace of technological change, that debate could change overnight.[48] One thing is a given: The dollar cost of changing to e-books will be a serious obstacle for needy community libraries and schools.

What Is the Role of the Librarian in the Coming Digital World?

The answer to that can be found in opposite corners of the U.S.: the rocky hillsides of Ashburnham, Massachusetts, and the Olympic National Forest, in the Pacific Northwest.

If you want to see an example of the future library, look to Cushing Academy in Ashburnham (population 6,000). With annual tuition of nearly $50,000, the 148-year-old ivy-covered boarding academy isn't your average school, but its library was facing usage problems just like the average town's or school's. So in 2009, Cushing converted its Fisher-Watkins Library to all digital.

The 450-student population (ninth grade to postgrad) had been using the "old" library as a study hall more than a reference or reading room. It's twenty-five thousand books sat idly on the shelves, mostly untouched for years. Realizing the faculty had moved on to the Internet's information services and that students were following suit, Cushing's library decided to join the crowd—or at least change its face enough to draw a crowd. Out went twenty thousand books (donated to faculty and area libraries), while five thousand reference volumes were retained. The book processing room was converted into the Cushing Cyber Café, open seven thirty a.m. to three thirty p.m. and now one of the most popular sites on campus. To draw the faculty back, their lounge and mailboxes were moved to renovated space in the library. The area previously occupied by bookshelves is now filled with tables, chairs, and collaborative space for students wired to the Internet. Noisier and busier than ever before, the library today is an information resource instead of a book depository.

Today Cushing students still read traditional books, all of which come with their tuition dollars and are distributed by their teachers. But what about recreational reading outside of class, like a James Patterson or Suzanne Collins novel? The library purchases these as e-books and downloads them to Kindles loaned to the student (minus any e-mail or Internet capabilities). By 2011, the library's monthly e-book bill from Amazon ($1,000) was the same as its bill before going digital. If a student is looking for a book unavailable as an e-book (which is seldom), local libraries are happy to loan a hard copy (often the very libraries who were beneficiaries when Cushing gave away its collection). And because the young families of faculty and staff are still served by the library, there are hundreds of picture books still available in the family section, coexisting like a small stable within a massive e-garage.

You might be inclined to say, "Sure, the wealthy Cushing Academies can afford that kind of stuff, but it's a long, long way down the road." Maybe, maybe not. While Cushing was ahead of the curve, other prestigious institutions are following in its shadow. New York Public Library is selling one of its main lending libraries and only a last-minute $8 million donation kept it from shipping three million books off-site to New Jersey; Harvard's library has reduced its staff by 30 percent. In short, the traditional library is going the route of the card catalog.

The change may be slow to begin with, but think of it in these terms: In 1920, a police patrolman named William Potts, frustrated by the burgeoning automobile traffic in downtown Detroit, invented and installed the first automatic traffic signal in America. The first piece of roadway technology cost $37. By the end of the year, Detroit had fifteen of them. The rest is history.

The future library will shrink in size but, judging from present needs and behavior, there will remain a critical need for skilled librarians. As Cushing's library director, Tom Corbett, told his faculty, "You had it a lot easier than today's students. If you were researching King Charles, all the information was organized and focused right in front of you on a shelf." Today's student is confronted with a mess of unorganized and sometimes unauthenticated information on the Internet. Studying, learning, and researching were a lot simpler yesterday.

Tree Octopus: "Cause for serious concern."

The librarian's role today? Think "Officer Potts" from two paragraphs ago—supervising the e-traffic. When young people approach the Internet today, too often they suspend disbelief and assume if it's online it must be true. And that brings us to the Olympic National Forest and the "tree octopus" study.

Attempting to raise awareness about the low level of student Web skills, researchers at the University of Connecticut selected forty-eight seventh-grade Web users, all of them carefully tested to be proficient Web users and readers, drawn from diverse but economically challenged schools in Connecticut and South Carolina. They were introduced to what they didn't know was a spoof page about a fictitious endangered species—the Pacific Northwest Tree Octopus[49]—and asked to evaluate its authenticity.

Only six of the forty-eight students rated the site doubtful, and those because they had been tipped off about the site by a previous lesson in another class. When those six were asked to prove their doubts, none could do so. The remaining forty-two students rated it "reliable." When told it was a hoax site and asked for evidence of such, they were unable to find traces of deceit, despite the site listing Sasquatch as the octopus's main predator and links to conservation groups like People for the Ethical Treatment of Pumpkins. All of this from students reputed to be their schools' most proficient online users.

Dr. Donald Leu, the lead researcher on the tree octopus project, commented, "These results are cause for serious concern because anyone can publish anything on the Internet and today's students are not prepared to critically evaluate the information they find there." He cited the present classroom instruction as "woefully lacking" when it comes to online literacy.[50]

Echoing those concerns, a two-year study at five university libraries found student online research efforts to be, in a word, clueless, if not horrid. Not one student consulted a university librarian for help. In other words, most already knew what they were doing? Nope. Only seven out of thirty conducted "well-executed" research. The rest usually relied on Google and floundered there, wasting long hours and ending up in dead-end searches, while ignoring options like Google Scholar or Google Book Search. Making matters worse, little or no guidance was offered by their professors, and most students were inclined to do only enough to get by. The report indicated a greater need for students to access librarians for help, for greater cooperation between faculty and library, and a need for better online research education.[51]

All right, you say, the college kids are immature about their online research, but not so with adult professionals. Five years after it appeared, I went in search of the original source material for the tree octopus study, but all I could find was a university press release and blog commentaries. Stymied, I e-mailed Dr. Leu at UConn, who sent me a link to the original paper, along with this e-mail:

> Good of you to ask. Despite extensive coverage on the blogosphere, in the newspapers and on CNN, you are only the 4th person to ask for the source. That was the point of the octopus study. Apparently adults are not much better than adolescents about evaluating sources online.

The "enough to get by" syndrome appears to have a wider infection radius than we thought. All of this demonstrates there's as much of a need for good librarians today as there was thirty years ago—before Google and the Internet were born. Considering how complicated things are today, we might need them even more. Or think of it from a more pragmatic, though slightly vulgar, point of view: The Internet's information crop has multiplied, but so has its "crap." The closest thing we have to a "crap detector" is a qualified librarian.[52]

How Accurate Is the Internet's Wikipedia Versus a *Real* Encyclopedia?

During its decade of existence, Wikipedia has taken considerable abuse from critics and elitists. Founded in 2001, it is now the seventh most visited Web site (Google, Facebook, and YouTube rank 1, 2, and 3), and it contains more than four million articles in two hundred languages, versus the online Encyclopaedia Britannica, with half a million articles in English. Wikipedia is entirely free online, while Britannica offers a limited amount of information free online and then requires a subscription for more details. (The latter's print edition retired in March 2012, much like an aging boxing champ no longer able to stay on his feet—weight: 129 pounds; age: 244 years; price: $1,395.)[53]

The bigger contrast, however, is in their respective "authors." Britannica has about four thousand authorities who contribute information to approximately one hundred editors. Wikipedia is entirely "volunteer" in its composition and editing. Anyone, with or without credentials, may contribute, add to, or edit articles. Although there were serious liabilities with this approach through 2005, a series of "checks and balances" have since been added to curb the abuses. Anyone who has tried recently to edit or contribute to a Wikipedia article will tell you it is not easy. Want to contribute a snide remark to a movie star's Wiki page? Don't bother. You'll need some serious coding skills and then have to get by even more serious editors. Furthermore, the entire history of the page's editing process can be found by clicking on "View history," eliminating "stealth" contributors.

Since many of the Wiki contributors are not credentialed, how many errors can one expect to find? Back in 2005, the journal *Nature* had a panel of experts examine forty-two scientific online articles from both Wikipedia and Encyclopaedia Britannica. Wikipedia averaged four errors and Britannica averaged three. The experts discovered a total of eight "serious" errors among the forty-two entries, four in Wikipedia and four in Britannica.[54]

Other than the authorship issue, the biggest online difference between Wikipedia and Britannica is in their scope. Take the name of the community in which you were born and enter it into each site. Britannica had no entry for my birth city (Orange, New Jersey) while Wikipedia had five pages and sixty footnote citations. No less an authority than the recently retired executive editor of the *New York Times* is on record citing Wikipedia as his favorite Web tool after search engines.[55]

Is Wikipedia perfect? No, but considering its size and scope, as well as audience size, a free Wikipedia is one of the wonders of the digital age and makes the entire world a better, smarter place. For most of history, expensive encyclopedias were tethered to the hard maple tables of libraries, unavailable for public circulation. With the arrival of Wikipedia, instant information sits in our very pockets. "Let's look it up right now" has replaced "We'll go to the library tomorrow" in parent-child conversation.

Chapter 7

Digital Learning:
Good News and Bad

What I worry about, as a sociobiologist, is not what
my kids are doing on the Internet but what all this
connectivity is doing to their brains.

—Anthony Wagner, Stanford professor[1]

Back in September 1950, at the dawn of the great television decade,
Motorola ran a series of national ads in which it promised a TV in the
home would bring families closer and improve student grades. A half
century later we all know how those promises panned out. In similar
fashion, digital learning is being promoted today as the cure-all for the
American (if not the world) classroom: Connect to the e-cloud and we're
saved and educated. U.S. schools are investing $2.2 billion a year in edu-
cational software, to say nothing of the e-tablet investments that parents
and teachers think will put their children on a faster, smarter track to
success. Can you hear the echoes of
TV in the 1950s?

While the past decade has produced more than a few advocates
supporting all things digital for kids
("At least they're reading online,
right?"), there's been simultaneous
growth in information on how
humans of all ages behave and learn
with digital devices. Since e-learning
is an integral part of today's home

and classroom, I thought this edition should include at least the rudiments of the new findings.

And in the spirit of full disclosure, I admit to using digital technology daily: iPad, iPod, laptop and desktop computers, and digital cameras. In researching and documenting this edition, I added more than seven hundred articles and papers to what I already had from previous editions, except most of the new papers were accessed via the Internet, using my local library card to connect to professional journals through the Connecticut state library and department of higher education. And all the papers fit on a tiny flash drive. Good-bye clippings and file drawers.

I have tried to keep the information here simple and straightforward. If you wish to challenge the findings or explore them further, just follow the footnotes. I also urge you to keep in mind that whenever new technology appears, there are "experts" playing soothsayer: Socrates once claimed the alphabet and writing would be the ruination of the mind and memory; Edison said motion pictures would replace textbooks; and TV executives predicted *Sesame Street* would solve our literacy woes. All were wrong. I'm sure some of the findings here will be wrong someday. The question is: Which ones?

E-Book Advantages in Learning

The vast majority of arguments I hear against e-books involve traditional readers declaring how much they'll miss the feel of the pages and the smell of the book. This is reminiscent of silent film fans mourning the demise of the pipe organ player.

Smell or no smell, the e-book is here to stay, for very legitimate reasons. It is a win-win situation: a moneymaker for the publisher and a money saver for the buyer. It also saves time, space, student spines, and trees, to say nothing of what it does for the visually impaired.

For decades schoolchildren have been straining under increasing weight loads of textbooks. A fully loaded student backpack tips the scales at twenty to thirty pounds. As states raised academic standards, more pages were added to cover the possible testing material.[2] No wonder school districts and colleges are moving to e-tablets that will hold all of a student's texts in a space weighing less than two pounds. Moreover, a science or math e-textbook can be quickly updated without buying new editions, the same way computer operating systems receive security updates.

And then there is the added life expectancy. When tax laws changed and publishing houses had to pay taxes on the books in their warehouse, books that were not consistent sellers went out of print faster. An e-book, however, has no physical presence (no more warehousing costs) and isn't taxed as inventory. Therefore it can stay in print for as long as the publisher and author have a contract. This greatly extends the life of the book and allows publishing houses to instantaneously bring out-of-print titles back to life (as is happening now)—thus the Lazarus effect. In fact, most of the classics are now available as free e-books from Gutenberg.org.[3]

While the e-book version adds years to the book's life, the e-tablet adds multimedia to the reading experience. Suppose the class is studying the civil rights movement. A hyperlink in the e-text on an iPad could bring up PBS's American Experience "Freedom Riders," a program that follows the trail of the four hundred black and white "riders" who set out to violate Jim Crow bus laws and make the struggle into a focal point for the entire nation.[4]

E-page hyperlinks will bring thousands of free tutoring lessons from Khan Academy to any student, anywhere in the world.[5] The child in rural Georgia can have the same online tutoring lessons Bill Gates's kids had.

Or think in terms of audio information available through e-book links—the voluminous archives from public radio. For example, almost as famous as *Catcher in the Rye* is its author, J. D. Salinger, and his reclusive lifestyle. Everyone told teenager Jim Sadwith not to bother reaching out to Salinger, that he didn't welcome visitors—stay away! Besides, they declared, you'll never find him. But the boy wanted to make a high school play based on the book and was sure Salinger would love the idea, so off he went in search of the recluse. More than forty years later, Sadwith told American Public Media's *The Story* about finding Salinger and what the author's reaction was. And as the adventure progressed, the boy dictated his exploits into a recorder and later submitted the tape to Harvard instead of the traditional college essay. (He got in.) Wouldn't that interview add dimensions for anyone studying the book? It's free online, accessed via hyperlink.[6]

Worried about the venerable tradition of autographed books? They've even found a way for authors to personalize and sign e-books.[7] The resources are unlimited, and none of them would add either a dime to the cost or a pound to the weight of the e-textbook.

E-Book Liabilities

Some of these downsides may change with time, but today they raise serious concerns.

How do you share or loan an e-book to a group of friends? How does a teacher stock her classroom library with e-books? Will there ever be used e-bookstores? (Think of how used bookstores prolong the life of a book by decades.) Where will low-income families stand in the land of $200 e-readers? The book cover that caught your eye on the bookstore shelf, that provoked you to pick it up and read the flap and first page? Gone. Those covers were a major factor in grabbing customers of all ages (see page 118). How soon before e-book batteries become the equivalent of printer ink cartridges? (Gotta have 'em; can't afford 'em.)

Still readable after 100 years.

And very worrisome, how long before today's e-book format is outdated, like those old Word documents you can no longer read with your latest version of Microsoft Word? Though their phrasing may be antiquated, books that were written two hundred years ago are still readable today. The same can't be said for many digital documents created twenty years ago, sometimes even just a few years ago.[8] Will the e-book formatting be outdated five years from now? Will we have to purchase updated software to reread our e-books? Do software companies have a track record for this kind of behavior? Tried to use a floppy disk recently?

The research clearly shows that we read more slowly (6 to 11 percent) from a screen than from paper.[9] As with automobile driving, humans may get better and faster at e-reading over the years—but that could take generations.

Science also shows we comprehend less while reading digital text than printed text. Here's why:

1. One cause appears to be the lack of permanent physical "landmarks" on a digital page versus paper.[10] Unlike paper text, which is like a landscape with roadside markers, e-text is like an ocean—harder to navigate. What we remember best from reading is usually aided by visual and geographic recall. That's why it's so difficult to navigate back through e-text without the book's search tool. The reader has little sense of whether the text in question was top of the page or bottom, front of the book, middle, or back.

2. More than digital reading, paper reading stimulates areas of the brain dealing with emotional involvement and spatial recall, thus leaving a "deeper footprint."[11]

Learning Online: Gaining or Draining?

As I write these words, major universities are firing and hiring presidents in a rush to climb aboard the "Online Learning" cruise ship.[12] Led by MIT and Stanford, online learning is either the latest phase or the future of learning, but more and more schools see the Internet as a virtual classroom that will save money, time, minds, and even campus parking.

Among the people who see future progress tied directly to the Internet is Cathy N. Davidson, a distinguished Duke University professor and vice provost.

In Davidson's book *Now You See It: How the Brain Science of Attention Will Transform the Way We Live, Work, and Learn*,[13] she offers support for digital learning, despite what doomsayers proclaim about digital multi-tasking:

- We're all born inattentive and have to learn attentiveness with age and experience, growing increasingly attentive to our important multiple needs if we need to.
- "[Multitasking] is the ideal mode of the twenty-first century. . . . On the Internet, everything links to everything and all of it is available all the time, at any time." We're entirely capable of handling those multiple challenges, she notes.
- Just as the desktop computer forced us to reorganize our work and play spaces, we now need to reorganize our minds. The brain's neural plasticity will allow that rewiring to happen handily.

In support of her argument, Davidson offers the Great Duke iPod Experiment. Back in 2003, she and her colleagues handed new iPods to 1,650 incoming Duke freshmen, challenging them to come up with educational uses for the device. Until that point, the iPod was largely seen as a glorified Walkman and music organizer. This class was arguably one of the last to recall life before and after the birth of the Internet. With all of their online experience during high school, who would be better equipped to see any education potential lurking inside the iPod? If an idea or product was to be turned over to "crowd sourcing" for improvement, why not start with this collection of bright young people?

As expected, ideas blossomed. According to Davidson, "The real treasure trove was to be found in the students' innovations. Working together, and often alongside their profs, they came up with far more learning apps for their iPods than anyone—even Apple—had dreamed possible."

The long and short of the Duke experiment was that by the time those freshmen were graduating in 2007, Apple was unveiling its "iTunes U," with thousands of free downloadable lectures and files from universities, libraries, and museums. By 2011, the numbers dwarfed any educational outreach effort in recorded history: more than 350,000 individual lectures downloaded 600 million times (half of them in 2010), free for download in 123 countries. Contributors to the lecture library include the faculties of Harvard, Yale, MIT, Duke, Cambridge, and Oxford, among more than a thousand institutions.

Some Words from the Doomsayers

For brevity's sake I'll list just five of the major liabilities some of the experts see in online learning, followed by their reasoning.

1. Kids will be kids. Wi-Fi or not, sophomores act sophomorically.
2. Educational software companies regularly either overpromise or lie about their products.
3. Multitasking diminishes achievement.
4. Constant connectedness undercuts thinking and creativity.
5. Hyperlinked text (online reading) impedes understanding.

Kids will be kids. Nate Stulman was a sophomore at Swarthmore College when he decided to monitor how his classmates were using their computers. Despite the fact that Swarthmore is one of the preeminent small colleges in the United States, Stulman discovered its students were using their computers in the same way millions of others do at lesser schools: playing games, e-mailing boyfriends and girlfriends, killing time in chat rooms, and uploading and downloading music (Facebook and Twitter hadn't been invented yet). Writing for the *New York Times* op-ed page,[14] Stulman concluded that many students are too immature to handle the distractions and temptations of the Internet, a fact largely unaddressed by those who think wiring the school is like wiring the brain. More than a few school districts that have handed laptops to their high school students have learned that digital connections do not hurry maturity.[15]

Educational software companies regularly either overpromise or lie about their products. On the same September day in 2011 when millions were being told by the Associated Press that six hundred school districts were launching iPad programs to put the latest technology in their students' hands,[16] the *New York Times* devoted a large chunk of its front page and two full pages inside to a more sobering technology story.[17] The Kyrene (Arizona) School District was entering year six in its technological classroom revolution, having poured $33 million into techno-smart gadgets. Conclusion: stuck in neutral.

Although above the state average, Kyrene's math and reading scores had shown negligible improvement in six years, despite all the clicking, mousing, and PowerPointing. This didn't surprise the experts, who pointed out there were few studies showing either positive or negative results from the digital investment in classrooms. The former executive director for education at the Bill & Melinda Gates Foundation told the *Times*, "The data is pretty weak. It's very difficult when we're pressed to come up with convincing data."

In fact, the number of government and independent studies documenting the ineffectiveness of education software to date is too long to be included here as anything but footnotes.[18] All their findings were summarized by one *New York Times* headline: "Inflating the Software Report Card,"[19] which is what ed-software salesmen appear to have been doing to the tune of $2.2 billion a year. When Stanford University's Center for Research on Education Outcomes (CREDO) project tracked four years' worth of reading scores for more than 73,000 Pennsylvania charter school students, it found 100 percent of the cyberschool students (who operate entirely online from home) did worse than their public counterparts in school.[20] Colorado's cyberstudent graduation rate was 12 percent versus 78 percent for public-schoolers.[21] Even Steve Jobs and Bill Gates, meeting shortly before Jobs's death in 2011, "agreed that, so far, computers had made surprisingly little impact on schools."[22]

Maybe all of that is why the private Waldorf schools in and around Silicone Valley are brimming with the children of executives and engineers from tech firms like Apple, Yahoo, and Google. The Waldorf philosophy is simple: no tech gadgets in the primary school. Their curriculum is about hands-on creativity and learning; the tech stuff can wait until high school or later. More incredible, the tech parents sign on and so do their kids.[23]

Multitasking diminishes achievement. It's possible that e-fans are overestimating both the gadgets and the kids. If the challenge is juggling, then a digital device is like a rubber ball that you're juggling between your hands. Add another ball to the mix and the process becomes more challenging. Add a third or fourth and you've got your hands full. It gets harder and harder to add more.

Now think digital devices juggled by the brain. Today's teenager is regularly juggling e-tablets, iPods, smartphones, and laptops, along with the TV in their bedroom.

From 2,272 text messages a month in 2008, American teenagers (ages 13–17) ballooned to 3,339 messages a month in 2010, an average of six per waking hour. Simply put, students in one of the most formative periods of their intellectual and emotional lives are interrupted 118 times a day for messages, totaling 90 minutes.[24] (Remember the role of distractions in Fraction of Selection, page 84.)

Still juggling the twenty-four-hour day, let's look at what the student is also doing while texting. The longest-running examination of children's media consumption is the Kaiser Family Foundation study.[25] When Kaiser reported on children's media multitasking in 2009, researchers found a daily increase of more than two hours since 2004: 10.7 hours of multimedia packed into 7.5 hours—all of it devoted to movies, music, TV, videos, and a little print. And that was *before* the birth of smartphones or e-tablets like the Kindle and iPad.

Exactly how much can the brain juggle before losing something more important than a rubber ball? Dr. Clifford Nass and Stanford researchers studied the impact of media multitasking on two groups of university students to see if there were any differences in their memory and performance.[26] While performing various tasks, they had to juggle media that included cell phone, Twitter, texting, video chatting, and Web surfing. The students, judged to be of comparable intelligence, were divided into heavy multitaskers and light multitaskers, depending on how much they were assigned to use simultaneously.

*E-critics say their concerns multiply by the
number of digital distractions.*

The heavy media multitaskers lost on every count, with deficits on all aspects of attention. Nass and his colleagues found the heavy users struggled to tell what was relevant or not, and were more easily distracted by irrelevant material. Their recall abilities showed scrambled recollections, and they were more disorganized in switching tasks. The same impairment findings have also held true for multitasking as simple as talking on a cell phone while driving a car.[27]

Constant connectedness undercuts thinking and creativity. Because so many teens and adults are connected 24-7 in their multitasking, there is very little downtime or disconnect.

What's wrong with that? The more you work, the more you accomplish, right? Not necessarily, say the experts.

Most creative artists and thinkers admit there comes a point when they must stop, put their tools aside, and think about something else (like biking or vacuuming) while the work "percolates." This allows the creative muse to speak to them. And since muses seldom shout, solitude is needed to hear them.[28] There are countless examples in history of significant discoveries or insights arriving during idle time, away from the workbench.[29] Einstein frequently abandoned a math problem and retreated to music to unwind the problem.

So what happens to the creative process when there is no disconnect time, when we and our children are constantly downloading, uploading, texting, YouTubing, Googling, or tweeting our 742 "friends"? Less "deep thinking" takes place, less creativity.[30] Where will the next Steve Jobs come from, or the next Edison, Salk, Spielberg, Ellington, or Steinbeck? It's unlikely he or she will come from noisy multitasking, that's for sure.

While we're all connected, we're also running down both batteries—the device's and our own. From recent scientific observations of both humans[31] and rats,[32] the research is very convincing that constant stimulation of the brain from multitasking debilitates brain function. In other words, it's a lot harder to have those "aha" moments if you don't have enough "ah" moments.

The student who is constantly connected, including sleeping with his or her cell phone on the pillow, is not allowing time for the day's learning and experiences to gestate, and this has the psychological field genuinely worried.[33] The afflicted are living widely in the present but only about an inch deep.

Hyperlinked text (online reading) impedes understanding. One of the most sobering examinations of the Internet's impact on our human thinking can be found in Nicholas Carr's book *The Shallows: What the Internet Is Doing to Our Brains.* With degrees from Dartmouth and Harvard, Carr is a frequent contributor to some of the most prestigious journals on both sides of the Atlantic and a member of the Encyclopaedia Britannica's editorial board. But he had a problem.

The Shallows was written in response to his conclusion that a decade of steady Internet usage had significantly "tinkered" with his brain, making it increasingly difficult to read complex narrative. His concentration continually drifted, his reading grew shallower, and his recall suffered.

The world of e-reading is aglow with distractions.

When Carr shared his problem with colleagues, distinguished writers and researchers, many confessed to similar problems, even to the extent that they had ceased to read long narratives altogether. They'd begun to read the way they were thinking—quick and skimming. Who needed to read at length? Google will do that for us.

In *The Shallows*, Carr devoted a carefully documented twenty-six-page chapter to the hazards of reading online. Here are a few of his sobering observations:

+ Hyperlinked (underlined) text both slows the reading process and impedes understanding.[34]
+ The torrential force of information and diversions facing the Internet reader overwhelms the brain, making "distractions more distracting."[35]
+ Among one hundred volunteers presenting a lesson via their computer browsers, half received a text-only version and half had text with a multimedia window on the lesson added. The text-only volunteers scored significantly higher on the posttest.[36]
+ Studies of eye movements while reading online show only about 18 percent of a Web page is actually read, with the average page view lasting 10 seconds or less.[37]

Carr's concerns about inattention during online reading are further supported by newspaper industry studies that track reader behavior. Visitors to online newspaper sites spent an average of 45 minutes per month at the sites, compared with print users of those newspapers, whose monthly use averaged 790 minutes.[38] The online readers seldom, if ever, read in depth.

Ah, the Promise of Microwaves!

In summary, in these early hours of the digital age, there is a mix of peril and promise. Research shows reading from paper makes for greater retention of facts than digital reading, although that may change with constant screen use through generations. On the other hand, e-tablets and screens are more entertaining, give us faster access to more information, and allow for easier use and greater dollar savings.

Those differences eventually may push e-reading into what one observer called the "microwave" mode. She recalled how twenty years ago we thought we'd be cooking entire meals in our microwaves but now we pretty much use them for warm-ups and popcorn—the big stuff still goes on the stove. Thus we may end up using e-books for easy recreational reading but traditional books for information we need to retain.[39]

As for expecting children to learn faster and deeper simply because we're buying them digital devices, "microwave learning" is no guarantee of well-done minds.

Chapter 8

Television and Audio: Hurting or Helping Literacy?

I believe television is going to be the test of the modern world, and that in this new opportunity to see beyond the range of our vision we shall discover either a new and unbearable disturbance of the general peace or a saving radiance in the sky. We shall stand or fall by television—of that I am quite sure.
—E. B. White, "Removal from Town," *Harper's* (October 1938)

WITH electronic media now the dominant force in a child's life outside of family (and for some, even larger than the family), it must be included in any book or discussion about literacy. While digital issues are addressed in the previous chapter, what about television? Most people thought the arrival of computers would dull TV's presence in the family, but so far that hasn't happened. So is its presence positive, negative, or null and void?

Do you remember the positive impact of Oprah's Book Club on book reading? A plus for TV there. Recall the positive role TV played in raising public awareness during the Vietnam War, the civil rights struggle, the aftermath of both 9/11 and Hurricane Katrina? Big pluses there, too.

Furthermore, in full disclosure, I own a television set and watch the nightly news, *Jeopardy, 60 Minutes,* Yankees games, and movies via Apple TV. As a form of entertainment and information, even diversion, television is harmless—in the right dosages. Media is like the medications in your medicine cabinet. Helpful as they might be, with children they need oversight and controls. Can that be done when the average home now contains 3.8 television sets? It's a serious challenge.

I also fully understand and sympathize with the complexities of modern family living: two working parents, often under considerable stress and time constraints, trying to raise and cope with the young—a family portrait that doesn't look the slightest bit like either the Cleavers or the Brady Bunch. For some parents, the TV may be the only crowd-control device they have—and they have my sympathies. But just because a family needs the device in order to survive, that doesn't mean its consequences are benign. They are not, for any family.

I will make a point twice in this chapter because of its importance: It is not so much what children are doing while they watch multiple hours of TV; it is the experiences they are not having that make the viewing so dangerous. With that in mind, let me share the story I offered to every parent audience for nearly twenty-five years.

It begins with a woman named Sonya Carson trying to raise two sons in inner-city Detroit as a single parent. One of twenty-four children, Mrs. Carson had only a third-grade education. A hardworking, driven woman, she toiled as a domestic and children's caregiver for wealthy families—sometimes working two or three jobs at a time to support her sons. Sometimes she worked so hard that she had to "get away to her relatives for a rest." Only years later did her sons discover that she was checking herself into a mental facility for professional help for depression.

Her sons, on the other hand, were not working themselves into any kind of frenzy. Both were on a slow boat to nowhere in the classroom. Bennie, the younger one, was the worst student in his fifth-grade class. As if raising two sons in one of the most dangerous cities in America was not enough, Mrs. Carson now faced the challenge of the boys' grades. She met it head-on.

"Bennie—you're smarter than this report card," she declared, pointing to his math score. "First thing, you're going to learn your times tables—every one of them!"

"Mom, do you know how many there are? It would take me a whole year!" he replied.

"I only went through the third grade and I know them all the way through my twelves," his mother answered. "And furthermore, you are not to go outside tomorrow until you learn them."

Her son pointed to the columns in his math book and cried, "Look at these things! How can anyone learn them?"

His mother simply tightened her jaw, looked him calmly in the eye, and declared, "You can't go out until you learn your times tables."

Bennie learned his times tables—and his math scores began to climb. His mother's next goal was to get the rest of his grades up. Her intuition pointed to the television that never seemed to be off when the boys were home. "From now on, you can only watch three television programs a week!" A week! (What Sonya Carson lacked in book sense she made up for with common sense that would be vindicated nearly thirty years later when major research studies showed a powerful connection between "over-viewing" and underachievement.)

She next looked for a way to fill the free time created by the television vacuum. She said, "You boys are going to the library and checking out two books. At the end of each week you'll write me a report on what you've read." (Only years later did the boys discover she couldn't read well enough to understand any of the reports.)

They didn't like it, of course, but they didn't dare refuse. And in reading two books a week, then talking about them with his mother, Bennie raised his reading scores. And because the entire curriculum was tied to reading, the rest of his report card began to improve. (It's worth noting that before his mother thought about changing schools, she changed her home. Politicians who pose vouchers or magnet schools as a solution ignore the pivotal role of the home.) Each semester, each year, Bennie's scores rose. And by the time he was a senior in high school he was third in his class, scoring in the ninetieth percentile of the nation.

With colleges like West Point, Yale, and Stanford waving scholarships in his face, but with only ten dollars in his pocket for application fees, Bennie let his choice fall to whichever school won the College Bowl television quiz that year (Yale). He spent four years there majoring in psychology, then went on to the medical schools at the University of Michigan and Johns Hopkins. Today, at age sixty-two, Dr. Ben Carson is one of the world's premier pediatric brain surgeons. When Johns Hopkins named him head of pediatric neurosurgery, he was, at age thirty-three, the youngest in the nation.

Ask Dr. Carson to explain how you get from a fatherless inner-city home and a mother with a third-grade education, along with being the worst student in your fifth-grade class, to being a world-famous brain surgeon with a brother who is an engineer. Again and again, he points to two things: his mother's religion (Seventh-Day Adventist) and the pivotal moment when she limited their television viewing and ordered him to start reading.

I had people in my audiences with three times the education of young Mrs. Carson and ten times her income—but not half her common sense and courage when it came to raising children. They're not "raising" children—they're "watching them grow up," and most of the watching occurs from the couch in front of a television set.

Dr. Ben Carson concedes his medical career could have been undone by the wrong dosage of TV.

There are two important things to remember about the Carson family's story: (1) Mrs. Carson didn't trash the set—she controlled it, and (2) with high expectations of her children, she demanded appropriate behavior from them. In controlling the dosage of TV, Mrs. Carson averted disaster. Dosage determines the impact of anything—from hurricanes and aspirin to reading and television.

The story of the Carson family is now available in every format, each adding a dimension to the inspiration: in book format, *Gifted Hands: The Ben Carson Story* by Ben Carson; also as an e-book and audiobook; and finally as an excellent Turner film starring Cuba Gooding Jr., available from Amazon. In addition, the Academy of Achievement offers an excellent online interview (audio and video) with Dr. Carson at http://www .achievement.org/autodoc/page/car1int-1.[1]

What Exactly Is So Wrong with Television?

Until recently, most critics could only point to "overdosing" as the problem. TV was just an innocent bystander to parent neglect or irresponsibility. New research, however, is getting closer to identifying TV as more of an accomplice. But even if the research fails to completely indict TV, it all points to the dangers of over-viewing among all age groups, with the youngest being the most prone to danger. The latest findings from media research don't bode well for the future classroom: Students between the ages of eight and eighteen now average 4 hours and 29 minutes a day viewing television, twice that of music or any other media format, and an increase of 38 minutes since the last study in 2004.[2]

Let's start with the youngest "viewers" and work upward.

1. While TV is sometimes portrayed as a "family event," it is often experienced in isolation as an infant. When six-month-old infants living at poverty level were monitored during more than four hundred television exposures, their mothers interacted with them only 24 percent of the time, most often during educational programs. Most programs they were exposed to, however, were not intended for infants. Overall, children from lower income levels watch more television and achieve at lower levels in school.[3] Could their focus have been harmed by heavy doses of early TV? Read on.

2. When the television viewing habits of 2,500 children were tracked and examined by researchers at Seattle Children's Hospital, the doctors concluded that for each hour of daily TV viewed by the child before age three, the risk of attention deficit hyperactivity disorder (ADHD) by age seven increased by 10 percent.[4] (ADHD is now the most common childhood behavioral disorder.)

3. Today's young parents, anxious to keep their child one step ahead of the neighbors' child, are buying into an electronic culture that is often one big suede shoe operation. Remember the hucksters who used to push their snake oil products off covered wagons and then moved to late-night infomercials? They just encamped in the nursery, promoting toys, DVDs, videos, and gadgets that will make your child into an infant Einstein. But considering the unhappy childhood of Einstein, who would want it? Apparently millions of parents, all of them ignorant of comments like this from the director of child research at one of the nation's biggest toy companies: "There is no proof that this type of toy helps children become smarter."[5] Child development experts caution against the do-all toys intended to boost IQ. As one critic explained, "The most useful toy is the one that requires the most activation on the part of a young child. The more they have to use their minds and bodies to make something work, the more they are going to learn." When Baby Einstein's parent company, Disney, was threatened with class action suits for misusing the "educational" label on the product, Disney defused the crisis by simply conceding, "Don't like it? Here's your money back."[6] That in itself didn't sound like there was an arsenal of support behind the product.

4. Once children are in school, the impact of heavy viewing is reflected in student achievements in both reading and math. In a study of 348 ethnically

diverse third-graders from six California schools, the presence of a television set in the child's bedroom was significantly associated with lower math, reading, and language arts scores.[7] (See the chart below.) Kaiser media studies show bedroom TVs always correlate to more viewing hours.[8]

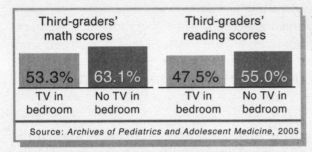

Third-graders' math scores		Third-graders' reading scores	
53.3%	63.1%	47.5%	55.0%
TV in bedroom	No TV in bedroom	TV in bedroom	No TV in bedroom
Source: *Archives of Pediatrics and Adolescent Medicine*, 2005			

A TV in the child's bedroom spells more viewing and lower scores. Based on the study "The Remote, the House, and the No. 2 Pencil,"

By age eight, 71 percent of children not only lived in a home with three televisions but also had a TV in their bedroom, resulting in an additional hour of TV viewing daily[9] and two additional hours of general exposure.[10] If a video game is in the bedroom, the child plays thirty-two minutes more daily, and the availability of a bedroom computer doubles the usage when compared with no computer in the bedroom.

Nor is it just an academic problem. In 1999, sleep researchers working with parents and teachers of 495 students in kindergarten through fourth grade found that those with televisions in their bedrooms were far more apt to have difficulty falling asleep and woke up more often during the night, thus impeding school performance later.[11]

5. Like the elephant in the room that no one wanted to talk about, the black-white reading gap existed for decades before federal requirements forced everyone to break down their scores demographically. The ensuing uproar brought outcries and attention to the problem. As evidenced in the first three chapters of this book, poverty plays a significant role in that gap. But when poverty was accounted for and still black scores were low, researchers began digging for other causes. Among other things, there was a definite TV connection. The case in point was the study of an academically oriented high school in the middle-class white-black community of Shaker Heights, Ohio.[12]

In this situation, black children of parents with at least one graduate degree still scored 191 points below their white counterparts in similar family circumstances. Among the reasons offered: Middle-class black children watched twice as much TV as their white counterparts.

The research, conducted by Ronald F. Ferguson, an African-American and lecturer in public policy at Harvard, showed that this first generation of children of black achievers watched twice as much TV as their white classmates: three hours a day compared with one and a half hours. The Kaiser study in 2010[13] showed national results similar to Ferguson's, but also found that black children were far more likely to have TVs in their bedrooms and viewed almost two hours more daily.

6. In 2005, New Zealand researchers published results of a twenty-six-year study of 980 children born between 1972 and 1973. The group included full representation of every socioeconomic level.

Based on the study "Association of Television Viewing During Childhood with Poor Educational Achievement,"

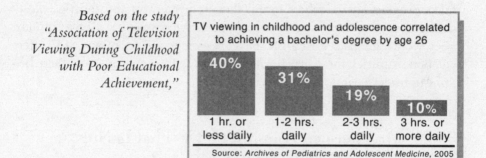

TV viewing in childhood and adolescence correlated to achieving a bachelor's degree by age 26

40%	31%	19%	10%
1 hr. or less daily	1-2 hrs. daily	2-3 hrs. daily	3 hrs. or more daily

Source: *Archives of Pediatrics and Adolescent Medicine*, 2005

Data were obtained from the families at ages five, seven, eight, eleven, thirteen, and fifteen, while interviews were used at age twenty-six to determine each member's educational achievement level. Adjusting for IQ, socioeconomic status, and childhood behavioral problems, the children's schooling level by age twenty-six was directly related to how much they viewed TV throughout childhood (see chart). Children who viewed less than one hour a day were the most likely to achieve a college degree. The researchers noted, "These findings indicate that excessive television viewing is likely to have a negative impact on educational achievement. This is likely to have far-reaching consequences for an individual's socioeconomic status and well-being in adult life."[14]

7. Beginning around the age of three, television does help in developing vocabulary, especially educational TV. But by ten years of age, little of what the average child hears on television is adding to his everyday vocabulary. He's heard it all before. Each decade has seen a decline in TV vocabulary level. In *The Inarticulate Society*, Tom Shachtman measured and compared the language structure of the *CBS Evening News* in a

thirty-year period between 1963 and 1993 (from Cronkite to Rather).[15] For the 1963 program, Shachtman found its sentences usually ran eighteen to twenty-five words, had dependent clauses, and included abstract words like *unanimous*, *compulsory*, and *protestations*. The overall vocabulary was on the level of the front page of the *New York Times*, and aimed at individuals with working vocabularies of nine thousand to ten thousand words, the level of well-written language. By 1993, the program's language level had deteriorated to that of common conversation (about 848 everyday words) and seldom used abstract terms, and short sentences or phrases predominated. The program, as well as the commercials, had dropped from the level of the well-prepared high school graduate in 1963 to junior high school level in 1993. In a 2009 study of eighty-eight television programs, researchers found that 98 percent of the shows' vocabulary consisted of the Common Lexicon, the words we use all the time. In other words, for native English speakers over ten years of age, TV offers few opportunities for learning new words.[16] It can, however, help beginning readers—if you use the right tools.

Is There an Amount of TV That Is Not Harmful to Children?

Before looking at the recommended dosage, it's important to understand that the greatest academic damage may be in what is *not* being done during those thirty-one and a half hours a week of sitting inertly in front of the TV: the games not played, the chores not done, the drawings not drawn, the hobbies not worked, the friends not made or played with, the homework not done, the bikes or skateboards not ridden, the balls not caught, the books not read, and the conversations not held. I hear parents call it "my babysitter"—but if there were a babysitter who interrupted your child's natural growth that much, you'd never hire him or her again, right?

The American Academy of Pediatrics recommends a limit of ten hours a week, and no TV for children under two. This was based on a research analysis of twenty-three TV-learning studies of 87,025 children in England, Japan, Canada, and five areas of the United States between 1963 and 1978.[17] The findings for schoolchildren showed no detrimental effects on learning (and some positive effects) from TV viewing up to ten hours a week; however, after that, the scores begin to decline. The average student today watches three times the recommended dosage.

Presidents, schools, and religious institutions have largely failed when it comes to solving the TV problem in society and the home. They've failed to use the bully pulpits to sound the alarm, perhaps because so many are addicted to the medium themselves. The past twenty years have seen a parade of Democratic and Republican presidents decrying the state of education and extolling the virtues of testing, yet none had the courage to say, "As for you parents watching this State of the Union address, I happen to know from the research[18] that 64 percent of you watch television while you and your families eat dinner, and almost half of you have the TV set on every waking hour you're at home. More than half of you put no limits on your children's viewing, yet by every measure available, the more TV your children watch, the lower their school scores. I have a simple question for you: Parents—have you completely lost your minds?"

I may not live long enough to see a president with that kind of courage, but how about the school superintendents and clergy? What can a school district or church or synagogue do to publicize the dangers in overviewing? You could start with this chapter. My Web site offers a free single-page pamphlet that summarizes some of the facts here. Distribute it; put it in your school or parish newsletter.[19] If only five families take it to heart, it's at least five minds saved.

How Do You Manage a Family's Viewing?

This reply also applies to family use of the Internet and computers. It really comes down to management of time and family.

My family's restricted viewing began in 1974, at about the time I'd begun to notice a growing television addiction in my fourth-grade daughter and kindergarten-age son. (They are now forty-seven and forty-three.) Even our long-standing read-aloud time each night had begun to deteriorate because, in their words, it "took too much time away from the TV."

One evening while visiting Marty and Joan Wood, of Longmeadow, Massachusetts, I noticed that their four teenage children went right to their homework after excusing themselves from the dinner table.

I asked the parents, "Your television broken?"

"No," replied Marty. "Why?"

"Well, it's only six forty-five and the kids are already doing homework."

Joan explained, "Oh, we don't allow television on school nights."

"That's a noble philosophy—but how in the world do you enforce it?" I asked.

"It is a house law," stated Marty. And for the next hour and a half, husband and wife detailed for me the positive changes that had occurred in their family and home since they put that "law" into effect.

That evening was a turning point for my family. After hearing the details of the plan, my wife, Susan, agreed wholeheartedly to back it. "On one condition," she added.

"What's that?" I asked.

"You be the one to tell them."

After supper the next night, we brought the children into our bedroom, surrounded them with pillows and quilts, and I calmly began, "Jamie . . . Elizabeth . . . Mom and I have decided there will be no more television on school nights in this house—forever."

Their reaction was predictable: They started to cry. What came as a shock to us was that they cried for four solid months. Every night, despite explanations on our part, they cried. We tried to impress upon them that the rule was not meant as a punishment; we listed all the positive reasons for such a rule. They cried louder.

The peer group pressure was enormous, particularly for Elizabeth, who said there was nothing for her to talk about during lunch at school since she hadn't seen any of the shows her friends were discussing. There was even peer pressure on Susan and me from neighbors and friends who thought the rule was needlessly harsh.

As difficult as it was at first, we persevered and resisted the pressure on both fronts. We lived with the tears, the pleadings, the conniving. And after three months we began to see things happen that the Woods had predicted. Suddenly we had the time each night as a family to read aloud, to read to ourselves, to do homework at an unhurried pace, to learn how to play chess and checkers and Scrabble, to make plastic models that had been collecting dust in the closet for years, to bake cakes and cookies, to write thank-you notes to aunts and uncles, to do household chores and take baths and showers without World War III breaking out, to play on the parish sports teams, to draw and paint and color, and—best of all—to talk to one another, ask questions, and answer questions.

Our children's imaginations were coming back to life.

For the first year, the decision was a heavy one, but with time it grew lighter. Jamie, being younger, had never developed the acute taste for television that Elizabeth had over the years, and he lost the habit fairly easily. It took Elizabeth longer to adjust.

Over the years the plan was modified until it worked like this:

1. The television is turned off at supper time and not turned on again until the children are in bed, Monday through Thursday.

2. Each child is allowed to watch one school-night show a week (subject to parents' approval). Homework and chores must be finished beforehand.
3. Weekend television is limited to any two of the three nights. The remaining night is reserved for homework and other activities. The children make their selections separately.

We structured the TV diet to allow the family to control the television and not the other way around. Perhaps this particular diet won't work for your family, but any kind of control is better than none. Unfortunately, "none" is the norm in 65 percent of American families.[20]

Don't Kids Need the Entertainment Break That Electronic Media Offer?

Everyone needs a break. But when you're talking about seven and a half hours a day (the total number of hours the average eight- to eighteen-year-old spends in front of entertainment media a day, including video and computer games),[21] that's more than a break. That's the equivalent of watching *Gone with the Wind* 730 times a year. Give me a break!

In his autobiography, *A Life in the Twentieth Century*, the esteemed historian Arthur Schlesinger Jr. notes that he had read 598 books by the age of fourteen and viewed 482 movies between ages fourteen and nineteen.[22] If the latter sounds high, it's not. It amounts to 90 minutes a week compared with 3,150 minutes of weekly entertainment for most American children today. It's not the entertainment that softens the mind; it's the dosage.

What About the Mechanical Reading Tutor You Mentioned Earlier?

Let's begin in the place that has achieved the highest performance with the device, Finland.[23] As I pointed out in chapter 1, Finland's children don't start formal schooling until age seven, yet they achieve the highest reading scores in the world.[24] Part of that success can be attributed to a mechanical device that Finnish children use, perhaps more often than any other nation. Surprisingly, these high-scoring children also watch fairly large amounts of television—far more time than they spend reading books. Their daily viewing is about two-thirds of what American children watch, which is the highest in the world.[25]

The device used to be pretty expensive in the United States ($250), but the price has dropped since 1993—when it went to zero dollars. Free. In fact, it comes built into every television set sold in America. It's the closed-captioning chip you access through the TV remote.

Almost half of all Finnish TV shows are our old sitcoms like *Gilligan's Island*, *Bonanza*, *The Brady Bunch*, *The Partridge Family*, and *Hogan's Heroes*. There are so many shows that the Finns can't afford to dub Finnish into all the sound tracks, so they just run them in English with Finnish closed-captioning or subtitles.

This means that nearly half of everything a nine-year-old Finn wants to watch is going to be in a foreign language. In order to understand it, she'll have to be able to read Finnish and be able to read Finnish fast! In chapter 1, I wrote about the importance of motivation in learning anything. Whereas motivation propels American teens to learn to drive a car, it pushes kids in Finland to learn to read—they want to understand those TV shows.

It stands to reason that moderate doses of captioned television can do no harm to students, and most likely it will help greatly with reading. There is enough research to indicate significant gains in comprehension and vocabulary development (especially among bilingual students) when receiving instruction with educational television that is captioned.[26]

In 2003, a first-grade teacher told me about a young girl entering her class in September:

> On the first day of school, she was already reading on a third-grade level. That's always unusual, but what made it more so was that her parents were both deaf. Normally the hearing child of deaf parents is language deficient and therefore behind—but this child was three years ahead. I could hardly wait to conference with the parents.

They beamed when I told them of their daughter's achievement and they explained that she'd had closed-captioning all her life.

There are several other factors that make closed-captioning so effective as a reading tutor. In chapter 2, I wrote about the 30:1 ratio of visual receptors over auditory receptors in the brain. In other words, the chances of a word (or sentence) being retained in our memory bank are thirty times greater if we see it instead of just hear it. There's that sponge effect again.

Now recall the observations in chapter 6 about the print climate of at-risk children. Closed-captioning is basically a government program that puts the equivalent of a daily newspaper or weekly magazine in the home— for free. The number of words flowing across the screen in the course of three hours of closed-captioned TV is more than the average adult would read in a daily newspaper or a weekly newsmagazine. Enabling the TV's closed-captioning is the equivalent of a newspaper subscription, but unlike the subscription, it costs nothing.

Although a child may be too young to read yet, all the books, magazines, and newspapers in the home are acclimating him or her to the world of print. The same thing happens with closed-captioning. In fact, you could argue that the characters on the TV show are reading aloud the closed-captioning to the child.

Pasi Sahlberg, a leading member of Finland's Ministry of Education, has long tied the country's students' reading progress to its decision to require all foreign programs on TV to be closed-captioned.[27] Strangely, since George H. W. Bush signed the Television Decoder Circuitry Act back in 1990, making the closed-captioning chip mandatory in U.S. sets, not one of his three successors has promoted the use of the device as an aid for children's reading. My guess is they either didn't like it because there are no tests to go along with the captioning or they think Finnish children's brains are built differently than U.S. children's. Either way, their silence is embarrassing.

Do Audiobooks Count as Reading?

When parents ask me if stories on tape are okay for their five-year-old, I respond: "If the audio is used as a full-time substitute for a literate parent, no, they're not okay. But if used to supplement your readings or used by children whose parents are illiterate or unavailable, they are excellent!"

As Americans spend more and more time in their cars and listening to

iPods, audiobook recordings have become a major player in the publishing industry, especially with the average round-trip commute lasting
fifty minutes. The recorded book is a perfect example of how technology
can be used to make this a more literate nation.

While audiobooks lack the immediacy of a live person who can hug a
child and answer questions, they fill an important gap when the adult is not
available or busy. Even when used as background noise while a child is
playing, their verbal contents are still enriching his vocabulary more than
television would with its abbreviated sentences. So by all means begin
building your audio library with songs, rhymes, and stories. Community
libraries and bookstores now have a growing assortment for all ages. You
should definitely consider recording the stories yourself and encouraging
distant relatives to do the same and send them as gifts (check out Sony and
Olympus recorders for less than $50). What could be more personal and last
as long? And I might add, for long family car trips, audiobooks are the
greatest "peacekeepers" short of the UN.

One of the early (and sometimes current) fears was that audiobooks
would make readers "print lazy," similar to Plato's anxiety that print would
shrivel our memory muscles. Such fears are baseless; in fact, the opposite is
true. The heaviest users are among the most literate people in America, according to a national survey.[28] Among the study's findings:

- Seventy-five percent were college graduates and 41 percent had ad-
  vanced degrees.
- Eighty percent had an annual family income of $51,000 or higher.
- Eighty-six percent read at least one newspaper daily.
- Twenty-one percent read at least twenty-five books a year.

Your local library can be your cheapest resource for audiobooks and
will search area libraries for titles it doesn't have.

There is a distinct difference between an audiobook player and a DVD
player. The recent addition of the DVD player to family transportation
does nothing but deprive the child of yet another classroom: conversation
with parents or the shared intellectual experience of listening to an audiobook communally. Unlike the DVD, audio recordings can be experienced by those in both the front and back of the car. This allows the parent
to pause a disc and ask, "Why do you think he did that? What do you
think he meant by that?" That doesn't happen with a DVD because it's
playing only in the back of the vehicle. The child and the movie might as
well be on another planet.

While on the subject of listening while traveling: When you run out of audiobooks, consider old-time radio dramas. There is a Web site, www .otrcat.com/all.htm, that offers thousands of these old shows as MP3 files burned to a CD for as little as twenty cents a show. It's one of the best bargains on the Web and keeps children focused, nurtures listening skills, and exercises their imaginations far better than DVDs.

As of this writing, the future of audiobooks is in digital downloads, with CDs fading among younger generations so fast that the esteemed Recorded Books, LLC discontinued its retail sales and rentals in 2011, but continued their library and school CD business. Traditional book sales in 2010 rose by 2.7 percent and CD audiobooks dropped 11 percent, but digital audiobook downloads rose a whopping 38.8 percent.[29]

Could audiobooks help students who are English Language Learners to bolster their lack of exposure to English? See what they're doing in San Bruno Park School District, page 67.

Chapter 9

Dad—What's the Score?

Do not train boys to learning by force and harshness,
but lead them by what amuses them, so that they may better
discover the bent of their minds.

—Plato

I WAS taking a vacation walk on a beach recently when I noticed the sand castles. The first one was pretty impressive. Watching the father and sons constructing the scene, handful by handful, I guessed the father to be an architect or an engineer. Had to be, I thought.

Continuing my walk, I encountered another family bent over a sand castle. In fact, there were more than a dozen castles yet to be seen—some good, some poor, and a few spectacular.

Together, they had me thinking there was a common denominator among the best of them—a father (or older male) usually was involved. If dad was there, the boys were more involved and succeeding. When the adult male was missing, so, too, was the achievement among the boys, and the castles were inferior.

I couldn't help but connect those thoughts to the current problems we have with young boys and schooling. I'm sure there is no quick remedy, but we as a culture had better come up with some solutions pretty soon. As one critic put it, you can't make much progress as a country if only one gender is working at it.[1]

Some say it's a boy problem; others claim it's a male or father problem. Before we explore that, let's at least concede it's not an entirely *new* issue, at least if we're to believe Plato's quote at the beginning of this chapter. Apparently even in 350 B.C., the little guys had an attitude problem about learning.

In case you've been off the planet for the past several decades, let me bring you up-to-date on our boys and their school woes.

- In a 2008 study of reading tests in forty-five states, the girls exceeded the boys at every grade level.[2]
- Unlike four decades ago, it is now common for girls to dominate a high school's highest academic positions (valedictorian), class leadership positions, advanced placement spaces, and school activities.[3] While the girls are assuming responsibilities, the boys are playing sports or video games.
- For the first time in history, women exceed their male counterparts in most collegiate achievements, from enrollment and graduation to earning advanced degrees, and the gap is widening annually.[4] About the only

Where have all the boys gone? Not to the front of the class.

significant area in which males dominate in college is "dropout," where they lead by a 3:2 ratio.

Tom Chiarella is one of the best long-form writers in the country today, covering everything from food to cinema, from sports to architecture. He's also a visiting professor at DePauw University, and it was the male culture he witnessed on college campuses that provoked him to write an article for *Esquire* titled "The Problem with Boys . . . Is Actually a Problem with Men." It's a piece so powerful I'd recommend pediatricians print out copies and hand it to every new father they encounter. Chiarella summarizes his concerns that if you're a boy in this country today:

> You're twice as likely as a girl to be diagnosed with an attention-deficit or learning disorder. You're more likely to score worse on standardized reading and writing tests. You're more likely to be held back in school. You're more likely to drop out of school. If you do graduate, you're less likely to go to college. If you do go to college, you will get lower grades and, once again, you will be less likely to graduate. You'll be twice as likely to abuse alcohol, and until you are twenty-four, you are five times as likely to kill yourself. You are more than sixteen times as likely to go to prison.[5]

Those of us who have witnessed this young male crisis know it's not a boy thing. It's a man thing. Boys don't raise themselves—at least they're not supposed to.

Naturally there is a vocal group of male defenders who say it's all a mirage. They blame minority boys, claiming their scores lower the overall male average.[6] While it's true that black boys have the lower reading scores, that can't account for the lack of white male participation in school activities, leadership positions, and graduation rates. The public schools in Maine are 96 percent white, yet the male-female achievement gap is among the five widest in the U.S. at both the high school and college levels.[7]

The other excuses include: girls' brains develop sooner; school rules are biased against male behavior; girls are naturally more organized than boys;[8] and fathers are either absent or more interested in the scorecard than the report card. Some of those excuses have a kernel of truth in them, but they cannot account for the overall poor performance of so many boys at a wide range of ages in so many circumstances. But one of the explanations deserves more serious attention: *the men who are supposed to raise boys—fathers.*

Sea Changes in the Male World

For nearly thirty years I did parent programs in all of the fifty states, and regardless of the community, there was always a shortage of fathers attending, usually by a 10:1 (mothers:fathers) ratio. Maybe they were all tending to business, so to speak, and they obviously didn't think school was any of their business.

The three things most dads think they understand best are boys, business, and sports. In case they haven't looked lately, there have been some sea changes in those areas. You've already read the changes in boys, so let's look at the other two, starting with business.

The world is now flat. How's that for a sea change? As Thomas Friedman described it in his book *The World Is Flat*, twenty-five years ago the power structure of the world consisted of highs and lows: The countries with the power and knowledge were at the top of the mountains and the rest were down in the valleys. A handful of countries (the United States, Britain, Germany, and Japan) ruled the world's economy because they monopolized the information and power.

Then came the Internet. Suddenly the countries down in the valleys were connected to the information network and the work flow.[9] These included India, Eastern Europe, South Korea, Brazil, and China. Don't believe it? Walk through Toys R Us and pick up any ten toys, checking each for where it was made. My last count: China, ten out of ten. The world's workforce became "flattened." No more disconnected valleys.

Has anyone told Dad? The world of hills and valleys is gone.

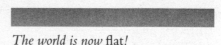

The world is now flat!

As Friedman reports, twenty-five thousand U.S. tax returns were processed in India in 2003, outsourced by U.S. companies who wanted them done cheaply and correctly. Within two years, that number ballooned to four hundred thousand. India now graduates seventy thousand accountants a year. These are not necessarily smarter accountants than those in the United States, but they're not dumber and they sure are cheaper.

Almost none of them are watching the clock either, unlike many male college students in the U.S.

Since 2000, U.S. manufacturing has lost six million jobs, or one-third of its workforce, most of them males. For the first time in history, women hold the majority of jobs in the U.S., and the Bureau of Labor Statistics reports women hold more than half the U.S. managerial jobs.[10]

The only people who don't understand the sea change in business are the fathers and sons watching their third straight hour of ESPN, still clinging to the image of the male who doesn't need to play school—just play ball. It's been thirty years since that idea had any wings, but too many males are still trying to make it fly. Where once the only thing that mattered for men was what they could get out of the ground with their hands, it's now what they can get out of their heads that counts.[11] And without classroom success, today's male faces an impossible challenge from both intelligent women on the home front and foreigners willing to do the same job for less while sitting in an office in Bangalore or Singapore.

The third change started right there in front of the family TV set. Remember what I said earlier about the change in boys' scores? We know what caused the rise in the girls' scores—their mothers' value systems about education changed forty years ago. Mothers now expect more of their daughters' brains. But how do we explain the nosedive on the part of the boys since 1970? Is it a coincidence that in that same year, 1970, we saw the birth of a national TV phenomenon called *Monday Night Football*? Prior to that, Madison Avenue pretty much thought it was a waste of time trying to advertise to men late at night—they were all asleep in their La-Z-Boys. Then along comes *MNF* and they've got millions of guys doing high fives in their chairs at eleven p.m. It didn't take long for the networks to catch on that sports at night could bring in a boatload of advertising dollars and thus was born ESPN, then ESPN2, followed by channels for golf, rodeo, NASCAR, wrestling, the NBA, the NFL, MLB, extreme sports—you name it, all sports, all the time, 24-7. And that's your third sea change.

The impact on the young male from seeing so many adult role models worshipping daily and nightly at the altar of ESPN has played a damaging role in male attitudes about school. Girls read and write; guys hit, throw, catch, shoot, and fish. By 2000, moms were taking their daughters to work, but dads were only taking their sons to ball games. Ever see them in the library or bookstore?

The game-time mentality seems immune to even college tuition costs. In a nine-year study of nonathlete grade point averages at a traditional football powerhouse (University of Oregon), during fall semesters when the football team won more games, student averages dropped significantly due to increased partying and drinking. (Males suffered larger declines than did females.) Conversely, losing seasons saw scores improve.[12]

Fathers and sons banking on an NBA or NFL career might reflect on the average career length in those leagues: less than four years.

None of this is to suggest that a healthy, balanced interest in sports by father and son is wrong. In my mind, nothing could be further from the truth (coming from the guy who was the source of the Basketball Hall of Fame archives recording of Wilt Chamberlain's 100-point game).[13] Many of the successful and balanced people we meet can point to lessons learned from sports and coaches, lessons seldom taught in classrooms—lessons about teamwork, practice, and tenacity. It was those lessons, combined with classroom lessons, that enabled their success. In the next chapter of this book, I relate the critical role sports played in my own reading life as a teenager, but they were only a *part*, not the whole.

In short, the father who can find his way only to ball games with his kids is a "boy-man," whereas the father who can find his way to a ball game *and* to the library or bookshelf can be called a "grown man." Fathers need to understand that sports and school are not mutually exclusive. We can do both.

The strange thing about "reluctant reading daddies" is they're found at all education levels. When poverty-level families and university-educated families were compared, fathers in both groups read to the children only 15 percent of the time, mothers 76 percent, and others 9 percent.[14] That could change if we publicized studies like the one conducted in Modesto, California, which showed that (1) boys who were read to by their fathers scored significantly higher in reading achievement, and (2) when fathers read recreationally, their sons read more and scored higher than did boys whose fathers did little or no recreational reading. When the dads were surveyed, only 10 percent reported having fathers who read to them when they were children.[15]

So how do we get fathers more involved with reading and school? How about having them read this chapter? Not the whole book (unless they want to)—just this chapter. And maybe the next one, which is the shortest in the book and has information about how my father, some "secret stuff," and a rich man's sports magazine all motivated me so strongly to be a reader.

If Dad is lost as to what to read (since he might not have been a reader as a child), the list of books in the Treasury at the back of this volume will help. The books listed are more likely to hook the reluctant reader than create a future English professor. We have a glut of English professors, but a genuine shortage of male lifetime readers.

If you're a father who has never been much of a reader, change that pattern for the next generation in your family. Start with the picture books and work your way up to the novels, side by side with your kids. Here are four picture books from the list: *Captain Abdul's Pirate School* by Colin McNaughton, *How FAST Is It?* by Ben Hillman, *The Secret Shortcut* by Mark Teague, and *Snip Snap! What's That?* by Mara Bergman. Want something a little more challenging, something that will spark a conversation? There is a small picture book of thirty-six pages titled *Six Men* by David McKee, which begins very simply: "Once upon a time there were six men who traveled the world searching for a place where they could live and work in peace." The rest of the book pretty much explains half the front page of any daily newspaper or evening's newscast. When you're done reading those books, your first response will probably be, "Where were books like that when I was a kid?" Need to slip in some sports? On page 216 there's a list of terrific sports picture books you never had as a kid. For older children, try the short novel *Stone Fox* by John Reynolds Gardiner. Check out *Hatchet* by Gary Paulsen. Dip anyplace into *Uncle John's Bathroom Reader for Kids Only!* You'll be surprised at what you've been missing all these years. I'll bet you missed David Lubar's short story "Kid Appeal" in *Guys Read: Funny Business*, a humor collection for boys. Here's one paragraph:

> There are lots of things that make someone a great best friend, like loyalty and courage. Dwight's totally loyal. He'd never tell on me, no matter what I did. Even though he got six weeks of detention, Dwight never admitted he had help when he dumped twenty packs of cherry Kool-Aid into the school's new fishpond. I swear

we thought there weren't any fish in it yet. I guess it's a good thing only two of them were hiding in there at the time. They looked real pretty right before they turned belly up. It was sort of like a Dr. Seuss story. One fish, two fish. Red Fish, dead fish.[16]

Dad—when you read to a child you get a second chance in life: to meet and enjoy the books you missed out on as a kid. Who knows, you might even meet some of your childhood buddies along the way—like Dwight. Or look at it this way: Reading to your child is really just another form of coaching, except this one allows snuggling.

Chapter 10

A Hyper Kid's Road to Reading

How a Father, a Five-Cent Book,
Secret Stuff, and One Young Teacher Led to This Book

IT would be nice to think my father knew what he was doing, but I doubt it. (He died before I could ask him.) He was probably just trying to keep things from getting worse. The problem was me, and the fact that we lived in a second-floor apartment and I was out of control a lot of the time, causing enough collateral damage in the complex to provoke some of the residents to get up a petition to have us evicted. Fortunately there were enough people who liked my parents (a lot more than liked me) to nullify the petition.

So my father would come home from work at night (he worked in sales for a manufacturing company, the only non–college graduate in his department) and my mother would hand me over to him as though they were doing a prisoner swap. "Here, take him," she would say. Years later she told me, "They didn't have the term in those days, but if they did, you'd have been the poster child for hyperactivity."

With time my father found something that calmed and focused me—he read to me. He read the library picture books we had in the house, but mostly he read what *he* liked to read—the evening newspaper and *The Saturday Evening Post*. It became a nightly ritual, and by the time I was four years old we were doing the comics page every night. (Those pages eventually became such an integral part of my life and my brother's, we'd give them up for Lent—our ultimate sacrifice.)

In the beginning, my father had to explain things like the satire in Al Capp's *Li'l Abner* strip, but gradually it all fell into place. I got the humor

*Jim sharing a comic book with
an injured friend, circa 1945.
He claims no culpability in
the injury. A likely story.*

and eventually understood the relationship between Dagwood and his boss, Mr. Dithers. *Li'l Abner* set the stage for my later readings of *Mad* magazine. Years later, in the Berkshire Hills of Massachusetts, a long line of people waiting behind me forbade my telling an aged Norman Rockwell about the hours my father and I had spent poring over his *Post* covers and their meanings. But I wanted to.

Most important, those nightly readings helped me understand what reading was really all about. By the time I reached first grade, I knew this reading stuff was going to be worth whatever I had to go through to get it—all those flash cards and work sheets.

But there was one memorable stop before first grade, an afternoon when I met my oldest literary friend. It's a book called *Junior Literature*, and it sits across the room from me as I write this. On its flyleaf is penciled "5¢" in red. It's a junior high school English textbook, published a decade before I was born. Its contents include works by Frost, Longfellow, Twain, Whittier, and Kipling, along with Jonathan Swift, Anatole France, William Cullen Bryant, and Theodore Roosevelt.

Most junior and senior high schools would take a pass on it as a text today. But one day in 1946, on my way home from kindergarten at Connecticut Farms Elementary School (Union, New Jersey), I passed the public library next door to the school and thought, Whoaa! There were tables on the front lawn and books were not only out on the tables, they were for sale! It was my very first encounter with a yard sale, or the annual book sale common at most public libraries today. While the situation was confusing to me (I thought they were selling the library books), of one thing I was certain: Right in front of me was a book whose title I couldn't read, nor could I read anything in its 613 pages, but I wanted it. Furthermore, it was only a nickel!

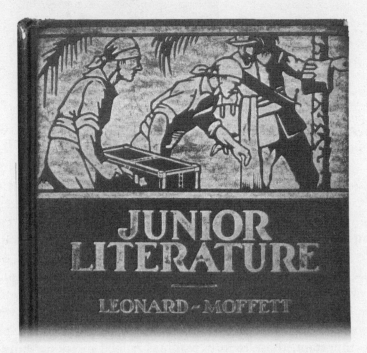

Why did I want it? First, there were three pirates on the cover, embossed in gold. Second, inside were more pirates, as well as kings, archers, swords, and damsels in distress. And third, it cost as little as a comic book. I raced the two blocks home, secured the nickel from my mother, and fled back, fearing it would be sold. But it was still there—the first book I ever bought all by myself.

In the years that followed, that book and I were like neighbors—not especially close at the start, but it was reassuring to have each other there. I sensed from the start the book was different from others, that there was important stuff in it, like having a college professor living next door, someone you didn't just drop in on unannounced. As I matured, we became closer, and I would read a short piece here and there when I'd run out of "regular" books and the library was closed. I didn't realize it was a textbook until I was in high school. Nonetheless, by then we were old friends.

It was the first book I totally owned, and its draw was adventure—pirates, knights, etc. You could say it was a "guy thing." The same thing would later draw me to comic books, of which eventually I would have the largest collection in the neighborhood and trade them endlessly with friends. In fact, although we didn't own our own house until I was in seventh grade and every car my Dad bought until late in life was a used car, our home was awash in print: encyclopedias, newspapers, and magazines. The mailman once complained good-naturedly to my father that my mother subscribed to more magazines than anyone else on his route and it was breaking his back. Long before we could read, the Trelease boys were big print perusers, paging through the magazines and catalogs that came in the mail almost every day.

A behavior update here: Along the way I calmed down considerably, although my mother still complained I was a "street angel/house devil," and she was more right than wrong.

The calming was a good thing, because the next stop after Connecticut Farms kindergarten was first grade at St. Michael Parish School across town. This was 1947, the war was over, and classrooms were overflowing. At least they were in St. Mike's, especially my first-grade class: one Dominican nun (Sr. Elizabeth Francis), one room, ninety-four kids. Teacher's aide? Yup. He was hanging on the cross in the front of the room. It was all she needed. That and a look that could melt glass.

I don't know how the other kids felt about the flash cards Sister was holding up in front of the room, sounding out letters as we chanted them back to her, but I thought they were boring. (Not that I shared those thoughts with her.) I just sat there waiting for the good stuff to start— stuff like *The Saturday Evening Post*. She did finally begin to read aloud to us, and not what you'd expect. Not picture books—Lord knows we had enough of those with Dick and Jane readers. She read chapter books to us (see page 59), and we loved them enough to give up recess if she'd just read one more chapter, please, Sister, please?

So with little pain or suffering, and in spite of the horrendous pupil-teacher ratio in the class, I learned to read. And life was good and the books got better and better, especially Jack London's *Call of the Wild* in fourth grade (unassigned). It was the best ever, and all others would be compared with it for the rest of my life.

The young adult novelist Bob Lipsyte, writing about book subjects that interest boys, has observed that competition is one of the items that drive males, and especially boys, in many of their life choices.[1] In my case it was going to play a pivotal role in my reading. I should explain, St. Michael's had no physical education classes or teams. Thus, until we moved into our first house, in North Plainfield, New Jersey, I'd never played on a single team. Oh, we had little pickup games in the vacant lot behind the apartments but nothing organized—no uniforms or caps, no umpires or coaches.

That put me at a decided disadvantage when I arrived in North Plainfield, where almost every boy played sports and every sport was taught in PE class by a Pied Piper–like teacher named Harold "Bud" Porter (who would become my hero and friend). While I had watched sports on TV, there were only six channels in those days and limited sports. How was I going to catch up on all that I had missed in sports?

Into this breach stepped Henry Luce, founder of *Time* and *Life* magazines. Luce had just created a weekly sports magazine called *Sports Illustrated*, something people thought would become Luce's folly. It was a publication, I learned later, that Luce was using to impress his wealthy sporting friends in the Hamptons and Greenwich. I don't know if it impressed them, but it was just what this adolescent needed. Not only would it fill my sports void, it had advertisements for stuff like deodorant and shaving cream. This meant it was written for grown-ups; therefore I suspected whatever was in *SI* (as it was known to its devoted readers) had to be the God's honest truth. Soon my younger brother, Brian, joined me in devouring every issue.

There were several things about *SI*, however, that we didn't know at the time. Since the target audience was Hamptonites, its stories were, shall we say, on the rich side. If you were to look into the *SI* vault of covers (http://sportsillustrated.cnn.com/vault/article/home/m/1/index.htm), you would find a preponderance of cover stories on horse racing, golf, tennis, dog shows, bowling, bullfighting, steeplechasing, and sailing. (Only six basketball stories versus seventeen clothing articles in 1954.) Wait a minute, my brother and I wondered, this is sports? We thought sports were baseball and basketball, but—maybe we were wrong. There's all this other stuff, too. So we better read it if we're going to be real sportsmen.

I should add that *SI* had hired some fancy writers to do its reporting (and impress the folks in the Hamptons), people like Herbert Warren Wind, John Underwood, John Gerald Holland, and Whitney Tower. All these years later their names reek of richness. Here's how Wind, recruited from *The New Yorker*, described the maturing of the Masters golf tourney:

> In just about a score of years, the Masters, which started out in 1934 as just a notable competition, has grown so inexorably in prestige and honest glamour that today it has come to eclipse the National Open in the stir it arouses, and this stir is sufficient to place the event in just about the same category as the World Series (inaugurated in 1903) and the Kentucky Derby (first run in 1875) as a full-fledged national sports classic.

In case you weren't keeping score, that's an eighty-word sentence, normally not a thirteen-year-old's reading fare. But I was willing to wade through it to get the scoop on this guy Ben Hogan. That's an important point. Personal interest can be a powerful driving force with boys, whether that interest is sports, auto repair, model racing, war, music, or computers. The window of opportunity through which you can reach his mind might only stay open a short while, so allow as much through it as the child is willing to consume.

I like to think of those *SI* writers as my early writing coaches. Most people are affected one way or another by the words and people they hang around with. Few people write doggerel after reading good literature. Granted, they may not write exactly like Dickens after reading him, but they certainly recognize the difference between him and junk. Exposure to great writing can only have a positive effect, especially if the writing is willingly absorbed.

The first time my own name appeared in print was in *Sports Illustrated*, November 28, 1955, when I was listed as a contributor to the U.S. Olympic team by purchasing a $10 membership card to make-believe Happy Knoll Country Club. For two years the magazine serialized a novel (*Life at Happy Knoll*) by the social critic and novelist J. P. Marquand, in which he satirically explored the machinations of the board members at a fictitious country club. Did this fourteen-year-old understand all the social commentary tucked into the series? No, but it gave me a good idea of how rich people maneuvered in their world and how decidedly different their secrets were from mine. You might call it "secret stuff" from the boardroom, and I gobbled it up.

Secret stuff is another driving force with boys (the stuff we think the grown-ups don't want us to know), and it was on my mind one day in ninth grade when I picked up a copy of *My Six Convicts: A Psychologist's Three Years in Fort Leavenworth* by Donald Powell Wilson. I'd stumbled on it in the adult section of the North Plainfield public library and the cover convinced me this was something really secret. I didn't know a single psychologist or convict but I was willing to bet there was a ton of stuff in there I wasn't supposed to know. Secret stuff.

A California professor, Jo Stanchfield, once told me that girls tend to be extrinsically motivated in their reading (favoring the choices of their peers, mom, and teacher), while boys are intrinsically motivated (favoring what they themselves are interested in). I agree. Call it selfish or pragmatic, but guys are drawn more to what interests them, not what interests the crowd. That certainly was the case with *Convicts*. And it was going to change my life.

The book was as revealing as I had hoped, and I used it as my first book report for my freshman English teacher, Mr. Alvin R. Schmidt. I can't recall ever writing a book report in the years before this, although there must have been others. I do know it was the first adult book I'd ever reported on. Not long after that, Mr. Schmidt summoned me to his desk after class and handed me a sealed envelope for my parents.

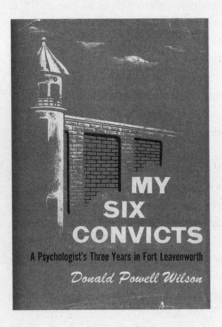

I was never what you would call an introverted child, so there might have been about a dozen things for him to contact my parents about at the end of a marking period, and I worried all the way home. My mother read the contents, a single page, stuffed it back in the envelope, and said, "We'll talk about it when your father gets home." Must be really bad, I thought.

She waited until after dinner and sent my brothers out of the room before giving my father the letter. I watched him read it, watched his eyes fill up. I winced at the trouble I must be in. Then he handed me the piece of paper.

This note is to inform you that James's work and attitude during the first marking period in English 1 have been "tops." It has been a pleasure working with "Jim," and I'm sure that he'll maintain the fast pace that he has set. Jim expresses himself very well in writing and speaking and has served as an inspiration to his class.

My congratulations to both of you.

—Very truly yours, A. R. Schmidt

I'd been in school nine years by that time, and no teacher had ever sent home such a note. As I look back on it now, I think: Here was a second-year teacher (I later learned) who was talking about "gifted and talented" nearly twenty years before the concept came into vogue, who had the decency and sense to send a note to the manufacturer to let them know the product was working.

I never forgot that man or his note. Here was someone, besides my own family, who thought I was special. It was something I tucked away in my heart. At the end of that school year I moved away to Massachusetts (Mr. Schmidt wrote, of his own accord, to my new school to make sure they put me in a journalism class), and the year after that Mr. Schmidt switched to another district and we lost touch. One day in 1975 I was driving my widowed mother someplace and asked her, "Mom, do you remember that teacher I had in New Jersey years ago who sent that note home to you and Dad?"

There was a pause and then she said quietly, "I'll never forget it." We talked a bit about Mr. Schmidt, wondering where he had gone, and then we left the subject. But the next day when I dropped by, she had the original letter from Mr. Schmidt, dated twenty years ago that week. What I had tucked away in my heart, my mother had tucked away in a dresser drawer as a family heirloom. Today it rests in my dresser drawer.

I mention all of that for several reasons. Certainly the recognition I received for my writing and speaking (he insisted we give speeches in class throughout the year) was important for my adolescent self-image. No grade on a paper could mean as much as that note home. Second, Mr. Schmidt was a very young teacher without a long list of degrees after his name but he possessed an intangible that makes for a great teacher: His students loved him, respected him, and would have walked through walls for him. There is no accreditation exam that can measure such qualities in a teacher. No matter how much money you dangle as a merit raise in front of a teacher, you cannot create that kind of magic extrinsically.[2]

Mr. Schmidt and I found each other again years later when the first edition of this book came out and I dedicated it to him and my children. He told me that dedication made not only his day and his week, but his nearly thirty years in education. Several years later I attended his retirement party in Cranford, New Jersey, and the next morning I drove to make a presentation in a small town in New Hampshire, an afternoon in-service for about twenty-five teachers. In the course of the presentation I mentioned Mr. Schmidt and his impact. At the break, a young teacher approached me and said, "I grew up in Cranford, New Jersey, and had Mr. Schmidt in eighth grade. He's the reason I'm a teacher today."

There is much talk these days about applying the business paradigm to schools and measuring teachers' effectiveness by their students' test scores. The practice is deeply scarring the profession, driving out some of the best we have. (Imagine if we told police we were going to pay them on the basis of the crime rate: Lower crime rate equals higher pay. Nobody would want to police urban America; everybody would head for the suburbs.) Whenever I read of such measures, I think of the impact Mr.

Schmidt had on his classes. How could you begin to measure his effectiveness with a test?

So there you have it—one kid's route to reading. Did you notice it wasn't a solo journey? All the traveling company I had—family, libraries, teachers—ensured I reached my destination safely. And while there's no single road map to reading that works for everyone, there are people along the route who always make it easier, by reading to us daily, providing plenty of rich print around us, and offering encouraging words—words, not tests.

As Maya Angelou once said: "People will forget what you said, people will forget what you did, but people will never forget how you made them feel."

And it is the feel we get from great parenting, great teaching, and great reading that changes our lives. Male or female, it's a feeling we remember forever.

Treasury of Read-Alouds

How to Use the Treasury

AN essential element in reading aloud is what you choose to read. Not everyone reading this book is familiar with children's literature, either yesterday's or today's. Some readers are new parents or teachers, and others are veterans to the experience; some are looking for standards, and others are seeking newer titles. To meet that diversity, I've tried to strike a balance between old and new in compiling this list.

For this edition, I've tried where possible to eliminate out-of-print titles from the main listings, allowing room for good new titles without making the book too cumbersome.

I recognize the danger in compiling any book list, but only a thousand-page volume could do justice to the titles that deserve mention. Rather than being comprehensive, this list is intended as a starter and time-saver. Try to remember that these are read-aloud titles, which eliminates some books that are difficult to read aloud or, because of the subject matter, are best read silently to oneself—like Robert Cormier's *The Chocolate War* (subject) or Mark Twain's *Tom Sawyer* (dialect). Other books even among the missing here may otherwise be well written but have an abundance of obscene language, something that would put a teacher reading that book aloud greatly at risk. Also among the missing are books that are shallow on narrative and top-heavy with dialogue, making them difficult to read unless you have a knack for voices.

Many of the titles included here have been around for a decade or more, and that's a great credential. It means the book has a lasting message that people continue to buy or borrow. Books that don't continue to sell go out of print, so I've excluded those.

There are nine categories, and all books in the respective categories are listed alphabetically by title (the author/illustrator index to the Treasury at the end of the book will also help you locate books).

With each major title, I've included a listening level. Thus when you read "K–2," that refers to the grade level at which the child could hear and understand the story; it is not the reading level of the book (see page 38 for a discussion of reading versus listening levels). In the book's summary section, related titles are sometimes listed. If they have their own listing in the Treasury, I've added an annotation such as (n) beside the title to indicate where each can be found in the Treasury (see abbreviations listed below). Therefore, when *My Father's Dragon* (s)" appears as a related title, the "(s)" indicates that a full description of that book can be found in the Short Novels section of the Treasury.

♦ Picture Books (p)
♦ Short Novels (s)
♦ Novels (n)
♦ Poetry (po)
♦ Anthologies (a)
♦ Fairy and Folk Tales (f)

While trying to limit my selections to just those still in print, I know OP (out of print) is far less of a problem today than it was before used bookstores went online. With resources like Bookfinder.com, Alibris.com, and Amazon.com, it is nearly impossible to come up empty while searching for any book published in the past forty years.

Happy reading!

Treasury Contents

Wordless Books

These books contain no words; the story is told entirely with pictures arranged in sequence. Wordless books can be "read" not only by prereaders and beginning readers but also by adults (even illiterate or semiliterate) who want to read to children. They can "tell" the book, using the pictures for clues to the emerging plot. Books marked with an asterisk (★) are described at length in the Picture Books section of the Treasury.

Ah-Choo by Mercer Mayer (Dial, 1976)
A Ball for Daisy by Chris Raschka (Farrar, 2011)
Ben's Dream by Chris Van Allsburg (Houghton Mifflin, 1982)
A Boy, a Dog, and a Frog by Mercer Mayer (Dial, 1967)
Deep in the Forest by Brinton Turkle (Dutton, 1976)
Flotsam by David Wiesner (Clarion, 2006)
Frog Goes to Dinner by Mercer Mayer (Dial, 1974)
Frog on His Own by Mercer Mayer (Dial, 1973)
Frog, Where Are You? by Mercer Mayer (Dial, 1969)
Good Dog, Carl by Alexandra Day (Green Tiger, 1985)
Peter Spier's Rain by Peter Spier (Doubleday, 1982)
Sector 7 by David Wiesner (Clarion, 1997)
The Silver Pony by Lynd Ward (Houghton Mifflin, 1973)★
The Snowman by Raymond Briggs (Random House, 1978)
Time Flies by Eric Rohmann (Crown, 1994)
Tuesday by David Wiesner (Clarion, 1991)
Unspoken: A Story of the Underground Railroad by Henry Cole
    (Scholastic, 2012)

Predictable Books

These picture books contain word or sentence patterns that are repeated often enough to enable children to predict their appearance and thus begin to join in on the reading.

Are You My Mother? by P. D. Eastman (Random House, 1960)

Brown Bear, Brown Bear, What Do You See? by Bill Martin Jr. (Henry Holt, 1983)★

Chicka Chicka Boom Boom by Bill Martin Jr. and John Archambault (Simon & Schuster, 1989)

Chicken Soup with Rice by Maurice Sendak (Harper, 1962)

Do You Want to Be My Friend? by Eric Carle (Putnam, 1971)

Drummer Hoff by Barbara Emberley (Prentice-Hall, 1967)

Duck in the Truck by Jez Alborough (Harper, 2000)

The Flea's Sneeze by Lynn Downey (Henry Holt, 2000)

Goodnight Moon by Margaret Wise Brown (Harper, 1947)★

The House That Jack Built by Jeanette Winter (Dial, 2000)

I Know an Old Lady Who Swallowed a Pie by Alison Jackson (Dutton, 1997)

If You Give a Mouse a Cookie by Laura Numeroff (Harper, 1985)★

The Important Book by Margaret Wise Brown (Harper, 1949)

Jack and Jill's Treehouse by Pamela Duncan Edwards (Katherine Tegen Books, 2008)

The Little Old Lady Who Was Not Afraid of Anything by Linda Williams (Crowell, 1986)

Millions of Cats by Wanda Gag (Putnam, 1977)

The Napping House by Audrey Wood (Harcourt Brace, 1984)★

Pierre: A Cautionary Tale by Maurice Sendak (Harper, 1962)

Rolie Polie Olie by William Joyce (Harper, 1999)

Snip Snap! What's That? by Mara Bergman (Greenwillow, 2005)★

Ten Little Fingers and Ten Little Toes by Mem Fox (Harcourt, 2008)★

This Is the House That Was Tidy and Neat by Teri Sloat (Henry Holt, 2005)

This Is the Van That Dad Cleaned by Lisa Campbell Ernst (Simon & Schuster, 2005)

Tikki Tikki Tembo by Arlene Mosel (Holt, 1968)★

The Very Hungry Caterpillar by Eric Carle (Philomel, 1969)★

We're Going on a Bear Hunt by Michael Rosen (Atheneum, 1992)★

The Wheels on the Bus by Maryann Kovalski (Little, Brown, 1987)

Reference Books

How Animals Live: The Amazing World of Animals in the Wild
BY BERNARD STONEHOUSE AND ESTHER BERTRAM; JOHN FRANCIS, ILLUS.

Grades K and up   *96 pages*
Scholastic, 2004

This amounts to a Whitman's Sampler box of short but fascinating informational text about wildlife—including mammals, reptiles, birds, insects, and fish. It offers strange but true facts in single paragraphs about how they are born and how they parent, cooperate, fight, defend, and hide themselves. Typical is the description of the unique relationship between the courser bird and crocodiles. The coursers serve as flossing agents by picking the meat from between the teeth of crocodiles. In turn, the crocs recognize the good dental plan offered by the birds and refrain from eating them. Related book: *Amazing Animals* by Ingrid and Dieter Schubert.

Scholastic Children's Encyclopedia

Grades 2–6   *710 pages*
Scholastic, 2004

There are more than six hundred entries with two thousand photographs, diagrams, charts, and maps. In addition, "Key Facts," "Did You Know?" and "Amazing Facts!" boxes offer information in bite-size but entertaining chunks. An excellent single-volume encyclopedia for preschool through first grade is *DK First Encyclopedia*, with seven hundred photos and descriptions (166 pages).

The Worst-Case Scenario Survive-O-Pedia Jr. Edition
BY DAVID BORGENICHT, MOLLY SMITH, BRENDAN WALSH, AND
ROBIN EPSTEIN; CHUCK GONZALES, ILLUS.

Grades 3 and up   *141 pages*
Chronicle, 2011

Not a day goes by without reports of a disaster that provokes the question: What would I do in such circumstances? Caught in a tornado, avalanche, tsunami, blizzard, mud slide, quicksand, earthquake, or a falling elevator? Here's your survival manual. Suffering from bee stings, amnesia, mob violence, piranhas, or parachute malfunction? Fear not—there are coping strategies. This is a fast-paced photo- and infographic-filled collection of sixty-five worst cases (each taking two pages) that is as addictive for young readers as that time-worn *Guinness Book of World Records*, except this is a thousand times more informative. And they won't forget its "fast facts" either, like: Ninety-five percent of passengers survive airline accidents; only one human being has been killed by wolves in the past one hundred years; and maritime tragedies in the Bermuda Triangle are no more frequent than in any other part of the Atlantic.

Picture Books

Aesop's Fables
BY JERRY PINKNEY
Grades 2–5   *85 pages*
North-South, 2000
Aesop's fables offer us not only wisdom but also an introduction to the characters, ideas, and images that turn up again and again in the literary tradition. This volume includes more than sixty of Aesop's most famous tales. The most economical collection is *Aesop's Fables*, selected and adapted by Jack Zipes. Related books: *Fables* (contemporary) by Arnold Lobel; *Fox Tales: Four Tales from Aesop* by Amy Lowry; *Lousy Rotten Stinkin' Grapes* (p); *Mouse & Lion* by Rand Burkert; and *The Town Mouse and the Country Mouse* retold by Helen Ward.

Alexander and the Terrible, Horrible, No Good, Very Bad Day
BY JUDITH VIORST; RAY CRUZ, ILLUS.
Grades K and up   *34 pages*
Atheneum, 1972
Everyone has a bad day once in a while, but little Alexander has the worst of all. Follow him from a cereal box without a prize to a burned-out night-light. Sequels: *Alexander, Who Used to Be Rich Last Sunday* and *Alexander, Who's Not (Do You Hear Me? I Mean It!) Going to Move*. Also by the author: *If I Were in Charge of the World and Other Worries*. Related books: *Are You Going to Be Good?* by Cari Best.

All About Alfie (series)
BY SHIRLEY HUGHES
Grades PreS–1   *128 pages*
Bodley Head, 2011
This collection features preschooler Alfie in four of his most popular stories (published individually over the years). Though set in England, the stories radiate the feeling of children everywhere—from facial expres-

sions and clothing to the crises that really matter to young children (birthday party companions). With spare text and glorious illustrations, these books contain plots that easily hold young children's attention. Other books about Alfie's family: *Annie Rose Is My Little Sister* and *The Big Alfie and Annie Rose Storybook*. Also by the author: *Don't Want to Go!* (p) and *Dogger*.

Andrew Henry's Meadow
BY DORIS BURN
Grades K–2   *48 pages*
Philomel, 2012; e-book
Back in the mid-nineteenth century, Henry David Thoreau took to the Massachusetts woods beside a pond at the edge of town. There he demonstrated his independence and self-reliance, eventually making himself famous when he published his notes as *Walden*. By a small stretch, one could say *Andrew Henry's Meadow* is a children's version of *Walden*. The author-illustrator created it while raising her family in an island cabin with neither electricity nor running water. In detailed black-and-white drawings, we follow the preteen Andrew Henry and his inventive efforts at making everyone's life in the family easier. Unfortunately no one at home appreciates his marvels, and he packs his tools and heads off through the woods to a meadow where he builds a little home for himself. Soon other kids from the neighborhood arrive—all of them unappreciated at home for their hobbies and sundry talents—and Andrew Henry builds them each a retreat tailored to meet their needs. And what happens when the children turn up missing? How do their parents and siblings respond? A heartwarming ending. Note: After being out of print for decades, this much-loved book from the sixties is now back in print. As of now Hollywood is laboring over a script for a movie based on the book, and one can only guess what monsters they'll generate in the meadow to threaten the innocents. Stick with the book for now.

April and Esme, Tooth Fairies
BY BOB GRAHAM
Grades PreS–K   *32 pages*
Candlewick, 2010
Seven-year-old April and her little sister, Esme, are the children of tooth fairies, anxious themselves to begin the exciting career of collecting those little teeth and delivering the coin rewards. They both assume that excitement is years away, until April receives a call on her cell phone: her very first order! Her parents give her all the reasons why she's too young

and the trip is too dangerous, but April argues a strong case until she and her sister are cautiously given permission. The excitement builds as they accomplish their goal—almost. Unfortunately the tooth's owner awakens and sees the fairies. April, however, is a tech-savvy tooth fairy and texts her mother for instructions on what to do. Also by the author: *A Bus Called Heaven* (p); *How to Heal a Broken Wing*; *Jethro Byrd, Fairy Child*; *Max*; and *Rose Meets Mr. Wintergarten*.

Arthur's Chicken Pox (series)
BY MARC BROWN
Grades PreS–1   *28 pages*
Little, Brown, 1994
Long before he was discovered by PBS, there was Arthur in print, a series of wildly popular stories about an aardvark family's warm and often hilarious adventures at home, at school, and in the neighborhood. There are numerous books to choose from, and children can relate to Arthur. In this adventure, he's got a case of chicken pox, along with all its lifestyle complications for the entire family.

Aunt Minnie McGranahan
BY MARY SKILLINGS PRIGGER; BETSY LEWIN, ILLUS.
Grades K–2   *30 pages*
Clarion, 1999
Everyone in the small Kansas farm town thought Aunt Minnie had lost her mind when she took in nine orphaned nieces and nephews in 1920. Based on the true story of one of the author's relatives, the tale describes Minnie's sometimes whimsical adventures with the children as they adjust to farm life and she adjusts to all of them.

Baby Brains
BY SIMON JAMES
Grades PreS–1   *24 pages*
Candlewick, 2004
This is a wonderful send-up of the super-baby syndrome that afflicts too many parents, but it is also a funny story for children. Mr. and Mrs. Brains do "everything right." Before this baby is born they read to him, play music and foreign-language tapes, even watch the news with the sound turned up. Thus, days after Baby Brains is born, he's sitting up reading the newspaper when his parents come down for breakfast. After breakfast he announces he'd like to go to school tomorrow, which he does, and he heads the class! It's not long before he joins the astronauts for

a trip into space, and that's where it all comes apart—but in a good way. Sequels: *Baby Brains Superstar* and *Baby Brains and Robomom*. Related books: The body equivalent of Baby Brains is Todd, a one-hundred-foot-tall toddler who has a unique view of the world. He's found in two books by Kevin Hawkes: *The Wicked Big Toddlah* and *The Wicked Big Toddlah Goes to New York*. Also by Simon James: *The Birdwatchers*; *Dear Mr. Blueberry*; *George Flies South*; *Leon and Bob*; *Sally and the Limpet*; and *The Wild Woods*.

Bella and Stella Come Home

BY ANIKA DENISE; CHRISTOPHER DENISE, ILLUS.

Grades PreS–K   *36 pages*
Philomel, 2010

In today's world, few children will escape the trauma of moving from one home to another. Because of all the emotions involved—some good, some not so good—moving is one of life's most indelible moments. Strangely, few children's picture books have captured or addressed that feeling. Here we have a little gem to answer the call.

Bella is a preschooler who looks like any one of thousands of preschoolers. She represents a huge congregation of little movers. Stella is Bella's small stuffed elephant and her only apparent friend in these hours of moving. As the story's uncertain moments unfold, Stella rises to the occasion and grows larger on the page. Together these two pals wade through the heartache of saying good-bye to the old house and the nervousness of walking into a new one.

Belle, the Last Mule at Gee's Bend

BY CALVIN ALEXANDER RAMSEY AND BETTYE STROUD; JOHN HOLYFIELD, ILLUS.

Grades 1–4   *32 pages*
Candlewick, 2011

An old black woman sits in the shade with a young black boy, watching an old gray mule in the field across the street. In the ensuing time and pages, the woman shares the tale of that mule, from the midnight hour when Martin Luther King Jr. visited that dirt-poor Alabama community of Gee's Bend to the day three years later when that mule was asked to pull the wagon carrying Dr. King's coffin through the streets of Atlanta. In between those two events, the woman offers a moving synopsis of the civil rights movement and what it meant to the nation's poor. Related books: *Boycott Blues* by Andrea Davis Pinkney; *Goin' Someplace Special* by Patricia McKissack; *Leon's Story* (s); *Molly Bannaky* (n); *More Than Anything Else* by Marie Bradby; *Freedom on the Menu: The Greensboro Sit-ins* by Carole Boston

Weatherford; *My Brother Martin* (p); *Uncle Jed's Barbershop* and *When Grandmama Sings*, both by Margaree King Mitchell; and *White Water* by Michael Bandy and Eric Stein. Also: Listen to the commentary of a woman who took three of her godchildren to meet Rosa Parks as she recalls their meeting: www.npr.org/templates/story/story.php?storyId=4987683. For older students, see *Roll of Thunder, Hear My Cry* (n).

Benny and Penny in the Big No-No!
BY GEOFFREY HAYES
Grades PreS–K   *30 pages*
Toon/Candlewick, 2009
Early easy-reader books can be an important bridge to print for beginning readers, if only they had plots that kids cared about. Not so with these Toon books and their comic book style, in which text is neatly clued by the pictures. Equally important, the characters have serious things happen to them here, things that all kids worry about—like bullies or lying or tantrums or broken toys. In this winner of the Theodor Seuss Geisel Award, the two mouse siblings give in to temptation and go into forbidden territory—the new neighbors' yard! Also by the author: *Benny and Penny in Just Pretend*; *The Bunny's Night-Light: A Glow-in-the-Dark Search*; *Benny and Penny in the Toy Breaker*; and *Patrick in a Teddy Bear's Picnic and Other Stories*. See also *Tintin in Tibet* (p).

The Biggest Bear
BY LYND WARD
Grades K–3   *80 pages*
Houghton Mifflin, 1952
Johnny adopts a bear cub fresh out of the woods, and its growth presents problem after problem—the crises we invite when we tame what is meant to be wild. Also by the author: *The Silver Pony* (p). Related books: *Capyboppy* by Bill Peet; *Harry's Pony* by Barbara Ann Porte; *The Josefina Story Quilt* by Eleanor Coerr; and *Rikki-Tikki-Tavi* (p).

Boys of Steel: The Creators of Superman (nonfiction)
BY MARC TYLER NOBLEMAN; ROSS MACDONALD, ILLUS.
Grades 3–7   *32 pages*
Knopf, 2008
Jerry and Joe, two nerdy bespectacled teenagers in Cleveland, spend their high school years writing and drawing things that can't be seen or experienced except in their own imaginations. Their peers avoid them and their teachers berate them. The country is mired in the Depression and families

are struggling to put bread on the table. Why can't these two kids "get real"? What the pair was about to create would very soon become "real"— a real super-cultural hit, known the world over, that would bring daily relief from the pain of reality. Jerry Siegel would write and Joe Shuster would draw a fictional character named Clark Kent, aka Superman. This is the story behind the fictional saga.

Brave Irene
BY WILLIAM STEIG
Grades K–5   28 pages
Farrar, Straus & Giroux, 1986
When Irene's dressmaker mother falls ill and cannot deliver the duchess's gown for the ball, Irene shoulders the huge box and battles a winter storm to make the delivery. Also by the author: *Sylvester and the Magic Pebble* (p). Related books on courage: *High as a Hawk: A Brave Girl's Historic Climb* (p); *Mirette on the High Wire* (p); and *When Jessie Came Across the Sea* (p).

Brown Bear, Brown Bear, What Do You See?
BY BILL MARTIN JR.; ERIC CARLE, ILLUS.
Grades PreS–K   24 pages
Henry Holt, 1983; e-book
This classic predictable book follows the question through various animals and colors. Sequel: *Polar Bear, Polar Bear, What Do You Hear?* Also by the author: *Barn Dance!*; *Chicka Chicka Boom Boom*; and *The Ghost-Eye Tree*. For other predictable books, see list on page 176.

A Bus Called Heaven
BY BOB GRAHAM
Grades PreS–1   140 pages
Candlewick, 2011
Stella is part of a crowd that's gathered around a hollowed-out bus abandoned in the middle of the street. Soon she has convinced everyone to push it into her driveway. Next step is a makeover, complete with paint, rugs, games, chairs, and mattresses. It's turned into a neighborhood clubhouse for all ages. Or it was—until a tow truck hauls it to the junkyard ("It's an obstruction!"). But they don't know Stella and her resourcefulness. The strong plot will allow the book to be read to a class without showing the pictures (which are multiple small images on large pages), but it's perfect for sharing with two to three children at once. After hearing it, a class will want to examine and reexamine closely, so put this

one where it can easily be reached. For other books by the author, see *April and Esme, Tooth Fairies* (p).

Captain Abdul's Pirate School
BY COLIN MCNAUGHTON
Grades 1–5   *32 pages*
Candlewick, 1994
Hoping to toughen up their children, parents send them off to pirate school—something like a contemporary military or prep school. With tongue-in-cheek humor (some of it scoundrel-crude), the kids shape up and then turn against the pirates. Prequel: *Jolly Roger and the Pirates of Captain Abdul*. Sequel: *Captain Abdul's Little Treasure*. Other pirate books: *How I Became a Pirate* by Melinda Long; and *Maggie and the Pirate* by Ezra Jack Keats.

The Carpenter's Gift
BY DAVID RUBEL; JIM LAMARCHE, ILLUS.
Grades K–4   *44 pages*
Random House, 2011; e-book
In the early hours of the Great Depression, a very poor young boy and his father leave their rural shack and head for New York City in hopes of selling some Christmas trees they've cut. Construction workers at Rockefeller Center take pity and offer them some space for the tree sales. At the end of the day, they've turned a small profit and donate the remaining trees to the Rockefeller workmen. The next day, Christmas, the workmen return the favor. This remarkable tale is less a book about Christmas and more about giving without looking for credit, and taking without forgetting. Related books: *Pop's Bridge* (p); and *Spuds* by Karen Hesse, also set in the Great Depression.

A Chair for My Mother
BY VERA B. WILLIAMS
Grades K–3   *30 pages*
Greenwillow, 1982
This is the first book in a trilogy of tender stories about a family of three women: Grandma, Mama, and daughter Rosa (all told in the first person by the child). In this book, they struggle to save their loose change in order to buy a chair for the child's mother—something she can collapse into after her waitressing job. In *Something Special for Me*, the glass jar's contents are to be spent on the child's birthday present. What an important decision for a little girl to make! After much soul-searching, she settles on a

used accordion. In *Music, Music for Everyone*, the jar is empty again. With all the loose change going for Grandma's medical expenses now, little Rosa searches for a way to make money and cheer up her grandma. Related book: *Bun Bun Button* by Patricia Polacco.

Chewy Louie
BY HOWIE SCHNEIDER
Grades PreS–K   *32 pages*
Rising Moon, 2000; e-book
My three-year-old grandson never laughed so hard at a book as he did at this one, the tale of a new puppy with a gigantic need to chew. Louie devours everything in sight, from food bowls, tables, chairs, toys, and the vet's pants, to the family car. Will they have to give Louie up to save their home? A wonderful ending proves Schneider understands kids and where their funny bones are. Related book: *The Best Pet of All* by David LaRochelle. Also by the author: *Wilky the White House Cockroach*.

Cloudy with a Chance of Meatballs
BY JUDI BARRETT; RON BARRETT, ILLUS.
Grades PreS–5   *28 pages*
Atheneum, 1978
In the fantasyland of Chewandswallow, the weather changes three times a day, supplying all the residents with food out of the sky. But suddenly the weather takes a turn for the worse; instead of normal-size meatballs, it rains meatballs the size of basketballs, and pancakes and syrup smother the streets. Something must be done! Sequel: *Pickles to Pittsburgh*. Also by the author: *Animals Should Definitely Not Act Like People*; *Animals Should Definitely Not Wear Clothing*; and *Never Take a Shark to the Dentist*.

The Complete Adventures of Peter Rabbit
BY BEATRIX POTTER
Grades PreS–1   *96 pages*
Puffin, 1984
Here are the four original tales involving one of the most famous animals in children's literature—Peter Rabbit. Children identify with his naughty sense of adventure and then thrill at his narrow escape from the clutches of Mr. MacGregor. Although all the Potter books come in a small format that is ideal because young children feel more comfortable holding that size (3" x 5"), this larger volume is the most affordable choice and still retains the Potter illustrations. The original story of Peter was contained in a get-well letter Potter wrote to a child; the story of that child and his

letter is explored in the picture book *My Dear Noel* by Jane Johnson and can be used as low as kindergarten level. Author study: a children's biography, *Beatrix Potter*, by Alexandra Wallner. There is a wealth of Potter information on the Web, beginning with www.peterrabbit.co.uk/.

Corduroy

BY DON FREEMAN

Grades PreS–2   *32 pages*
Viking, 1968; e-book

In this beloved story, a teddy bear searches through a department store for a friend. His quest ends when a little girl buys him with her piggy-bank savings. Also by the author: *A Pocket for Corduroy* and *Beady Bear*. Related books: *Ira Sleeps Over* (p) and *The Perfect Bear* (p).

A Day's Work

BY EVE BUNTING; RONALD HIMLER, ILLUS.

Grades K–4   *30 pages*
Clarion, 1994; e-book

A young Mexican American boy seeks work for his newly arrived grandfather, who speaks no English. In persuading a man that his grandfather knows how to garden, the boy tells a small lie that ends up causing them twice as much work. The lesson in truthfulness is apparent, but just as important is the tender relationship of the child with an old man who needs help in a frightening new land. Related book: *The Paperboy* by Dav Pilkey.

The Dinosaurs of Waterhouse Hawkins (nonfiction)

BY BARBARA KERLEY; BRIAN SELZNICK, ILLUS.

Grades 1 and up   *48 pages*
Scholastic, 2001

In 1856, artist and naturalist Waterhouse Hawkins, collaborating with a leading scientist, earned an extraordinary commission: to build a dinosaur park. Think Jurassic Park in Queen Victoria's time. On an island outside London, Hawkins began building his giant models. And giants they were. Just one of the creatures required thirty tons of clay, six hundred bricks, fifteen hundred tiles, and thirty-eight casks of cement. The finished product would astonish Victorian England and lead him to the United States, where he was invited to build more models, this time in Central Park. Unfortunately, in the middle of his work, the henchmen of the infamous (and jealous) Boss Tweed vandalized the project beyond recovery. To this day, shattered pieces from the original models are still buried beneath the soil in

Central Park. The illustrator won the 2008 Caldecott Medal for the novel/picture book *The Invention of Hugo Cabret*.

Don't Want to Go!

BY SHIRLEY HUGHES

Grades PreS–K   *32 pages*

Candlewick, 2010

Lily's mother is home sick with the flu and Dad must go off to work, which means Lily must spend the day at the home of her parents' friend. That is *not* what Lily wants. She is not big on changes or strangers. But Dad prevails and off they go, where she has a wonderful day—so good, in fact, she's not keen on returning home. Sequel: *Bobbo Goes to School*. Also by the author: *All About Alfie* (p) and *Dogger*. Related books: *Llama Llama Home with Mama* by Anna Dewdney; *A Sick Day for Amos McGee* by Philip C. Stead; and *A Visitor for Bear* by Bonny Becker.

Jim's Favorite Books in Rhyming Verse
(in order of complexity)

The Neighborhood Mother Goose (p) by Nina Crews

Ten Little Fingers and Ten Little Toes (p) by Mem Fox

Over in the Meadow by Olive A. Wadsworth

Chicka Chicka Boom Boom by Bill Martin Jr.

The Napping House (p) by Audrey Wood

The Wheels on the Bus by Maryann Kovalski

Where's My Truck? by Karen Beaumont

King Jack and the Dragon by Peter Bently

This Is the House That Was Tidy and Neat by Teri Sloat

Duck in the Truck by Jez Alborough

Sheep in a Jeep by Nancy Shaw

Jesse Bear, What Will You Wear? by Nancy White Carlstrom

The Day the Babies Crawled Away by Peggy Rathmann

Shoe Baby by Joyce Dunbar

Snip Snap! What's That? by Mara Bergman

Madeline by Ludwig Bemelmans

Micawber by John Lithgow

The Recess Queen by Alexis O'Neill

Kermit the Hermit by Bill Peet

If I Ran the Zoo (p) by Dr. Seuss

The Friend by Sarah Stewart

Casey at the Bat by Ernest L. Thayer, ill. by C. F. Payne

Who Swallowed Harold? by Susan Pearson

Eddie: Harold's Little Brother (nonfiction)

BY ED KOCH AND PAT KOCH THALER; JAMES WARHOLA, ILLUS.

Grades 1–3   *28 pages*

Putnam, 2005

Eddie idolized his older brother, not just because he was older but also because he was the best athlete in the neighborhood. Everyone wanted Harold on their team. The one they didn't want was Eddie. Harold insisted Eddie be chosen for one side or the other but eventually even he tired of Eddie's clumsiness. There was one skill that Eddie did have—he could talk about almost anything. When he talked about his brother's games, the boys were spellbound. So when a notice appeared about a public speaking contest, Harold was certain this was meant for Eddie and convinced him to give it a try. So Eddie wrote his speech, rehearsed it in front of the team, and entered the contest. What followed eventually led the never-at-a-loss-for-words Ed Koch to the mayor's office of New York City. For other picture book biographies, see *My Brother Martin* (p).

Elsie's Bird

BY JANE YOLEN; DAVID SMALL, ILLUS.

Grades K–3   *34 pages*

Philomel, 2010

In a tale as evocative as her Caldecott-winning *Owl Moon*, Jane Yolen gives us a story of things lost and things found, of the sounds we take for granted in our lives, and the difference between a house and a home. In the mid-1800s, young Elsie is Boston born and bred, soaking up every sound and scent of the city. When her mother dies Elsie's father moves himself and Elsie to a sod house on the Nebraska plains. This may be the right move for his aching heart, but it does nothing for Elsie except to drive her deeper into herself. Add to that the loneliness of the prairie and you have a very sad child. I won't spoil the ending except to say it's a turning point for both the story and Elsie, leaving the reader-aloud and audience with much to talk about. Also by the author: *Encounter* (p). Also by illustrator David Small: *The Gardener*. Related book: *Harry & Hopper* by Margaret Wild.

Encounter

BY JANE YOLEN; DAVID SHANNON, ILLUS.

Grades 3–7   *30 pages*

Harcourt Brace, 1992; e-book

In observance of the five hundredth anniversary of Columbus's arrival in the Western Hemisphere, Yolen viewed the arrival through the eyes of a Taino Indian boy on San Salvador who has a foreboding dream about the newcomers. But the boy's warnings are rejected by the tribe's elders. A thought-provoking book on imperialism and colonialism. Related reading: *Time* article, "Before Columbus," October 19, 1998, detailing recent archaeological discoveries about the Taino tribe in Caribbean digs. Related book: *Me, All Alone, at the End of the World* by M. T. Anderson.

Erandi's Braids
BY ANTONIO HERNÁNDEZ MADRIGAL; TOMIE DEPAOLA, ILLUS.
Grades PreS–2   30 pages
Putnam, 1999
It was once the custom for women in poor Mexican villages to sell their hair, which was then used for wigs and fancy embroidery. In this tale, Erandi's mother has decided to sell her hair in order to pay for a much-needed fishing net. The barber refuses, saying hers is too short, but that he would gladly take the child's braids. It is now the child's difficult decision to make. Related books: *The Legend of the Bluebonnet* (p); and *The Babe & I* by David A. Adler.

The Everything Book
BY DENISE FLEMING
Inf–Tod   64 pages
Henry Holt, 2000
After Mother Goose, all new parents should have this terrific book about everything important to a child—animals, shapes, colors, rhymes, finger games, food, faces, letters, traffic, and toys. The art is a rainbow feast for the eyes, but is done in a style very young children can easily absorb.

Franklin and Winston: A Christmas That Changed the World (nonfiction)
BY DOUGLAS WOOD; BARRY MOSER, ILLUS.
Grades 4 and up   36 pages
Candlewick, 2011
In the first month of World War II and just after Pearl Harbor, the two leaders of the free world, Winston Churchill and Franklin D. Roosevelt, met for the Christmas holidays at the White House, where they planned a war and partnership that would save the world. One was the victim of polio, the other the victim of a neglected childhood, both rising well above their prescribed stations. This book looks beyond the somber history pages to show the warm friendship between them, as well as Churchill's

personal foibles (two hot baths a day, *no* noise in the hallway outside his room).

Froggy Gets Dressed (series)

BY JONATHAN LONDON; FRANK REMKIEWICZ, ILLUS.

Grades PreS–K   *32 pages*
Viking, 2000

Young Froggy is so excited about the first snowfall, he rushes outside to play with his friends before realizing he's forgotten to get dressed! He's out of breath and back outside after all that dressing, when his mother shouts to remind him he's forgotten his long underwear! This popular series includes twenty-one books, dealing with those staples of childhood like tree houses, Halloween, soccer, baby sisters, sleepovers, bikes, T-ball, doctors, school, babysitters, eating out, and (gulp!) first kisses. Related book: *Catch That Baby!* by Nancy Coffelt.

Full, Full, Full of Love

BY TRISH COOKE; PAUL HOWARD, ILLUS.

Grades PreS–K   *24 pages*
Candlewick, 2003

This book is like sitting down to dinner with a very happy family. When little Jay Jay is dropped off at his grandmother's, he helps her prepare the big Sunday family dinner. Gran's home is full of love and kisses, but there's lots of work to be done, so Jay Jay will need to feed the fish, put out dishes, pick up the spilled candy, and be patient. And when everyone finally sits down for the meal, it is a very full one, filled with love and family.

Goodnight Moon

BY MARGARET WISE BROWN; CLEMENT HURD, ILLUS.

Inf–Tod   *30 pages*
Harper, 1947

This classic is based on a bedtime ritual sure to be copied by every child who hears it. Also by the author: *The Important Book*; *The Runaway Bunny*; and *The Sailor Dog*. Related bedtime books for infants and toddlers: *Can't You Sleep, Little Bear?* by Martin Waddell; *Goodnight, Goodnight Construction Site* by Sherri Duskey Rinker and Tom Lichtenheld; *Good Night, Gorilla* by Peggy Rathmann; *Hide and Squeak* by Heather Vogel Frederick; *Kiss Good Night* by Amy Hest; *Max's Bedtime* by Rosemary Wells; *The Napping House* (p); *Sleep Tight, Little Bear* by Martin Waddell; and *Tell Me the Day Backwards* by Albert Lamb.

Gossie (series)

BY OLIVIER DUNREA

Inf–Tod   *30 pages*

Houghton Mifflin, 2002; e-book

It is rare for a book aimed at this age group to remain in print for a decade, and in three different formats: hardcover, paperback, and e-book. A barnyard gosling, Gossie is full of the same curiosity that all infants and toddlers have—except she has more freedom to explore her environment. The stories are simple—lost boot, favorite toys, eating, avoiding nap time, etc.—with uncomplicated but luminous illustrations, and the books are a perfect fit and weight for little hands. The humorous touch in both story and illustrations makes the series a winner. Also in the series: *Gossie and Gertie*; *Ollie*; *Ollie the Stomper*; *BooBoo*; *Peedie*; *Gideon*; and *Gideon and Otto*. Related book: *Brown Bear, Brown Bear, What Do You See?* (p).

The Great Fuzz Frenzy

BY SUSAN STEVENS CRUMMEL; JANET STEVENS, ILLUS.

Grades PreS–1   *56 pages*

Harcourt Brace, 2005; e-book

This whimsical tale was born the day the authors watched a tennis ball roll into prairie-dog town. What would the dogs think it was? So they put themselves into the mind of those underground dogs confronted by a round lump of fuzz and just imagined. The result is a delightful romp that has many applications to human behavior—copycatting, greed, even early-warning signals. The large fold-out pages (which are not text heavy) and brightly colored illustrations will make this a read-aloud standard for years. Try to have a tennis ball nearby when reading this book.

Harvesting Hope: The Story of Cesar Chavez (nonfiction)

BY KATHLEEN KRULL; YUYI MORALES, ILLUS.

Grades 1–4   *48 pages*

Harcourt Brace, 2003

This is a stunning biography of the man who made some of the richest people in America listen to some of the poorest. Despite the limitations of a picture book, the author and illustrator are able to create a multidimensional image of a man who walked so proudly in the footsteps of Gandhi and Martin Luther King Jr., faced down the rich and powerful, and changed America. The book spans his childhood in the Arizona desert and the bitter loss of his family's farm to the backbreaking harvest years and the blossoming of his labor movement for indigent farmworkers. For other picture biographies, see *My Brother Martin* (p).

Henry's Freedom Box (nonfiction)
BY ELLEN LEVINE; KADIR NELSON, ILLUS.

Grades 2 and up   *40 pages*

Scholastic, 2007

By the start of the Civil War, more than sixty thousand of the four million slaves in the U.S. had escaped to freedom, most via the Underground Railroad. But the most unusual route was that chosen by Henry Brown. Brown had just seen his wife and three children sold in the slave market and now he figured he had nothing left to lose. With the help of a white doctor and a black friend, he had himself stuffed into a wooden crate and then mailed 350 miles from Richmond, Virginia, to Philadelphia. This extraordinary journey, during which he could not stretch, sneeze, or even cough, took twenty-seven hours. Related books: *Belle, the Last Mule at Gee's Bend* (p); *Heart and Soul: The Story of America and African Americans* by Kadir Nelson; and *Unspoken: A Story of the Underground Railroad* by Henry Cole.

Jim's Favorite Friendship Books

The Carpenter's Gift by David Rubel

Chester's Way by Kevin Henkes

Danitra Brown, Class Clown by Nikki Grimes

A Day's Work by Eve Bunting

Erandi's Braids by Antonio H. Madrigal

Evie & Margie by Bernard Waber

The Friend by Sarah Stewart

The Lemonade Club by Patricia Polacco

Marshall Armstrong Is New to Our School by David Mackintosh

Marven of the Great North Woods by Kathryn Lasky

Nora's Ark by Natalie Kinsey-Warnock

Otis and *Otis and the Tornado* by Loren Long

Somebody Loves You, Mr. Hatch by Eileen Spinelli

Uncle Jed's Barbershop by Margaree King Mitchell

Wallace's Lists by Barbara Bottner and Gerald Kruglik

Worst of Friends by Suzanne Tripp Jurmain

High as a Hawk: A Brave Girl's Historic Climb (nonfiction)

BY T. A. BARRON; TED LEWIN, ILLUS.

Grades 1–3   30 pages
Philomel, 2004

Famed mountain guide Enos Mills successfully led the campaign to create
Rocky Mountain National Park. His friends and correspondents ran from
Teddy Roosevelt and Kit Carson to Helen Keller and Booker T. Washington. But of the more than 250 trips he made as a guide to the top of the
park's highest ridge, he claimed the most memorable was the one he made
in 1905 with a determined eight-year-old girl named Harriet Peters, the
youngest ever. This is the true story of their journey to 14,255 feet, illustrated in the lush watercolors of the great Ted Lewin.

A House in the Woods

BY INGA MOORE

Grades Tod–K   42 pages
Candlewick, 2011

If there were a single book that could embody pure happiness, it would
be this volume. There is no great plot here—just a group of woodland animals sharing the work of building a warm house in the woods. No ca-
lamities to overcome, no bickering, no tears; just working, sharing,
creating, and peanut butter sandwiches as reward. And how does this add
up to one of the most comforting and beautifully illustrated bedtime stories
ever written? Read it and see. Also by the author: *The Reluctant Dragon* (s).
For other bedtime books, see *Goodnight Moon* (p).

The House on East 88th Street (series)

BY BERNARD WABER

Grades PreS–3   48 pages
Houghton Mifflin, 1962

When the Primm family discovers a gigantic crocodile in the bathtub of
their new brownstone home, it signals the beginning of a wonderful
friendship (and picture book series). As soon as the Primms overcome
their fright, they see him as your children will—as the most lovable and
human of crocodiles. Sequels (in this order): *Lyle, Lyle, Crocodile*; *Lyle and
the Birthday Party*; *Lyle Finds His Mother*; *Lovable Lyle*; *Funny, Funny Lyle*;
Lyle at the Office; and *Lyle at Christmas*. Five Lyle books have been combined into a single volume for *Lyle, Lyle, Crocodile Storybook Treasury*. Also
by the author: *Ira Sleeps Over* (p); *Courage*; *Evie & Margie*; and *The Mouse
That Snored*.

How BIG Is It? (nonfiction series)
BY BEN HILLMAN
Grades K–4   *48 pages*
Scholastic, 2007 and 2008
For the weakest humans on earth—children—few attributes are as coveted
as strength and size. Ben Hillman, an enterprising and creative filmmaker,
designer, writer, and illustrator, has taken his many talents and applied
them to these subjects. Coupling seamless Photoshop techniques with ingenious analogies, Hillman's books will rivet the attention of young and
old alike. Size and strength are everyday concepts, but both are largely invisible qualities until we make comparisons with other objects—and then
the reality hits home. For example, in *How BIG Is It?* when Hillman
wanted to demonstrate the bigness of a giant squid, he posed one on the
front lawn of an average house.

In *How STRONG Is It?* he demonstrates the relative strength of a
spider's web with this analogy: "If a spider could make a web where each
strand was as thick as a pencil, its web could stop a Boeing 747 in mid-
flight. There is no other substance that even comes close to this stopping
power." Among the twenty-two items Hillman attempts to strength-
measure are a hurricane, elephant, secret code, hair, martial arts kick,
volcano, and Hercules beetle. Other books in the series: *How FAST Is It?*
and *How WEIRD Is It?*

I Am So Strong
BY MARIO RAMOS
Grades Tod–K   *28 pages*
Gecko/Lerner, 2011
Give me a book with some good old-fashioned yelling in it, throw in a
handful of familiar characters like that wolf and Red Riding Hood and
those three pigs, add a couple of dwarfs, and then round it off with a baby
dinosaur and his *huge* mother. The end result is one terrific read-aloud.
Related books: *Beware of Boys* by Tony Blundell; and *King Hugo's Huge Ego*
by Chris Van Dusen.

I Stink!
BY KATE AND JIM MCMULLAN
Grades PreS–2   *32 pages*
Harper, 2002
More than sixty years ago, Virginia Lee Burton created a series of picture
books that introduced children to the civic lives of their cities and towns:

Katy and the Big Snow and *Mike Mulligan and His Steam Shovel* (p). Now comes *I Stink!* Quite a contrast, but still successful. Let's face it, times change. The McMullans give us not only an inside look at the mechanics of the modern garbage truck (something that'll fascinate most children) but also a taste (no pun intended) of what life would be like without it. Jim McMullan's flamboyant use of mashed-up, exploding, slithering, rumbling, and dripping typefaces lends both amusement and texture to the tale. Also by the authors: *I'm Bad!*; *I'm Big!*; *I'm Dirty!*; *I'm Fast!*; and *I'm Mighty!*

If I Ran the Zoo

BY DR. SEUSS
Grades PreS–4   *54 pages*
Random House, 1950
Little Gerald McGrew finds the animals at the local zoo pretty boring compared with the zany, exotic creatures populating the zoo of his imagination (just like a little lad imagined things while walking to and from school in Seuss's first book for children, *And to Think That I Saw It on Mulberry Street*). Dr. Seuss's father ran the zoo in Springfield, Massachusetts, for thirty-one years. Seuss author studies: "Oh, the Places You've Taken Us: RT's Tribute to Dr. Seuss," in the May 1992 issue of *Reading Teacher*; a children's biography, *Dr. Seuss: Young Author and Artist*, by Kathleen Kudlinski (Aladdin, 2005); and two adult biographies, *The Seuss, the Whole Seuss, and Nothing but the Seuss: A Visual Biography of Theodore Seuss Geisel* by Charles D. Cohen and *Dr. Seuss & Mr. Geisel* by Judith and Neil Morgan, the definitive book on his personal life. For a more academic approach to Seuss's work, see Philip Nel's *Dr. Seuss: American Icon*. Fans of Dr. Seuss also will enjoy the books of Bill Peet—see *The Whingdingdilly* (p).

If You Give a Mouse a Cookie

BY LAURA NUMEROFF; FELICIA BOND, ILLUS.
Grades PreS–K   *30 pages*
Harper, 1985
In a humorous cumulative tale that comes full circle, a little boy offers a mouse a cookie and ends up working his head off for the demanding little creature. Sequels: *If You Give a Moose a Muffin*; *If You Give a Pig a Pancake*; *If You Take a Mouse to the Movies*; *If You Give a Pig a Party*; *If You Give a Cat a Cupcake*; and *If You Give a Dog a Donut*. For other cumulative stories, see Predictable Books on page 176.

Ira Sleeps Over
BY BERNARD WABER
Grades K–6   48 pages
Houghton Mifflin, 1972
This is a warm, sensitive, and humorous look at a boy's overnight visit to
his best friend's house, centering on the child's quandary of whether or
not to bring his teddy bear. It makes for lively discussion about individual
sleeping habits, peer pressure, and the things we all hold on to—even as
grown-ups. In the sequel, Ira Says Goodbye, the two best friends experience
a childhood pain when one moves away. Waber is also the author of the
popular Lyle the Crocodile series, which begins with The House on East
88th Street (p), and Evie & Margie, about two female best friends. Related
books: Bun Bun Button by Patricia Polacco; Corduroy (p); Don't Want to Go!
(p); Have You Seen Duck? by Janet Holmes; I Lost My Bear by Jules Feiffer;
and Where's My Teddy? (p).

The Island of the Skog
BY STEVEN KELLOGG
Grades PreS–2   32 pages
Dial, 1973
Sailing away from city life, a boatload of mice discover the island of their
dreams, only to be pulled up short by the appearance of a fearful monster
already dwelling on the island. How imaginations can run away with us
and how obstacles can be overcome if we'll just talk with others are central
issues in this tale. Also by the author: The Mysterious Tadpole (p).

Johnny on the Spot
BY EDWARD SOREL
Grades 1 and up   28 pages
Simon & Schuster, 1998
Young Johnny and his adult neighbor accidentally invent a radio that
broadcasts events one day in advance. The conflict arises when Johnny is
sworn to secrecy and forbidden to interfere with the future—even if he
knows a calamity is about to occur. Created by one of America's premier
political artists, the story is both adventure and morality tale. Related
books: A Day's Work (p); The King and the Seed (p); and The Real Thief by
William Steig.

The King and the Seed
BY ERIC MADDERN; PAUL HESS, ILLUS.

Grades K–2   *24 pages*
Frances Lincoln, 2009

King Karnak has no heir to his throne. His solution is to hold a competition, and anyone in the kingdom may participate. The king gives each participant a single seed, tells them to grow something with it, and in six months he'll decide the heir to the throne by what they produce. Young Jack takes his seed and assumes he has an advantage; after all, he's a farmer's son and knows about seeds, planting, and cultivating. But no matter how hard he tries, he cannot make his seed grow. At last the king summons all the competitors to the castle to see their results. The long line to the king includes the grandest flowers and plants imaginable, excluding, of course, Jack, who has nothing to show and is the last to see King Karnak. There he confesses he has been able to grow nothing, which pleases the king no end, and Jack is named heir to the crown. The king explains he boiled all the seeds to prevent them from ever blooming. The other competitors had lied about their plants; only Jack had told the truth. Related books: *Clever Jack Takes the Cake* by Candace Fleming; and *Johnny on the Spot* (p).

The Legend of the Bluebonnet
RETOLD BY TOMIE DEPAOLA

Grades PreS–4   *30 pages*
Putnam, 1984

Here is the legend behind the bluebonnets that blanket the state of Texas—the story of the little Comanche Indian orphan who sacrificed her only doll in order to end the drought that was ravaging her village. Related books: *The Legend of the Indian Paintbrush* and *Erandi's Braids* (p). A complete listing of books by Tomie dePaola can be found at www.tomie .com. He has also written a series of autobiographical chapter books (in order): *26 Fairmount Avenue*; *Here We All Are*; *On My Way*; *What a Year*; and *Things Will Never Be the Same*. For author studies: *Tomie dePaola: His Art & His Stories* by Barbara Elleman.

The Library Lion
BY MICHELLE KNUDSEN; KEVIN HAWKES, ILLUS.

Grades PreS–K   *48 pages*
Candlewick, 2006

When the lion walks into the library, he is too ferocious for anyone to object, and the head librarian thinks, "If he obeys the rules, no problem."

But his roaring at the end of story time brings a sharp reprimand from her and he gets the message. Nonetheless, the circulation assistant, Mr. McBee, doesn't like his presence, even though the lion helps out by licking envelopes and dusting shelves with his tail. Finally McBee has enough cause to eject him—a roaring that disrupts the entire building, causing the lion to be banished. Only afterward is the cause discovered: The head librarian fell and broke her arm and the lion was roaring for help. Too late now—the embarrassed lion has departed to no-one-knows-where. Lions are no strangers to libraries: Look who's guarding the doors to the New York Public Library—lion statues Patience and Fortitude (http://www .nypl.org/help/about-nypl/library-lions). Related books: *But Excuse Me That Is My Book* by Lauren Child; *The Day Dirk Yeller Came to Town* by Mary Casanova; *Miss Dorothy and Her Bookmobile* by Gloria Houston; *Wild About Books* by Judy Sierra; *Words Set Me Free: The Story of Young Frederick Douglass* by Lesa Cline-Ransome.

Lilly's Purple Plastic Purse
BY KEVIN HENKES
Grades PreS–1   *30 pages*
Greenwillow, 1996

Few writers for children have as firm a grip on the pulse of childhood as does Kevin Henkes. His mice-children experience all the joys and insecurities of being a kid, but he manages to maintain a light touch throughout his stories. In this case, Lilly loves school and her teacher—until the day her antics distract the class and the teacher must temporarily confiscate her precious new plastic purse. Shattered, she's uncertain how to handle this small rebuke and seeks ways to show her hurt. With the help of her family, Lilly overcomes her embarrassment and hasty behavior, writes an apology, and soars on the good feelings that come from doing the right thing. Lilly also stars in: *Lilly's Big Day*; *Chester's Way*; and *Julius, the Baby of the World*. Also by the author: *Chrysanthemum*; *A Weekend with Wendell*; and *Wemberly Worried*.

The Little House
BY VIRGINIA LEE BURTON
Grades PreS–3   *40 pages*
Houghton Mifflin, 1942

This Caldecott Medal winner uses a little turn-of-the-century house to portray the urbanization of America. With each page, the reader-listener becomes the little house and experiences the contentment, wonder, concern, anxiety, and loneliness that the passing seasons and encroaching city bring. Many of today's children who daily experience the anxieties of city life will identify with the little house's eventual triumph. Also by the author: *Katy and the Big Snow*; and *Mike Mulligan and His Steam Shovel* (p). Related books: *Farewell to Shady Glade*; and *The Wump World* by Bill Peet.

The Little Old Lady Who Was Not Afraid of Anything
BY LINDA WILLIAMS; MEGAN LLOYD, ILLUS.
Grades PreS–1   *28 pages*
Harper, 1988
Walking through the dark woods toward home, the little old lady is approached by a succession of scary articles of empty clothing—gloves, hat, shoes, trousers, etc. She refuses to allow them to frighten her—until she encounters the last one, which sets her running. In the end, however, she solves the problem by making all the items into a scarecrow. Other scary but nonthreatening books for young children: *There's a Nightmare in My Closet* by Mercer Mayer; *Snip Snap! What's That?* (p); and *The Squeaky Door* retold by Margaret Read MacDonald.

Little Red Riding Hood
RETOLD BY TRINA SCHART HYMAN
Grades PreS–3   *32 pages*
Holiday, 1983
It's hard to imagine a better-illustrated version of this famous tale. The artist has given us a child and grandma who are every child and grandma, and a texture so rich you can almost smell the woods. Related books: *Flossie and the Fox* by Patricia McKissack (African-American version); *The Gunniwolf* by Wilhelmina Harper; *Lon Po Po* by Ed Young (Chinese version); and *Pretty Salma* by Niki Daly (African version). Parodies: *Betsy Red Hoodie* by Gail Carson Levine; and *Little Red Riding Hood: A Newfangled Prairie Tale* by Lisa Campbell Ernst. See page 294 for more story parodies.

Lost and Found: Three Dog Stories
BY JIM LAMARCHE
Grades PreS–K   *42 pages*
Chronicle, 2009
In one of these delightful dog stories, a child is lost and rescued by the dog; in the second, a dog is lost and then found by a child; and last, a dog owner and family are lost and then found. Three searches and three happy endings, all with the subtle message: Don't give up! Also by the illustrator: *The Carpenter's Gift* (p). Related books: *Charley's First Night* by Amy Hest; *Chewy Louie* (p); *Dogger* by Shirley Hughes; *George Flies South* by Simon

James; *Harry & Hopper* by Margaret Wild; and *Little Dog Lost* by Mônica Carnesi.

Lousy Rotten Stinkin' Grapes

BY MARGIE PALATINI; BARRY MOSER, ILLUS.
Grades K–3   *28 pages*
Simon & Schuster, 2009

The title here will grab any child's attention. With that kind of title, I was prepared for an original twist on the old Aesop's fable, and I wasn't disappointed. The original tale featured only a single character—the fox—but Palatini has added six forest neighbors to the cast, each enlisted by the sly fox to help get the just-out-of-reach grapes. Each tries to explain to him that there's an easier way to reach his goal, but he won't take any advice. It's his way or no way. In the original tale, he concedes defeat by grousing that the grapes probably were sour anyway—thus the origin of the phrase "sour grapes." The ending here is the same but the moral of the story is entirely different: Don't be a know-it-all. Related book: *Aesop's Fables* (p).

The Luck of the Loch Ness Monster

BY A. W. FLAHERTY; SCOTT MAGOON, ILLUS.
Grades K–3   *34 pages*
Houghton Mifflin, 2007; e-book

Young, wealthy Katerina-Elizabeth is both stubborn and a picky eater. Despite the warning of her parents, she refuses to eat her oatmeal breakfasts. En route by herself to visit her grandmother in Scotland, the child willfully dumps her oatmeal out the ocean liner's porthole window each morning, watching it promptly sink to the ocean floor. It's there that a small sea worm spots and swallows the sodden lump. He loves it! Looking for more, he follows the ship across the sea, dining each morning and growing larger by the day. The rest, as they say in Loch Ness, is history. Be sure to read the book's short postscript on the science of picky eating and then try the experiment on your family or class. Related books: *The Mysterious Tadpole* (p); *Plantzilla* by Jerdine Nolen; and for older children, *The Water Horse* (n).

Madeline (series)

BY LUDWIG BEMELMANS
Grades K–3   *30 pages*
Viking, 1939

This series of six books features a daring and irrepressible girl named

Madeline and her eleven friends, who all live together in a Parisian boarding school. The author's use of fast-moving verse, daring adventure, naughtiness, and glowing color keep it a favorite in early grades year after year. Other books in the series: *Madeline and the Bad Hat*; *Madeline and the Gypsies*; *Madeline in London*; *Madeline's Rescue*; and *Madeline's Christmas*.

Make Way for Ducklings
BY ROBERT MCCLOSKEY
Grades PreS–2   62 pages
Viking, 1941

In this Caldecott award–winning classic, we follow Mrs. Mallard and her eight ducklings as they make a traffic-stopping walk across Boston to meet Mr. Mallard on their new island home in the Public Garden. Also by the author: *Blueberries for Sal*; *Burt Dow: Deep-Water Man*; *Lentil*; and *One Morning in Maine*. Be sure to check out *Make Way for McCloskey: A Robert McCloskey Treasury*, a single-volume anthology containing six of his best works. Related books: *Chibi: A True Story from Japan* by Julia Takaya and Barbara Brenner; *John Philip Duck* by Patricia Polacco; and *Micawber* (p).

Marshall Armstrong Is New to Our School
BY DAVID MACKINTOSH
Grades PreS–1   30 pages
Abrams, 2011

Marshall is the new kid and sits next to the story's narrator—who thinks he's weird, to say the least. He doesn't eat what everyone else eats, doesn't play their games, and certainly doesn't dress like they do. Even his skin looks weird. And then everyone in class gets invited to Marshall's house for a party. Wow! What a cool guy he turned out to be. Related books: *Odd Boy Out: Young Albert Einstein* (p); *The Recess Queen* by Alexis O'Neill; and *Somebody Loves You, Mr. Hatch* (p).

Marven of the Great North Woods
BY KATHRYN LASKY; KEVIN HAWKES, ILLUS.
Grades K–4   36 pages
Harcourt Brace, 1997

In 1918, one of history's worst flu epidemics was sweeping across the world, killing tens of thousands. The Lasky family believed their ten-year-old son's chances of escaping the plague would be greater if he spent the winter far from the city of Duluth, Minnesota. So they packed Marven's bags and sent him by train to a logging camp in the Great North Woods. A true story of courage, history, and the warm friendship between a small Jewish city boy and a French Canadian giant.

Me and Momma and Big John

BY MARA ROCKLIFF; WILLIAM LOW, ILLUS.
Grades K–2, 1–3   *32 pages*
Candlewick, 2012

Momma is a single parent raising three children, providing for them with her new job as an apprentice stonecutter in New York City, working on the Cathedral of St. John the Divine, one of the largest churches in the world. Its construction began in 1892, and through the years the cathedral has earned two nicknames among its neighbors: "St. John the Unfinished" and "Big John." The story's young narrator has many questions, including why the church remains unfinished and how people will know his mother's stone from all the others. It is a gorgeously illustrated tale of art, worship, family, and pride. Related books: *Pop's Bridge* (p) and *A Day's Work* (p).

Micawber

BY JOHN LITHGOW; C. F. PAYNE, ILLUS.
Grades PreS–2   *24 pages*
Simon & Schuster, 2002

In this delightful picture book, brilliantly illustrated by C. F. Payne, we meet a squirrel named Micawber in New York's Central Park whose favorite haunt is the Metropolitan Museum of Art—to be more exact, the skylight on the museum's roof, where he can gaze with rapture at the works of Rembrandt, Titian, and Rubens. One day he sees an aspiring artist set up her easel and canvas in the gallery and begin to copy the masters. Suddenly a light dawns for Micawber. So this is how they make those pictures! In flawless, witty, rhyming verse we follow the squirrel as he follows the artist home to her apartment and borrows her paints each night while she sleeps to paint his own canvases. In the end, we open two double-page spreads to see the result of his nightly labors.

Mighty Jackie: The Strike-Out Queen (nonfiction)

BY MARISSA MOSS; C. F. PAYNE, ILLUS.
Grades 1–4   *36 pages*
Simon & Schuster, 2004

In March 1931, Jackie Mitchell's dream was finally going to come true: Jackie would get a chance to show the world's greatest hitters that a seventeen-year-old could throw a mighty mean curveball. All those barnyard practice throws would finally come to something, and not just against any team—against the mighty New York Yankees, led by Babe Ruth and Lou Gehrig, coming through Tennessee on a spring barnstorming tour. So when Jackie Mitchell struck out Babe and Lou in succession while pitching for the Chattanooga Lookouts, there was considerable excitement—and not just because Jackie was seventeen years old. The bigger story was that Jackie Mitchell was a girl! In this wonderful retelling, Moss and Payne bring to life a little-known but true story in American sport. Also by the author: *The Bravest Woman in America*; and *Nurse, Soldier, Spy: The Story of Sarah Edmonds, a Civil War Hero*. Related books: *Girl Wonder* by Deborah Hopkinson; *Mama Played Baseball* by David A. Adler; *Players in Pigtails* by Shana Corey; *She Loved Baseball: The Effa Manley Story* and *Brothers at Bat*, both by Audrey Vernick. For other picture book biographies, see *My Brother Martin* (p).

Mike Mulligan and His Steam Shovel
BY VIRGINIA LEE BURTON
Grades K–4   *42 pages*
Houghton Mifflin, 1939; e-book
This is the heartwarming classic about the demise of the steam shovel and how it found a permanent home with driver Mike. Also by the author: *Choo Choo*; *The Emperor's New Clothes*; *Katy and the Big Snow*; and *The Little House* (p). Related book: *Pop's Bridge* (p).

The Minpins
BY ROALD DAHL; PATRICK BENSON, ILLUS.
Grades K–4   *47 pages*
Viking, 1991
This is one of Dahl's final and most sensitive and dramatic works. When a small boy disobeys his mother and enters the dark forest, he meets not only the monster she predicted but also tiny matchstick-size people who inhabit all the trees. The tiny creatures enable his escape and help destroy the monster. Related book: *There's a Nightmare in My Closet* by Mercer Mayer.

Mirette on the High Wire
BY EMILY ARNOLD MCCULLY
Grades K–2   *30 pages*
Putnam, 1992
One hundred years ago in a small boardinghouse in Paris lived the Great Bellini, a daredevil tightrope walker who had lost his confidence. In the

weeks that followed, the innkeeper's daughter became enchanted with rope walking and was able to restore the man's lost confidence while becoming a star herself. Winner of the Caldecott Medal, the book was followed by *Starring Mirette & Bellini* and *Mirette & Bellini Cross Niagara Falls*. Also by the author: *The Bobbin Girl*. Related books: *Brave Irene* (p) and *The Man Who Walked Between the Towers* by Mordicai Gerstein.

Miss Nelson Is Missing! (series)
BY HARRY ALLARD; JAMES MARSHALL, ILLUS.
Grades PreS–4   *32 pages*
Houghton Mifflin, 1977
Poor, sweet Miss Nelson! Kind and beautiful as she is, she cannot control her classroom—the worst-behaved children in the school. But when Miss Nelson is suddenly absent, the children begin to realize what a wonderful teacher they had in her. Her substitute is wicked-looking, strict Miss Viola Swamp, who works the class incessantly. Wherever has Miss Nelson gone and when will she return? Sequels: *Miss Nelson Is Back* and *Miss Nelson Has a Field Day*.

Molly Bannaky (nonfiction)
BY ALICE MCGILL; CHRIS K. SOENTPIET, ILLUS.
Grades 3–8   *32 pages*
Houghton Mifflin, 1999
Benjamin Banneker was one of the first black American scientists, wrote the first black almanac, and was part of the federal panel that planned Washington, D.C., but the story behind the man is his grandmother. She came to America as a white indentured servant, having narrowly escaped the English gallows by proving she could read the Bible. In America, she fulfilled her seven years of servitude, later bought a farm, and then bought a newly arrived slave, whom she grew to love and then married. For the story of her famous grandson, see *Dear Benjamin Banneker* by Andrea D. Pinkney. Related book: *January's Sparrow* by Patricia Polacco.

Molly's Pilgrim
BY BARBARA COHEN; DANIEL MARK DUFFY, ILLUS.
Grades 1–4   *41 pages*
Morrow, 1983
Molly, an immigrant child and the target of her classmates' taunts, discovers she is more a part of America's Thanksgiving tradition than anyone in the class. This book is the basis for the 1985 Academy Award–winning best short film of the same title (previews available on YouTube and DVD

from Phoenix Learning Group). Related books: *An Outlaw Thanksgiving* by Emily Arnold McCully; *Thanksgiving at the Tappletons'* by Eileen Spinelli; *Thank You, Sarah: The Woman Who Saved Thanksgiving* (p); and *When Jessie Came Across the Sea* (p).

My Brother Martin: A Sister Remembers (nonfiction)

BY CHRISTINE KING FARRIS; CHRIS SOENPIET, ILLUS.

Grades 1–5   *30 pages*

Simon & Schuster, 2003

One unfortunate aspect of heroes and icons is that we put them on such high pedestals that they're out of children's reach; thus children can find little of themselves in them. Along comes Christine King Farris, older sister of Martin Luther King Jr., who regrets the loss of both her brother and those things that made him human. Thankfully, she has put her memories down in this fine little narrative—the events of one family's childhood years that molded, inspired, entertained, and sometimes frightened its three children, the human things we seldom find in the history books but that make heroes real to readers. Other outstanding picture book biographies: *A Boy Called Dickens* by Deborah Hopkinson; *The Boy Who Drew Birds: A Story of John James Audubon* by Jacqueline Davies; *Boys of Steel: The Creators of Superman* (p); *Eleanor* (Roosevelt) by Barbara Cooney; *Franklin and Winston: A Christmas That Changed the World* (p); *Harvesting Hope: The Story of Cesar Chavez* (p); *Here Come the Girl Scouts!* by Shana Corey; *Jim Henson: The Guy Who Played with Puppets* by Kathleen Krull; *Noah Webster and His Words* by Jeri Chase Ferris; *Nurse, Soldier, Spy* (p); *Roberto Clemente* by Jonah Winter; *Seed by Seed: The Legend and Legacy of John "Appleseed" Chapman* by Esmé Raji Codell; *Thank You, Sarah: The Woman Who Saved Thanksgiving* (p); *The Watcher: Jane Goodall's Life with the Chimps* by Jeanette Winter; *Words Set Me Free: The Story of Young Frederick Douglass* by Lesa Cline-Ransome; *Worst of Friends: Thomas Jefferson, John Adams, and the True Story of an American Feud* by Suzanne Tripp Jurmain; and the Turning Point series by Judith St. George, which includes: *Take the Lead, George Washington*; *Make Your Mark, Franklin Roosevelt*; *You're on Your Way, Teddy Roosevelt*; and *Stand Tall, Abe Lincoln*.

The Mysterious Tadpole

BY STEVEN KELLOGG

Grades PreS–4   *30 pages*

Dial, 1977

When little Louis's uncle in Scotland sends him a tadpole for his birthday, neither of them has any idea how much havoc and fun the pet will cause in Louis's home, classroom, and school swimming pool. The tadpole turns out to be a direct descendant of the Loch Ness monster (but what a cuddly monster this is!). Also by the author: *The Island of the Skog* (p). Related books: *The Best Pet of All* by David LaRochelle; *Jangles: A Big Fish Story* by David Shannon; *The Serpent Came to Gloucester* by M. T. Anderson; and *The Water Horse* (n).

Naming Liberty
BY JANE YOLEN; JIM BURKE, ILLUS.
Grades 2–5   *30 pages*
Philomel, 2008
In facing single pages, award-winning author Jane Yolen tells two parallel stories: One portrays a Jewish family in the Ukraine in the 1800s and the other pictures a young French sculptor named Frédéric Auguste Bartholdi. The converging tales paint an excellent portrait of both the American immigrant experience and the American dream. In Yolen's tale, the Ukrainian family battles the insecurities of new families arriving on American shores and Bartholdi with the political and financial forces standing in the way of his famous statue called Liberty. Related book: *When Jessie Came Across the Sea* (p) by Amy Hest.

The Napping House
BY AUDREY WOOD; DON WOOD, ILLUS.
Tod–PreS   *28 pages*
Harcourt Brace, 1984
One of the cleverest bedtime books for children, this simple tale depicts a cozy bed on which are laid in cumulative rhymes a snoring granny, a dreaming child, a dozing dog, and a host of other sleeping characters— until a sudden awakening at daybreak. The subtle lighting changes in the double-page illustrations show the gradual passage of time during the night and the clearing of a storm outside. See *Goodnight Moon* (p) for a list of bedtime books.

The Neighborhood Mother Goose
PHOTOGRAPHED BY NINA CREWS
Inf–PreS   *64 pages*
Dutton, 1989
Nina Crews took her camera into urban America and coupled Mother Goose with children of every hue, making it a rainbow's worth of traditional nursery rhymes peopled by children who have been traditionally

excluded from such volumes. Also by the photographer: *The Neighborhood Sing-Along* (po). Other Mother Goose collections: *The Everything Book* (p); *¡Pío Peep! Traditional Spanish Nursery Rhymes* selected by Alma Flor Ada and F. Isabel Campoy; and *Tomie dePaola's Mother Goose* by Tomie dePaola.

Nurse, Soldier, Spy: The Story of Sarah Edmonds, a Civil War Hero (nonfiction)

BY MARISSA MOSS; JOHN HENDRIX, ILLUS.

Grades 3–5   *48 pages*
Abrams, 2011

Under any circumstances, Frank Thompson—nurse, soldier, and spy— would have been an extraordinary Civil War soldier. When you discover Frank was not Frank—that "he" was a nineteen-year-old girl named Sarah Edmonds, the story goes beyond extraordinary. Sarah had begun dressing as a man to escape Canada and an arranged marriage, and she loved the newfound freedoms that came with her disguise. With the start of the Civil War and the need for soldiers, Sarah joined the Union army. Although hundreds of other women joined in disguises, Edmonds is the only one to have accomplished so much, come so close to being both shot and dis- covered, and finally to be voted by Congress as the only official woman veteran of the Civil War. This book offers a striking contrast with the headlines of today, when women serve as battlefield equals on the sands of the Middle East. Also by the author: *The Bravest Woman in America* and *Mighty Jackie: The Strike-Out Queen* (p). Related books: *Independent Dames: What You Never Knew About the Women and Girls of the American Revolution* by Laurie Halse Anderson; *The Librarian of Basra* by Jeanette Winter; and *Mama Played Baseball* by David Adler.

Odd Boy Out: Young Albert Einstein (nonfiction)

BY DON BROWN

Grades 2–7   *30 pages*
Houghton Mifflin, 2004

In this simple but insightful biographical picture book on the life of the great scientist, the author offers hope for every child who marches to a different drum, who doesn't blossom on time, who isn't good at sports, who believes in daydreaming about things that no one else can even imagine, and who is the class outsider. And for those who think they know the story already, that Einstein worked on the atom bomb—wrong. He was barred from working on it because his pacifist leanings prevented him from receiving a security clearance. This is picture book biography at its very best, from an author-illustrator whose work places him at the very front of the field. Related book: *Marshall Armstrong Is New to Our School* (p). Also by the author: *American Boy: The Adventures of Mark Twain*; *Uncommon Traveler: Mary Kingsley in Africa*; *Rare Treasure: Mary Anning and Her Remarkable Discoveries*; *Alice Ramsey's Grand Adventure*; *Ruth Law Thrills a Nation*; and *Teedie: The Story of Young Teddy Roosevelt*. For other picture book biographies, see *My Brother Martin* (p).

An Orange for Frankie

BY PATRICIA POLACCO
Grades K and up   *40 pages*
Philomel, 2004

We start with a family of nine on Christmas Eve, a father missing in a snowstorm, a boxcar of hungry and freezing hobos, one missing sweater, and a lost Christmas orange—all of it neatly tied into a happy holiday ending. Based on the author/artist's family history, this is as good as holiday stories get! Related books: *The Carpenter's Gift* (p); *Mim's Christmas Jam* by Andrea Davis Pinkney; *The Polar Express* by Chris Van Allsburg; *Spuds* by Karen Hesse; and *The Story of Holly and Ivy* by Rumer Godden.

Otis

BY LOREN LONG
Grades PreS–1   *36 pages*
Philomel, 2009

Otis is a throwback. A small but diligent tractor, Otis is the life of the barnyard and the best friend of a lonely calf residing in the barn's adjoining stall. When his day's labors are done, they sit in the shade of the apple tree to contemplate their happy lives. But their happiness is suddenly interrupted when the farmer purchases a brand-new yellow tractor, which quickly relegates Otis to the scrap-heap weed patch outside the barn. He is now outdated, unemployed, and too sad to play with his friend.

The calf, in turn, wanders down to the pond, only to get stuck in the mud. Either unable or unwilling to work herself out of the mire, she becomes the focus of a community-wide rescue effort. But neither the farmhands, the new tractor, nor the fire department can extricate her from the mud. Suddenly Otis is seen making his way down the hillside and soon a happy ending is in sight. Sequel: *Otis and the Tornado*. Related books: *The Story of Ferdinand* by Munro Leaf; *The Little House* (p) and *Mike Mulligan and His Steam Shovel* (p) by Virginia Lee Burton; and *Smokey* by Bill Peet.

The Perfect Bear

BY GILLIAN SHIELDS; GARY BLYTHE, ILLUS.

Grades PreS–K   *26 pages*

Simon & Schuster, 2008

When he was sitting on the store's shelf, the little white bear was so perfect they placed a sign beside him: Do Not Touch. He not only thought he was perfect, he thought that was his name—Do Not Touch. Then the little girl receives him as a gift and his life begins to change. Not only is he being touched, he is getting dirty and rusty (the key in his music box). Poor bear is miserable and can't make the little girl understand. The real understanding comes only when bear learns that it is not what we have showing outside but what we have inside that counts. Related books: *Bun Bun Button* by Patricia Polacco; *Corduroy* (p); *Dogger* by Shirley Hughes; and *Ira Sleeps Over* (p).

Peter and the Winter Sleepers

BY RICK DE HAAS

Grades PreS–K   *26 pages*

North-South, 2011

Peter is living in a lighthouse with his grandmother and his dog just as the first winter storm arrives. When the snow begins to pile up, they have to bring the chicken and goat inside. Fine enough, until the snow continues and a rabbit comes scratching at the door. In he comes. Followed by an owl, a bat, a hedgehog, squirrels—well, there was soon a lighthouse full. And the snow keeps coming—along with a dangerous red fox. Related books: *Nora's Ark* by Natalie Kinsey-Warnock; and *Otis and the Tornado* by Loren Long. For younger children: *The Snowy Day* by Ezra Jack Keats.

The Pied Piper of Hamelin

BY MICHAEL MORPURGO; EMMA CHICHESTER CLARK, ILLUS.

Grades K–5   *64 pages*

Candlewick, 2011

Through the ages there have been many versions of the legend of Hamelin and the piper who led away the children when he was left unpaid. Here is yet another version, but this one has particular relevance to our times and it comes from one of the most decorated British authors in children's literature, Michael Morpurgo. This version of Hamelin shows hundreds of neglected or abandoned children, wealthy townspeople who detest the poor, corrupt politicians, and a community overrun by garbage and refuse—which invites the invasion of rats. Enter the Pied Piper with his promise. The plot then takes the traditional path, including the lame boy who falls behind and returns to the village with the sad news. But from there, Morpurgo offers a different slant, a parable very much for our time. It is handsomely illustrated, with oversize pages. Also by the author: *Kaspar the Titanic Cat* (n) and *Kensuke's Kingdom* (n).

Pink and Say
BY PATRICIA POLACCO
Grades 3 and up   *48 pages*
Philomel, 1994

Based on an incident in the life of the author-illustrator's great-great grandfather, this is the tale of two fifteen-year-old Union soldiers—one white, one black. The former is wounded while deserting his company; the latter has been separated from his black company and stumbles upon the left-for-dead white soldier. The pages that follow trace this sad chapter in American history about as well as it's ever been told for children, beginning with a visit to the black soldier's mother, who is living on a nearby plantation ravaged by the war. There the wounded boy is nursed to both health and full courage, while discovering the inhumanity of slavery. Related books: *January's Sparrow* by Patricia Polacco; *Nurse, Soldier, Spy* (p); and *Thunder at Gettysburg* by Patricia Lee Gauch. For other books by the author, see: *An Orange for Frankie* (p).

Please, Baby, Please
BY SPIKE LEE AND TONYA LEWIS LEE; KADIR NELSON, ILLUS.
Inf–Tod   *28 pages*
Simon & Schuster, 2002

This talented husband-and-wife author team offers a witty but very true-to-life picture of a rambunctious toddler's day, following her many moods from daybreak to bedtime. Toddlers will love seeing themselves in this child, especially in her more mischievous moments. The recurring use of "please" has a better chance of teaching and instilling the meaning of that lovely word than any other means. Sequel: *Please, Puppy, Please*. Related book: *Catch That Baby!* by Nancy Coffelt.

Pop! The Invention of Bubble Gum (nonfiction)
BY MEGHAN MCCARTHY
Grades K–2   *32 pages*
Simon & Schuster, 2010; e-book

Nonfiction is always a challenge for read-aloud, either because the material is often dry or because it is interesting to only a small selection of the audience. This is especially true of younger children with shallower back-grounds. So with a sigh of relief we welcome this book. First, the subject matter is near and dear to the heart of everyone who can chew: bubble gum. Second, and just as important, McCarthy offers a tasty tale that is little known and easily digested.

Back in the 1920s, a young accountant, Walter Diemer, went to work in a Philadelphia gum and candy factory. Shortly thereafter he found an experimental laboratory set up in the adjoining office, a lab where they were trying to produce a new kind of gum. When Walter was asked to keep an eye on one of the lab kettles, he found the temptation to exper-iment on his own too much to resist. What follows is the evolution of bubble gum, complete with a history of gum that goes all the way back to the Greeks. Also by the author: *City Hawk: The Story of the Pale Male*; *The Incredible Life of Balto*; *Seabiscuit the Wonder Horse*; and *Strong Man: The Story of Charles Atlas*. Related book: *The Kid Who Invented the Popsicle* (n).

The Poppy Seeds

BY CLYDE ROBERT BULLA
Grades K–2   *34 pages*
Puffin, 1994
A selfish old man who scorns the friendship and needs of his neighbors is finally reached through the kindness of a Mexican child who attempts to plant poppies in the man's yard.

Pop's Bridge

BY EVE BUNTING; C. F. PAYNE, ILLUS.
Grades K–2   *32 pages*
Harcourt Brace, 2006; e-book
Robert and Charlie watch as their fathers work on the construction of the "impossible" Golden Gate Bridge in San Francisco. Back in the 1930s, critics were saying it could never be built because of the width, the winds, and the waves. Robert's father is a high-iron man, walking the catwalks high above the fifty-foot waves. Charlie's father is a painter, facing the same dangers, but Robert quietly believes his father's job is more important than a painter's. Only when a tragedy strikes the thousand-man crew does he realize everyone confronts the same dangers, regardless of their jobs. Not only are we living a piece of American history here, we also explore the bonds of friendship and families. Related book: *The Recess Queen* by Alexis O'Neill.

Regards to the Man in the Moon

BY EZRA JACK KEATS

Grades PreS–3   *32 pages*

Four Winds, 1981

When the neighborhood children tease Louie about the junk in his backyard, his father shows him how imagination can convert rubbish into a spaceship that will take him to the farthest galaxies. The next day, Louie and his friend Susie hurtle through space in their glorified washtub and discover that not even gravity can hold back a child's imagination. The settings for Ezra Jack Keats's books are largely the inner city, but the emotions are those of all children. *Keats's Neighborhood: An Ezra Jack Keats Treasury* is an excellent anthology containing ten of Keats's best, including *The Snowy Day; Goggles!; Whistle for Willie; Peter's Chair;* and *Apt. 3.* Included is an excellent essay on Keats by Anita Silvey. Related books: *The Junkyard Wonders* by Patricia Polacco; and for younger children, *Red Wagon* by Renata Liwska.

Richard Wright and the Library Card (nonfiction)

BY WILLIAM MILLER; GREGORY CHRISTIE, ILLUS.

Grades 2–5   *32 pages*

Lee & Low, 1999

Growing up in segregated Mississippi in the 1920s, young Richard Wright had an insatiable hunger for print that only a library card could satisfy. Unfortunately, his skin color prevented him from owning one. So as a young janitor, the future author of *Native Son* and *Black Boy* conspired with a white man to beat the system. Related books for younger students: *More Than Anything Else* (Booker T. Washington learns to read) by Marie Bradby; *Tomás and the Library Lady* by Pat Mora, the childhood story of Tomás Rivera, the son of migrant workers who became a university chancellor; and *Words Set Me Free: The Story of Young Frederick Douglass* by Lesa Cline-Ransome.

Rikki-Tikki-Tavi

BY RUDYARD KIPLING; ADAPTED AND ILLUSTRATED BY JERRY PINKNEY

Grades K–4   *44 pages*

Morrow, 1997

Rikki is a fearless mongoose adopted by a family in India to protect their child. In no time, he is tested by the cunning cobra snakes that live in the garden. Made famous by Kipling a century ago, this tale features a ferocious fight between the mongoose and snakes and is not for the timid.

The Rough-Face Girl

BY RAFE MARTIN; DAVID SHANNON, ILLUS.

Grades 1–4   *32 pages*
Puffin, 1998

There are more than seven hundred different versions of Cinderella from various cultures. This is a retelling of the Algonquin Indian version, complete with the evil sisters who try to betray "Cinderella." In this case, she is known as the rough-face girl, because sparks from the campfire have scarred her face through the years. Another retelling of Cinderella can be found in *Mufaro's Beautiful Daughters* by John Steptoe. Other books about Native Americans: *The Boy Who Lived with the Seals* by Rafe Martin; *Knots on a Counting Rope* by Bill Martin Jr. and John Archambault; and *The Legend of the Bluebonnet* (p). For other picture book fairy tales, see page 292.

The Secret Shortcut (series)

BY MARK TEAGUE

Grades PreS–K   *32 pages*
Scholastic, 1996

Wendell and Floyd are in trouble with their teacher for being late for school every day. She doesn't understand how hard they're trying: Every shortcut they take to save time is a turn for the worse. They meet pirates one day, a plague of frogs the next, even spacemen. It's their last secret shortcut—the jungle route—that turns out to be the best and muddiest of all. Sequels: *Lost & Found* and *One Halloween Night*.

The Seven Silly Eaters

BY MARY ANN HOBERMAN; MARLA FRAZEE, ILLUS.

Grades K–3   *38 pages*
Harcourt Brace, 1997

There are seven children in the Peters family and, unfortunately, each has a different favorite food that must be specially prepared or the child will not eat. Mrs. Peters is at her wits' end and worn to a frazzle trying to cook these specialties three times a day. When her birthday arrives, she's certain her children won't remember it—but she's wrong. They're up all night scheming, and their birthday present accidentally solves her cooking dilemma forever. Also by the author/poet: *Forget-Me-Nots* and *A House Is a House for Me*. Also by the illustrator: *A Couple of Boys Have the Best Week Ever*.

The Silver Pony

BY LYND WARD
Grades PreS–4   *176 pages*
Houghton Mifflin, 1973

A classic wordless book (and the longest published for children), this is the heartwarming story of a lonely farm boy and the flights of fancy he uses to escape his isolation. His imaginative trips take place on a winged pony and carry him to distant parts of the world to aid and comfort other lonely children. Also by the author: *The Biggest Bear* (p). For more wordless books, see the list on page 175.

Six Men

BY DAVID MCKEE
Grades K and up   *36 pages*
North-South, 2011

It is the rare artist who can take thirty-six small pages, fill them with simple words and simple black-and-white line drawings, and end up with a classic myth explaining the cravings of our species for peace and war. From its first page and its single sentence, we know this is something special: "Once upon a time there were six men who traveled the world searching for a place where they could live and work in peace." How that quest grows into a war with their neighbors is the story of civilization, a tale powerful enough to make audiences of any age stop and wonder. This is a book for not only our time, but all times. Related book: *The Story of Ferdinand* by Munro Leaf.

Snip Snap! What's That?

BY MARA BERGMAN; NICK MALAND, ILLUS.
Grades PreS–K   *30 pages*
Greenwillow, 2005

This is a happy mix of *We're Going on a Bear Hunt* (p), *The Little Old Lady Who Was Not Afraid of Anything* (p), and *There's a Nightmare in My Closet* by Mercer Mayer. An alligator comes calling at the children's door. As it and they move from room to room, the question is asked, "Were they afraid?" eliciting the response (louder and louder each time), "You bet they were!" Until they gather their courage and turn on the creature, driving him out. Was he scared? This is great fun with a group or class. Related book: *The Squeaky Door* retold by Margaret Read MacDonald.

Somebody Loves You, Mr. Hatch

BY EILEEN SPINELLI; PAUL YALOWITZ, ILLUS.

Grades K and up   30 pages

Simon & Schuster, 1991

This book about friendship and loneliness has been in print for twenty years! Mr. Hatch is a lonely little man who has no friends. But one day a box of Valentine chocolates is delivered to him by mistake, changing his life forever. Related books: *The Lemonade Club* by Patricia Polacco; and *Marshall Armstrong Is New to Our School* (p). For more friendship books, see the list on page 192.

The Story of Little Babaji

BY HELEN BANNERMAN; FRED MARCELLINO, ILLUS.

Grades Tod–K   68 (small) pages

Harper, 1996

Reset in India (where it originally was written in 1899), redrawn with Indian characters, and with the offending names removed, this is nearly word for word the original *Story of Little Black Sambo*. The original version rightly fell from favor in the 1950s, but this retelling corrects the earlier offenses and allows children to enjoy the battle of wits between the child and the boy-eating tigers. Other versions of this tale include: *Little Britches and the Rattlers* by Eric A. Kimmel; and *Pancakes for Supper* by Anne Isaacs.

The Story of Ruby Bridges (nonfiction)

BY ROBERT COLES; GEORGE FORD, ILLUS.

Grades 1–5   26 pages

Scholastic, 1995

From the pen of a Pulitzer Prize–winning research psychiatrist comes the true story of six-year-old Ruby Bridges, one of four black children selected by a federal judge to integrate the New Orleans public schools in 1960. Escorted to the school doors by federal marshals, Ruby had to pass through a gauntlet of curses and spittle. Whispering prayers and backed by her parents' love, the child withstood the daily attacks without bitterness. Ruby Bridges herself expands on Coles's work in *Through My Eyes*, updating the story and including photographs taken during and after the integration conflict. For related books, see *Roll of Thunder, Hear My Cry* (n).

The vestiges of Ruby's story have been seen in literature through the years. It was a searing event in Steinbeck's *Travels with Charley* and is widely believed to be the inspiration for Norman Rockwell's famous illustration *The Problem We All Live With*. Both the Rockwell and Steinbeck connections can be found online at http://kenlairdstudios.hubpages.com/hub/The-Problem-We-All-Live-With-Norman-Rockwell-the-truth-about-his-famous-painting.

The Super Hungry Dinosaur

BY MARTIN WADDELL; LEONIE LORD, ILLUS.

Grades Tod–PreK   *32 pages*

Dial, 2009

A small boy and his dog are playing in the backyard when a super hungry dinosaur arrives and announces he's going to eat up the boy. The ensuing simple tale details how the lad and his dog outwit and tame the dinosaur. And any damage done by the dinosaur's rampage is fixed by the exasperated creature before he can have lunch (cooked by Mom). Martin Waddell uses the same simple storytelling here that made his earlier book *Owl Babies* so successful, and illustrator Leonie Lord turns what could have been a threatening story into an exciting but nonthreatening adventure. Together they have created the perfect toddler/preschool book.

High-Scoring Sports Picture Books

All-Star! Honus Wagner and the Most Famous Baseball Card Ever by Jane Yolen

America's Champion Swimmer: Gertrude Ederle by David A. Adler

Baseball Saved Us by Ken Mochizuki

Brothers at Bat by Audrey Vernick

Casey at the Bat by Ernest Thayer (C. F. Payne, illus.)

Eddie, Harold's Little Brother by Ed Koch and Pat Koch Thaler

The Greatest Skating Race by Louise Borden

Major Taylor: Champion Cyclist by Lesa Cline-Ransome

Mighty Jackie: The Strike-Out Queen by Marissa Moss

A Nation's Hope: The Story of Boxing Legend Joe Louis by Matt de la Peña

Oliver's Game by Matt Tavares

Roberto Clemente by Jonah Winter

Salt in His Shoes: Michael Jordan in Pursuit of a Dream by Deloris Jordan and Roslyn M. Jordan

Shoeless Joe & Black Betsy by Phil Bildner

Teammates by Peter Golenbock

There Goes Ted Williams by Matt Tavares

Wilma Unlimited: How Wilma Rudolph Became the World's Fastest Woman by Kathleen Krull

Sylvester and the Magic Pebble

BY WILLIAM STEIG

Grades PreS–4   30 pages

Simon & Schuster, 1969

In this contemporary fairy tale and Caldecott Medal winner, young Sylvester finds a magic pebble that will grant his every wish as long as he holds it in his hand. When a hungry lion approaches, Sylvester wishes himself into a stone. The pebble drops to the ground and he can't reach it to wish himself normal again. The subsequent loneliness of both Sylvester and his parents is portrayed with deep sensitivity, making all the more real their joy a year later when they are happily reunited. Also by the author: *The Amazing Bone*; *Brave Irene* (p); *Doctor De Soto*; *Pete's a Pizza*; *The Toy Brother*; and *Zeke Pippin*.

Ten Little Fingers and Ten Little Toes

BY MEM FOX; HELEN OXENBURY, ILLUS.

Inf–Tod   36 pages

Harcourt, 2008

Here are two widely accepted facts among early childhood educators: (1) children gravitate first to rhyming words (thus the success of Mother Goose and Dr. Seuss); and (2) children gravitate to images of other children, especially babies to babies. Apply those facts to the most recent efforts of the popular Mem Fox and illustrator Helen Oxenbury and you end up with what may become their biggest picture book success ever. With the multiethnic flavor of the book and boys and girls equally present, I can't think of a better gift for the new baby. It is available also as a board book. Also by the author: *Two Little Monkeys*. Related books: *Gossie* (p); *Ten Little Babies* by Gyo Fujikawa; and *The Neighborhood Mother Goose* (p).

Thank You, Sarah: The Woman Who Saved Thanksgiving (nonfiction)

BY LAURIE HALSE ANDERSON; MATT FAULKNER, ILLUS.

Grades K–3   40 pages

Scholastic, 2002

By the middle of the 1800s, only New England states were observing Thanksgiving, to the chagrin of Sarah Hale, widowed mother of five and the editor of America's most popular women's magazine. So she began a campaign to make the day a national holiday, an effort that fell on the deaf ears of four straight presidents. Hale had not only written them letters but also urged her readers to do the same—and they did, by the tens of thousands, all to no avail. They couldn't vote, so no president had to listen to them. Then came the fifth president, a man carrying a great sorrow in his heart but still aware of how much he and we should be grateful for— Abraham Lincoln. Also by the author: *Independent Dames: What You Never Knew About the Women and Girls of the American Revolution*. Related books: *Molly's Pilgrim* (p) and *Milly and the Macy's Parade* by Shana Corey, which uses a fictionalized young girl to uncover the origins of the famous Macy's Thanksgiving Day Parade. Based on a true anecdote, the tale revolves around a thousand Macy's employees who are recent immigrants and homesick for lands where costume parades and street festivals are the norm.

There's Going to Be a Baby

BY JOHN BURNINGHAM; HELEN OXENBURY, ILLUS.
Grades PreS–K   *46 pages*
Candlewick, 2010
Of all the books about new siblings, this is the best. Mother tells her little boy that she is going to have a baby, and then entertains his questions, including what will the baby "do." The mother then offers a list of various occupations the child might someday enjoy while the boy's imagination runs wild with a baby sibling working at the zoo or doctoring or landscaping or banking, with many humorous results. In the end, the boy shares his conclusions with Grandpa as they approach the hospital for their first visit with the new arrival. Also by the illustrator: *Ten Little Fingers and Ten Little Toes* (p) and *King Jack and the Dragon*. Related book: *Catch That Baby!* by Nancy Coffelt.

Thomas' Snowsuit

BY ROBERT MUNSCH; MICHAEL MARTCHENKO, ILLUS.
Grades PreS–4   *24 pages*
Annick, 1985
Thomas hates his new snowsuit, much to the dismay of his mother, his teacher, and his principal—all of whom find him a most determined fellow. But children will find the situation just plain funny and loaded with old-fashioned slapstick. Also by the author: *The Boy in the Drawer; David's Father; 50 Below Zero; I Have to Go!; Moira's Birthday; Mortimer;* and *The Paper Bag Princess*.

Tikki Tikki Tembo

BY ARLENE MOSEL; BLAIR LENT, ILLUS.
Grades PreS–3 40 pages
Henry Holt, 1968
This little picture book tells the amusing legend of how the Chinese people stopped giving their first-born sons incredibly long first names and started giving all children short names. Related books with Asian settings: *Beautiful Warrior: The Legend of the Nun's Kung Fu* by Emily Arnold McCully; *The Boy Who Drew Cats* retold by Arthur A. Levine; *Crow Boy* by Taro Yashima; *The Emperor and the Kite* by Jane Yolen; *Kamishibai Man* by Allen Say; and *The Voice of the Great Bell* by Lafcadio Hearn.

Tintin in Tibet (comic book)

BY HERGÉ
Grades 2–4 62 pages
Little, Brown, 1975
When you've been in print for nearly eighty years, translated into eighty languages, praised by presidential advisers (Arthur Schlesinger Jr.), and made into movies by Peter Jackson and Stephen Spielberg, you must be special. Tintin is just that. He's the boy detective/reporter who hopscotches the globe in pursuit of thieves and smugglers. Loaded with humor, adventure, and marvelous artwork (seven hundred pictures in each issue), *Tintin* has special appeal for parents who want to assist their child in reading: Each *Tintin* contains more than eight thousand words. Having heard *Tintin* read aloud, children will want to obtain his other adventures and read them by themselves, oblivious to the fact that they are reading so many words in the process. Because of the size of the pictures, *Tintin* is best read aloud to no more than two children at a time. Furthermore, a comic book should be read aloud to the child only a few times—to show the child how a comic book works so that then he can read to himself.

Beginning in 1994, *Tintin*'s American publisher began issuing the comics in hardcover, three to a volume. Related books in comic format: *Bone #1: Out from Boneville* (series) by Jeff Smith; and Little Lit, an excellent series of stories told in comic format, selected and edited by Art Spiegelman and Françoise Mouly: *Folklore & Fairy Tale Funnies*; *Strange Stories for Strange Kids*; and *It Was a Dark and Silly Night*.

Toy Boat

BY RANDALL DE SÈVE; LOREN LONG, ILLUS.

Grades PreS–K   32 pages
Philomel, 2007

A young boy builds a toy boat out of a can, a cork, a yellow pencil, and some white cloth. Together they bathe, sleep, and play together. But beneath the surface, the little boat yearns to make it on his own, out of reach and on the high seas—not unlike *The Little Engine That Could* or *Little Toot*. All children will identify with this tale because it's analogous to the yearning of any child to be done with "baby stuff" and get on with becoming a grown-up—or at least a "big kid." Books like this offer a gentle warning: Take it easy, kid; it's not all fun 'n' games out there. Enjoy the comforts of home while you have them. This is a common thread in Bill Peet's books, including: *The Caboose Who Got Loose*; *Fly Homer Fly*; *Smokey*; and *The Whingdingdilly* (p).

The True Story of the Three Little Pigs

BY JOHN SCIESZKA; LANE SMITH, ILLUS.

Grades K and up   28 pages
Viking, 1989

For two hundred years we've taken the word of the three little pigs as gospel truth. But when the author presents the infamous wolf's side of the story, we get an implausible but entertainingly different point of view. This book began a wave of fairy-tale parodies by other authors, many of which are listed on page 294. Related books: *The Three Little Aliens and the Big Bad Robot* by Margaret McNamara; *The Three Little Wolves and the Big Bad Pig* by Eugene Trivizas; and *The Three Pigs* by David Wiesner.

The Ugly Duckling

BY HANS CHRISTIAN ANDERSEN; ROBERT INGPEN, ILLUS.

Grades 1 and up   34 pages
Penguin, 2005

It is a special book that unites one of the world's great storytellers with one of the world's great illustrators, and that's what this classic volume does brilliantly in a traditional telling of the ugly duckling, ridiculed by his brothers and sisters, who leaves home in search of beauty and finds it within himself. Related books: *Chicken Big* by Keith Graves; *Eleanor* (Roosevelt) by Barbara Cooney; *Marshall Armstrong Is New to Our School* (p); *The Ugly Truckling* by David Gordon; Jane Yolen's picture book biography, *The Perfect Wizard: Hans Christian Andersen*, author of the original ugly duckling; and *Thumbelina* adapted by Brad Sneed.

The Very Hungry Caterpillar

BY ERIC CARLE

Grades Tod–1   *38 pages*

Philomel, 1969

What an ingenious book! It is a simple, lovely way to teach a child at once the days of the week, how to count to five, and how a caterpillar becomes a butterfly. First, this is a book to look at, with bright, bright pictures. Then it is something whose pages beg to be turned—pages that have little round holes in them made by the hungry little caterpillar. And as the number of holes grows, so does the caterpillar. Other books by the author: *The Grouchy Ladybug*; *Mister Seahorse*; *The Very Busy Spider*; *The Very Clumsy Click Beetle*; and *The Very Lonely Firefly*.

Wagon Wheels

BY BARBARA BRENNER; DON BOLOGNESE, ILLUS.

Grades K–2   *64 pages*

Harper, 1993

In four short chapters, this story can be read either as a long picture book or as an introduction to chapter books. Three young black brothers follow a map to their father's homestead on the western plains. The children brave storms, fires, and famine to reach their goal. For other historical fiction and nonfiction picture books, see page 205.

We're Going on a Bear Hunt

BY MICHAEL ROSEN; HELEN OXENBURY, ILLUS.

Grades Tod–K   *32 pages*

Atheneum, 1992

A family hunts a bear through field, river, swamp, forest, and snowstorm (with predictable, appropriate sounds and movement). When they find him, he hunts them back home via the same route and sounds. See the list of predictable/cumulative books on page 176. For an affectionate look at bears: *You Can Do It, Sam* (p). A similar tale with an alligator and greater tension in the story: *Snip Snap! What's That?* (p).

When Jessie Came Across the Sea

BY AMY HEST; P. J. LYNCH, ILLUS.

Grades 1–5   *32 pages*

Candlewick, 1997

The courageous and bittersweet tale of American immigration is told in the story of a Jewish orphan girl from Eastern Europe who receives a one-way ticket to America from the village rabbi. This great opportunity is tempered by the fact she must leave her grandmother, the only relative she has in the world. The girl's courage in the New World and her eventual reunion with her grandmother make this an inspiring story. Related books: *Molly's Pilgrim* (p); *Naming Liberty* (p); *Streets of Gold* retold by Rosemary Wells; and the novel *Lupita Mañana* by Patricia Beatty.

Where the Wild Things Are

BY MAURICE SENDAK

Grades K–3   *28 pages*

Harper, 1963

This is the 1963 Caldecott winner that changed the course of modern children's literature. Sendak creates a fantasy about a little boy and the monsters that haunt and fascinate children. The fact that youngsters are not the least bit frightened by the story, that they love it as they would an old friend, is a credit to Sendak's insight into children's minds and hearts. Also by the author: *In the Night Kitchen*. Related books: *The Super Hungry Dinosaur* (p); and *There's a Nightmare in My Closet* by Mercer Mayer.

Where's My Teddy? (series)

BY JEZ ALBOROUGH

Grades PreS–K   *24 pages*

Candlewick, 1997

Alborough has created three popular books in this series about little Eddie and the giant bear who lives in the park. Here, in their first encounter, Eddie mistakenly ends up with the bear's teddy and the bear has his. Though each is equally afraid of the other, they both finally end up with the right teddy. In the second book (*It's the Bear!*), Eddie's mother is a nonbeliever until she and the bear come face-to-face (reminiscent of Robert McCloskey's *Blueberries for Sal*). In the third book (*My Friend Bear*), their fear of each other is happily resolved when each realizes how much they have in common—including that needless fear of each other and a love of their teddies. Related book: *Bun Bun Button* by Patricia Polacco.

Where's My Truck?

BY KAREN BEAUMONT; DAVID CATROW, ILLUS.

Grades Tod–PreS   *30 pages*

Dial, 2011

In rhyming verse, we follow the travails of little Tommy, who has lost his favorite red truck. He looks everywhere—inside, outside, high, and low—and begs his father, mother, sister, brother, all to no avail. And then Tommy notices, over by the fence where his dog is digging . . . Also by the author-illustrator team: *Doggone Dogs!*; *I Ain't Gonna Paint No More!*; and *I Like Myself!* Related books: *Have You Seen Duck?* by Janet Holmes. For PreS–K: *Bun Bun Button* by Patricia Polacco; *Dogger* by Shirley Hughes; *Little Blue Truck* and *Little Blue Truck Leads the Way* by Alice Schertle; and *Shoe Baby* by Joyce Dunbar.

Where's Waldo? (series)

BY MARTIN HANDFORD
Grades PreS–4   26 pages
Little, Brown, 1987

Waldo is a hiker on a worldwide trek who plays hide-and-seek with the reader-viewer, who has to find him as he threads his way through thousands of people populating a dozen different landscapes. Children will spend hours searching the pages for Waldo and the checklist of more than three hundred items at the end of the book. Also note that in each scene Waldo loses one of his twelve personal items. Books like this stretch children's attention spans while polishing visual discrimination. (They should also be required equipment for anyone taking a child under six to a restaurant or church.) Sequels: *The Great Waldo Search*; *Where's Waldo? The Fantastic Journey*; and *Where's Waldo? In Hollywood*.

The writer/photographer team of Jean Marzollo and Walter Wick offer a similar challenge with the I Spy photo book series, including: *I Spy Extreme Challenger!*; *I Spy Gold Challenger!*; and *I Spy Year-Round Challenger!* Walter Wick created a less challenging series of "search and find" books for younger children, which includes: *Can You See What I See?*; *Can You See What I See? Dream Machine*; *Can You See What I See? Cool Collections*; and *Can You See What I See? Toyland Express*.

The Whingdingdilly

BY BILL PEET
Grades PreS–5   60 pages
Houghton Mifflin, 1970

Using animals to make his points, Bill Peet explores the human condition in a way that helps us all to better understand each other. Typical is this book: Discontented with his life as a dog, Scamp envies all the attention given to his beribboned neighbor—Palomar, the wonder horse. But when a backwoods witch changes Scamp into an animal with the feet of an elephant, the neck of a giraffe, the tail of a zebra, and the nose of a rhinoceros, he gets more attention than he bargained for: He ends up a most unhappy circus freak. But all ends well, and tied into the ending is a subtle lesson for both Scamp and his readers: Be yourself!

Among Peet's most popular titles are: *Big Bad Bruce*; *The Caboose Who Got Loose*; *Eli*; *Encore for Eleanor*; *Farewell to Shady Glade*; *Fly, Homer, Fly*; *How Droofus the Dragon Lost His Head*; *Kermit the Hermit*; *Randy's Dandy Lions*; and *The Wump World*. See also *Bill Peet: An Autobiography*, a Caldecott Honor winner with an illustration on each of its 180 pages.

The Wolf Who Cried Boy

BY BOB HARTMAN; TIM RAGLIN, ILLUS.

Grades K–3   *30 pages*

Putnam, 2002

In this clever takeoff on the traditional tale (see *The Boy Who Cried Wolf* retold by B. G. Hennessy), we meet Little Wolf, a stubborn cub with an appetite for junk food like "chipmunks and dip." His parents, on the other hand, insist that he eat the nourishing foods they serve, like three-pig salad. They do concede, however, that in the good old days before Little Wolf was born, when shepherd boys were plentiful, there was nothing as tasty as boy chops, baked boy-tato, and boys-n-berry pie! All of this whets both Little Wolf's appetite and his imagination, so the next day he sounds the alarm that he's spotted a boy. By the time his parents finish a long and fruitless search, their dinner is burned and they must content themselves with junk food. Which is just what Little Wolf wanted in the first place! So he tries it again the next day—and we all know what's coming: a Boy Scout! Related books: *I Am So Strong* by Mario Ramos; and *Betsy Who Cried Wolf!* by Gail Carson Levine. For a list of other picture book parodies, see page 294.

The Wretched Stone

BY CHRIS VAN ALLSBURG

Grades 2–7   *30 pages*

Houghton Mifflin, 1991

When the crew members of a clipper ship sailing tropical seas discover a desert island, they also find a large gray stone, luminous and with one smooth side. When it is brought on board, an eerie change begins to envelop the ship. Fascinated by the rock, the crew members gradually desert their work and leisure activities, spending more and more time gazing in silent numbness at the rock—despite the protestations of their captain. A powerful allegory about the effects of television on society.

Van Allsburg's other books include: *Ben's Dream*; *The Garden of Abdul*

Gasazi; *Jumanji*; *Just a Dream*; *The Mysteries of Harris Burdick*; *The Polar Express*; *The Stranger*; *The Sweetest Fig*; *Two Bad Ants*; *The Widow's Broom*; *The Wreck of the Zephyr*; and *The Z Was Zapped* (an unusual alphabet book).

You Can Do It, Sam (series)

BY AMY HEST, ANITA JERAM, ILLUS.

Grades Tod–PreS   *28 pages*

Candlewick, 2003

If ever a picture book series deserved the adjective *cozy*, this is it. Mrs. Bear and her cub Sam are baking little cakes together, licking bowls, packing the cakes, and finally driving through the snow to deliver them as surprises to neighbors. The title comes from Sam's concern over whether he can carry each package all the way to the doorstep by himself. This is the third book in the series. Also in the series: *Kiss Good Night* and *Don't You Feel Well, Sam?* For older children, Amy Hest is also the author of *When Jessie Came Across the Sea* (p). Related book: *Maudie and Bear* by Jan Ormerod.

Short Novels

Jim's Favorite Kindergarten Novels
(in order of difficulty)

Two Times the Fun by Beverly Cleary

Look Out, Jeremy Bean! by Alice Schertle

Junie B. Jones and the Stupid Smelly Bus by Barbara Park

The Chalk Box Kid by Clyde Robert Bulla

Dinosaurs Before Dark by Mary Pope Osborne

My Father's Dragon by Ruth Stiles Gannett

Mostly Monty by Johanna Hurwitz

The Stories Julian Tells by Ann Cameron

Chocolate Fever by Robert Kimmel Smith

James and the Giant Peach by Roald Dahl

The Water Horse by Dick King-Smith

Baseball in April
BY GARY SOTO
Grades 6 and up   *107 pages*
Harcourt Brace, 1990

A product of the Latino community in Fresno, California, Soto grew up with a cement factory across the street, a junkyard next door, and a raisin factory at the end of the street. This collection of eleven short stories is largely based on his early teen years, filled with the bittersweet laughter and tears found in all adolescent lives. Also by the author: the short story collections *Living Up the Street*; *Local News*; and *Help Wanted*.

Be a Perfect Person in Just Three Days!
BY STEPHEN MANES
Grades 2–5   *76 pages*
Yearling, 1996

If any subversive person is interested in sneaking in a little laughter among the many serious books these days about orphans, vampires, and post-apocalyptic children, this is for that person. A young boy, tired of being the brunt of everyone's taunts, begins a do-it-yourself course in becoming perfect—with hilarious and unpredictable results. Conclusion: Nobody's perfect, even the popular kids.

The Bears' House
BY MARILYN SACHS
Grades 4–6   *82 pages*
iUniverse, 2008

A perfect vehicle for a classroom discussion of values, this novel portrays a ten-year-old girl whose mother is ill and can no longer care for her family after the father deserts them. The girl decides to tend to the family while suffering the taunts of classmates because she sucks her thumb, wears dirty clothes, and smells. To escape, she retreats to the fantasy world she has created in an old dollhouse in her classroom. Sequel: *Fran Ellen's House*. Related books: *The Great Gilly Hopkins* by Katherine Paterson; and *The Hundred Dresses* (s).

The Best Christmas Pageant Ever
BY BARBARA ROBINSON
Grades 2–6   *80 pages*
Harper, 1972; e-book

What happens when the worst-behaved family of kids in town comes to Sunday school and muscles into all the parts for the Christmas pageant? The results are zany and heartwarming; a most unusual Christmas story. Sequels: *The Best School Year Ever* and *The Best Halloween Ever*. There is also an excellent CD recording of the three novels, narrated by Broadway's Elaine Stritch: *The Best Barbara Robinson CD Audio Collection Ever*.

A Blue-Eyed Daisy
BY CYNTHIA RYLANT
Grades 4–8   *99 pages*
Simon & Schuster, 1985; e-book
This is about a warm yet bittersweet year in the life of an eleven-year-old girl and her family in the hills of West Virginia as she experiences her first kiss, has a brush with death, comes to understand her good but hard-drinking father, and begins to grow into the person you'd love to have as a relative. Related books: *Because of Winn-Dixie* (n); and *Ida Early Comes Over the Mountain* by Robert Burch.

Cam Jansen: The Mystery of the Dinosaur Bones (series)
BY DAVID ADLER
Grades 1–3   *56 pages*
Puffin, 1997; e-book
Thanks to Cam Jansen's photographic memory, little escapes her notice in this easy mystery series that now comprises more than twenty books. You might say she's a grade school Nancy Drew, but with far fewer pages per book. In this volume, when Cam's class visits the museum's dinosaur room, she quickly notes that three of the skeleton's bones are missing. This is an excellent introduction to the mystery genre. For the next older audience, go to *Encyclopedia Brown and the Case of the Carnival Crime* by Donald J. Sobol, starring the local police chief's ten-year-old son, who is always too smart for the crime crowd. Each book in the ongoing series contains nearly a dozen six-page crimes and their solutions.

Chocolate Fever
BY ROBERT K. SMITH
Grades 1–3   *94 pages*
Dell, 1978
Henry Green doesn't just like chocolate—he's crazy about it. He even has chocolate sprinkles on his cereal and chocolate cake for breakfast. He thus is a prime candidate to come down with the world's first case of "chocolate fever." Funny, with a subtle message about moderation. *Jelly Belly*, also by the author, uses humor and insight to describe the self-image

problems of an overweight child. In both *Jelly Belly* and *The War with Grandpa*, Smith paints a powerful picture of the relationship between child and grandparent.

Dinosaurs Before Dark (series)

BY MARY POPE OSBORNE

Grades K–2   *76 pages*

Random House, 1992; e-book

In this first book of the popular time-travel series (with three- to four-page chapters), young Annie and Jack discover a tree house that transports them back in time to the age of dinosaurs. The journey is filled with fantasy adventure while exploring scientific, cultural, or historic places and events.

The Friendship

BY MILDRED TAYLOR

Grades 4 and up   *53 pages*

Dial, 1987

The Logan children, from *Roll of Thunder, Hear My Cry* (n), witness the searing cruelty of bigotry during this story set in 1933 in rural Mississippi, where two men (one white, one black) see their onetime friendship destroyed by violence when the black man dares to call the other by his first name. Readers should be aware of racial epithets in the context of the story. For other books by the author and related titles, see *Roll of Thunder, Hear My Cry* (n).

Frindle

BY ANDREW CLEMENTS

Grades 3–6   *105 pages*

Simon & Schuster, 1996; e-book

This book will have you laughing out loud by paragraph five, nodding in affirmation of its wisdom throughout, and wiping the tears away at its end. The story is what education, family, and relationships are supposed to be about, never mind what a good book can do for the reading appetite. And—it's fall-down funny. Oh, yes, it's about the dictionary, too. (So be sure to have a copy of the picture book *Noah Webster and His Words* by Jeri Chase Ferris nearby.) No author rivals Clements in capturing the soul of the American classroom. Also by the author: *About Average*; *Extra Credit*; *The Jacket*; *The Janitor's Boy*; *The Landry News*; *The Last Holiday Concert*; *Lost and Found*; *Lunch Money*; *No Talking*; *The Report Card*; *Troublemaker*; and *A Week in the Woods*.

Gooney Bird Greene (series)

BY LOIS LOWRY

Grades K–2   *88 pages*

Houghton Mifflin, 2002; e-book

Gooney Bird Greene is the antithesis of Junie B. Jones in civil behavior but a carbon copy in uniqueness and irrepressibility. Second-grader Gooney Bird is smart, mature, kind, and in charge at all times—or at least she wants to be, which sometimes presents a challenge for the teacher. But on the first day in her new school it's clear she is mysterious and interesting. Her clothes are unusual. Her hairstyles are unusual. Even her lunches are unusual. On her second day at school, she was wearing a pink ballet tutu over green stretch pants, and she had three small red grapes, an avocado, and an oatmeal cookie for lunch. Just as Gooney wins over her classmates and teacher, she'll win over her readers. Sequels: *Gooney Bird and the Room Mother*; *Gooney the Fabulous*; *Gooney Bird Is So Absurd*; and *Gooney Bird on the Map*. The Newbery-winning Lowry has long been one of our most gifted writers for children, and this series proves again her great versatility.

The Half-a-Moon Inn

BY PAUL FLEISCHMAN

Grades 2–6   *88 pages*

Harper, 1980

A chilling fantasy-adventure story about a mute boy separated from his mother by a blizzard and later kidnapped by the wicked proprietress of a village inn. Fast-moving, white-knuckle reading.

Herbie Jones (series)

BY SUZY KLINE

Grades 1–4   *95 pages*

Putnam, 1985

Third-grader Herbie and his irrepressible pal Raymond meet the challenges and trials of third grade—from escaping the bottom reading group to escaping the girls' bathroom. All of it is done with a blend of sensitivity and humor, topped off with some sidesplitting "gross-outs." Also by the author: *Herbie Jones and the Birthday Showdown*; *Herbie Jones and the Class Gift*; *Herbie Jones and the Dark Attic*; *Herbie Jones and the Monster Ball*; *Herbie Jones and Hamburger Head*; and *What's the Matter with Herbie Jones?* For younger readers, see Kline's Horrible Harry series.

The Hundred Dresses

BY ELEANOR ESTES

Grades 3–6   *78 pages*

Harcourt Brace, 1944

Wanda Petronski comes from the wrong side of the tracks and is the object of class jokes, until her classmates sadly realize their awful mistake and cruelty. But by then it's too late. Though written more than sixty years ago, the book has a message about peer pressure that has lost none of its power or relevance in an age of bullying. Related book: *The Bears' House* (s).

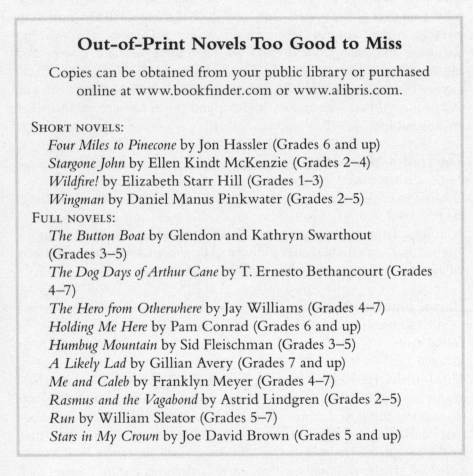

Out-of-Print Novels Too Good to Miss

Copies can be obtained from your public library or purchased online at www.bookfinder.com or www.alibris.com.

SHORT NOVELS:

Four Miles to Pinecone by Jon Hassler (Grades 6 and up)

Stargone John by Ellen Kindt McKenzie (Grades 2–4)

Wildfire! by Elizabeth Starr Hill (Grades 1–3)

Wingman by Daniel Manus Pinkwater (Grades 2–5)

FULL NOVELS:

The Button Boat by Glendon and Kathryn Swarthout (Grades 3–5)

The Dog Days of Arthur Cane by T. Ernesto Bethancourt (Grades 4–7)

The Hero from Otherwhere by Jay Williams (Grades 4–7)

Holding Me Here by Pam Conrad (Grades 6 and up)

Humbug Mountain by Sid Fleischman (Grades 3–5)

A Likely Lad by Gillian Avery (Grades 7 and up)

Me and Caleb by Franklyn Meyer (Grades 4–7)

Rasmus and the Vagabond by Astrid Lindgren (Grades 2–5)

Run by William Sleator (Grades 5–7)

Stars in My Crown by Joe David Brown (Grades 5 and up)

Junie B. Jones and the Stupid Smelly Bus (series)

BY BARBARA PARK

Grades K–1   70 pages

Random House, 1992; e-book

Don't be put off by the title of this book, part of a wonderfully funny series (more than thirty books to date). Junie B. is Ramona, Little Lulu, and Lucy all rolled into one determined kindergartner. The twenty-two million copies sold in the Junie series is proof positive how popular she is. Related book: *Gooney Bird Greene* (s). Park's other books, like *Mick Harte Was Here* (s) and *Skinnybones* (s), are aimed at older students and demonstrate why she's consistently a state award winner with children. See page 117 for a discussion of the Junie B. series and its issues.

Keeper of the Doves

BY BETSY BYARS

Grades 3–6   121 pages

Viking, 2002; e-book

This could be among the best work of Byars's distinguished career. The bulk of this tale, which takes place in 1897, focuses on a precocious girl named Amen (the last of five daughters), and follows her from birth to age eight. There is much humor, thanks to the mischievous twins assigned to raise Amen. They are just two years older and prone to exaggeration and great flights of fancy. Always lurking in the background is the mysterious Mr. Tominski, the wild-eyed recluse who saved Amen's father's life when the latter was a boy, thus earning him a place of refuge with the family but not exemption from the torment of the twins. And when their ill-considered words about him possibly cause his accidental death, Amen and the reader have much to think about. For other books by the author, see *The Midnight Fox* (n).

Kindred Souls

BY PATRICIA MACLACHLIN

Grades 2–5   117 pages

Harper, 2012

Like her famous Newbery winner, *Sarah, Plain and Tall*, this novella is set on the American plains but in contemporary times. It's a plain farm, populated by six people and a dog that appeared one day out of nowhere. The central characters are eighty-eight-year-old grandfather Billy, his youngest grandson, Jake, and Lucy the dog. Off on the farm's hillside are the decayed remains of the sod house that Billy grew up in, a site that brings back the happiest of memories for the old man. Gradually it's decided that young Jake will attempt to rebuild the sod house as a favor for his grandfather, something the boy feels is beyond his capabilities. When Billy needs to be temporarily hospitalized, the whole family pitches in to finish the house as a gift for him. A warm and loving portrait of what family can be and how affection works as a powerful force when decent, loving people rub against one another all day long, willing to go the extra mile for each other.

Lafcadio, the Lion Who Shot Back

BY SHEL SILVERSTEIN
Grades 2–6   *90 pages*
Harper, 1963
Lafcadio decides he isn't satisfied being a lion—he must become a marksman and man-about-town and painter and world traveler and . . . He tries just about everything and anything in hopes of finding happiness. If only he'd try being himself. A witty and thought-provoking book, it was Silverstein's first for children; for his other titles, see *Where the Sidewalk Ends* (po). Related book: *Malcolm at Midnight* (n).

Lawn Boy

BY GARY PAULSEN
Grades 4–7   *96 pages*
Wendy Lamb Books, 2007; e-book
Lawn Boy, unlike most of Paulsen's other books, is very funny, and is probably the only children's novel that can explain the fragile nature of the U.S. economy. Talk about being ahead of the curve: Paulsen wrote this a full two years before the world economy collapsed.

In a nutshell, this is a ninety-six-page, first-person novella about a preteen who's been given his late grandfather's old riding lawn mower. The boy comes from a loving family but his folks are busy, like many parents today. His neighbors are just as busy with their lives, and need help with their yard work. Before he knows it, he's got more lawn jobs than he can handle—working mornings, afternoons, and evenings. That's when he gets even luckier. There's a down-on-his-luck e-trader who wants to trade his skills with the stock market for the kid's skill with the mower: You do the lawn, and instead of paying you, I'll invest some money for you. And it works—big-time. And that is just the beginning. Sequel: *Lawn Boy Returns*.

Leon's Story (nonfiction)

BY LEON WALTER TILLAGE

Grades 2–6   *105 pages*

Farrar, Straus & Giroux, 1997

For years, the custodian at a Baltimore school has spellbound the children with his story of growing up in segregated North Carolina, how families and community managed to survive, and then the tumultuous civil rights years when they unleashed the dogs. This is his amazingly simple but powerful true story. Related books: *From Miss Ida's Porch* by Sandra Belton; and *Uncle Jed's Barbershop* by Margaree King Mitchell.

The Littles (series)

BY JOHN PETERSON

Grades 1–4   *80 pages*

Scholastic, 1970

Children have always been fascinated by the idea of "little people"—from leprechauns to Lilliputians, from Thumbelina to hobbits. Unfortunately, much of the famous fantasy literature is too sophisticated for reading aloud to young children. This series is the exception—fast-paced short novels centering on a colony of six-inch people who live inside the walls of the Bigg family's home and have dramatic escapades with gigantic mice, cats, gliders, and telephones. There have been eleven books in the series. Related books: For older students, *The Borrowers* by Mary Norton; *The Indian in the Cupboard* (n); and *Stuart Little* (n).

Look Out, Jeremy Bean!

BY ALICE SCHERTLE; DAVID SLONIM, ILLUS.

Grades K–1   *60 pages*

Chronicle, 2009

Jeremy Bean will ring absolutely true with parents, teachers, and children. When his class is asked to bring in their "collections," Jeremy is worried: He has no collection. What can he share with his classmates? The gentle-humored book is broken down into three chapters, each dealing with a different challenge with short subchapters, making it an ideal read for classes with short attention spans. Typical is when Jeremy overhears his mother tell someone that she has to get after the "dust bunnies" under the beds. He thinks there must be some kind of rabbit under his bed and begins laying traps to catch it. Related book: *Mostly Monty* (s).

234 The Read-Aloud Handbook

Mick Harte Was Here

BY BARBARA PARK
Grades 3–5   88 pages
Knopf, 1995; e-book

This is Barbara Park at her serious best (as opposed to the whimsy of Junie B. Jones). Told through the eyes of an angry, grieving, yet plucky and funny thirteen-year-old sister, it's the story of her younger brother's death from a bike accident, which would have ended otherwise had he been wearing a helmet. Park fills it with warm and often hysterically funny recollections of this terrific boy, who could unnerve anyone with his creative antics. Far from maudlin, it has won numerous children's-choice state awards. See also *Skinnybones* (s).

Missy Violet and Me

BY BARBARA HATHAWAY
Grades 5–8   100 pages
Houghton Mifflin, 2004

Mothers and fathers will have to make their own judgments about their children's readiness for this book. Because of the tangential subject matter, this book might best be shared with same-sex classes. Even with those constrictions, it's too good to eliminate from this collection of recommended books. Viney was eleven the summer she was apprenticed to Missy Violet, the black community's beloved midwife. The setting is the deep rural South at a time when there were still community members who could remember slavery and blacks were called "colored." Through this young girl's eyes, we see community magnified as she learns to not only "catch babies," but to be responsible and follow instructions. She also discovers how some people struggle to pay their bills. The book is never unnecessarily graphic and is quite gentle in its approach; it also brims with the humor and customs of the time and community, including when the children decide to imitate the local preacher while playing in the yard, only to be overheard by the meanest woman in town. For those who have never lived rural or in a community where its members desperately need each other, this volume of one hundred pages will be a warm, eye-opening experience. Baby catching is but a small part of it, while Missy Violet's wisdom is a huge part—something dearly missing in many neighborhoods today, white, black, or otherwise. Sequel: *Letters to Missy Violet*.

The Monster's Ring (Magic Shop series)

BY BRUCE COVILLE
Grades 2–4   *87 pages*
Pantheon, 1982

Just the thing for Halloween reading, this is the Jekyll-and-Hyde tale of timid Russell and the magic ring he buys that can turn him into a monster. Not a make-believe monster, but one with hairy hands, fangs, and claws, one that roams the night, one that will make short order of Eddie the bully, and one that will bring out the worst in Russell. An exciting fantasy of magic gone awry, this is part of the Magic Shop series, which includes: *Jeremy Thatcher, Dragon Hatcher*; *Jennifer Murdley's Toad*; and *The Skull of Truth*.

Mostly Monty

BY JOHANNA HURWITZ
Grades K–2   *96 pages*
Candlewick, 2007

This is the author's latest creation in a career of gentle family stories. Monty is an asthmatic who is overly protected by his family, leaving him with few social contacts, not even pets (allergies). All of this is going to change in first grade, where he discovers not only his own talents (reading first in his class) but his first friends. Along the way, his little adventures with the school's Lost and Found section are giving him the confidence to start a hobby and a neighborhood club. Sequels: *Mighty Monty* and *Amazing Monty*. For other books by the author, see *Rip-Roaring Russell* (s).

My Father's Dragon (series)

BY RUTH S. GANNETT
Grades K–2   *78 pages*
Knopf, 1948; e-book

This is the little fantasy novel that has stood the test of time—surviving in print for more than a half century. The three-volume series is bursting with hair-raising escapes and evil creatures. The tone is dramatic enough to be exciting for even mature preschoolers but not enough to frighten them. The narrator relates the tales as adventures that happened to his father when he was a boy. This is an excellent transition series for introducing children to longer stories with fewer pictures. The rest of the series, in order: *Elmer and the Dragon* and *The Dragons of Blueland*. All three tales are combined in a single volume, *My Father's Dragon: 60th Anniversary Edition*. Related dragon books for young readers: *The Best Pet of All* by

David LaRochelle; *The Book of Beasts* by E. Nesbit, abridged by Inga Moore; *The Serpent Came to Gloucester* by M. T. Anderson; and *The Reluctant Dragon* (s).

On My Honor
BY MARION DANE BAUER
Grades 5–9   *90 pages*
Clarion, 1986; e-book
When his daredevil best friend drowns in a swimming accident, Joel tells no one and returns home to deny the reality and truth of the tragedy. This gripping drama of conscience and consequences is also a story of choices— the ones we make and those we refuse to make. Related book: *A Taste of Blackberries* by Doris B. Smith.

Owls in the Family
BY FARLEY MOWAT
Grades 2–6   *108 pages*
Little, Brown, 1961
No child should miss the author's reliving of his rollicking boyhood on the Saskatchewan prairie, where he raised dogs, gophers, rats, snakes, pigeons, and owls. It is an era we will never see again. Mowat would grow up to become a world-famous writer and naturalist (author of *Never Cry Wolf*, book and film). Also by the author: *Lost in the Barrens*. Related books: *Capyboppy* by Bill Peet; *Gentle Ben* (n); and *My Side of the Mountain* (n).

Pearl Verses the World
BY SALLY MURPHY; HEATHER POTTER, ILLUS.
Grades 2–5   *73 pages*
Candlewick, 2011
There is a Pearl in every classroom, sometimes more than one; sometimes she's a girl, sometimes a boy. They're alone and invisible, seldom selected for anyone's playground group. And that's been just fine with Pearl because she's always had her family—Mom, Granny, and herself, all she ever needed. Unfortunately, that is changing as Granny grows more ill and nears death. This is a realistic, though never maudlin, look at how one family copes with change and grief, as well as how friendship and community aid in coping. The tale is told as a first-person prose poem (Pearl hates rhyming, despite her teacher's prompting). Although Pearl is portrayed as being around eight or nine years old, her feelings are those of anyone meeting a family loss. This book is a shining example of literature

as healer and helper. Related books on death: *The Tenth Good Thing About Barney* by Judith Viorst; and for older children: *Mimi* (n); and *A Taste of Blackberries* by Doris B. Smith.

The Reluctant Dragon
BY KENNETH GRAHAME; ERNEST H. SHEPARD, ILLUS.
Grades 2–4   *57 pages*
Holiday House, 1989
The author of the classic *Wind in the Willows* gives us here a simple boy-and-dragon story. The dragon is not a devouring dragon but a reluctant one who wants nothing to do with violence. The boy is a scholar, well versed in dragon lore and torn between his desire to view a battle between the dragon and St. George and the desire to protect his dragon friend. Related books: *The Book of Beasts* and *The Book of Dragons*, both by E. Nesbit; *My Father's Dragon* (s); *Saint George and the Dragon* retold by Margaret Hodges; and *The Story of Ferdinand* by Munro Leaf.

The Rifle
BY GARY PAULSEN
Grades 6 and up   *104 pages*
Harcourt Brace, 1995
This short biography of a weapon, from its artistic birth on the eve of the Revolutionary War to the present time, offers a moving portrait of the many people whose paths intersect with the rifle during its 230-year history. Although the weapon is always at the center of this tale, American history shares much of the stage as the rifle's role changes with the social structures of the times. Also by the author: *Hatchet* (n) and *Woods Runner*. Related books: *Gunstories: Life-Changing Experiences with Guns* by S. Beth Atkin; and *Scorpions* (n).

Rip-Roaring Russell (Russell and Elisa series)
BY JOHANNA HURWITZ
Grades K–2   *96 pages*
Morrow, 1983
In this delightful introduction to chapter and series books, we follow little Russell, his younger sister, Elisa, and their family and friends through preschool, kindergarten, and primary grades. Hurwitz understands children and families, and no one can resist loving the characters in her books. The series of books about Elisa can be read by themselves as well, beginning with *Russell and Elisa*. After this first book, the series reads in this order: *Russell Sprouts*; *Russell Rides Again*; *Russell and Elisa*; *E Is for Elisa*; *Make*

Room for Elisa; Ever-Clever Elisa; Elisa in the Middle; and *Summer with Elisa.* Also by the author: *Mostly Monty* (s).

Shoeshine Girl

BY CLYDE ROBERT BULLA
Grades 1–4   *84 pages*
Harper, 1989
A spoiled ten-year-old girl, having driven her parents to the edge, is sent to spend the summer with her aunt. Immediately she's in trouble for conning a neighboring child into giving her a loan. Determined to have spending money, she lands a job at a local shoeshine stand, and there she receives a maturing dose of reality and responsibility. Related books: *Bud, Not Buddy* (n); *The Pinballs* (n); and *Troublemaker.*

Skinnybones

BY BARBARA PARK
Grades 3–5   *112 pages*
Knopf, 1982; e-book
Park creates characters who may not always be lovable, but they are remarkably alive and interesting as they deal with losing ball games, moving, camp, or sibling rivalries. Best of all, they are funny—not cutesy or caustic, but genuinely and interestingly funny. Typical (along with Junie B. Jones) is Alex Frankovitch of *Skinnybones*, who is an uncoordinated smart aleck who throws tantrums; he's also a laugh a minute. Sequel: *Almost Starring Skinnybones.* Also by the author: *Junie B. Jones and the Stupid Smelly Bus* (s) and *Mick Harte Was Here* (s).

The SOS File

BY BETSY BYARS, BETSY DUFFEY, AND LAURIE MYERS
Grades 1–3   *72 pages*
Henry Holt, 2004
Placing a folder at the front of the classroom, the teacher gives his students a chance for extra credit: All they have to do is write an essay or story about a traumatic moment—a time they had to call 911 or were so frightened they could barely speak or walk. Each of his eleven students accepts the challenge, writing tales that are entirely believable for primary-grade students. Some raise the hairs on the neck (like the pair who meet a black bear on their hike), some make you laugh (like the student with the ungoverned appetite who ate the candy bars instead of selling them for fund-raising), and several are quite poignant. Each tale runs an average of three pages; they are excellent examples of short narrative.

Soup (series)

BY ROBERT NEWTON PECK

Grades 4–6   *96 pages*

Knopf, 1974; e-book

Two Vermont pals share a talent for getting themselves into trouble. The stories are set in the rural 1930s, when life was simpler and the days were longer. But the need for a best friend was just as great then as now. There are a dozen books in the series. For older readers: *A Day No Pigs Would Die* (n). Related book: *Herbie Jones* (s).

Stone Fox

BY JOHN R. GARDINER

Grades 1–7   *96 pages*

Crowell, 1980; e-book

A million-copy seller in its thirty years, this is a story that, like its ten-year-old orphan hero, never stands still. Based on a Rocky Mountain legend, the story recounts the valiant efforts of young Willy to save his grandfather's farm by attempting to win the purse in a local bobsled race. Pushing the plot is a big dose of loyalty: grandson to grandfather, dog to his young master. For a list of other dog stories, see page 242.

The Stories Julian Tells (series)

BY ANN CAMERON

Grades K–3   *72 pages*

Pantheon, 1981; e-book

The author takes six short stories involving Julian and his brother and weaves them into a fabric that glows with the mischief, magic, and imagination of childhood. Though centered on commonplace subjects like desserts, gardens, loose teeth, and new neighbors, these stories of family life are written in an uncommon way that will both amuse and touch young listeners. Sequels: *Julian's Glorious Summer*; *Julian, Secret Agent*; *More Stories Julian Tells*; and *The Stories Huey Tells*.

The Stray

BY DICK KING-SMITH

Grades 1–4   *139 pages*

Dell, 2002

One day, on a nearly deserted beach, an old woman (Henny Hickathrift) who had walked away from an old age home and hopped a train to the seaside took her cane and wrote in the sand: "I am a stray old woman."

That inscription soon leads five redheaded siblings to the old woman. It's Henny's seventy-fifth birthday and the children insist she come home with them to celebrate in style. The afternoon visit stretches into a week, then a month, and finally becomes permanent as the family grows to love her. In the style the author has made his trademark in books like *Babe: The Gallant Pig*, this is a warm celebration of family and aging. Also by the author: *The Invisible Dog*; *A Mouse Called Wolf*; *Pigs Might Fly*; *The School Mouse*; and *The Water Horse* (n).

Two Times the Fun
BY BEVERLY CLEARY
Grades PreS–K   *92 pages*
Harper, 2005; e-book
Beverly Cleary raised a set of twins, so she knows the breed well. Couple that with her witty insight into the workings of family life and you've got everything that makes this collection of four stories work so well. Jimmy and Janet are four-year-olds with two distinct approaches to things like dog biscuits, new boots, holes in the ground, and personal possessions. Originally separate picture books, these four tales work perfectly in the short novel category for preschoolers.

The Whipping Boy
BY SID FLEISCHMAN
Grades 3–6   *90 pages*
Greenwillow, 1986
The brattish medieval prince is too spoiled ever to be spanked, so the king regularly vents his anger on Jeremy, a peasant "whipping boy." When circumstances lead the two boys to reverse roles à la *The Prince and the Pauper*, each learns much about friendship and sacrifice. Painted with Fleischman's broad humor, this is a fast-paced Newbery-winning melodrama with short, cliffhanger chapters. Also by the author, who is known for injecting the perfect amount of humor into his historic novels: *The Ghost in the Noonday Sun*; *By the Great Horn Spoon!*; *Jim Ugly*; and *Humbug Mountain* (my favorite).

Who Was Steve Jobs? (nonfiction series)
BY PAM POLLACK AND MEG BELVISIO; JOHN O'BRIEN, ILLUS.
Grades 2–5   *100 pages*
Grosset & Dunlap, 2012
After nonfiction picture books, one of the best pathways for children into deeper nonfiction is biography. Too often, however, biographies for children

in grades 2–4 are top-heavy with detail. Here in the "Who Was . . . " series, children can taste the worlds of science, art, music, and history without drowning in detail. Each of the volumes is 100 pages. If that seems too long for second-graders, nearly every page has an illustration on it, reducing the text to about 50 full pages. As here with *Who Was Steve Jobs?* the book offers an overview of the person's entire life, along with notes on contemporary figures and events that affected him (in this case, his rival Bill Gates, and Jobs's connection to the Beatles and *Star Wars*). The amount of detail is just right for grades 2–4. With almost 50 volumes to date, the series' subjects run the gamut from King Tut and Marco Polo to Helen Keller and Steve Jobs. For picture book biographies, see *My Brother Martin: A Sister Remembers* (p).

Full-Length Novels

Adam Canfield of the Slash
BY MICHAEL WINERIP
Grades 5–8   *326 pages*
Candlewick, 2005; e-book
An African-American girl named Jennifer is the bright, levelheaded co-editor of Harris Elementary/Middle School's student newspaper, the *Slash*. Coeditor Adam Canfield is a bright but un-levelheaded eighth-grader. Together they're a veritable Woodward and Bernstein. Author Michael Winerip (a Pulitzer Prize–winning education writer for the *New York Times*) has placed his coeditors in wealthy Tremble, suburbia brimming with overscheduled kids too busy to play, school administrators and real estate agents too focused on test scores, and a husband-wife team that owns both the cable company and the local newspaper and is thus able to slant news and views as they wish. This is a superb introduction to modern journalism and some contemporary issues the author has dealt with as a reporter. Sequels: *Adam Canfield: Watch Your Back!* and *Adam Canfield: The Last Reporter.*

The Adventures of Pinocchio
BY CARLO COLLODI; ROBERTO INNOCENTI, ILLUS.
Grades 1–5   *144 pages*
Knopf, 1988; e-book
Unfortunately, most children's familiarity with this 1892 classic comes from the emasculated Disney and TV versions. Treat your children to the original story of the poor wood-carver's puppet who faces all the temptations of childhood, succumbs to many, learns from his follies, and gains

his boyhood by selflessly giving of himself for his friends. The Knopf edition, the most lavishly illustrated ever, is the real *Pinocchio*.

The Bad Beginning (series)

BY LEMONY SNICKET

Grades 2–4   *162 pages*

Harper, 1999; e-book

Contrary to the title, this is a splendid beginning to an enormously popular series that follows the "riches-to-rags" tale of three resilient orphans who no sooner overcome one Dickensian misfortune and villain than even darker ones appear. The children must and do resist these threats with determined quick wits. Sending up the moralistic Victorian adventure tales of a century ago, as well as old-time Saturday movie serials, the author's asides to the reader-listener are humorous, helpful, and enlightening (especially with vocabulary). Since the success of this series, there has been a wave of published imitations, none of which compare even closely to its originality or humor. And forget the movie.

Bambi

BY FELIX SALTEN

Grades 2–5   *191 pages*

Aladdin, 1988; e-book

Don't be misled by the Disney version of this tale. Salten's original forest is far deeper than the film's. Intended as a protest against hunting, the story follows the young roe deer from birth to the arrival of danger—man. This is an accessible classic for children, but definitely for experienced listeners. If you insist upon an abridged version, find Janet Schulman's (Atheneum).

Jim's Favorite Dog Novels

Big Red by Jim Kjelgaard

Call of the Wild by Jack London

A Dog Called Kitty by Bill Wallace

Foxy by Helen Griffith

Hurry Home, Candy by Meindert DeJong

Kavik the Wolf Dog by Walt Morey

Lassie Come-Home by Eric Knight

Old Yeller by Fred Gipson

Shiloh by Phyllis Naylor

Stone Fox by John Reynolds Gardiner

Where the Red Fern Grows by Wilson Rawls

Woodsong by Gary Paulsen

Because of Winn-Dixie

BY KATE DICAMILLO

Grades 2–5   *182 pages*
Candlewick, 2000; e-book

Ten-year-old Opal Buloni is not only the new kid in town, she's also a preacher's kid. She picks up a stray dog at the neighborhood Winn-Dixie grocery (that's how it gets its name) and charms her daddy into letting her keep him. She also charms everyone she meets, collecting the weirdest assortment of cast-off grown-ups and kids you'll ever meet and grow fond of. The movie is a good translation of the book. Also by the author: *The Tale of Despereaux*. Related books: *A Blue-Eyed Daisy* (s); *Close to Famous* (n); *Ida Early Comes over the Mountain* by Robert Burch; *Lily's Crossing* (n); and *Riding Freedom* by Pam Muñoz Ryan.

Black Beauty

BY ANNA SEWELL; CHARLES KEEPING, ILLUS.

Grades 4–8   *214 pages*
Farrar, Straus & Giroux, 1990; e-book

In this classic animal novel, and the first with an animal as narrator, the author vividly describes the cruelty to horses during the Victorian period, as well as giving a detailed picture of life at that time. Related books: *The Black Stallion* (series) by Walter Farley; *Dream of Night* (n); *Hoofbeats: Katie and the Mustang* by Kathleen Duey; *King of the Wind: The Story of the Godolphin Arabian* by Marguerite Henry; and *Riding Freedom* by Pam Muñoz Ryan.

Bridge to Terabithia

BY KATHERINE PATERSON

Grades 4–7   *128 pages*
Crowell, 1997; e-book

Few novels for children have dealt with so many emotions and issues so well: sports, school, peers, friendship, death, guilt, art, and family. This popular Newbery winner deserves to be read or heard by everyone. Also by the author: *The Great Gilly Hopkins*. Related book: *The Pinballs* (n).

Bud, Not Buddy

BY CHRISTOPHER PAUL CURTIS

Grades 4–8   *243 pages*
Delacorte, 1999; e-book

After escaping a succession of bad foster homes, ten-year-old Buddy sets out to find the man he suspects to be his father—a popular jazz musician in Grand Rapids, Michigan. Told in the first person, this engaging Newbery winner brims with humor and compassion while offering a keen insight into the workings of a child's mind during the Great Depression. Also by the author: *The Mighty Miss Malone* (n). Related books: *City of Orphans* (n); *A Family Apart* (n); *No Promises in the Wind* by Irene Hunt; and *Roll of Thunder, Hear My Cry* (n).

Caddie Woodlawn
BY CAROL RYRIE BRINK
Grades 4–6   *286 pages*
Simon & Schuster, 1935
You take *Little House on the Prairie*; I'll take *Caddie Woodlawn*. Ten times over, I'll take this tomboy of the 1860s with her pranks, her daring visits to Indian camps, her one-room schoolhouse fights, and her wonderfully believable family. Try to pick up the 1973 edition, with Trina Schart Hyman's illustrations. For experienced listeners. Sequel: *Magical Melons*. Related book: *Riding Freedom* by Pam Muñoz Ryan.

The Call of the Wild
BY JACK LONDON
Grades 6 and up   *126 pages*
Multiple publishers; e-book
This 1903 dog story, set amid the rush for gold in the Klondike, depicts the savagery and tenderness between man and his environment in unforgettable terms. The Whole Story edition includes extensive sidebars and illustrations that add greatly to the story's setting in time and place. For experienced listeners. Also by the author: *White Fang* (look for the edition illustrated by Ed Young). Related book: *Where the Red Fern Grows* (n). For a list of great dog stories, see page 242.

The Cay
BY THEODORE TAYLOR
Grades 2–6   *144 pages*
Doubleday, 1969; e-book
An exciting adventure about a blind white boy and an old black man shipwrecked on a tiny Caribbean island. The first chapters are slow but it builds with taut drama to a stunning ending. Sequel/prequel: *Timothy of the Cay*. Also by the author: *The Bomb* (atomic); *Sniper*, an outstanding suspense story set at a "big cat" preserve in Southern California; *Ice Drift*; and *A Sailor Returns*. Related books: *Hatchet* (n) and *Kensuke's Kingdom* (n).

Charlotte's Web: 50th Anniversary Edition

BY E. B. WHITE; GARTH WILLIAMS, ILLUS.

Grades K–4   *213 pages*

Harper, 2002

One of the most acclaimed books in children's literature, it is loved by adults as well as children. The tale centers on the barnyard life of a young pig who is to be butchered in the fall. The animals of the yard (particularly a haughty gray spider named Charlotte) conspire with the farmer's daughter to save the pig's life. While there is much humor in the novel, the author uses wisdom and pathos in developing his theme of friendship within the cycle of life.

For a half century this modern classic didn't include a single sentence about the author in the hardcover edition. The only mention was his byline on the cover. With this fiftieth anniversary edition we have some information to bring the man alive for young readers: how he lived, how he wrote, and samples of his editing and concerns while he wrote. Also by the author: *Stuart Little* (n). Beverly Gherman's *E. B. White: Some Writer!* is an excellent children's biography of the author. Related books: *Babe: The Gallant Pig* by Dick King-Smith; *Spiders!* by the editors of *Time for Kids*, an excellent picture book on the world of spiders; *The Cricket in Times Square* by George Selden; *Malcolm at Midnight* (n); and *Poppy* (n).

The City of Ember

BY JEANNE DUPRAU

Grades 4–7   *288 pages*

Random House, 2003; e-book

More than 240 years before the story opens, a great holocaust confronted the population of earth. To save the species, one group created a huge underground city, Ember, that would be safe from the ravages above. Because it was complete with giant storehouses of supplies and a huge generator, humanity could survive. These forefathers also conceived a means by which the inhabitants would be able to extricate themselves from their underground tomb after 200 years, estimating that by then the surface would be habitable again. Detailed instructions were given to the mayor, who, in turn, would pass them to his successor. The book picks up the story almost 250 years later. Those instructions have long been misplaced and forgotten, and so has much of history. The people know only their life underground and live increasingly meager existences with dwindling supplies and energy.

But the youngest generation is chafing under the regimentation of the old order, even wondering if there might be something beyond the here and now, pondering, "What if—?" Two such people are twelve-year-olds Doon and Lina. The latter has stumbled on some strange but ancient instructions in her grandmother's closet, and the former is a born rebel and questioner but sentenced to spend the rest of his life repairing the plumbing in the bowels of the city. Together they begin the journey outward and upward that will save their civilization—if they can ever get anyone to follow them. Sequels: *The People of Sparks*; *The Prophet of Yonwood*; and *The Diamond of Darkhold*. There is also a graphic novel version by Dallas Middaugh and Niklas Asker. Related books: *The Giver* by Lois Lowry; *Journey Outside* by Mary Q. Steele; and *When the Tripods Came* (n).

City of Orphans

BY AVI

Grades 5–8   *350 pages*

Atheneum, 2011; e-book

It's 1893 on the Lower East Side of New York City and the tenements are brimming with poor immigrants, most of them living lives of desperation, others dying by the wayside. In the middle of this mix we find the Geless family, including the story's main character, thirteen-year-old Maks. As a school dropout, he's earning eight cents a day selling newspapers on street corners, then turning the money over to help support his family—the same thing his older sisters do with their money. As the narrative plays out (told through the vernacular of a working-class New Yorker of that time whose English is less than perfect, not unlike the technique used in Tom Sawyer), we meet the realities of life in America—where the streets were never paved with gold and dreams sometimes came true but most often did not—and the primal power of family bonding. Indeed, as we live through five days in the Geless household, we encounter all the hardships and indignities of poverty. The book is arranged in ninety-one two-page chapters, perfect for short readings. Related film: *Newsies*, the Disney film musical based on the 1899 newsboys strike against the newspaper barons Pulitzer and Hearst. See also the *New York Times* article "Read All About It! Kids Vex Titans!" by Dan Barry, March 5, 2012, about the Broadway show based on the same events. A Google search for "Lewis Hine + newsboys" will give you hundreds of original newsboy images from that era, taken by the famous photographer/sociologist.

Claudette Colvin: Twice Toward Justice (nonfiction)

BY PHILLIP HOOSE

Grades 7 and up   *124 pages*

Macmillan, 2009; e-book

One can safely say no revolution of any size was ever neat and tidy. There are always misunderstandings, infighting, and backbiting, along with eventual triumph. Such is the case in this highly honored (National Book Award and Newbery Honor) nonfiction chronicle of Claudette Colvin's pivotal role in the great Montgomery bus boycott. Rosa Parks got all the attention and fame nine months later but Colvin was there first, a fifteen-year-old in 1955 who refused to move for a white woman bus passenger. She was promptly arrested and manhandled by police. And even though it was Colvin's courageous and articulate testimony before the federal court (quickly affirmed by the Supreme Court) that broke the back of the Montgomery bus company, Colvin spent the next thirty-five years in obscurity, tending elderly nursing home patients in New York City, while the fame and glory went to people like Medgar Evers, Martin Luther King Jr., and Rosa Parks. What went wrong for the young girl? Why was her courage ignored by the movement and scorned by her classmates and neighbors? This is a brilliant young adult volume on adolescence, race, politics, and American history—and every page is documented truth. Related book: *Roll of Thunder, Hear My Cry* (n).

Close to Famous

BY JOAN BAUER

Grades 7–9   *250 pages*

Viking, 2011; e-book

Twelve-year-old Foster McFee is lovable and determined, just like her mother. Which gives you the feeling right from the get-go that things are going to work out for the two of them. But not before there are some rough spots. First they have to start life over again in a new town, Culpepper, West Virginia, where they're hiding out from Foster's mother's abusive boyfriend, an Elvis impersonator. Culpepper is struggling with the letdown from the promises that the new penitentiary would bring all kinds of jobs for the local folks. So the town is devoid of hope, which is frustrating to Foster, who envisions herself as a TV chef. How do you build a career on a hopeless town? The same goes for her new friend Macon, who has his eye set on becoming a film documentarian. And then things begin to fall into place as Foster starts a cupcake business through the local café. And true to form, the abusive boyfriend resurfaces, as do an assortment of bad guys, good guys, and as warm a collection of neighbors since Kate Di-Camillo's *Winn-Dixie*. If you don't bring in cupcakes while you're reading this book, you're missing a big opportunity. Also by the author: *Hope Was Here* and *Rules of the Road* (n).

Danny, the Champion of the World
BY ROALD DAHL
Grades 3–5   *196 pages*
Knopf, 1975
In what might be Dahl's most tender book for children, a motherless boy and his father—"the most wonderful father who ever lived"—go on an adventure together. Teachers and parents should explain the custom and tradition of poaching in England before going too deep into the story (Robin Hood was a poacher). Also by the author: *James and the Giant Peach* (n). Related book: Try comparing the experiences of Danny with those of Leigh Botts, the boy in *Dear Mr. Henshaw* (n).

Darby
BY JONATHON SCOTT FUQUA
Grades 2–4   *240 pages*
Candlewick, 2002
To get a quick grip on this book, think of it as *To Kill a Mockingbird* for nine-year-olds—except *Darby* is told with the immediate feelings and words of a girl who is nine and who hasn't achieved the wisdom that comes with hindsight. It takes us back to 1926 and the American South, specifically Marlboro County, South Carolina. And though Darby Carmichael acts as if the world revolves around her, she is beginning to notice other forces in her small universe—some of which she can't control. She is writing the book to explain the good and terrible things that happened that year in her family and community.

Truthfulness is at the heart of this novel, from the time that Darby is inspired by her best friend to become a newspaper writer. The friend, Evette, is the daughter of a black tenant farmer on Darby's father's farm. It wasn't fashionable for a white girl to have a black best friend in that time and place, but sometimes friendships grow like wildflowers. Ever since Evette told her that newspaper writers must always write the truth, Darby has been writing short articles for the local paper and has become a little celebrity in the community. Then the Carmichaels' redneck neighbor assaults a black boy he finds stealing a chicken, a beating that results in the boy's death. This opens Darby's eyes to the unfair differences between whites and blacks in her town, and she and her friend write an essay that unsettles family, friends, and community. Readers-aloud should not be put off by the size of the book (240 pages); the page dimensions are small, and the text is double-spaced, so it's really about 140 pages in length. Related books: *Adam Canfield of the Slash* (n) and *Roll of Thunder, Hear My Cry* (n).

A Day No Pigs Would Die
BY ROBERT NEWTON PECK
Grades 6 and up   *150 pages*
Knopf, 1972; e-book
Set among Shaker farmers in Vermont during the 1920s, this is the poignant story of the author's coming-of-age at thirteen, his adventures, fears, and triumphs. As a novel of life and death, it should be read carefully by the teacher or parent before it is read aloud to children. A very moving story for experienced listeners. Sequel: *A Part of the Sky.* Also by the author: the Soup series (s).

Dear Mr. Henshaw
BY BEVERLY CLEARY
Grades 3–6   *134 pages*
Morrow, 1983; e-book
In this 1984 Newbery winner, Beverly Cleary departs from her Ramona format to write a very different but every bit as successful book—one of the finest in her long career. Using only the letters and diary of a young boy, Leigh Botts, the author traces his personal growth from first grade to sixth. We watch the changes in his relationship with his divorced parents, his schools (where he always ends up the friendless "new kid"), an author with whom he corresponds over the years, and finally the changes in himself. Along with the usual Cleary humor, there is also genuine sensitivity to the heartaches that confront the growing number of Leigh Bottses in our homes and classrooms. Sequel: *Strider.* Also by the author: *Ramona the Pest* (n). Related books: *Danny, the Champion of the World* (n) and *Thank You, Jackie Robinson* (n).

Deltora Quest: The Forests of Silence (series)
BY EMILY RODDA
Grades 1–5   *131 pages*
Scholastic, 2000
Here is a fantasy series for those not ready for the complexity or length of the Harry Potter series. The author has borrowed the traditional quest motif from classical literature and coupled it with a little bit of King

Arthur, *The Lord of the Rings*, Narnia, and even *Star Wars*. In the land of Deltora, an evil shadow lord takes over the land when the kingdom's protective stones are stolen and dispersed. To the rescue comes an unlikely trio of teen warriors (two males, one female) who set out to recover the stones and save the kingdom. Each book uncovers more stones but also enormous obstacles that block their recovery. The series has sold more than fifteen million copies and is broken into three distinct "miniseries": Deltora Quest, Deltora Shadowlands, and Dragons of Deltora.

Dream of Night

BY HEATHER HENSON

Grades 4–8   *218 pages*

Atheneum, 2010; e-book

Make no mistake: This is no cookie-cutter horse story. Old Jess is feeling her age these days, weary of caring for rejected horses and foster kids who inflict too much pain. So this just might be the last time around for her. First, she's boarding a former champion thoroughbred she's rescued from an abusive owner. Unless she finds a way to defuse Dream of Night's angry temperament soon, euthanasia may be the only option. And then there's Shiloh, an angry, uncommunicative twelve-year-old girl who has bounced among a series of foster homes. Unless Jess can also defuse this boarder's rage, a juvenile institution will be the next stop. Complicating matters, neither boarder wants anything to do with the other. Teens of either gender will find this a believable and riveting narrative. *New York Times* coverage of one alleged abuse case can be found online at http://www.nytimes.com/2009/04/05/sports/othersports/05horses.html. The opposite of Dream of Night's life is that of the great Triple Crown winner Seattle Slew. The black colt with the crooked leg was turned over to Paula Turner for training and right away she sensed something special in him, although her view may have been biased by a childhood favorite book called *The Black Stallion*. She told her heartwarming story, "Training a Champion," to American Public Media's *The Story* in 2011, online at http://thestory.org/archive/the_story_050611_full_show.mp3/view. Related books: *Black Beauty* (n); *The Georges and the Jewels* by Jane Smiley; and *The Pinballs* by Betsy Byars.

Dugout Rivals

BY FRED BOWEN

Grades 3–5   *128 pages*

Peachtree, 2010

Twelve-year-old Jake has labored for a couple of years with a mostly losing baseball team, but this year promises to be different. First, the team is loaded with experienced players, and second, Jake will be taking over at the coveted shortstop position. To make it even better, they've got a new kid, named Adam, who is the best player Jake and his teammates have ever seen. As expected, the team begins to win. The unexpected part is that Adam also plays shortstop, and pitches. Jake is suddenly playing in the shadow of a superstar, something he's never had to deal with before. To complicate matters, Adam is just as nice as he is athletic. Other novels by the author: *Throwing Heat*; *Hardcourt Comeback*; *Soccer Team Upset*; *T. J.'s Secret Pitch*; and *Touchdown Trouble*. Also by the author: *No Easy Way: The Story of Ted Williams and the Last .400 Season*. Related baseball novels: *Thank You, Jackie Robinson* (n) and *Finding Buck McHenry* (n).

A Family Apart (series)
BY JOAN LOWERY NIXON
Grades 3–7   *162 pages*
Bantam, 1987

The popular Orphan Train Adventures series is based on the years between the Civil War and the Great Depression, when 150,000 homeless children were shipped west to families willing to give them shelter. Some were looking to adopt a first child, some were reaching out to enlarge their present family, and some were looking for unpaid laborers, under the guise of family. This opening book in the series follows the six Kelly children from New York City to Missouri after their widowed mother turns them over to the Children's Aid Society, which sends them to Missouri and parcels them out to farm families. Much of the book focuses on thirteen-year-old Frances and her attempts to masquerade as a boy in order to be "adopted" by the same family that takes her youngest brother. Also in the series: *Caught in the Act*; *In the Face of Danger*; *A Place to Belong*; *A Dangerous Promise* (Civil War); *Keeping Secrets*; and *Circle of Love*.

Finding Buck McHenry
BY ALFRED SLOTE
Grades 3–6   *250 pages*
Harper, 1991

Eleven-year-old Jason, baseball card collector extraordinaire, is convinced that school custodian Mr. Mack Henry is really the legendary Buck McHenry of Negro League fame. Before either of them can stop it, the idea steamrolls out of control. The author creates a rich blend of baseball history, peer relationships (male and female), family, and race relations while never losing sight of a good story. Also by the author: *Hang Tough, Paul Mather*. See also the excellent paperback series by Dan Gutman about a boy who time-travels using his baseball cards: *Jackie & Me* (Jackie Robinson); *Satch & Me* (Satchel Paige); and *Honus & Me* (Honus Wagner). See also *Just as Good: How Larry Doby Changed America's Game* by Chris Crowe; *Thank You, Jackie Robinson* (n); and *We Are the Ship: The Story of Negro League Baseball* by Kadir Nelson.

Freak the Mighty
BY RODMAN PHILBRICK
Grades 6–9   *165 pages*
Scholastic, 1993

Many popular entertainment tales have involved teams—Batman and Robin, the Lone Ranger and Tonto, Luke Skywalker and Han Solo. Each member is usually of vastly different stature. In that tradition comes the team of Max and Kevin, two unlikely teenage heroes. Middle-schooler Max is gigantic, powerful, and a remedial student. The wisecracking Kevin suffers from a birth defect that limits his growth and keeps him on crutches; his body cannot grow to more than a few feet in height, but his mind has expanded to brilliant proportions. The two become fast friends and give themselves the nickname Freak the Mighty (Kevin and Max respectively). Their adventures run the gamut from escaping street bullies and outwitting school authorities to educating Max and surviving his homicidal father. While some parts are implausible, the friendship between the two is a thing of beauty, and Max's first-person voice rings true as he painfully explores the anxieties of adolescence. Sequel: *Max the Mighty*.

From the Mixed-up Files of Mrs. Basil E. Frankweiler
BY E. L. KONIGSBURG
Grades 4–7   *62 pages*
Macmillan, 1967; e-book

A bored and brainy twelve-year-old girl talks her nine-year-old brother into running away with her. To throw everyone off their trail, Claudia chooses the Metropolitan Museum of Art in New York City as a refuge, and amid centuries-old art they sleep, dine, bathe, and pray in regal secret splendor. An exciting story of hide-and-seek and a wonderful art lesson to boot. For experienced listeners. Related runaway books: a city boy hides in the wilderness in *My Side of the Mountain* (n); a city boy hides in the subway system in *Slake's Limbo* (n).

Gentle Ben
BY WALT MOREY
Grades 3–6   *192 pages*
Dutton, 1965

A young boy adopts a huge bear and brings to his family in Alaska all the joys and tears such a combination might invite. Though the struggle to save animals from ignorant but well-intentioned human predators is one that has been written many times over, Morey's handling of characters, plot, and setting makes this an original and exciting tale. He supports the pace of his story with many lessons in environmental science, from salmon runs to hibernation. Also by the author: *Canyon Winter*; *Hero*; *Kavik the Wolf Dog*; and *Scrub Dog of Alaska*. Related book: *The Year of Miss Agnes* by Kirkpatrick Hill.

The Girl with the Silver Eyes
BY WILLO DAVIS ROBERTS
Grades 4–8   *181 pages*
Aladdin, 2011

There is something about nine-year-old Katie that sets her apart, besides the strange pupils in her eyes. Her secret is she has paranormal powers as a result of her mother's exposure to factory chemicals during pregnancy. Written as a suspense story, it's also a moving study of a child who marches to a different drummer and the pain that comes with such marches. It's an attention grabber, for sure.

Good Old Boy
BY WILLIE MORRIS
Grades 5–8   *128 pages*
Yoknapatawpha, 1981

If Mark Twain had been writing *Tom Sawyer* in the 1940s, this is the book he'd have written. One of the South's most distinguished authors gives us the heartwarming tale of growing up in a town on the banks of the Mississippi. For experienced listeners. Sequel: *My Dog Skip*, upon which the movie is loosely based, but read the book first. Related books: *The Adventures of Tom Sawyer* by Mark Twain and *Soup* (s). See if you can find the long-out-of-print *Humbug Mountain* by Sid Fleischman at your library. It is a wonderful companion to *Tom Sawyer* or *Good Old Boy*. For a view of how African-American girls saw the world in those times: *Missy Violet and Me* (s).

The Great Turkey Walk

BY KATHLEEN KARR
Grades 4–8   *199 pages*
Scholastic, 1998

Set in the time of cattle drives and the Kansas Territory, this comic-novel tall tale follows fifteen-year-old Simon Green as he journeys nine hundred miles from Missouri to Denver. But it's no ordinary journey. First, muscular but soft-headed Simon has just "graduated" from third grade after four years there. Second, he's herding a thousand turkeys. Third, he's accompanied and assisted by a recovering alcoholic and a runaway slave. En route, they encounter rustlers; Indians whose territory they've accidentally violated; Simon's no-account long-lost father, who is bent on stealing the turkeys; target-hungry U.S. cavalry; and a deranged woman. And one last ingredient to make it an even tastier tale of redemption: The venture is being bankrolled by Simon's fourth-grade teacher with her life's savings. Mark Twain would have given this a five-star review. Related books: Sid Fleischman's *By the Great Horn Spoon!*; *Humbug Mountain*; and *Chancy and the Grand Rascal*.

Harry Potter and the Sorcerer's Stone (series)

BY J. K. ROWLING
Grades 2–8   *309 pages*
Scholastic, 1998; e-book

Harry is the best thing to happen to children's books since the invention of the paperback. While the series' plot is surely original, it follows in the path of C. S. Lewis's dual Narnia world, George Lucas's *Star Wars* struggles with the "dark side," and Dorothy's search for the Wizard of Oz. It is also blessed with an abundance of Roald Dahl's cheeky childhood humor.

Harry is the orphan child of two famous wizards, who died mysteriously when he was very young. Rescued at age eleven from abusive relatives, he is sent to Hogwarts School (sorcery's equivalent of an elite boarding school), where he experiences high adventure as he and his friends (boy and girl) struggle with classes in potions, charms, and broom flying, all the while battling a furtive faculty member working for the dark side.

This is not an easy read-aloud, and the reader-aloud should be aware that the first two chapters of the first book are a bit complicated, as they set the scene for Harry's dual world. Definitely for experienced listeners, the books grow darker in content as they proceed toward the final volume. Actor Jim Dale has done a masterful job of recording (unabridged) all of the Potter books for Listening Library/Random House.

Other books in the series (in order): *Harry Potter and the Chamber of Secrets*; *Harry Potter and the Prisoner of Azkaban*; *Harry Potter and the Goblet of Fire*; *Harry Potter and the Order of the Phoenix*; *Harry Potter and the Half-Blood Prince*; and *Harry Potter and the Deathly Hallows*. Younger fans of Harry will enjoy: *Deltora Quest* (n); *The Lion, the Witch, and the Wardrobe* (n); and the Redwall series, beginning with *Martin the Warrior* (n). Older fans may be ready for *The Hobbit* by J. R. R. Tolkien.

Two years after J. K. Rowling unveiled the world of Harry Potter, Anthony Horowitz (of Alex Rider fame) offered a marvelous send-up of the Rowling series in *Groosham Grange*. Monty Python couldn't have done it better. Horowitz presents thirteen-year-old David Eliot, an adolescent goof-off who is burdened with two of the most self-serving parents in the world. David's underachievements leave his parents little choice but to send him to Groosham Grange (a parody of Hogwarts), set on an obscure island with fifty-foot cliffs. There he'll join other banished boarding students, who must sign their names in blood and reside in stone-cold rooms, and are taught by a faculty that includes only one normal-looking member. Needless to say, they attend school on Christmas Day. It's all done with great tongue-in-cheek. Sequel: *Return to Groosham Grange: The Unholy Grail*.

Hatchet: 20th Anniversary Edition (series)

BY GARY PAULSEN

Grades 6 and up   195 pages
Bradbury, 2007; e-book

The lone survivor of a plane crash in the Canadian wilderness, a thirteen-year-old boy carries three things away from the crash: a fierce spirit, the hatchet his mother gave him as a gift, and the secret knowledge that his mother was unfaithful to his father. All play an integral part in this Newbery Honor survival story for experienced listeners. Sequels: *The River*; *Brian's Winter*; *Brian's Return*; and *Brian's Hunt*. Having received about four hundred letters a week with *Hatchet*-related queries, Paulsen's answered them in one book: *Guts*, detailing the true-life events that inspired the series. Related survival books: *The Cay* and *Ice Drift*, both by Theodore Taylor; *Incident at Hawk's Hill* (n); the Island series by Gordon Korman; *Kensuke's Kingdom* (n); and *Winter Camp* by Kirkpatrick Hill.

Other books by Paulsen: *The Foxman* (a precursor to *Harris and Me*); *Mr. Tucket* (n); *The Rifle* (s); *Soldier's Heart*; *The Tent*; a survival-at-sea novel, *The Voyage of the Frog*; and *Woods Runner*. Paulsen also has written a memoir for children of his relationships with dogs, *My Life in Dog Years*. A Paulsen author profile is available at www.trelease-on-reading.com/paulsen.html.

Holes
BY LOUIS SACHAR
Grades 4–8   233 pages
Farrar, Straus & Giroux 1998; e-book

Holes is an adventure tale, a mystery, a fantasy, and a quest book. (It captured a rare literary triple crown: Newbery, National Book, and Horn Book awards—all in the same year.) An important ingredient in this success is Sachar's wit. Set in a juvenile detention station in the Texas desert, it traces the sad life of fourteen-year-old Stanley Yelnats, who has just been sentenced (mistakenly) for stealing a pair of sneakers. Not only has the friendless, hopeless Stanley been haunted all his life by a dark cloud of events, so has his family. Indeed, there is a family legend that his grandfather's long-ago selfishness in Latvia has rusted every golden opportunity for the family since then. Forced by the abusive camp police to dig holes all day long in the baking desert, he experiences an epiphany, makes his first friend, and gradually discovers courage he never knew he had. In so doing, he slowly and painfully unwinds the century-old family curse. The movie based on the book was exceptionally well received by critics and families, perhaps because the author himself wrote the screenplay. Sequel: *Small Steps*. Also by the author: *Sideways Stories from Wayside School* (n). Related book: *Maniac Magee* (n).

Homer Price
BY ROBERT MCCLOSKEY
Grades 2–5   160 pages
Viking, 1943

A modern children's classic, this is a collection of humorous tales about a small-town boy's neighborhood dilemmas. Whether telling how Homer foiled the bank robbers with his pet skunk or of his uncle's out-of-control doughnut maker, these six tales will long be remembered. Sequel: *Centerburg Tales*. Related books: *Good Old Boy* (n) and *Soup* (s).

I Was a Rat!
BY PHILIP PULLMAN; KEVIN HAWKES, ILLUS.
Grades 3–5   75 pages
Dell, 2002

This is pure melodramatic parody and a slapstick adventure as only Philip Pullman can offer it. From the first chapter, when a nameless and homeless boy knocks on the door of a childless couple at ten p.m. and declares he used to be a rat, the reader-listener is hooked. And you stay that way as

Pullman pulls you through a series of madcap chapters filled with threatening (but not too threatening) sewers, asylums, schools, jails, laboratories, courtrooms, and carnivals, all populated by Dickensian characters, kind and cruel. One might say this is Stuart Little meets Cinderella as written by Dickens and Roald Dahl. Other fairy-tale parodies, page 294.

In the Year of the Boar and Jackie Robinson
BY BETTE BAO LORD
Grades 1–5   *169 pages*
Harper, 1984
Over the course of the year 1947, we watch a nine-year-old Chinese immigrant girl as she and her family begin a new life in Brooklyn. Told with warmth and humor and based on the author's own childhood, Shirley Temple Wong's cultural assimilation will ring true with any child who has had to begin again—culturally or socially. To know this little girl is to fall in love with her—and her neighbors and classmates. (One of the students in Bette Bao Lord's childhood New York classroom was the future children's novelist Avi.)

Incident at Hawk's Hill
BY ALLAN W. ECKERT
Grades 6 and up   *174 pages*
Little, Brown, 1971
An extremely timid six-year-old who wandered away from his family's farm in 1870 is adopted by a ferocious female badger, à la Mowgli in *The Jungle Book*. The boy is fed, protected, and instructed by the badger through the summer, until the family manages to recapture the now-wild child. Definitely for experienced listeners. When reading this aloud, paraphrase a large portion of the slow-moving prologue. In the sequel, *Return to Hawk's Hill*, young Ben is again missing, this time adrift in a canoe in Indian territory among the feared Cree. Related books: *Hatchet* (n) and *My Side of the Mountain* (n).

The Indian in the Cupboard (series)
BY LYNNE REID BANKS
Grades 2–6   *182 pages*
Doubleday, 1981; e-book
A witty, exciting, and poignant fantasy tale of a nine-year-old English boy who accidentally brings to life his three-inch plastic American Indian. Once the shock of the trick wears off, the boy begins to realize the immense responsibility involved in feeding, protecting, and hiding a

three-inch human being from another time (1870s) and culture. Anyone concerned about the political correctness of the series may feel relieved by reading the review by Native American author Michael Dorris in the *New York Times Book Review* (May 16, 1993). Sequels: *The Return of the Indian*; *The Secret of the Indian*; *The Mystery of the Cupboard*; and *The Key to the Indian*.

Inventing Elliot

BY GRAHAM GARDNER

Grades 9 and up   *181 pages*
Dial, 2004

This rich and disturbing first novel describes the web that entangles a fourteen-year-old boy at an English high school. He's new, having come from another school, where he'd been singled out for physical abuse by the dominant clique. At this new school, he's determined to be anonymous among the hundreds of other students. But soon he's spotted by a secret society of boys who rule the school with a reign of terror, right under the noses of the faculty. When the boys invite Elliot to join their society, he realizes this time it's inclusion instead of exclusion. Joining would certainly secure his safety, but it would also destroy whatever self-worth he has. This is the chasm faced every day by whistle-blowers in all walks of life. I must report that it concludes on a very hopeful but suspenseful note. Caution: Readers-aloud should be aware there is brief sexual innuendo along with graphic violence, though not gratuitous. Related books: *Ghetto Cowboy* by G. Neri; *Killing Mr. Griffin* (n); *Plague Year* (n); and *Scorpions* (n).

James and the Giant Peach

BY ROALD DAHL

Grades K–6   *120 pages*
Knopf, 1961

Four-year-old James, newly orphaned, is sent to live with his abusive aunts and appears resigned to spending his life as their humble servant. Then a giant peach begins growing in the backyard. Waiting inside that peach is a collection of characters that will captivate your audience as they did James. Few books hold up over six grade levels as well as this one does, and few authors for children understand their world as well as Dahl did. Also by the author: *The BFG*; *Danny, the Champion of the World* (n); *Fantastic Mr. Fox*; *Matilda*; *The Minpins*; *The Wonderful Story of Henry Sugar*; and *The Roald Dahl Treasury*, a collection of his best work. Related book: *Malcolm at Midnight* (n).

Journey to the River Sea

BY EVA IBBOTSON

Grades 4–7   *299 pages*

Viking Penguin, 2001; e-book

In 1910, we find Maia, a wealthy orphan girl, residing at the Mayfair Academy for Young Ladies, a setting very reminiscent of Frances Hodgson Burnett's *Sara Crewe* or *A Little Princess*. When Maia's legal guardian informs her that a worldwide search has produced her only living relatives (her father's second cousin and his family, including twin daughters her age), who live on a rubber plantation in the Amazon, her imagination takes flight. The opportunity to see the world's largest river, to explore the exotic jungles of Brazil, to spend her childhood hours and dreams with twin cousins—it's a young girl's dream come true. Wrong, of course. The plantation-owning Carters are deeply in debt, the father is a leach looking for Maia's inheritance, the wife is a shrew, and the twins are nothing short of vipers. How Maia extricates herself from this predicament, with the aid of a mysterious Indian boy with a large British inheritance, a homesick child actor, and a host of savvy natives, makes for an old-fashioned melodrama that has you rooting out loud for Maia and hissing her relatives all the way down the Amazon. Also by the author: *The Star of Kazan* (n) and *One Dog and His Boy*. Related books: all of Frances Hodgson Burnett's children's novels; *Riding Freedom* by Pam Muñoz Ryan; and *Understood Betsy* (n).

Kaspar the Titanic Cat

BY MICHAEL MORPURGO; MICHAEL FOREMAN, ILLUS.

Grades 2–5   *200 pages*

Harper, 2012

Fourteen-year-old Johnny Trott is the savvy orphan bellboy at London's swanky Savoy Hotel when he's spotted by a Russian countess and designated to care for her prized black cat, Kaspar. Soon a tragedy leaves him the sole protector of the cat, which he must hide in his room against the hotel rules. Unfortunately Kaspar refuses to eat without his countess and is starving to death—until Lizziebeth, an eight-year-old American heiress, arrives on the scene and saves the day, though not before her dangerous impulsiveness requires her to be publicly rescued from the rooftop by Johnny. No good melodrama should be without a villain and Morpurgo provides a dandy in Skullface, the feared head housekeeper. When it's time for Lizziebeth and her parents (and Kaspar) to depart for America, their ship is the *Titanic* (with Johnny aboard as a working stowaway). Of course, all survive, including the cat. Better yet, it's not even the end of the book. The description of the *Titanic* sinking is based on careful research and includes realistic portrayals of the crew's heroics. For other books by the author, see *Kensuke's Kingdom* (n).

Kensuke's Kingdom
BY MICHAEL MORPURGO
Grades 3–5   *164 pages*
Scholastic, 2003

Because childhood can sometimes be a case of survival, children seem to gravitate to survival books, as proven by Paulsen's success with the Hatchet series (n). This volume ranks with the best of that genre.

Michael is twelve years old when he and his dog are washed overboard from the family's yacht and into the Coral Sea off Australia. Clinging to the dog and a soccer ball, the boy is washed up on a tropical island. While appearing uninhabited, the island has a host of animals, plants, and fish that might keep him alive. It also contains another resident—a very old and very angry Japanese man named Kensuke Ogawa, a navy doctor who has been on the island since the end of World War II. Initially, Kensuke was marooned there when his ship sank, but eventually he was there by choice, more than fifty-five years after his home in Nagasaki was bombed with one of the first atomic bombs. The rest is his story and Michael's. Entwined with the modern survival story are issues of war and peace, brotherhood, family ties, art, nature, and hope. Related books: *Baseball Saved Us* by Ken Mochizuki (a story from the Japanese internment camps); *The Cay* (n); *Robinson Crusoe* by Daniel Defoe (one of the Scribner Illustrated Classics series [abridged, thank you], illustrated by N. C. Wyeth); and three books by Gary Paulsen: *The Foxman*; *Hatchet* (n); and *The Voyage of the Frog*. Also by the author: *Kaspar the Titanic Cat* (n); *The Pied Piper of Hamelin* (p); *Private Peaceful*; *War Horse*; and *The War of Jenkins' Ear*.

The Kid Who Invented the Popsicle (nonfiction)
BY DON L. WULFFSON
Grades 1–5   *128 pages*
Puffin, 1999

Here are the true but little-known stories behind the invention of one hundred everyday items: animal crackers, aspirin, balloons, Band-Aids, barbed wire, baseball caps, blue jeans, doughnuts, Frisbees, miniature golf, marshmallows, phonographs, ice-cream sundaes, supermarkets, and yo-yos. Since none of these items takes more than a page to describe, this is the kind of book you keep in the car to bring into restaurants to read while the family is waiting for the meal; it's also perfect for brief classroom fill-ins. Sequel: *The Kid Who Invented the Trampoline* (fifty more items). Related books: In *Girls Think of Everything*, Catherine Thimmesh tells the story of fifty-nine inventions by women, from dishwashers and diapers to fire escapes and windshield wipers; *Hooray for Inventors!* by Marcia Williams; *Marvelous Mattie* by Emily A. McCully; *Odd Boy Out: Young Albert Einstein* (p); and *So You Want to Be an Inventor?* by Judith St. George.

Killing Mr. Griffin
BY LOIS DUNCAN
Grades 7 and up   224 pages
Little, Brown, 1978; e-book
This young adult novel offers a chilling dissection of peer pressure and group guilt. Because of the subject matter and occasional four-letter words, care should be used in its presentation. The story deals with five high school students who attempt to scare their unpopular English teacher by kidnapping him. When their carefully laid plans unravel toward a tragic catastrophe, they find themselves unable to handle the situation. For experienced listeners. Also by the author: *I Know What You Did Last Summer*. Related books: *Deathwatch* by Robb White; *Inventing Elliot* (n); *On My Honor* (s); *Plague Year* (n); and *Wolf Rider* (n).

The Land I Lost
BY HUYNH QUANG NHUONG
Grades 2–6   126 pages
Harper, 1982
Most American children today know Vietnam only as a word associated with a bitter war that divided the nation. The author of this remembrance grew up there, one of eight children in a farming family along a river, not far from the jungle. This is the dramatic and affectionate tale of how the citizens of his tiny hamlet worked together to survive the constant assaults from wild animals and a climate that would destroy lesser souls. Each of the fifteen chapters is an adventure into a long-lost world. Sequel: *Water Buffalo Days*.

Lassie Come-Home
BY ERIC KNIGHT
Grades 4 and up   200 pages
Square Fish, 2007
This 1947 classic dog story reads so easily, the words ringing with such feeling, that you'll find yourself coming back to it year after year. As with

many dog stories, there are the usual themes of loss, grief, courage, and struggle—but here they are taken to splendid heights. Set between the Scottish Highlands and Yorkshire, England, in the early 1900s, the novel describes the triumphant struggle of a collie to travel one hundred miles to return to her young master. Unfortunately, Hollywood and television have badly damaged the image of this story with their tinny, affected characterization. This is the original Lassie story. For a list of dog stories, see page 242.

Lily's Crossing
BY PATRICIA REILLY GIFF
Grades 3–6   *180 pages*
Delacorte/Dell, 1997; e-book
This coming-of-age novel focuses on the summer of 1944 and one feisty yet frightened young girl in a Long Island beach community. With her beloved father shipped overseas and her best friend moved away, Lily befriends a Hungarian refugee, Albert. Together they experience the great fears and small triumphs that keep children afloat during war years. Lily, reader and future writer, learns the hard way that tall tales, spun out of control, can become dangerous lies. And Albert finds in Lily a friend who will change his life forever. This is a multiple award winner, including Newbery Honor. Related books: *Alan and Naomi* by Myron Levoy; and *Because of Winn-Dixie* (n).

The Lion, the Witch, and the Wardrobe (Narnia series)
BY C. S. LEWIS
Grades 3–6   *186 pages*
HarperCollins, 1950; e-book
Four children discover that the old wardrobe closet in an empty room leads to the magical kingdom of Narnia—a kingdom filled with heroes, witches, princes, and intrigue. This is the most famous (but second) of seven enchanting books in the Chronicles of Narnia series, which can be read as adventures or as Christian allegory. The series in chronological order: *The Magician's Nephew; The Lion, the Witch, and the Wardrobe; The Horse and His Boy; Prince Caspian; The Voyage of the Dawn Treader; The Silver Chair;* and *The Last Battle. The Land of Narnia* by Brian Sibley is an excellent guide to Narnia. Many reasonable comparisons have been made between the dual world of Narnia and the Harry Potter (n) books. See also *Martin the Warrior* (n).

The Lion's Paw
BY ROBB WHITE
Grades 4–7   *243 pages*
A. W. Ink, 1946
Take three runaways—orphaned brother (age nine) and sister (thirteen) and the son of a missing-in-action naval officer (fifteen)—place them aboard a sailboat in Florida's inland waterways, and then put their fate in the hands of a veteran adventure writer. The result is a nautical adventure novel like they used to write. In fact, it was written in 1946 in the heat of WWII. (Note: There are three references to "the Japs" in the context of the war.) It was out of print for decades but is again available. You'll find no wasted words here, no smart-mouthed dialogue that reads like a TV sitcom— just three determined kids evading authorities, bounty hunters, and alligators. For experienced listeners. Also by the author (for teens): *Deathwatch*. Related books: *The Cay* (n); and *The Voyage of the Frog* by Gary Paulsen.

Listening for Lions
BY GLORIA WHELAN
Grades 3–8   *194 pages*
Harper, 2005; e-book
From an outstanding writer of historical fiction comes this tale set in 1919 in British East Africa, where thirteen-year-old Rachel was living an idyllic life with her medical-missionary parents until the Great Flu Epidemic struck. Suddenly orphaned, Rachel ends up in the hands of two wealthy, plotting neighbors, who have lost their own daughter to the flu. Their intention was to send their daughter back to England in hopes her visit would move the heart of her grandfather—and then loosen his purse strings (he disowned the girl's ne'er-do-well father years ago). Now they're manipulating the grieving Rachel into posing as their deceased daughter and sending her off to the grandfather's estate with the warning that any bad news could send the old man to his grave. In England, a wonderful relationship grows between the man and child, making it all the harder for her to tell him the truth. Reminiscent of *The Secret Garden* and *Little Lord Fauntleroy*, this tale of a plucky young lady is a delightful page-turner and character study. Related book: *The Star of Kazan* (n).

Loser
BY JERRY SPINELLI
Grades 4 and up   *218 pages*
HarperCollins, 2002; e-book

There are Donald Zinkoffs in every neighborhood, in every classroom, and in many, if not most, families. They go by a variety of names: bumbler, dope, klutz, loser. As Jerry Spinelli points out in the first chapter of *Loser*, these people are largely ignored by the outside world until one day somebody notices them and labels them. Not since *The Hundred Dresses* (1944), Eleanor Estes's timeless novel of a poor girl's trial by classroom prejudice, has anyone grabbed this subject of the odd-child-out with such force. Donald is not retarded, nor is he ADHD. He's just a little out of focus, not enough to send him to special education classes but enough to leave him without a best friend.

Donald also has a giant sense of humor. His appreciative laughter and choice of clothing send early warning signals to his first-grade teacher. Just as important for this story, he is the son of loving but not overbearing parents. Indeed, it is their abiding, unconditional love (along with the affection of two master teachers) that allows the boy to grow a heart that abounds in exuberant love for everything and everyone around him. Spinelli's irreverent humor will have middle-grade readers doubled over (to say nothing of the adult who tries to read it aloud). It is this humor that pulls the reader through the first half of the book, each chapter provoking you to wonder what will come next. It also prevents the story from becoming a tale of despair.

In light of today's "bullying" and "hazing" headlines, this is a novel for our times. Related book: *A Corner of the Universe* by Anne Martin. Also by the author: *Maniac Magee* (n).

Lupita Mañana
BY PATRICIA BEATTY
Grades 4–8   *192 pages*
Harper, 2000
After the death of her father, thirteen-year-old Lupita emigrates illegally to the United States. In slums, under cover of night, in damp freight cars, across the desert, plucky Lupita—posing as a boy—learns the meaning of fear as immigration police haunt her thoughts night and day. Here is the hope and heartbreak of poor families everywhere. Related books: *City of Orphans* (n); in a much lighter though still serious vein, *The Unforgotten Coat* by Frank Cottrell Boyce (author of *Millions*) portrays a family of illegal Mongolians and their children's efforts to fit in with a class of sixth-graders in Liverpool, England.

Malcolm at Midnight
BY W. H. BECK; BRIAN LIES, ILLUS.
Grades 2–4   *265 pages*
Houghton Mifflin, 2012
When the teacher purchased Malcolm from the pet shop, he thought he
was just a large mouse. Wrong. And when Malcolm ended up in the fifth
grade as the classroom pet, he thought he had gone to heaven. Wrong.
Malcolm is a rat, a species with a particularly bad reputation, something
he spends the book trying to overcome. And just in case you think the
teachers run the school—wrong again. In this school, the Midnight
Academy rules—a collection of all the classroom pets that meets outside
their cages each midnight to debate and investigate school issues. A warm,
humorous adventure with many illustrations. Related books: *Charlotte's
Web* (n); *James and the Giant Peach* (n); *Poppy* (n); *Stuart Little* (n); and *The
Water Horse* (n).

Maniac Magee
BY JERRY SPINELLI
Grades 5–9   *184 pages*
Little, Brown, 1990
One of the most popular Newbery winners, this is the tale of a legendary
twelve-year-old runaway orphan and athlete extraordinaire, who touches
countless families and peers with his kindness and wisdom. Could he be a
modern Huck Finn? The book deals with racism, homelessness, and com-
munity violence in a most effective, almost allegorical manner. Also by
the author: *Crash*; *The Library Card*; *Loser* (n); *Space Station Seventh Grade*;
Stargirl; and *Wringer*. Spinelli's autobiography: *Knots in My Yo-Yo String:
The Autobiography of a Kid*.

Martin the Warrior (Redwall series)
BY BRIAN JACQUES
Grades 4–7   *376 pages*
Philomel, 1994
The Redwall series is in the tradition of *The Hobbit*, but for younger readers.
Built around an endearing band of courageous animals inhabiting an old
English abbey, the books describe their fierce battles against evil creatures.
There is high adventure galore, cliffhanger chapter endings, gruesome be-
havior by evil outsiders, and rollicking fun. For experienced listeners. *Martin
the Warrior* is a prequel, going back to the founding of the abbey, and should
be read first, followed by *Redwall* and then the rest of the series. Related

books: *Harry Potter and the Sorcerer's Stone* (n) and *The Lion, the Witch, and the Wardrobe* (n). For grades 6 and up: *The Hobbit* by J. R. R. Tolkien.

The Midnight Fox

BY BETSY BYARS
Grades 4–6   *160 pages*
Viking, 1968

From the very beginning, young Tommy is determined he'll hate his aunt and uncle's farm, where he must spend the summer. His determination suffers a setback when he discovers a renegade black fox. His desire to keep the fox running free, however, collides with his uncle's wish to kill it, and the novel builds to a stunning moment of confrontation and courage. Also by the author: *Cracker Jackson*; *Keeper of the Doves* (s); *The Pinballs* (n); *The SOS File* (s); and *Trouble River*.

The Mighty Miss Malone

BY CHRISTOPHER PAUL CURTIS
Grades 5–8   *320 pages*
Wendy Lamb Books, 2012

Revisiting some of the territory he made familiar to us with his Newbery-winning *Bud, Not Buddy*, the author offers here a plucky eleven-year-old African-American girl narrating her family's journey through the Great Depression. A determined optimist, Deza Malone is mighty in word and thought, never to be outtalked and shining in the classroom—when there is one. And unlike her counterpart in *Buddy*, Deza is surrounded by one mighty sacrificing family that encounters in the 1930s what many families are facing in today's Great Recession. Many people were reduced to riding filthy, dangerous freight trains to get from place to place, as do the Malones en route to a shantytown. PBS's *American Experience* spotlighted that experience in "Riding the Rails," online at http://www.pbs.org/wgbh/americanexperience/films/rails/player/. As bad as the times were, they were worse for people of color. See "Added Obstacles for African Americans," online at http://www.pbs.org/wgbh/americanexperience/features/general-article/rails-added-obstacles/. For related books, see *Bud, Not Buddy* (n).

Mimi

BY JOHN NEWMAN
Grades 4–8   *186 pages (small)*
Candlewick, 2011

We meet this family—a father, two teens, and one primary-grader—five months after the mother died in a traffic accident. The tale is seen through the witty but penetrating eyes of Mimi, the youngest. No one is finished grieving; they are all going through the motions, especially Dad, who is on leave from his job and tuned out to everyone's needs except his own. This isn't a depressing tale, but instead one about family dysfunction and humans working their way out of the wreckage of a tragedy. The author is a classroom teacher who has obviously met a few struggling families. In this case, it's a supporting cast of relatives, teachers, and classmates who come to the rescue. There are gobs of laughter as well as pure wisdom in these pages ("'You said that with your head, love, not with your heart— so it doesn't count,' said Dad" after an angry outburst by the teenage daughter). For related books on grief, see *Pearl Verses the World* (s).

Mockingbird

BY KATHRYN ERSKINE
Grades 6 and up   *235 pages*
Putnam, 2010; e-book

With autism cases tripling in the past several decades, this book is long overdue. Ten-year-old Caitlin has Asperger's syndrome and tells her own story in a most compelling voice. People on the autism spectrum normally don't handle interpersonal communication or social issues easily, and *Mockingbird* offers its readers (and listeners) a deep insight into one girl's mind and heart, far closer than they might ever come with an actual classmate.

Not only does Caitlin have to cope with Asperger's, she's also struggling to understand the tragedy that recently struck her family when her older brother was one of the victims in a fatal school shooting. While Caitlin is loved by her widower father, her brother was the pride of his life and she's trying to fill the family void left by his death—not an easy task for anyone, let alone someone for whom empathy is a foreign emotion. As the book progresses, we see the efforts of her teachers, counselor, father, and classmates in trying to bring closure to the struggling child, giving us an opportunity to view all of them through the child's eyes. And while there are many wrenching moments, the book is not without its honestly humorous moments as she struggles with literal interpretations of classmates' and teachers' words and actions.

Because of the serious nature of the book and its subjects, I would hesitate in sharing it with children as young as the narrator (ten) unless he or she is very mature. One cannot come away from this book without both a greater understanding of autism and a greater empathy for those suffering with social disorders. This tale will grab you by the throat, give you a good shake, and then set you cheering for the human spirit. In a related novel, *Wonder* by R. J. Palacio, a spunky boy with a deeply deformed face who has been previously homeschooled is enrolled at a neighborhood middle school. Like *Mockingbird*, his story enables readers and listeners to crawl into a "different" child's skin and soul for a more complete view of the world.

The Moon over High Street

BY NATALIE BABBITT

Grades 6 and up   *148 pages*

Scholastic, 2012

In a publishing age awash in wizardry, apocalypses, dystopias, and teenage vampires, it's easy to forget there is anything left resembling old-fashioned storytelling about normal people. And that's what we have here in the tale of a twelve-year-old orphan boy, Joe, raised lovingly by his homespun grandmother in the 1960s. This summer Joe has gone downstate to visit his aunt in a small town filled with common midwestern folk. Across the street from Joe's aunt is a family with a girl his age, and they become fast friends. Out of the blue, Joe is given the chance of a lifetime, something people play the lottery for every day: The millionaire in town would like to adopt him, send him to the finest schools, let him live on wealthy High Street, and eventually give him the family factory to run. There is only one string attached. This is a wise but simple novel about ambition, friendship, family, wealth, and hubris. What are we willing to do to be happy? It has a feel-good ending that leaves us wondering about the rest of Joe's life.

The Mouse and the Motorcycle (series)

BY BEVERLY CLEARY

Grades K–2   *158 pages*

Morrow, 1965; e-book

When young Keith and his family check into a run-down motel one day, the mice in the walls are disappointed. They'd hoped for young children, messy ones who leave lots of crumbs behind. What Ralph S. Mouse gets instead is a mouse-size motorcycle. He and the boy guest become fast friends and embark on a series of hallway-to-highway escapades that make this tale a longtime favorite. Sequels: *Runaway Ralph* and *Ralph S. Mouse*. Also by the author: *Ramona the Pest* (n). Related books: *Malcolm at Midnight* (n); *Poppy* (n); and *Stuart Little* (n).

Mr. Popper's Penguins

BY RICHARD AND FLORENCE ATWATER; ROBERT LAWSON, ILLUS.

Grades 2–4   *140 pages*

Little, Brown, 1938; e-book

When you add twelve penguins to the family of Mr. Popper, the house-painter, you've got immense food bills, impossible situations, and a freezer full of laughs. The short chapters will keep your audience hungry for more. Don't confuse this book with the movie—two very different stories. Related books: *Capyboppy* by Bill Peet; *Owls in the Family* (s); and *The Water Horse* (n) by Dick King-Smith.

Mr. Tucket (series)

BY GARY PAULSEN

Grades 2–8   *166 pages*

Dell, 1997; e-book

We meet fourteen-year-old Francis Tucket just after he's been captured by an Indian raiding party while his family was heading to Oregon via wagon train. In typical Paulsen fashion, Francis is not going to remain captive for long, but it'll take him five books to reach his destination by way of war, starvation, and every imaginable threat on the American frontier. After *Mr. Tucket*, the series includes (in order): *Call Me Francis Tucket*; *Tucket's Ride*; *Tucket's Gold*; and *Tucket's Home*. All five books have been compiled into a single large paperback, *Tucket's Travels*. These are a little more accessible for a younger age than is *Hatchet* (n).

Mrs. Frisby and the Rats of NIMH (series)

BY ROBERT C. O'BRIEN

Grades 4–6   *232 pages*

Atheneum, 1971

In this unforgettable fantasy–science fiction tale, we meet a group of rats that has become superintelligent through a series of laboratory injections. Though it opens with an almost fairy-tale softness, it grows into a taut and frighteningly realistic tale. A decade after its publication, the author's fiction grew closer to fact with a breakthrough in genetic engineering; see the December 27, 1982, issue of *Newsweek*, "The Making of a Mighty Mouse." Sequels: *Racso and the Rats of NIMH* and *R-T, Margaret, and the Rats of NIMH*, both by Jane L. Conly (Robert C. O'Brien's daughter). Also by O'Brien: *The Silver Crown*.

My Brother Sam Is Dead
BY JAMES LINCOLN COLLIER AND CHRISTOPHER COLLIER
Grades 5 and up   *251 pages*
Simon & Schuster, 1974

In this Newbery-winning historical novel, the inhumanity of war is examined through the experiences of one divided Connecticut family
during the American Revolution. Told in the words of a younger brother,
the heartache and passions hold true for all wars in all times, and the authors' balanced accounts of British and American tactics allow readers to
come to their own conclusions. Related Revolutionary War books: *The
Fighting Ground* by Avi; *Sarah Bishop* (n); and *Toliver's Secret* (n). Related war
books: *Otto of the Silver Hand* (n) and four books by Gary Paulsen: *The
Foxman*; *The Rifle* (s); *Soldier's Heart*; and *Woods Runner*.

My Side of the Mountain
BY JEAN CRAIGHEAD GEORGE
Grades 3–8   *178 pages*
Dutton, 1959

A modern teenage Robinson Crusoe, city-bred Sam Gribley describes
his year surviving as a runaway in a remote area of the Catskill Mountains. His diary of living off the land is marked by moving accounts of the
animals, insects, plants, people, and books that helped him survive. For
experienced listeners. Sequels: *On the Far Side of the Mountain*; *Frightful's
Mountain*; and *Frightful's Daughter*. For other survival books, see *Hatchet* (n).

Nothing but the Truth: A Documentary Novel
BY AVI
Grades 7 and up   *177 pages*
Orchard, 1991

In this Newbery Honor winner, a ninth-grader decides to irritate his
teacher until she transfers him to another class. But what begins benignly
soon escalates into a slanderous attack on the teacher when parents,
faculty, media, and school board members join the conflict. In the end,
everyone loses. Told exclusively through documents—memos, letters, and
diary entries—this is a dramatic example of how freedom of speech can
also be abused. Also by the author: *The True Confessions of Charlotte Doyle*
(n). Related books: *Inventing Elliot* (n) and *Plague Year* (n).

Nothing to Fear

BY JACKIE FRENCH KOLLER

Grades 4 and up   *279 pages*

Harcourt Brace, 1991

This is a good old-fashioned historical novel that grabs you right by the heart and throat. Set in the Depression, it follows the travails and triumphs of a poor Irish family—especially young Danny and his mother—as they try to hold on against all odds. This is a vivid depiction of life in the 1930s, but the acts of love and courage displayed by the Garvey family are repeated daily in many families wherever poverty abides. Related books: *Bud, Not Buddy* (n) and *The Mighty Miss Malone* (n), both by Christopher Paul Curtis; *City of Orphans* (n); and *No Promises in the Wind* by Irene Hunt.

Number the Stars

BY LOIS LOWRY

Grades 4–7   *137 pages*

Houghton Mifflin, 1989; e-book

In 1943, as the occupying Nazi army attempted to extricate and then exterminate the seven thousand Jews residing in Denmark, the Danish people rose up as one in a determined and remarkably successful resistance. Against that backdrop, this Newbery winner describes a ten-year-old Danish girl joining forces with her relatives to save the lives of her best friend and her family. Related books: *Darkness over Denmark* by Ellen Levine is an excellent nonfiction companion to this book, with photos of Denmark and the resistance fighters; the popular novel *Snow Treasure* by Marie McSwigan is about Norwegian children smuggling gold past the Nazis; also *The Little Ships* and *The Greatest Skating Race*, both by Louise Borden.

Otto of the Silver Hand

BY HOWARD PYLE

Grades 5–8   *132 pages*

Dover, 1967; e-book

First published in 1888 and written by one of the leading figures of early American children's literature, this is an ideal introduction to the classics. Intended as a cautionary tale about warfare (and inspired by the wounded Union soldiers he saw on railroads during the Civil War), Pyle's story describes a young boy's joy and suffering as he rises above the cruelty of the world, while caught between warring medieval German tribes. Though the language may be somewhat foreign to the listener at the start, it soon adds to the flavor of the narrative. For experienced listeners. Related books: *Castle Diary* by Richard Platt, the yearlong diary of a young page serving in the castle of his uncle in 1285 (a large picture book with rich text and illustrations describing everyday life); and *Matilda Bone* by Karen Cushman, about a female apprentice bonesetter in a medieval village.

Peppermints in the Parlor
BY BARBARA BROOKS WALLACE
Grades 3–7   *198 pages*
Atheneum, 1980; e-book
When the newly orphaned Emily arrives in San Francisco, she expects to be adopted by her wealthy aunt and uncle. What she finds instead is a poverty-stricken aunt held captive as a servant in a shadowy, decaying home for the aged. Filled with Dickensian flavor, this novel has secret passageways, tyrannical matrons, eerie whispers in the night, and a pair of fearful but plucky kids. Sequel: *The Perils of Peppermints*. Following the success of this book, the author produced four more in the same genre: *Cousins in the Castle*; *Ghosts in the Gallery*; *The Twin in the Tavern*; and *Sparrows in the Scullery*.

The Pinballs
BY BETSY BYARS
Grades 5–7   *136 pages*
Harper, 1977
Brought together under the same roof, three foster children prove to each other and the world that they are not pinballs to be knocked around from one place to the next; they have a choice in life—to try or not to try. The author has taken what could have been a maudlin story and turned it into a hopeful, loving, and very witty book. Short chapters with easy-to-read dialogue. Related books: *Bud, Not Buddy* (n); *A Family Apart* (n); *Maniac Magee* (n); and *Touch Blue* by Cynthia Lord.

Plague Year
BY STEPHANIE S. TOLAN
Grades 7 and up   *198 pages*
Fawcett, 1991; e-book
When Bran arrives in his aunt's neatly manicured middle-class town, his clothes, hairstyle, and manner make him the immediate target of the high school's "jock" crowd. That he can handle, but a month later a tabloid newspaper announces his secret—that his father is about to go on trial in New Jersey as an accused serial killer. Suddenly, the town is consumed by

Bran's presence and the danger this "bad seed" poses for its children, and mob mentality takes over for common sense and justice. Reading like today's headlines, it is fast paced and thought provoking, and offers powerful examples of all that is good and bad in school and community. Related books: *Inventing Elliot* (n); *Nothing but the Truth* (n); and *Tangerine* by Edward Bloor.

Poppy (series)

BY AVI

Grades K–4   160 pages

Orchard, 1995; e-book

Like an evil dictator, a great horned owl keeps the growing deer mouse population in Dimwood Forest under his fierce control, eating those who disobey his orders. When he kills her boyfriend, little Poppy dares to go where no mouse has gone before—to the world beyond Dimwood. Indeed, she uncovers the hoax the evil owl has perpetrated through the years and leads her frightened family to the promised land. Told with wit and high drama, this is an excellent start to the tales from Dimwood Forest that have followed: *Poppy & Rye*; *Ragweed*; *Ereth's Birthday*; *Poppy & Ereth*; and *Poppy's Return*. Older fans of this series will enjoy *Martin the Warrior* (n); younger fans, *Charlotte's Web* (n).

Ramona the Pest (series)

BY BEVERLY CLEARY

Grades K–4   144 pages

Morrow, 1968; e-book

Not all of Beverly Cleary's books make good read-alouds, though children love to read her silently. Some of her books move too slowly to hold read-aloud interest, but that's not the case with the Ramona series, which begins with *Ramona the Pest*. The book follows this outspoken young lady, a forerunner of Junie B. Jones with a better grasp of grammar, through her early months in kindergarten. Children will smile in recognition of Ramona's encounters with the first day of school, show-and-tell, seat work, a substitute teacher, Halloween, young love—and dropping out of kindergarten. Long chapters can easily be divided. Early grades should have some experience with short novels before trying Ramona. The sequels follow Ramona as she grows older and, with her family, experiences the challenges of modern life: *Ramona and Her Father*; *Ramona and Her Mother*; *Ramona Quimby, Age 8*; *Ramona Forever*; and *Ramona's World*. Also by the author: *Dear Mr. Henshaw* (n); *The Mouse and the Motorcycle* (n); and for pre-schoolers, *Two Times the Fun* (s).

Roll of Thunder, Hear My Cry (series)

BY MILDRED TAYLOR
Grades 5 and up   *276 pages*
Dial, 1976

Filled with the lifeblood of a black Mississippi family during the Depression, this Newbery winner depicts the pride of people who refuse to give in to threats and harassments from white neighbors. The story is narrated by daughter Cassie, age nine, who experiences her first taste of social injustice and refuses to swallow it. Along with her family, her classmates, and neighbors, she will stir listeners' hearts and awaken many children to the tragedy of prejudice and discrimination. For experienced listeners. Caution: There are several racial epithets used in the dialogue. Other books in the series: *The Land* (a prequel to *Roll of Thunder*); *Let the Circle Be Unbroken*; *The Road to Memphis*; and four short novels, *The Friendship* (s), *Mississippi Bridge*, *Song of the Trees*, and *The Well*. Also by the author: *The Gold Cadillac*.

Related nonfiction titles: *Getting Away with Murder: The True Story of the Emmett Till Case* by Chris Crowe; *Heart and Soul: The Story of America and African Americans* by Kadir Nelson; *More Than Anything Else* (Booker T. Washington learns to read) by Marie Bradby; *Rosa Parks: My Story* by Rosa Parks; and *Words Set Me Free: The Story of Young Frederick Douglass* by Lesa Ransome.

Roll of Thunder, Hear My Cry is an excellent introduction to the American civil rights movement, something that now can be turned into a multimedia experience. Consider the wide array of options available for expanding on the book:

- **Video recommendations:** *Once Upon a Time . . . When We Were Colored* is an affectionate look back at life in a black Mississippi neighborhood from the mid-1940s to the dawn of the civil rights movement, based on the autobiographical novel by Clifton Taulbert. See also *4 Little Girls*, Spike Lee's acclaimed 1997 documentary about the turning point in the civil rights movement—the bombing of the 16th Street Baptist Church (for grades 7 and up); and *The Untold Story of Emmett Louis Till*, Keith A. Beauchamp's documentary film about one of the most horrific murders in the civil rights era (for grades 7 and up).
- **Audio:** See Duke University's oral history project composed of the memories of those who lived in the segregated South: "Behind the Veil." Different portions of that collection can be heard on the Internet at American RadioWorks, in the documentary *Remembering Jim Crow*. The RadioWorks

site also includes excellent slide shows of images taken during the period; see http://americanradioworks.publicradio.org/features/remembering/; also American RadioWorks, http:americanradioworks.publicradio.org/features/sayitplain/index.html. American Public Media's radio program *The Story*, with Dick Gordon, features interviews with non-famous people who have lived in and behind the headlines. Most of the program's civil rights interviews can be found at http://thestory.org/special-features/dedicated-to-the-proposition-the-march-to-equality-1.

Rules of the Road

BY JOAN BAUER

Grades 6 and up   *201 pages*
Putnam/Puffin, 1998

Jenna Boller is a savvy sixteen-year-old salesgirl at a Chicago shoe store when she is spotted by the crusty matriarch of the shoe chain and given an unusual summer job: driving her from Chicago to Dallas. Considering Jenna just got her driver's license, this is no small challenge. Along the way, they visit various stores in the chain, assess the strengths and weaknesses of each, and discover that the shoe company is the object of a takeover bid by a cheapskate rival chain. In Dallas, the bid comes to a head and Jenna's courage—something she honed while coping all her life with an alcoholic father—comes to the rescue. The rules of the road, as applied here, are the rules of life, family, and business that keep us balanced when unexpected curves appear. This is a wise, witty, and moving novel that has deservedly won awards and praise. Sequel: *Best Foot Forward*. Also by the author: *Close to Famous* (n) and *Hope Was Here*.

Sarah Bishop

BY SCOTT O'DELL

Grades 5 and up   *184 pages*
Houghton Mifflin, 1980; e-book

Based on a historic incident, this is the story of a determined young girl who flees war-torn Long Island after her father and brother are killed at the outbreak of the Revolutionary War. In the Connecticut wilderness, she takes refuge in a cave, where she begins her new life. *Sarah Bishop* makes an interesting comparative study with two other read-aloud novels dealing with children running away: *Slake's Limbo* (n) and *My Side of the Mountain* (n). Each depicts the subject of the runaway at a different point in history. For experienced listeners. O'Dell's stories often focus on independent, strong-willed young women. For related Revolutionary War titles, see *My Brother Sam Is Dead* (n).

Scorpions
BY WALTER DEAN MYERS
Grades 7 and up   *216 pages*
Harper, 1988; e-book

This award-winning novelist has drawn upon his childhood in Harlem to give us a revealing and poignant look at an African-American family facing the daily pressures of urban poverty. While seventh-grader Jamal Hicks struggles to resist the pressures to join a neighborhood gang, he is watching his family being torn apart by the crimes of an older brother and a wayward father. Moreover, his relationship with school is disintegrating under a combination of his own irresponsibility and an antagonistic principal. Unable to resist the peer pressure, Jamal makes a tragic decision involving a handgun. Readers-aloud should be aware that some of the book's dialogue is written in black dialect.

In 1993, NPR gave a tape recorder to two boys living in Chicago public housing and allowed them to produce a documentary eventually called *Ghetto Life 101*. Several years later, the two boys again recorded their life in the projects, this time after a five-year-old had been hurled to his death from a fourteenth-floor window by two other young children. If ever there was audio to add another dimension to Myers's urban novel *Scorpions*, these two NPR programs are it. They can still be heard online at http://soundportraits.org/on-air/ghetto_life_101/.

Also by the author: *Bad Boy: a Memoir.* Related books: Sheila P. Moses offers a moving, inspiring, more contemporary tale of urban black life in her novels *Joseph* and *Joseph's Grace*, in which we follow a teenager as he battles to stay safe and sane while his mother disintegrates and he tries to figure out whom to trust in his family and peer group; also *Ghetto Cowboy* by G. Neri.

Myers's *Monster* won the Michael L. Printz Award for Young Adult literature in 2000 but may not be a suitable read-aloud for all adolescents and public classrooms. Written in the form of a screenplay and diary, the story focuses on a young black male charged with murder in a Harlem drugstore. The scenes, which shift between the courtroom and detention center, are unflinching and visceral in their descriptions. Any collection of urban teens (or older) will find much to discuss in this docudrama. For an NPR interview with Myers, see "To Do Well in Life, You Have to 'Read Well,'" *Morning Edition*, January 10, 2012, online at http://www.npr.org/2012/01/10/144944598/to-do-well-in-life-you-have-to-read-well.

The Secret Garden

BY FRANCES HODGSON BURNETT; INGA MOORE, ILLUS.

Grades 2–5   *278 pages*

Candlewick, 2007; e-book

Few books spin such a web of magic about their audiences as does this 1911 children's classic about the sulky orphan who comes to live with her cold, unfeeling uncle on the windswept English moors. Wandering the grounds of his immense manor house one day, she discovers a secret garden, locked and abandoned. This leads her to discover her uncle's invalid child hidden within the mansion, her first friendship, and her own true self. While this is definitely for experienced listeners, try to avoid the abridged versions, since too much of the book's flavor is lost in those. The Inga Moore illustrated version is by far the best full edition to date. Also by the author: *Little Lord Fauntleroy*; *A Little Princess*; and *The Lost Prince*. Two recent books by Eva Ibbotson are so reminiscent of Burnett's genre, you'd almost think she'd come back from the dead: *The Star of Kazan* (n) and *Journey to the River Sea* (n). Other books: *Mandy* by Julie Edwards; and *Understood Betsy* (n).

Sideways Stories from Wayside School

BY LOUIS SACHAR

Grades 2–5   *124 pages*

Random House, 1990

Thirty chapters about the wacky students who inhabit the thirtieth floor of Wayside School, the school that was supposed to be built one story high and thirty classes wide, until the contractor made a mistake and made it thirty stories high! If you think the building is bizarre, wait until you meet the kids who inhabit it. Sequels: *Wayside School Is Falling Down* and *Wayside School Gets a Little Stranger*. Also by the author: *Holes* (n); *Johnny's in the Basement*; and *There's a Boy in the Girls' Bathroom*. Other humorous novels: *Skinnybones* (s); *Be a Perfect Person in Just Three Days!* (s); *The Best Christmas Pageant Ever* (s); and *Tales of a Fourth-Grade Nothing* (n).

The Sign of the Beaver

BY ELIZABETH GEORGE SPEARE

Grades 3 and up   *135 pages*

Houghton Mifflin, 1983; e-book

This is the story of two boys—one white, the other American Indian—and their coming-of-age in the Maine wilderness during the Colonial period. It is also a study of the awkward relationship that develops when the starving white boy is forced to teach the reluctant Indian to read in order for both of them to survive. Related books on the relationship between white settlers and Indian neighbors: *Encounter* (p); *Sing Down the Moon* by Scott O'Dell; *Weasel* (n); and *Woods Runner* by Gary Paulsen.

Slake's Limbo

BY FELICE HOLMAN
Grades 5–8   *117 pages*
Atheneum, 1984

A fifteen-year-old takes his fears and misfortunes into the New York City subway one day, finds a hidden construction mistake in the shape of a cave near the tracks, and doesn't come out of the underground system for 121 days. The story deals simply but powerfully with the question, Can anyone be an island unto himself? It is also a story of survival, personal discovery, and the plight of today's homeless. This book makes interesting comparative study with three other books that discuss running away, hiding, and personal discovery: *Inventing Elliot* (n); *My Side of the Mountain* (n); and *Sarah Bishop* (n).

The Star of Kazan

BY EVA IBBOTSON
Grades 2–5   *405 pages*
Dutton, 2004; e-book

If you've been yearning for the good, solid, old-fashioned storytelling that made *The Secret Garden* and *Anne of Green Gables* the favorites of devoted readers for a century, look no further than this book. Near the turn of the previous century in Austria and Germany, a young girl is being raised by two maiden Austrian housekeepers, who discovered her as an abandoned baby in a church. Young Annika now lives with them in the house where they work for three finicky professors. It's an idyllic life for all, though the child does dream that someday her mother will return to claim the child she misplaced. And then the great upheaval: The woman who abandoned the child twelve years earlier arrives to claim her.

But all is not what it appears, and the ensuing chapters are filled with disappointment, deceit, cruel relatives, sheltering servants, buried treasure, scheming lawyers, loyal friends, and perilous last-minute rescues.

One of Ibbotson's favorite tools is foreshadowing, and she plants intriguing clues in chapters that usually end with a cliffhanger. Ibbotson also offers here a clear sense of the creeping infection called nationalism that would envelop Germany in the coming years and lead to two world wars. An integral part of both the setting and the plot is the world-famous

Lipizzaner stallions and their home at the Spanish Riding School of Vienna. There is an excellent nine-minute YouTube video of the horses in performance: http://www.youtube.com/watch?v=vY3wmWT-sb8. Also by the author: *Journey to the River Sea* (n) and *One Dog and His Boy*. Related books: *The Secret Garden* (n) and *Understood Betsy* (n).

Stormbreaker (Alex Rider series)

BY ANTHONY HOROWITZ

Grades 5–8   *234 pages*

Philomel, 2000; e-book

When fourteen-year-old Alex Rider is informed that his bachelor uncle/guardian has died in an auto accident, he's understandably distressed. But he's also perplexed by the news that he wasn't wearing his seat belt—something he was fanatical about. He's even more confused when two men show up at the funeral wearing loaded shoulder holsters under their jackets. Why guns at a bank manager's funeral? Before long his questions bring him into Britain's top-secret intelligence agency, and he may not make it out alive. As someone has noted elsewhere, if James Bond had a kid relative, it would have been Alex Rider. This first book in the fast-paced, increasingly popular series by Horowitz has, like most thrillers, a certain amount of violence, though none of it is gratuitous. Books like this are very likely to produce a kid who likes to read at least as much as he likes to play video games. Sequels: *Point Blank*; *Skeleton Key*; *Eagle Strike*; *Scorpia*; *Ark Angel*; *Snakehead*; *Crocodile Tears*; and *Scorpia Rising*. The author's own father and Alex's uncle share much in common. Listen as Horowitz describes his family's tragic financial loss, as well as how he researches each novel, online at http://www.ttbook.org/book/anthony-horowitz-fiction-children. Two years after the much-heralded arrival of Harry Potter, Horowitz wrote a comical send-up called *Groosham Grange*, about a Hogwarts-type school set on an island, with every enrollee a school misfit and only one normal-looking faculty member. Sequel: *Return to Groosham Grange: The Unholy Grail*.

Stuart Little

BY E. B. WHITE

Grades K–3   *130 pages*

Harper, 1945

Stuart is a very, very small boy (two inches) who looks exactly like a mouse. This leaves him at a decided disadvantage living in a house where everyone else is normal size, including the family cat. White's first book for children, it is filled with beautiful language and lots of adventures as

Stuart struggles to find his way in the world—an important job for all children, even if they don't look like a mouse. Also by the author: *Charlotte's Web* (n). Related books: *The Mouse and the Motorcycle* (n), and the Dimwood Forest tales by Avi, beginning with *Poppy* (n).

Tales of a Fourth-Grade Nothing
BY JUDY BLUME
Grades 3–5   *120 pages*
Dutton, 1972; e-book
A perennial favorite among schoolchildren, this novel deals with the irksome problem of a kid brother whose hilarious antics complicate the life of his fourth-grade brother, Peter. Sequels: *Superfudge* (caution: *Superfudge* deals with the question, Is there a Santa Claus?); *Fudge-a-Mania*; and *Double Fudge*. Also by the author: *Freckle Juice*.

Thank You, Jackie Robinson
BY BARBARA COHEN
Grades 5–7   *126 pages*
Lothrop, 1988
In the late 1940s, we meet young Sam Green, a rare breed known as the True Baseball Fanatic and a Brooklyn Dodger fan. His widowed mother runs an inn, and when she hires a sixty-year-old black cook, Sam's life takes a turn for the better. The two form a fast friendship and begin to explore the joys of baseball in a way the fatherless boy has never known. A tender book that touches on friendship, race, sports, personal sacrifice, and death. Related books: *Finding Buck McHenry* (n); *In the Year of the Boar and Jackie Robinson* (n); *Just as Good: How Larry Doby Changed America's Game* by Chris Crowe; *Teammates* by Peter Golenbock; and an excellent paperback series by Dan Gutman, including *Jackie & Me*, about a boy who time-travels using his baseball cards.

Theodore Boone: Kid Lawyer (series)
BY JOHN GRISHAM
Grades 6–9   *263 pages*
Dutton, 2010; e-book
Theo Boone is the thirteen-year-old only child of two successful lawyers, both of whom give Theo lots of encouragement but not a lot of attention. What gets his attention is the local court system, where he's become a little legend among the judges, lawyers, and clerks for his love of all things legal. He has even taken to doling out legal advice free of charge to his eighth-grade classmates. This first adventure in the series

finds Theo involved in a controversial local murder trial, since he's just discovered information that would surely convict the defendant but for a couple of large liabilities: (1) the trial has already started (all evidence is supposed to be presented before the trial begins), and (2) the person who gave him the information is an illegal immigrant. The same smooth, believable style Grisham has brought to multiple adult best sellers is here in his first YA title, offering keen insights to the workings of a small-city legal system. Sequels: *Theodore Boone: The Abduction* and *Theodore Boone: The Accused*.

Toliver's Secret
BY ESTHER WOOD BRADY
Grades 3–5   *166 pages*
Crown, 1988
During the Revolutionary War, ten-year-old Ellen Toliver is asked by her ailing grandfather to take his place and carry a secret message through British lines. What he estimates to be a simple plan is complicated by Ellen's exceptional timidity and an unforeseen shift by the British. The book becomes a portrait of Ellen's personal growth—complete with a heart-stopping crisis in each chapter. Related books: *The Little Ships* and *The Greatest Skating Race*, both by Louise Borden.

The True Confessions of Charlotte Doyle
BY AVI
Grades 4 and up   *215 pages*
Orchard, 1990
Winner of a Newbery Honor medal, this is the exciting tale of an obstinate thirteen-year-old girl who is the lone passenger aboard a merchant ship sailing from England to the United States in 1832. The crew is bent on mutiny, the captain is a murderer, and within weeks the girl is accused of murder, tried by captain and crew, and sentenced to hang at sea. Avi is at his finest with this first-person adventure, exploring history, racism, feminism, and mob psychology.

Other books by Avi: *City of Orphans* (n); *Crispin: The Cross of Lead*; *The Good Dog*; *Nothing but the Truth* (n); *Poppy* (n); and *Wolf Rider* (n).

Tuck Everlasting
BY NATALIE BABBITT
Grades 4–7   *124 pages*
Farrar, Straus & Giroux, 1975; e-book
A young girl stumbles upon a family that has found the "fountain of

youth," and in the aftermath there is a kidnapping, a murder, and a jail-break. This touching story suggests a sobering question: What would it be like to live forever? We all make decisions and sometimes those decisions affect us for the rest of our lives. For experienced listeners. Also by the author: *The Moon over High Street* (n) and *The Search for Delicious*.

The Twenty-one Balloons
BY WILLIAM PÈNE DU BOIS
Grades 4–6   *80 pages*
Viking, 1947; e-book
This long-ago Newbery winner is a literary smorgasbord; there are so many different and delicious parts one hardly knows which to mention first. The story deals with a retired teacher's attempts to sail by balloon across the Pacific in 1883, his crash landing and pseudo-imprisonment on the island of Krakatoa, and, finally, his escape. The book is crammed with nuggets of science, history, humor, invention, superior language, and marvelous artwork. For experienced listeners.

Understood Betsy
BY DOROTHY CANFIELD FISHER
Grades 2–5   *229 pages*
Henry Holt, 1999; e-book
Written in 1917 by one of America's most celebrated writers, this is the classic story of a timid, almost neurotic orphan child, Betsy, being raised by her overprotective city-dwelling aunts. Then a family illness requires the child be sent to live with stiff-necked rural relatives in Vermont and she must stand on her own two feet, do chores, and speak for herself—all of which causes a heartwarming metamorphosis. As a novel, even as a psychological or his-torical profile, the book is enormously successful. One of its original inten-tions was to promote the Montessori method of education at the beginning of the twentieth century. Related books: *Journey to the River Sea* (n); *Mandy* by Julie Edwards; *The Secret Garden* (n); and *The Star of Kazan* (n).

The Water Horse
BY DICK KING-SMITH
Grades K–2   *120 pages*
Dell Yearling, 2001
Eight-year-old Kirstie and her five-year-old brother, Angus, discover what they think is some kind of egg that needs to be saved in the bathtub. Their guess is more than correct. With a head and neck that look like that of a horse, the body of a turtle, and the tail of a crocodile, the creature is

about the size of a newborn kitten. But it won't stay that size for long. What they have inadvertently hatched is the future Loch Ness monster.

Dick King-Smith, author of the popular *Babe: The Gallant Pig*, gives us not a monster story here but an affectionate look at what might have been if there really was a Loch Ness monster and if it had been raised by two affectionate children, a cooperative mom, a seafaring father, and a once grumpy but now knowledgeable grandfather. Each short chapter deals with the increasing challenges faced by the family as the creature grows larger, requires increasing amounts of food, and needs to learn that not all people are its friends. But how to train a "monster"? Also by the author: *The Stray* (s). Walden Media made a very successful film loosely based on the book, online at: www.walden.com/movie/the -water-horse-legend-of-the-deep-4/. Related books: *The Luck of the Loch Ness Monster* (p) and *The Mysterious Tadpole* (p).

Weasel

BY CYNTHIA DEFELICE
Grades 2–6   *119 pages*
Atheneum, 1990
Set in Ohio in 1839, this realistic look at the American frontier focuses on a widower and his two children as they confront racism, violence, and the elements. Most of the challenge comes in the person of Weasel, a former government "Indian fighter" who captures both father and son. A fast-paced, first-person adventure story, it also describes the plight of the American Indian and America's own "ethnic cleansing." Also by the author: *The Apprenticeship of Lucas Whitaker*. Related books: *The Buffalo Knife*, *Flaming Arrows*, *The Perilous Road*, and *Winter Danger*, all by William O. Steele; *The Sign of the Beaver* (n); and *Woods Runner* by Gary Paulsen.

A Week in the Woods

BY ANDREW CLEMENTS
Grades 3–6   *190 pages*
Simon & Schuster, 2002; e-book
A master of the school setting, Clements gives us a fifth-grade nature trip into the woods, a wealthy know-it-all new kid in town, and a science teacher. The teacher is a decent, hardworking man but he's not perfect. And sometimes when you've been in a business for twelve years and you're the best at what you do, you're tempted to think you know it all. It's an easy trap to fall into. This teacher, who thinks he's seen all kinds of kids, thinks he's got the new kid figured out perfectly and that what the kid needs is a hard lesson or two.

The teacher may be an expert at reading kids' behavior, but he's misread this child's heart. In resolving the conflict, Clements gives us a solid dose of outdoor survival tips, as well as tips on how classmates might make the life of newcomers a lot easier. For other books by the author, see *Frindle* (s).

When the Tripods Came (Tripods series)
BY JOHN CHRISTOPHER
Grades 5 and up   *151 pages*
Dutton, 1988
An updating of H. G. Wells's *The War of the Worlds*, this is the prequel to one of modern science fiction's most popular juvenile series: the Tripods. When invaders from space take over earth and begin implanting brain-control devices among the humans, a group of rebellious teens lay the groundwork for the invaders' destruction. The series includes (in order): *The White Mountains*; *The City of Gold and Lead*; and *The Pool of Fire*. Related book: *City of Ember* (n).

When the Whistle Blows
BY FRAN CANNON SLAYTON
Grades 6 and up   *162 pages*
Philomel, 2009; e-book
This fine first novel traces one family's life in a small West Virginia town that is so dependent upon its trains and steam engines that it literally lives and dies by them. And there is some of both in this volume. Each of the book's chapters is set on Halloween night for seven successive years, 1943 through 1949. Each episode finds the book's protagonist, Jimmy Cannon, a little older and a little wiser but still yearning to work the rails—much to his rail machinist father's dismay. The railroad's days are coming to an end, declares the father, but Jimmy turns a deaf ear. By novel's end, however, the father's prescience is clearly evident. In this respect, the changing times of the 1940s are reflected in the employment ruptures today in American industry.

As the book spans the years, Jimmy's Halloween adventures move from giggly preteen stuff to sobering adult, from a cemetery prank to a gut-wrenching high school football contest, and, finally, to Jimmy's father's death. This is a pulsating slice of small-town America as it used to be (and still is in parts of rural America).

Where the Red Fern Grows
BY WILSON RAWLS
Grades 3 and up   *212 pages*
Doubleday, 1961; e-book

A ten-year-old boy growing up in the Ozark Mountains, praying and saving for a pair of hounds, finally achieves his wish. He then begins the task of turning the hounds into first-class hunting dogs. It would be difficult to find a book that speaks more definitively about perseverance, courage, family, sacrifice, work, life, and death. The long chapters are easily divided, but bring a box of tissues for the final ones. Wilson Rawls wrote only one other book, another delightful re-creation of his childhood in the Ozarks: *Summer of the Monkeys*. The author's recitation of the story of his life ("Dreams Can Come True") is available on CD; for details, see www .trelease-on-reading.com/rawls.html. For other dog books, see page 242.

Wolf Rider: A Tale of Terror

BY AVI
Grades 7 and up   *224 pages*
Aladdin, 2000
This is breathtaking, plausible, and compelling reading and always my first recommendation for "reluctant-reader" teens. When fifteen-year-old Andy accidentally receives a random phone call from a man claiming he's killed a college coed, nobody believes him. And when everyone writes it off as a prank, Andy sets out to find the anonymous caller in a race against death and the clock. Read any version of "The Boy Who Cried Wolf" before reading aloud this book. Caution: There is a small number of expletives in the text. For other books about and by Avi, see *The True Confessions of Charlotte Doyle* (n). Related books: *Inventing Elliot* (n); *Killing Mr. Griffin* (n); and *Plague Year* (n).

The Wonderful Wizard of Oz

BY L. FRANK BAUM
Grades 1 and up   *260 pages*
numerous publishers; e-book
Before your children are exposed to the movie version, treat them to the magic of this 1900 book, which many regard as the first American fairy tale as well as among our earliest science fiction. (Incidentally, the book is far less terrifying for children than the film version.) The magical story of Dorothy and her friends' harrowing journey to the Emerald City is but the first of many books about the Land of Oz. Among those sequels, one is regarded as the best—*Ozma of Oz*. Author studies: Michael Patrick Hearn's *The Annotated Wizard of Oz (Centennial Edition)* (W. W. Norton, 2000) and *L. Frank Baum: Creator of Oz* by Katharine M. Rogers (St. Martin's, 2002). On the Web: www.eskimo.com/~tiktok/index.htm.

The Year of Miss Agnes
BY KIRKPATRICK HILL
Grades 2–5   *128 pages*
Aladdin, 2002; e-book

Set in a remote and impoverished Alaskan bush village in 1948, this heart-warming story is told through the eyes of a ten-year-old Athabascan village girl, Fred, who watches as the new schoolteacher arrives. Everyone assumes that Miss Agnes will leave like the rest have. After all, how could she stand the smell? They're wrong, of course. She stays and takes over not just the one-room schoolhouse but also the hearts of everyone in the village, including Fred's deaf sister, who's never been to school. Out go all the old ways and in come records, pictures from all over the world, maps, and a Robin Hood read-aloud—anything to inspire learning in the bush. You'll be surprised by how Alaskan village kids can relate to Sherwood Forest. Miss Agnes demonstrates that programs don't teach, teachers do, and what an example she is! Also by the author: *Toughboy and Sister* and *Winter Camp*, a survival story.

Poetry

The Cremation of Sam McGee
BY ROBERT W. SERVICE; TED HARRISON, ILLUS.
Grades 4 and up   *32 pages*
Kids Can Press, 1987; e-book

Once one of the most memorized poems in North America, this remains the best description of the sun's strange spell over the men who once toiled in the North for gold. Also by the author and illustrator: *The Shooting of Dan McGrew.* Two excellent collections of Service's poetry: *Best Tales of the Yukon* (e-book) and *Collected Poems of Robert Service* (Putnam).

Danitra Brown, Class Clown
BY NIKKI GRIMES; E. B. LEWIS, ILLUS.
Grades 4–7   *32 pages*
HarperCollins, 2005

One of today's most acclaimed poets, Grimes uses fourteen short poems to trace the school year for two African-American friends, touching the highs and lows for the pair, who are as different as night and day in their outlooks. The title comes from the poem in which Zuri passes a note that is intercepted by a boy and read aloud to the class. Danitra knows this will be more embarrassment than Zuri can stand, so she immediately jumps up and acts like a clown in front of the class, offering just enough distraction to save her friend.

Dirt on My Shirt
BY JEFF FOXWORTHY; STEVE BJORKMAN, ILLUS.
Grades K–3   28 pages
HarperCollins, 2008
The popular comedian-songwriter takes us through the neighborhood and family, uncovering the funny foibles of one and all, with watercolor art by one of today's underappreciated illustrators. Be sure to check out the copyright page for a list of hidden objects in the illustrations.

Honey, I Love
BY ELOISE GREENFIELD; DIANE AND LEO DILLON, ILLUS.
Grades PreS–3   42 pages
Harper, 1976
Sixteen short poems about the things and people children love: friends, cousins, older brothers, keepsakes, mother's clothes, music, and jump ropes. Set against an urban background, the poems elicit both joyous and bittersweet feelings.

If You're Not Here, Please Raise Your Hand: Poems About School
BY KALLI DAKOS; G. BRIAN KARAS, ILLUS.
Grades 1–8   64 pages
Simon & Schuster, 1990; e-book
As a classroom teacher, Kalli Dakos has been down in the trenches with all the silliness, sadness, and happiness of elementary school. Can't you tell just from the title? Also by the author: *Don't Read This Book Whatever You Do! More Poems About School.*

I've Lost My Hippopotamus
BY JACK PRELUTSKY; JACKIE URBANOVIC, ILLUS.
Grades K–4   140 pages
Greenwillow, 2012
Jack Prelutsky was deservedly the nation's first children's poet laureate, with more than forty books to his credit. With Jackie Urbanovic's witty ink drawings on every page, this is among his best collections of short poems. The subject matter includes great wordplay (as always) and some of the most whimsical creatures you've never met: wiguanas, penguinchworms,

buffalocusts, kangarulers, and flemingoats. Among the more than one hundred subjects, there are the silly improbables: it's raining in my bedroom; the troll's not at the bridge today; my pencil will not write; and my weasels have the measles, all with Prelutsky twists, including one poem about the plight of a child whose *u*'s all come out upside down (they look like *n*'s). Also by the author: *The Dragons Are Singing Tonight*; *The New Kid on the Block*; *A Pizza the Size of the Sun*; *The Random House Book of Poetry for Children* (po); and *Read-Aloud Rhymes for the Very Young* (po). Prelutsky fans are almost always Silverstein fans—see *Where the Sidewalk Ends* (po).

Mother Goose. See *The Neighborhood Mother Goose* (p), page 206.

The Neighborhood Sing-Along
PHOTOGRAPHED BY NINA CREWS
Grades Tod–K   *64 pages*
HarperCollins, 2011
Those favorite childhood singsongs from the classroom, bedroom, and playground ("Do Your Ears Hang Low?" or "The Wheels on the Bus") are all illustrated in glorious color with children of every hue from every kind of neighborhood. What Crews did for nursery rhymes with *The Neighborhood Mother Goose* she's done equally well with song. Every home and classroom should own this.

Oh, How Sylvester Can Pester!
BY ROBERT KINERK; DRAZEN KOZJAN, ILLUS.
Grades K–3   *26 pages*
Simon & Schuster, 2011; e-book
One of the casualties of the modern age is manners, among young and old. Since demonstrations work better than lectures, these twenty poems have just enough humor and logic to work with the young (and maybe their elders, too). Detailed here are our failings at the table and theater, with our hands, our tongues, and even our clothes. Related book: *Dude, That's Rude! (Get Some Manners)* by Pamela Espeland and Elizabeth Verdick.

Poems I Wrote When No One Was Looking
BY ALAN KATZ; EDWARD KOREN, ILLUS.
Grades 1–5   *145 pages*
McElderry, 2011
From the poet who gave us the series of song parodies (*Take Me Out of the Bathtub and Other Silly Dilly Songs*) comes more laughter in short rhyming

verse. Everything is fair game here, from parents to peers, language, snow days, and even dad's GPS. Also by the author: *Oops!*

The Random House Book of Poetry for Children

SELECTED BY JACK PRELUTSKY; ARNOLD LOBEL, ILLUS.
Grades K–5   *248 pages*
Random House, 1983

One of the best children's poetry anthologies ever, showing that poet Jack Prelutsky recognizes the common language of children. The 572 selected poems (from both traditional and contemporary poets) are short—but long on laughter, imagery, and rhyme. They are grouped into fourteen categories that include food, goblins, nonsense, home, children, animals, and seasons.

Read-Aloud Rhymes for the Very Young

COLLECTED BY JACK PRELUTSKY; MARC BROWN, ILLUS.
Grades Tod–K   *88 pages*
Knopf, 1986

Here are more than two hundred little poems (with full-color illustrations) for little people with little attention spans, to help both to grow. Related book: *A Little Bitty Man* by Halfdan Rasmussen.

Where the Sidewalk Ends

BY SHEL SILVERSTEIN
Grades K–8   *166 pages*
Harper, 1974

Without question, this is the best-loved collection of poetry for children, selling more than two million hardcover copies in twenty-five years. When it comes to knowing children's appetites, Silverstein was pure genius. The titles alone are enough to capture children's attention: "Band-aids," "Boa Constrictor," "Crocodile's Toothache," "The Dirtiest Man in the World," and "Recipe for a Hippopotamus Sandwich." Here are 130 poems to either touch children's hearts or tickle their funny bones. Also by the author: *A Light in the Attic* and the short novel *Lafcadio, the Lion Who Shot Back* (s). Silverstein fans are usually fans of Jack Prelutsky—see *I've Lost My Hippopotamus* (po).

See page 187 for Jim's Favorite Books in Rhyming Verse

Anthologies

Guys Read: Thriller

EDITED BY JON SCIESZKA; BRETT HELQUIST, ILLUS.
Grades 4–8   *288 pages*
Walden Pond Press, 2011; e-book
Ten years ago the best-selling children's writer Jon Scieszka created a
mission called Guys Read, with the goal of reaching and motivating reluctant young male readers (online at www.guysread.com). One problem
to overcome was the lack of Mad stuff (as in *Mad* magazine) in books, the
kind of laugh-out-loud, milk-from-the-nose stuff that boys like to talk
about and read. So far the movement has given birth to three anthologies
of stories from top authors, including this latest collection of short thriller
pieces (e.g., body on the tracks) from authors like Anthony Horowitz,
Walter Dean Myers, and James Patterson. Other books in the series: *Guys
Write for Guys Read*; *Guys Read: Funny Business*; and *Guys Read: The Sports
Pages*. Related books: *Grossology: The Science of Really Gross Things!* by
Sylvia Branzei; *Mightier Than the Sword: World Folktales for Strong Boys* (f);
and *Uncle John's Bathroom Reader for Kids Only!* (a).

Hey! Listen to This: Stories to Read Aloud

BY JIM TRELEASE
Grades K–4   *410 pages*
Penguin, 1992
Here are forty-eight read-aloud stories from the top authors of yesterday
and today. Arranged in categories such as school days, food, families, folk
and fairy tales, and animals, the selections include entire chapter excerpts as
well as complete stories. There are also full-page biographical profiles of
the authors. Also by the author: *Read All About It!* (a), an anthology for
grades five and up. On the Web: www.trelease-on-reading.com/hey.html.

Read All About It!

BY JIM TRELEASE
Grades 5 and up   *487 pages*
Penguin, 1993
For parents and teachers at a loss for what to read to preteens and teens,
here are fifty selections—from classics to newspaper columns, fiction and
nonfiction, humor and tragedy. Each story is introduced by a biographical
profile of the author—like "Whatever Happened to Harper Lee?" (*To Kill*

a Mockingbird). Also by the author: *Hey! Listen to This* (a), an anthology for grades K–4. On the Web: www.trelease-on-reading.com/aai.html.

Scary Stories to Tell in the Dark
COLLECTED BY ALVIN SCHWARTZ; STEPHEN GAMMELL, ILLUS.
Grades 5 and up   *112 pages*
Lippincott, 1981

Dipping into the past and the present, the author presents twenty-nine American horror stories and songs guaranteed to make your listeners cringe. The text includes suggestions for the reader-aloud on when to pause, when to scream, even when to turn off the lights. The selections run the gamut from giggles to gore and average two pages in length. In addition, a source section briefly traces each tale's origin in the United States. (Discretion is advised because of the subject matter.) Sequels: *More Scary Stories to Tell in the Dark* and *Scary Stories 3: More Tales to Chill Your Bones*.

Uncle John's Bathroom Reader for Kids Only!
BY THE BATHROOM READERS' INSTITUTE
Grades 3–7   *324 pages*
Bathroom Readers' Press

I've been a fan of this series since it started with adult editions (more than a dozen at last count), and it's a delight to see the editors recognize the importance of young bathroom readers. To be honest about the title, this is an even better bedroom or kitchen table reader. Consider the variety covered in this edition: ubiquitous "body music" articles (burps and hiccups); the truth behind Aesop's fables, the Pony Express, the dollar bill, yo-yos, Popsicles, snowboards, Sylvester and Tweety, Bugs Bunny, and Little League; amazing kids' accomplishments; the history of bathrooms; toys that flopped; everything you ever needed to know about lightning. Look for it in Humor/Reference, but be sure to look for the "for Kids" tag. (It won't be in the children's section.) Also in the series: *Uncle John's Top Secret Bathroom Reader for Kids Only!*; *Uncle John's Electrifying Bathroom Reader for Kids Only!*; *Uncle John's Did You Know? Bathroom Reader for Kids Only!*; and *Uncle John's Facts to Annoy Your Teacher Bathroom Reader for Kids Only!*

Fairy and Folk Tales

Household Stories by the Brothers Grimm

TRANSLATED BY LUCY CRANE; WALTER CRANE, ILLUS.

Grades 2 and up   *269 pages*

Dover (paperback), 1963; e-book

This collection of fifty-three tales contains the Grimms' most popular works in a translation that is easily read aloud and includes more than one hundred illustrations. The maturity and listening experience of your audience should determine its readiness to handle the subject matter, complexity of plot, and language of these unexpurgated versions. A simpler collection for younger children is *Treasured Classics* (f).

Individual Grimm volumes: *The Elves and the Shoemaker* retold by Freya Littledale; *The Four Gallant Sisters* retold by Eric A. Kimmel; *Hansel and Gretel* retold by Rika Lesser; *Iron Hans* illustrated by Marilee Heyer; *Rapunzel* retold by Barbara Rogasky; *Rose Red and the Bear Prince* retold by Dan Andreasen; *Rumpelstiltskin* retold by Paul O. Zelinski; *Seven at One Blow* retold by Eric A. Kimmel; *The Sleeping Beauty* retold by Trina Schart Hyman; and *Snow White & Rose Red* illustrated by Gennady Spirin.

Mightier Than the Sword: World Folktales for Strong Boys

COLLECTED AND TOLD BY JANE YOLEN

Grades 3–6   *100 pages*

Harcourt Brace, 2003

Folktale expert Jane Yolen offers fourteen tales from around the world, each demonstrating that male heroes can overcome adversity by using their wits instead of their swords.

The People Could Fly: American Black Folktales

BY VIRGINIA HAMILTON; LEO AND DIANE DILLON, ILLUS.

Grades 3–6   *174 pages*

Knopf, 1985

Rich with rhythm, energy, and humor, these twenty-four stories were kept alive by slave tellers and include Bruh Rabbit, Gullah, and freedom-trail adventures. Related book: *Tales of Uncle Remus* retold by Julius Lester.

Rapunzel

ADAPTED BY PAUL O. ZELINSKY

Grades 1–4   *32 pages*

Dutton, 1997

Of all the fairy-tale picture books in the marketplace, this is perhaps the most lushly illustrated and thus deserving of its Caldecott Medal. Borrowing from both the Grimms and previous versions from France and Italy, Zelinsky's retelling might make it the best of all, especially when coupled with his Italian Renaissance oil illustrations of the fair damsel locked in the tower by the evil sorceress. No other illustrator has captured as many Caldecott honors as Zelinksy, including runner-up awards for *Hansel and Gretel*; *Rumpelstiltskin*; and *Swamp Angel*.

Red Ridin' in the Hood and Other Cuentos

BY PATRICIA SANTOS MARCANTONIO; RENATO ALARCÃO, ILLUS.

Grades 4 and up   *181 pages*

Farrar, Straus & Giroux, 2005

When the author was growing up as a Mexican American in Colorado, she loved the traditional fairy tales but mourned the absence of Latino culture in them. She solved that problem by writing these eleven versions as though they were set in the barrio itself. The title story, "Red Ridin' in the Hood," has a contemporary urban-Latino setting: Roja's mother has dispatched her with food for her ill *abuelita* (grandmother), along with instructions to wear the new red dress her *abuelita* made for her, to take the bus, and to avoid Forest Avenue. Instead, the daughter saves the bus fare and travels down Forest Avenue, where a brown low-rider Chevy begins to follow her. Very well written, these tales are closer to the Grimms' versions than Disney's, and the illustrations are not for the meek.

Snow White

BY THE BROTHERS GRIMM; CHARLES SANTORE, ILLUS.

Grades K–2   *32 pages*

Simon & Schuster

There have been many illustrated versions of this timeless classic by the Grimms, but few can match Santore's artwork in this volume. It's a masterpiece.

Treasured Classics

ILLUSTRATED BY MICHAEL HAGUE

Grades K–2   *132 pages*

Chronicle, 2011

Here are fourteen classic fairy tales, with the retelling kept to less than six pages each and coupled with lavish illustrations. These are more intended to familiarize children with the likes of *Cinderella*, *The Gingerbread Man*, *Jack and the Beanstalk*, etc., and are not scholarly tellings.

Jim's Favorite Fairy-Tale Parodies

Betsy Red Hoodie by Gail Carson Levine

Beware of Boys by Tony Blundell

Cinder-Elly by Frances Minters

Cindy Ellen: A Wild Western Cinderella by Susan Lowell

The Cowboy and the Black-eyed Pea by Tony Johnston

The Giant and the Beanstalk by Diane Stanley

The Gingerbread Girl by Lisa Campbell Ernst

Goldie and the Three Bears by Diane Stanley

Goldilocks and the Three Dinosaurs by Mo Willems

Goldilocks Returns by Lisa Campbell Ernst

I Am So Strong by Mario Ramos

I Was a Rat! (n) by Philip Pullman

Jim and the Beanstalk by Raymond Briggs

Kate and the Beanstalk by Mary Pope Osborne

Little Lit: Folklore & Fairy Tale Funnies edited by Art Spiegelman and Françoise Mouly (comic book)

Little Red Riding Hood: A Newfangled Prairie Tale by Lisa Campbell Ernst

Nobody Asked The Pea by John Warren Stewig

The Paper Bag Princess by Robert Munsch

The Principal's New Clothes by Stephanie Calmenson

Rumpelstiltskin's Daughter by Diane Stanley

Sleeping Ugly by Jane Yolen

Somebody and the Three Blairs by Marilyn Tolhurst

The Three Little Aliens and the Big Bad Robot by Margaret McNamara and Mark Fearing

The Three Little Rigs by David Gordon

The Three Little Wolves and the Big Bad Pig by Eugene Trivizas

The True Story of the Three Little Pigs by John Scieszka

The Ugly Truckling by David Gordon

The Wolf Who Cried Boy by Bob Hartman

The Wolf's Story by Toby Forward

Notes

Introduction

1. *A Nation at Risk: The Imperative for Educational Reform*, National Commission on Excellence in Education, 1983, Superintendent of Documents, U.S. Government Printing Office, Washington, DC 20402, http://www.casb.org/_literature_91465/ERC-NationatRisk.
2. This was highly flawed thinking, because the Japanese economic bubble burst by 1991, leading to what became known as "the lost decade." The collapse had nothing to do with its schools, but much to do with corporate greed.
3. Tamar Lewin, "College May Become Unaffordable for Most in U.S.," *New York Times*, December 3, 2008.
4. "College Students' Borrowing Hits an All-time High," *Morning Edition*, National Public Radio, November 3, 2011.
5. *The State of America's Children 2011, Report* (p. 330) (Washington, DC: Children's Defense Fund, 2011), http://www.childrensdefense.org/child-research-data-publications/state-of-americas-children-2011/.
6. Michael Winerip, "Off to College, Perfect Score in Hand," *New York Times*, August 20, 2003.
7. An allusion to the fictional town of Mudville from Ernest Thayer's poem, "Casey at the Bat," http://en.wikipedia.org/wiki/Casey_at_the_Bat.
8. Claudia Wallis, "How to Make a Better Student," *Time*, October 19, 1998, pp. 78–96, plus phone interview.
9. Michael Hout and Stuart W. Elliott, *Incentives and Test-Based Accountability in Education*, National Research Council, National Academies Press, 2011, Washington, DC 20001. See also Jonathan Kantrowitz, "Current Test-Based Incentive Programs Have Not Consistently Raised Student Achievement," May 26, 2011, http://educationresearchreport.blogspot.com/

2011/05/current-test-based-incentive-programs.html; and Valerie Strauss, "Report: Test-Based Incentives Don't Produce Real Student Achievement," *The Answer Sheet* (blog), *Washington Post*, May 28, 2011, http://www.washingtonpost.com/blogs/answer-sheet/post/report-test-based-incentives-dont-produce-real-student-achievement/2011/05/28/AG39wXDH_blog.html.

10. June Kronholz, "Preschoolers' Prep," *Wall Street Journal*, July 12, 2005. See also "Growing Tutoring Business in the U.S.," Part 1, *Morning Edition*, National Public Radio, June 6, 2005; "Tutoring Industry Grows Due to No Child Left Behind Act," *Morning Edition*, National Public Radio, June 7, 2005; Mary C. Lord, "Little Scholars Big Business as More Parents Seek to Give Kids an Edge; Learning Centers Thrive," *Boston Globe*, April 10, 2005; and Susan Saulny, "A Lucrative Brand of Tutoring Grows Un-checked," *New York Times*, April 4, 2005.

11. Alina Tugend, "Rethinking College Prep Costs in Tough Times," *New York Times*, February 28, 2009, http://www.nytimes.com/2009/02/28/your-money/paying-for-college/28shortcuts.html.

12. Wendy Mogel, "The Dark Side of Parental Devotion: How Camp Can Let the Sun Shine," *Camping Magazine*, January/February 2006, http://www.acacamps.org/campmag/0601darkside. See also Wendy Mogel, *The Blessings of a B Minus: Using Jewish Teachings to Raise Resilient Teenagers* (New York: Scribner, 2010).

13. "Schools Drop Nap Time for Testing Preparation," Associated Press, *Atlanta Journal-Constitution*, October 3, 2003.

14. Dirk Johnson, "Many Schools Putting an End to Child's Play," *New York Times*, April 7, 1998. The quote is from former Atlanta schools superintendent Benjamin O. Canada.

15. Kim Severson, "Systematic Cheating Is Found in Atlanta's School System," *New York Times*, July 6, 2011, www.nytimes.com/2011/07/06/education/06atlanta.html. See also Heather Vogell, "Investigation into APS Cheating Finds Unethical Behavior Across Every Level," *Atlanta Journal-Constitution*, July 6, 2011; Valerie Strauss, "Shocking Details of Atlanta Cheating Scandal," *The Answer Sheet* (blog), *Washington Post*, July 7, 2011, http://www.washingtonpost.com/blogs/answer-sheet/post/shocking-details-of-atlanta-cheating-scandal/2011/07/06/gIQAQPhY2H_blog.html; and Maureen Downey, "State Report on Dougherty: 'Acceptance of Wrongdoing and a Pattern of Incompetence That Is a Blight on the Community,'" *Get Schooled* (blog), *Atlanta Journal-Constitution*, December 20, 2011, http://blogs.ajc.com/get-schooled-blog/2011/12/20/state-report-on-dougherty-acceptance-of-wrongdoing-and-a-pattern-of-incompetence-that-is-a-blight-on-the-community/.

16. David Bornstein, "Hard Times for Recess," *New York Times*, April 4, 2011, http://opinionator.blogs.nytimes.com/2011/04/04/hard-times-for-recess/. Bornstein cites more than 250 studies that find a clear connection between adequate recess time and better academic scores, along with improved social and emotional indicators for children. See also J. R. Ruiz, F. B. Ortega et al., "Physical Activity, Fitness, Weight Status, and Cognitive Performance in Adolescents," *Journal of Pediatrics* 157 no. 6 (2010):

917–22; and Gretchen Reynolds, "How Exercise Fuels the Brain," *Well* (blog), *New York Times*, February 22, 2012, http://well.blogs.nytimes.com/2012/02/22/how-exercise-fuels-the-brain/.

17. Sara Rimer, "Less Homework, More Yoga, from a Principal Who Hates Stress," *New York Times*, October 29, 2007, http://www.nytimes.com/2007/10/29/education/29stress.html.

18. Winnie Hu, "Busy Students Get a New Required Course: Lunch," *New York Times*, May 24, 2008. More often than not these students catch the "busy-busy" virus from their parents. When a *New York Times* essay described the malady as largely self-infected, it struck such a loud chord with readers (more than 800 online comments), it quickly became the *Times'* most frequently e-mailed story; see http://opinionator.blogs.nytimes.com/2012/06/30/the-busy-trap/.

19. Kate Zernike, "Ease Up, Top Universities Tell Stressed Applicants," *New York Times*, December 7, 2000.

20. Since their first attempt in 1956 (Dwight Eisenhower over Adlai Stevenson), the only election miscalculation by U.S. schoolchildren was in 1992, George H. W. Bush versus Bill Clinton. See also http://www.reuters.com/article/2008/09/18/idUS171414+18-Sep-2008+PRN20080918. *Weekly Reader* ceased publication in 2012 after 110 years as a classroom tradition.

21. Jay Mathews, "Let's Have a 9-Hour School Day," *Washington Post*, August 16, 2005.

22. Using weekdays, weekends, and summers, the KIPP charter schools extend the school day by 70 percent. See Caroline Hendrie, "KIPP Looks to Re-create School Success Stories," *Education Week*, October 30, 2002. See also Jay Mathews, "Study Finds Big Gains for KIPP Charter Schools Exceed Average," *Washington Post*, August 11, 2005.

23. Julian E. Barnes, "Unequal Education," *Newsweek*, March 29, 2004, pp. 67–75.

24. William Johnson, "Confessions of a 'Bad' Teacher," *New York Times*, March 4, 2012; Michael Winerip, "Hard-Working Teachers, Sabotaged When Student Test Scores Slip," *New York Times*, March 5, 2012.

25. Lesley Mandel Morrow, "Home and School Correlates of Early Interest in Literature," *Journal of Educational Research* 76, no. 4 (1983): 221–30.

26. Leonard Pitts Jr., "My First Reader Started Me Down Path to Award," *Miami Herald*, April 9, 2004.

27. Jim Trelease offers a free single-page brochure for parents at his Web site that tells the story of Mrs. Pitts and her Pulitzer-winning son, as well as the triumphant saga of Mrs. Sonya Carson and her brain-surgeon son, Ben, in their rise from poverty. The brochure, "Two Families Every Parent Should Meet," highlights the efforts of these two parents and what other parents can learn from them. It is available at http://www.trelease-on-reading.com/brochures.html.

28. Jerry West, Kristin Denton, and Elvira Germino-Hausken, *America's Kindergartners: Findings from the Early Childhood Longitudinal Study, Kindergarten Class of 1998–99, Fall 1998*, Office of Educational Research and Improvement, NCES 2000-070 (Washington, DC: U.S. Department of Education, 2000).

29. Martha J. Bailey and Susan M. Dynarski, "Gains and Gaps: Changing Inequality in U.S. College Entry and Completion." Cambridge, MA: National Bureau of Economic Research, Working Paper No. 17633, 2011, http://www.nber.org/papers/w17633.

30. There may be a small percent who make it on their own, but without at least one encouraging family member or teacher, they are rarities. Two recent volumes have followed the trail of four such college graduates, detailing the extraordinary luck and support they received from near-strangers. See *A Hope in the Unseen: An American Odyssey from the Inner City to the Ivy League* by Ron Suskind; and *The Pact: Three Young Men Make a Promise and Fulfill a Dream* by Sampson Davis, George Jenkins, Rameck Hunt, and Lisa Frazier Page.

31. The brochures can be found online at http://www.trelease-on-reading.com/brochures.html; they are intended for use by nonprofit groups only.

32. On April 5, 2010, Dick Gordon of American Public Media's radio program *The Story* interviewed Jim Trelease about the time Abigail Van Buren ("Dear Abby") wrote up his book and their subsequent dinner together. The show can be heard online at http://thestory.org/archive/the_story_1008_The_Woman_Behind_the_Mask.mp3/view; it is the second interview under "The Woman Behind the Mask," with a play or download option at the bottom of the page. Jim's interview with *The Story* about having coffee with longtime Dodger announcer Vin Scully can be found at http://thestory.org/archive/the_story_Gay_Bashing.mp3/view, near the bottom of the page.

33. Adriana Lleras-Muney, "The Relationship Between Education and Adult Mortality in the United States," *Review of Economic Studies* 72, no. 1 (2005), http://www.econ.ucla.edu/alleras/research/papers/mortalityrevision2.pdf; Gina Kolata, "A Surprising Secret to a Long Life: Stay in School," *New York Times*, January 3, 2007.

34. Mary A. Foertsch, *Reading In and Out of School*, Educational Testing Service/Education Information Office (Washington, DC: U.S. Department of Education, May 1992); Keith E. Stanovich, "Does Reading Make You Smarter? Literacy and the Development of Verbal Intelligence," *Advances in Child Development and Behavior* 24 (1993): 133–80, http://www.ncbi.nlm.nih.gov/pubmed/8447247; and Anne Cunningham and Keith Stanovich, "Reading Can Make You Smarter!" *Principal*, November/December 2003, pp. 34–39, http://gse.berkeley.edu/faculty/aecunningham/Readingcanmakeyousmarter!.pdf.

35. Richard C. Anderson, Elfrieda H. Hiebert, Judith A. Scott, and Ian A. G. Wilkinson, *Becoming a Nation of Readers: The Report of the Commission on Reading*, U.S. Department of Education (Champaign-Urbana, IL: Center for the Study of Reading, 1985). See also Diane Ravitch and Chester Finn, *What Do Our 17-Year-Olds Know?* (New York: Harper & Row, 1987).

36. "Students Cite Pregnancies as a Reason to Drop Out," Associated Press, *New York Times*, September 14, 1994.

37. Michael Greenstone and Adam Looney, "Where Is the Best Place to Invest $102,000—In Stocks, Bonds, or a College Degree?" The Hamilton Project/ Brookings Institution, November 9, 2011, http://www.brookings.edu/ papers/2011/0625_education_greenstone_looney.aspx. See chart here. See also Melissa Lee, "When It Comes to Salary, It's Academic," *Washington Post*, July 22, 1994.

38. "Trends in Reading Scores by Parents' Highest Level of Education," in M. Perie, R. Moran, and A. D. Lutkus, *NAEP 2004 Trends in Academic Progress: Three Decades of Student Performance in Reading and Mathematics*, U.S. Department of Education, Institute of Education Sciences, National Center for Education Statistics (Washington, DC: U.S. Government Printing Office, 2005), pp. 36–38.

39. Kolata, "A Surprising Secret to a Long Life." See also James P. Martin, "The Impact of Socioeconomic Status on Health over the Life-Course," *Journal of Human Resources* 42, no. 4 (2007): 739–64; Katherine Bouton, "Eighty Years Along, a Longevity Study Still Has Ground to Cover," *New York Times*, April 19, 2011; Howard S. Friedman and Leslie R. Martin, *The Longevity Project: Surprising Discoveries for Health and Long Life from the Landmark Eight-Decade Study* (New York: Hudson Street Press, 2011); Eugene Rogot, Paul D. Sorlie, and Norman J. Johnson, "Life Expectancy by Employment Status, Income, and Education in the National Longitudinal Mortality Study," *Public Health Reports* 107, no. 4 (1992): 457–61; Jack M. Guralnik et al., "Educational Status and Active Life Expectancy Among Older Blacks and Whites," *New England Journal of Medicine* 329, vol. 2 (1993): 110–16; and E. Pamuk et al., *Health, United States, 1998: Socio-economic Status and Health Chartbook* (Hyattsville, MD: National Center for Health Statistics, 1998).

40. Students scoring A's, B's, or C's don't drop out. The ones who cannot read well enough to achieve those grades are the most likely to withdraw. It is the very rare performer who quits while still hitting home runs.

41. See note 35 and chart.

42. Jake Cronin, *The Path to Successful Reentry: The Relationship Between Correctional Education, Employment and Recidivism*, University of Missouri Columbia, Institute of Public Policy, Report 15-2011, http://ipp.missouri .edu/Publications/281. Also Paul E. Barton and Richard J. Coley, "Captive Students: Education and Training in America's Prisons," Educational Testing Service (Princeton, NJ: ETS Policy Information Center, 1996); Ian Buruma, "What Teaching a College-Level Class at a Maximum-Security Correctional Facility Did for the Inmates—and for Me," *New York Times Magazine*, February 20, 2005.

43. These figures vary in the literature. See Barton and Coley, "Captive Students" and the National Institute for Literacy (NIFL), *Correctional Education Facts*, http://lincs.ed.gov/facts/archive/Correctional.

44. Edward B. Fiske, "Can Money Spent on Schools Save Money That Would Be Spent on Prisons?" *New York Times*, September 27, 1989; National Institute for Literacy, *Correctional Education Facts*; (n. 43) Cronin, *The Path to Successful Reentry*.

45. Cronin, *The Path to Successful Reentry.*

46. Greenstone and Looney, "Where Is the Best Place to Invest"; David Leonhardt, "Even for Cashiers, College Pays Off," *New York Times*, June 26, 2011.

47. Chris Farrell, "A College Degree Is Still Worth It," *Bloomberg Businessweek*, March 20, 2011, http://www.businessweek.com/investor/content/mar2011/pi20110318_071224.htm.

48. Start with Diane Ravitch, *The Death and Life of the Great American School System: How Testing and Choice Are Undermining Education* (New York: Basic Books, 2010). In a 2012 essay ("How Much Testing?") on Ravitch's blog, Prof. Stephen Krashen offers an excellent summary of testing needs, results, and liabilities, http://dianeravitch.net/2012/07/25/stephen-krashen-how-much-testing/.

49. Michael Winerip, "10 Years of Assessing Students with Scientific Exactitude," *New York Times*, December 19, 2011, http://www.nytimes.com/2011/12/19/education/new-york-city-student-testing-over-the-past-decade.html.

50. Roach's experience can be found at http://www.washingtonpost.com/blogs/answer-sheet/post/revealed-school-board-member-who-took-standardized-test/2011/12/06/gIQAbIcxZO_blog.html; a public service video featuring interviews with Roach and honor students who have failed Florida's state reading test can be seen at http://teacher.ocps.net/daniel.stanley/Site/FCAT_PSA.html. See also what happens when two Ph.D.s take the New York third-grade Language Arts practice test: Anne Stone and Jeff Nichols, "Dear Governor: Lobby to Save a Love of Reading," *New York Times SchoolBook* (blog), January 20, 2012, http://www.nytimes.com/schoolbook/2012/01/20/dear-governor-lobby-to-save-a-love-of-reading/. When the celebrated essayist and novelist Naomi Shihab Nye tried to answer the questions about her own essay used in the tenth-grade Texas state exam, she came up empty on three of the five questions; see Rick Casey, "Author Used in TAKS Flunks Test," *Houston Chronicle*, February 27, 2005, http://www.chron.com/news/casey/article/Casey-Author-used-in-TAKS-flunks-test-1643105.php.

Chapter 1: Why Read Aloud?

1. M. Perie, R. Moran, and A. D. Lutkus, *NAEP 2004 Trends in Academic Progress: Three Decades of Student Performance in Reading and Mathematics,* U.S. Department of Education, Institute of Education Sciences, National Center for Education Statistics (Washington, DC: U.S. Government Printing Office, 2005).

2. Victoria J. Rideout, Ulla G. Foehr, and Donald F. Roberts, *Generation M2: Media in the Lives of 8- to 18-Year-Olds* (Menlo Park, CA: The Henry J. Kaiser Family Foundation Study, publication #8010, 2010), p. 30, http://www.kff.org/entmedia/8010.cfm.

3. "American Time Use Survey—2010 Results," Table 11, Bureau of Labor Statistics, U.S. Department of Labor, http://www.bls.gov/news.release/atus.nr0.htm.

4. Tom Bradshaw, Bonnie Nichols, Kelly Hill, and Mark Bauerlein, *Reading at Risk: A Survey of Literary Reading in America*, Research Division, Report No. 46 (Washington, DC: National Endowment for the Arts, 2004), http://www.nea.gov/pub/ReadingAtRisk.pdf.

5. National Household Education Survey (NHES), National Center for Education Statistics (Washington, DC: U.S. Government Printing Office, 1999).

6. B. D. Rampey, G. S. Dion, and P. L. Donahue, *NAEP 2008 Trends in Academic Progress* (NCES 2009–479). U.S. Department of Education, Institute of Education Sciences, National Center for Education Statistics (Washington, DC: U.S. Government Printing Office, 2009).

7. Stephen Krashen, "Reading for Pleasure," *Language Magazine*, December 2011. Krashen argues there has been no decline in reading by students; it's just been transferred from print to digital. Be that as it may, it has not raised the scores an iota. I argue in chapter 7 that it has damaged the scores by "continuous partial attention."

8. "U.S. Teen Mobile Report: Calling Yesterday, Texting Today, Using Apps Tomorrow," *NielsenWire* (blog), October 14, 2010, http://blog.nielsen .com/nielsenwire/online_mobile/u-s-teen-mobile-report-calling -yesterday-texting-today-using-apps-tomorrow/; Katie Hafner, "Texting May Be Taking a Toll," *New York Times*, May 25, 2009; and Amanda Lenhart, *Teens and Mobile Phones*, Pew Internet & American Life Project, April 20, 2010, http://www.pewinternet.org/~/media//Files/Reports/ 2010/PIP-Teens-and-Mobile-2010-with-topline.pdf. See chapter 7 for more on this.

9. Nicholas Carr, *The Shallows: What the Internet Is Doing to Our Brains* (New York: W. W. Norton, 2010), pp. 133–35.

10. Laura Rogerson Moore, "On the Same Page," *NAIS Independent School Magazine* online feature, Winter 2008, http://www.nais.org/publications/is-magazinearticle.cfm?ItemNumber=150424. The average college enrollee has spent only three hours a week reading anything for high school: see "Getting Students Ready for College: What Student Engagement Data Can Tell Us," the High School Survey of Student Engagement (Bloomington: Indiana University Press, 2005), http://www.indiana.edu/~ceep/hssse/ images/Getting%20Students%20Ready%20for%20College%20-% 202005.pdf.

11. Andrew Sum et al., *Getting to the Finish Line: College Enrollment and Graduation, A Seven Year Longitudinal Study of the Boston Public Schools Class of 2000*, Center for Labor Market Studies (Boston: Northeastern University Press, 2008).

12. Lisa W. Foderaro, "CUNY Adjusts Amid Tide of Remedial Students," *New York Times*, March 4, 2011.

13. M. D. R. Evans, Jonathan Kelley, Joanna Sikorac, and Donald J. Treimand, "Family Scholarly Culture and Educational Success: Books and Schooling in 27 Nations," *Research in Social Stratification and Mobility* 28, no. 2 (2010): 171–97, http://www.sciencedirect.com/science/article/ pii/S0276562410000090. See also http://www.rodneytrice.com/sfbb/ articles/home.pdf.

14. Richard C. Anderson, Elfrieda H. Hiebert, Judith A. Scott, and Ian A. G. Wilkinson, *Becoming a Nation of Readers: The Report of the Commission on Reading*, U.S. Department of Education (Champaign-Urbana, IL: Center for the Study of Reading, 1985), p. 23. *Becoming a Nation of Readers* is still in print. Copies can be obtained by contacting Brenda Reinhold at the University of Illinois-Champaign, College of Education, 217 244 4613, reinhold@illinois.edu. Cost: $7.50, plus handling fee of $2.50 and shipping.

15. Ibid., p. 51.

16. Keith E. Stanovich, "Matthew Effects in Reading: Some Consequences of Individual Differences in the Acquisition of Literacy," *Reading Research Quarterly* 21, no. 4 (1986): 360–407; Richard Anderson, Linda Fielding, and Paul Wilson, "Growth in Reading and How Children Spend Their Time Outside of School," *Reading Research Quarterly* 23, no. 3 (1988): 285–303.

17. *The Nation's Report Card: Reading 2011* (NCES 2012–457), Institute of Education Sciences, U.S. Department of Education (Washington, DC: National Center for Education Statistics, 2011), p. 2.

18. See page 121.

19. Jeanne S. Chall and Vicki A. Jacobs, "The Classic Study on Poor Children's Fourth-Grade Slump," *American Educator* 27, no. 1 (2003), http://www.aft.org/newspubs/periodicals/ae/spring2003/hirschsbclassic.cfm.

20. Gordon Rattray Taylor, *The Natural History of the Brain* (New York: Dutton, 1979), pp. 59–60.

21. Stanovich, "Matthew Effects in Reading"; Anderson, Fielding, and Wilson, "Growth in Reading and How Children Spend Their Time Outside of School"; Richard L. Allington, "Oral Reading," in *Handbook of Reading Research*, P. David Pearson, ed. (New York: Longman, 1984), pp. 829–64; Warwick B. Elley and Francis Mangubhai, "The Impact of Reading on Second Language Learning," *Research Quarterly* 19, no. 1 (1983): 53–67; Irwin Kirsch, John de Jong, Dominique LaFontaine, Joy McQueen, Juliette Mendelovits, and Christian Monseur, *Reading for Change: Performance and Engagement Across Countries—Results from PISA 2000*, Organisation for Economic Co-operation and Development (OECD), http://www.oecd.org/dataoecd/43/54/33690904.pdf; Foertsch, *Reading In and Out of School*.

22. Warwick B. Elley, *How in the World Do Students Read?* (Hamburg: International Association for the Evaluation of Educational Achievement, 1992). This document has been available as a PDF file from ERIC (Education Resources Information Center), http://www.eric.ed.gov/PDFS/ED360613.pdf. However, in 2012 security concerns at ERIC caused them to block access to most PDFs until they could be secured. Once that is done, the above url should work.

23. *The Nation's Report Card: Reading 2009* (NCES 2010–458). U.S. Department of Education, Institute of Education Sciences, National Center for Education Statistics. (Washington, DC: U.S. Government Printing Office, 2009).

24. Sabrina Tavernise, "Poor Dropping Further Behind Rich in School," *New York Times*, February 10, 2012.

25. Sarah Ransdell, "There's Still No Free Lunch: Poverty as a Composite of SES Predicts School-Level Reading Comprehension," *American Behavioral Scientist*, July 14, 2011, http://abs.sagepub.com/content/early/2011/07/14/0002764211408878.abstract?papetoc. For other research on the crippling role of poverty in children's learning, see David C. Berliner, "Sorting Out the Effects of Inequality and Poverty, Teachers and Schools, on America's Youth," in *Educational Policy and the Socialization of Youth for the 21st Century*, ed. S. L. Nichols (New York: Teachers College Press, 2013); Patrice L. Engel, Lia C. H. Fernald, Harold Alderman, Jere Behrman, Chloe O'Gara, Aisha Yousafzai, Meena Cabral de Mello et al., "Strategies for Reducing Inequalities and Improving Developmental Outcomes for Young Children in Low-Income and Middle-Income Countries," *The Lancet* 378, no. 9799 (2011): 1339–53, http://www.thelancet.com/journals/lancet/article/PIIS0140-6736(11)60889-1/fulltext; Helen F. Ladd and Edward B. Fiske, "Class Matters. Why Won't We Admit It?" *New York Times*, December 12, 2011; and Sam Dillon, "Districts Pay Less in Poor Schools, Report Says," *New York Times*, December 1, 2011. Also worth looking at is the work of Michael Marder, a physics professor at the University of Texas, whose "hobby" is investigating the impact of poverty on school scores throughout the United States. He has created astounding visualization charts that can be seen at http://uteachweb.cns.utexas.edu/Marder/Visualizations.

26. LynNell Hancock, "Why Are Finland's Schools Successful?" *Smithsonian*, September 2011, p. 94. See also Jenny Anderson, "From Finland, a Story of Educational Success in Going Against the Tide," *New York Times*, December 13, 2011; "The Finland Phenomenon: Inside the World's Most Surprising School System," *The Best of Our Knowledge* 1090, WAMC Radio, Public Broadcasting, Albany, NY, http://www.publicbroadcasting.net/wamc/news.newsmain?action=article&ARTICLE_ID=1821173; Lizette Alvarez, "Suutarila Journal: Educators Flocking to Finland, Land of Literate Children," *New York Times*, April 9, 2004; Sean Coughlan, "Education Key to Economic Survival: Finland Has Often Been Hailed as One of the Most Successful Education Systems in Europe," *BBC News*, November 23, 2004, http://news.bbc.co.uk/1/hi/education/4031805.stm.

27. *PISA 2009 Results: Learning Trends: Changes in Student Performance Since 2000* (Volume 5), Organisation for Economic Co-operation and Development (OECD), 2010, p. 27, http://dx.doi.org/10.1787/9789264091580-en.

28. Michael Winerip, "Military Children Stay a Step Ahead of Public School Students," *New York Times*, December 12, 2011.

29. Elley, *How in the World Do Students Read?*

30. Ina V. S. Mullis, Michael O. Martin, Eugene J. Gonzalez, and Ann M. Kennedy, *PIRLS 2001 International Report: IEA's Study of Reading Literacy Achievement in Primary School in 35 Countries* (Chestnut Hill, MA: International Association for the Evaluation of Educational Achievement/International Study Center, Boston College, 2003), p. 95.

31. Kristen Denton and Jerry West, *Children's Reading and Mathematics Achievement in Kindergarten and First Grade* (Washington, DC: U.S. Department of Education, NCES, 2002), pp. 16, 20, http://nces.ed.gov/pubs2002/2002125.pdf.

32. Ibid.

33. L. B. Gambrell, "Creating Classroom Cultures That Foster Reading Motivation," *Reading Teacher* 50, no. 1 (1996): 14–25.

34. Adriana G. Bus, Marinus H. van IJzendoorn, and Anthony D. Pellegrini, "Joint Book Reading Makes Success in Learning to Read: A Meta-analysis on Intergenerational Transmission of Literacy," *Review of Educational Research* 65, no. 1 (1995): 1–21.

35. Warwick B. Elley, "Vocabulary Acquisition from Listening to Stories," *Reading Research Quarterly* 24 (1989): 174–87.

36. Mullis, Martin, Gonzalez, and Kennedy, *PIRLS 2001 International Report*; Francesca Borgonovi and Guillermo Montt, "Parental Involvement in Selected PISA Countries and Economies," OECD Education Working Papers, No. 73 (2012), pp. 18–19, 58, http://dx.doi.org/10.1787/5k990rk0jsjj-en; and *Let's Read Them a Story! The Parent Factor in Education*, OECD/PISA report (2012), http://www.oecd.org/document/48/0,3746,en_2649_35845621_50282672_1_1_1_1,00.html.

37. OECD, *PISA 2009 Results: Overcoming Social Background: Equity in Learning Opportunities and Outcomes, Vol. II* (2010), p. 95, http://dx.doi.org/10.1787/9789264091504-en.

38. For more on monastic table reading, see Eric Hollas, "Food for Thought: Monastic Table Reading," *Abbey Banner*, Spring 2003, pp. 10–11.

39. International Reading Association, "Reign of the Reader," *Reading Today*, December 2001/January 2002, p. 30; Gary R. Mormino and George E. Pozzetta, *The Immigrant World of Ybor City: Italians and Their Latin Neighbors in Tampa, 1885–1985* (Gainesville: Florida Sand Dollar Books, University Press of Florida, 1998); Edward Rothstein, "Connections: What It Takes to Bring Tears to an Unsentimental Reader's Eyes," *New York Times*, June 15, 2002; "Reading 2: Ybor City's Cigar Workers," *ParkNet*, National Park Service, http://www.cr.nps.gov/nr/twhp/wwwlps/lessons/51ybor/51facts2.htm.

40. Miguel Barnet, "Rolling by the Book," *Cigar Aficionado*, June 2008, pp. 193–95, http://www.cigaraficionado.com/webfeatures/show/id/3155#.

41. Elton G. Stetson and Richard P. Williams, "Learning from Social Studies Textbooks: Why Some Students Succeed and Others Fail," *Journal of Reading* 36, no. 1 (1992): 22–30.

42. Sam Dillon, "Schools Cut Back Subjects to Push Reading and Math," *New York Times*, March 26, 2006.

43. Jerry West, Kristin Denton, and Elvira Germino-Hausken, *America's Kindergartners: Findings from the Early Childhood Longitudinal Study, Kindergarten Class of 1998–99, Fall 1998*, Office of Educational Research and Improvement, NCES 2000-070 (Washington, DC: U.S. Department of Education, 2000). The narrow background knowledge of the poor is explored movingly by Samuel G. Freedman as he follows a group of former inmates, now group-home residents, on a trip to a bookstore, a first-time experience for many—see Samuel G. Freedman, "Tasting Freedom's Simple Joys in the Barnes & Noble," *New York Times*, August 2, 2006, http://www.nytimes.com/2006/08/02/education/02EDUCATION.html.

44. Betty Hart and Todd Risley, *Meaningful Differences in the Everyday Experience of Young American Children* (Baltimore, Brookes Publishing, 1996). For a downloadable six-page condensation of the book: Betty Hart and Todd R. Risley, "The Early Catastrophe: The 30 Million Word Gap by Age 3," *American Educator* (American Federation of Teachers), Spring 2003, http://www.aft.org/pdfs/americaneducator/spring2003/TheEarlyCatastrophe.pdf. This can be freely disseminated to parents, according to the AFT Web site. See also Ginia Bellafante, "Before a Test, a Poverty of Words," *New York Times*, October 7, 2012, p. MB; and Paul Chance, "Speaking of Differences," *Phi Delta Kappan*, March 1997, pp. 506–7.

45. George Farkas and Kurt Beron, "Family Linguistic Culture and Social Reproduction: Verbal Skill from Parent to Child in the Preschool and School Years," paper delivered March 31, 2001, to annual meetings of the Population Association of America, Washington, DC, http://www.eric.ed.gov:80/ERICWebPortal/contentdelivery/servlet/ERICServlet?accno=ED453910. Also Karen S. Peterson, "Moms' Poor Vocabulary Hurts Kids' Future," *USA Today*, April 12, 2001.

46. This is printed at the bottom of the article: "Articles may be reproduced for noncommercial personal or educational use only; additional permission is required for any other reprinting of the documents." That entire spring issue is an easy-to-understand treasure of research on children's language and reading comprehension, free for downloading at http://www.aft.org/pdfs/americaneducator/spring2003/TheEarlyCatastrophe.pdf.

47. M. Suzanne Zeedyk, "What's Life in a Baby Buggy Like?: The Impact of Buggy Orientation on Parent-Infant Interaction and Infant Stress," National Literacy Trust, University of Dundee, Dundee, Scotland (2008), http://www.literacytrust.org.uk/assets/0000/2531/Buggy_research.pdf. See also M. Suzanne Zeedyk, "One Ride Forward, Two Steps Back," *New York Times*, March 2, 2009.

48. Donald P. Hayes and Margaret G. Ahrens, "Vocabulary Simplification for Children: A Special Case for 'Motherese,'" *Journal of Child Language* 15 (1988): 395–410. One departure from the Hayes-Ahrens study is the deterioration of television's vocabulary since their original study. Tom Shachtman, in a thirty-year study of the *CBS Evening News*, found its language level had dropped from complex sentences with abstract words in 1963 to simple declarative sentences with few abstractions or rare words in 1993; in other words, from post–high school level down to junior high school level. His study also found daytime talk shows to be on the language level of ten-year-olds. See Tom Shachtman, *The Inarticulate Society: Eloquence and Culture in America* (New York: Free Press, 1995), pp. 115–42.

49. Caroline Hendric, "Chicago Data Show Mixed Summer Gain," *Education Week*, September 10, 1999, pp. 1, 14. See also Diane Ravitch, "Summer School Isn't a Solution," *New York Times*, March 3, 2000.

50. *Time*, February 1, 1988, pp. 52–58. See also Mark D. O'Donnell, "Boston's Lewenberg Middle School Delivers Success," *Phi Delta Kappan*, March

1997, pp. 508–12. The *Kappan* article describes how O'Neill didn't affect just the language arts curriculum. He also spearheaded a physical rebirth in the school and a remarkable six-week physical education program built around Project Adventure, an intense climbing regimen. There is also a detailed description of O'Neill's adventures with an often inept school department and an obstructionist custodial union, and the resulting triumph of the school. For his work at Lewenberg, O'Neill was named one of the inaugural recipients of the Heroes in Education award, presented by *Reader's Digest* to educators with original and effective methods.

51. Howard W. French, "Tokyo Dropouts' Vocation: Painting the Town," *New York Times*, March 12, 2000: "In the place of the nose-to-the-grindstone ethic of long study hours and single-minded focus on exams and careers that helped build postwar Japan, the motto of the current 15- to 18-year-olds seems to be that girls and boys just want to have fun." Since 1997, Japan has seen its school dropout rate increase by 20 percent. See also Norimitsu Onishi, "An Aging Island Embraces Japan's Young Dropouts," *New York Times*, June 6, 2004; and Miki Tanikawa, "Free to Be," *New York Times*, January 12, 2003.

52. David Snowdon, *Aging with Grace: What the Nun Study Teaches Us About Leading Longer, Healthier, and More Meaningful Lives* (New York: Bantam, 2001), pp. 117–18; Kathryn P. Riley, David A. Snowdon, Mark F. Desrosiers, and William R. Markesbery, "Early Life Linguistic Ability, Late Life Cognitive Function, and Neuropathology: Findings from the Nun Study," *Neurobiology of Aging* 26, no. 3 (2005): 341–47. See also Pam Belluck, "Nuns Offer Clues to Alzheimer's and Aging," *New York Times*, May 7, 2001.

Chapter 2: When to Begin (and End) Read-Aloud

1. These remarks were made during an interview (September 3, 1979) with Dr. Brazelton conducted by John Merrow for Options in Education, a coproduction of National Public Radio and the Institute for Educational Leadership of George Washington University.

2. Anthony J. DeCasper and Melanie J. Spence, "Prenatal Maternal Speech Influences Newborns' Perception of Speech Sounds," *Infant Behavior and Development* 9, no. 2 (1986): 133–50.

3. Marjory Roberts, "Class Before Birth," *Psychology Today*, May 1987, p. 41; Sharon Begley and John Carey, "The Wisdom of Babies," *Newsweek*, January 12, 1981, pp. 71–72.

4. Birgit Mampe, Angela D. Friederici, Anne Christophe, and Kathleen Wermke, "Newborns' Cry Melody Is Shaped by Their Native Language," *Current Biology* 19, no. 23 (2009): 1994–97.

5. Dorothy Butler, *Cushla and Her Books* (Boston: Horn Book, 1980).

6. Alice Ozma, *The Reading Promise: My Father and the Books We Shared* (New York: Grand Central Publishing, 2011). You can find book recommendations for creating your own streak at Ozma's Web site, http://www.makeareadingpromise.com/streak.html. See also Michael Winerip, "A Father-Daughter Bond, Page by Page," *New York Times*, March 21, 2010;

and "Father–Daughter Reading Streak Lasts Nearly 9 Years," *Weekend Edition Saturday*, National Public Radio, June 18, 2011, http://www.npr .org/2011/06/18/137223191/father-daughter-reading-streak-lasts -nearly-9-years.

7. LynNell Hancock, "Why Are Finland's Schools Successful?" *Smithsonian*, September 2011, p. 94. See also "The Finland Phenomenon," WAMC Radio; Lizette Alvarez, "Educators Flocking to Finland, Land of Literate Children," *New York Times*, April 9, 2004; Coughlan, "Education Key to Economic Survival"; Gerald W. Bracey, "American Students Near the Top in Reading," *Phi Delta Kappan*, February 1993, pp. 496–97. You'll find everything you need to know about the Finnish reading philosophy in the following: Leonard B. Finkelstein, "Finland's Lessons: Learning Thrives in a Land Where It Is Respected," *Education Week*, October 18, 1995, p. 31; Viking Brunell and Pirjo Linnakylä, "Swedish Speakers' Literacy in the Finnish Society," *Journal of Reading*, February 1994, pp. 368–75; Pirjo Linnakylä, "Subtitles Prompt Finnish Children to Read," *Reading Today* (October/November 1993), p. 31.

8. Elley, *How in the World Do Students Read?*

9. John Merrow, *Options in Education*, National Public Radio, September 3, 1979.

10. David Elkind, *The Hurried Child: Growing Up Too Fast Too Soon*, 3rd ed. (Cambridge, MA: Perseus/DaCapo, 2001).

11. Dolores Durkin, *Children Who Read Early* (New York: Teachers College, 1966); Margaret M. Clark, *Young Fluent Readers* (London: Heinemann, 1976). See also Anne D. Forester, "What Teachers Can Learn from 'Natural Readers,'" *Reading Teacher* 31, no. 2 (1977): 160–66.

12. Ina V. S. Mullis, Michael O. Martin, Eugene J. Gonzalez, and Ann M. Kennedy, *PIRLS 2001 International Report: IEA's Study of Reading Literacy Achievement in Primary School in 35 Countries*, (Chestnut Hill, MA: International Association for the Evaluation of Educational Achievement, International Study Center, Boston College, 2003), http://pirls.bc.edu/isc/ publications.html.

13. Ina V. S. Mullis, John A. Dossey, Jay R. Campbell, Claudia A. Gentile, Christine Sullivan, and Andrew Latham, *NAEP 1992 Trends in Academic Progress, Office of Educational Research and Improvement* (Washington, DC: U.S. Department of Education, 1994). See also Paul E. Barton and Richard J. Coley, *America's Smallest School: The Family* (Princeton, NJ: Educational Testing Service, Policy Information Center, 1992), pp. 12–19, http://www. ets.org/Media/Education_Topics/pdf/5678_PERCReport_School.pdf.

14. Ibid., pp. 105–24.

15. Andrew Biemiller, "Oral Comprehension Sets the Ceiling on Reading Comprehension," *American Educator*, Spring 2003, http://www.aft.org/ newspubs/periodicals/ae/spring2003/hirschsboral.cfm.

16. Nell K. Duke, "For the Rich It's Richer: Print Experiences and Environments Offered to Children in Very Low- and Very High-Socioeconomic Status First-Grade Classrooms," *American Educational Research Journal* 37, no. 2 (2000): 441–78.

17. Jerome Kagan, "The Child: His Struggle for Identity," *Saturday Review*, December 1968, p. 82. See also Steven R. Tulkin and Jerome Kagan, "Mother-Child Interaction in the First Year of Life," *Child Development*, March 1972, pp. 31–41.
18. Further examples of "concept-attention span" can be found in Kagan, "The Child: His Struggle for Identity," p. 82.
19. Norman Herr, "Internet Resources to Accompany the Sourcebook for Teaching Science: Television and Health," California State University, Northridge, http://www.csun.edu/science/health/docs/tv&health.html.
20. Morrow, "Home and School Correlates of Early Interest in Literature." See page xviii for chart on this study.
21. Anderson et al., *Becoming a Nation of Readers*, p. 51.
22. G. Robert Carlsen and Anne Sherrill, *Voices of Readers: How We Come to Love Books* (Urbana, IL: National Council of Teachers of English, 1998), http://www.eric.ed.gov/PDFS/ED295136.pdf.
23. In the interest of fairness, four different factors were taken into account by reading specialist Kathy Nozzolillo in determining the Harris-Jacobson reading level for the script: semantic difficulty, syntactic difficulty, vocabulary, and sentence length.
24. Biemiller, "Oral Comprehension." See also Thomas G. Devine, "Listening: What Do We Know After Fifty Years of Research and Theorizing?" *Journal of Reading*, January 1978, pp. 296–304.
25. The original dust jacket copy for *The Cat in the Hat* included the words "Many children . . . will discover for the first time that they don't need to be read to anymore," as noted in Judith and Neil Morgan's *Dr. Seuss and Mr. Geisel* (New York: Random House, 1995), p. 155.
26. Carl B. Smith and Gary M. Ingersoll, "Written Vocabulary of Elementary School Pupils," ERIC document ED323564, pp. 3–4.
27. John Holt treated this concept at length in "How Teachers Make Children Hate Reading," *Redbook*, November 1967.
28. Stephen Krashen, *The Power of Reading*, 2nd ed. (Portsmouth, NH: Libraries Unlimited and Heinemann, 2004). See also William Powers, John Cook, and Russell Meyer, "The Effect of Compulsory Writing on Writing Apprehension," *Research in the Teaching of English* 13, no. 3 (1979): 225–30; and Harry Gradman and Edith Hanania, "Language Learning Background Factors and ESL Proficiency," *Modern Language Journal* 75, no. 1 (1991): 39–51.
29. Deborah Salahu-Din, Hillary Persky, and Jessica Miller, The Nation's Report Card: Writing 2007 (NCES 2008-468), National Center for Education Statistics, Institute of Education Sciences, U.S. Department of Education (Washington, DC: NCES, 2008).
30. Arthur N. Applebee, Judith A. Langer, Ina V. S. Mullis, Andrew S. Latham, and Claudia A. Gentile, *NAEP 1992 Writing Report Card*, Educational Testing Service (Washington, DC: U.S. Department of Education, 1994). This document is now available from ERIC, http://www.eric.ed.gov/ERICWebPortal/contentdelivery/servlet/ERICServlet?accno=ED370119. See also Dana Gioia, ed., *To Read or Not to Read: A Question of*

National Consequence: Executive Summary, Research Report no. 47, (Washington, DC: National Endowment for the Arts, 2007), p. 13.

31. Jacques Barzun, *Begin Here* (Chicago: University of Chicago Press, 1991), pp. 114–16. Barzun is one of the grand old men of American letters (author of thirty books, including a National Book Award finalist, *From Dawn to Decadence: 500 Years of Western Cultural Life*, at age ninety-two) and former dean of graduate faculty and provost of Columbia University. He is a renowned authority in education and philosophy, to say nothing of detective fiction and baseball, whose advice should never be taken lightly.

32. Eric R. Kandel, James H. Schwartz, and Thomas M. Jessell, eds., *Principles of Neural Science*, 3rd ed., Center for Neurobiology and Behavior, College of Physicians and Surgeons of Columbia University and the Howard Hughes Medical Institute (Norwalk, CT: Appleton & Lange, 1991): "The visual system is the most complex of all the sensory systems. The auditory nerve contains about 30,000 fibers, but the optic nerve (visual) contains one million, more than all the dorsal root fibers entering the entire spinal cord!"

33. Dillon, "Schools Cut Back Subjects."

34. Daniel Goleman, *Emotional Intelligence* (New York: Bantam, 1995).

35. In 2011, twenty teens from Great Neck, Long Island, New York, were accused of paying as much as $3,500 to older students to take their SAT exams. Although parents of the students claimed no knowledge of the cheating, I do wonder where the high school seniors got $3,500 in loose change for the payoffs. Since Great Neck is one of the state's more affluent suburbs (long considered the backdrop for Fitzgerald's *The Great Gatsby*), I'm guessing the parents were very good tippers for family chores like dishwashing, vacuuming, and leaf raking.

36. Paul K. Piff et al., "Higher Social Class Predicts Increased Unethical Behavior," *PNAS* (2012), www.pnas.org/content/early/2012/02/21/1118373109 .full.pdf+html; Jennifer E. Stellar et al., "Class and Compassion: Socioeconomic Factors Predict Responses to Suffering," *Emotion* 12, no. 3 (2012): 449–59, http://www.apa.org/pubs/journals/releases/EMO-class-and-com passion.pdf; and Gerben A. van Kleef et al., "Power, Distress, and Compassion Turning a Blind Eye to the Suffering of Others," *Psychological Science*, 19, no. 12 (2008): 1315–21, http://socrates.berkeley.edu/~keltner/publica tions/vankleef.2008.pdf.

37. Irwin Kirsch, John de Jong, Dominique LaFontaine, Joy McQueen, Juliette Mendelovits, and Christian Monseur, *Reading for Change: Performance and Engagement Across Countries*, pp. 106–10, OECD, http://www.oecd.org/ dataoecd/43/54/33690904.pdf.

38. Annie Murphy Paul, "Your Brain on Fiction," *New York Times* Sunday Review, March 18, 2012. See also Maja Djikic, Keith Oatley et al., "On Being Moved by Art: How Reading Fiction Transforms the Self," *Creativity Research Journal* 21, no. 1 (2009): 24–29, http://dx.doi.org/10.1080/ 10400410802633392; and Raymond Mar, Keith Oatley et al., "Bookworms Versus Nerds: Exposure to Fiction Versus Non-Fiction, Divergent Associations with Social Ability, and the Simulation of Fictional Social Worlds," *Journal of Research in Personality* 40, no. 5 (2006): 694–712.

Chapter 3: The Stages of Read-Aloud

1. "Three Core Concepts in Early Development," video, Center on the Developing Child, Harvard University, http://developingchild.harvard.edu/resources/multimedia/videos/.

2. "Early Childhood Adversity, Toxic Stress, and the Role of the Pediatrician," policy statement from American Academy of Pediatrics, 2012, http://pediatrics.aappublications.org/content/129/1/e224.full.html. See also Nicholas D. Kristof, "A Poverty Solution That Starts with a Hug," *New York Times* Sunday Review, January 7, 2012; L. Alan Sroufe, "Ritalin Gone Wrong," *New York Times* Sunday Review, January 29, 2012; Paul Tough, "The Poverty Clinic," *The New Yorker*, March 21, 2011, pp. 25-32.

3. Dr. Shonkoff's eighty-one-minute lecture video on this subject for the State of Washington in 2010, "Leveraging an Integrated Science of Development to Strengthen the Foundations of Health, Learning, and Behavior," can be found online (video at the top of the page) at www.casey.org/resources/events/earlylearning/wa/speakers/shonkoff.htm.

4. Peter W. Jusczyk and Elizabeth A. Hohne, "Infants' Memory for Spoken Words," *Science*, September 26, 1997, pp. 1984–85.

5. Anthony J. DeCasper and Melanie J. Spence, "Prenatal Maternal Speech Influences Newborns' Perception of Speech Sounds," *Infant Behavior and Development* 9, no. 2 (1986): 133–50. See also Gina Kolata, "Rhyme's Reason: Linking Thinking to Train the Brain?" *New York Times*, February 19, 1995.

6. "The Experience of Touch: Research Points to a Critical Role," *New York Times Science Times*, February 2, 1988.

7. Linda Lamme and Athol Packer, "Bookreading Behaviors of Infants," *Reading Teacher* 39, no. 6 (1986): 504–9; Michael Resnick et al., "Mothers Reading to Infants: A New Observational Tool," *Reading Teacher* 40, no. 9 (1987): 888–94.

8. Warwick B. Elley, "Vocabulary Acquisition from Listening to Stories," *Reading Research Quarterly* 24, no. 2 (1989): 174–87.

9. Keith E. Stanovich, "Matthew Effects in Reading: Some Consequences of Individual Differences in the Acquisition of Literacy," *Reading Research Quarterly*, Fall 1986, pp. 360–407.

10. Joannis K. Flatley and Adele D. Rutland, "Using Wordless Picture Books to Teach Linguistically/Culturally Different Students," *Reading Teacher* 40, no. 3 (1986): 276–81; Donna Read and Henrietta M. Smith, "Teaching Visual Literacy Through Wordless Picture Books," *Reading Teacher* 35, no. 8 (1982): 928–52; J. Stewig, *Children and Literature* (Chicago: Rand McNally, 1980), pp. 131–58.

11. Foertsch, *Reading In and Out of School*.

12. Anderson, Fielding, and Wilson, "Growth in Reading."

13. Nell K. Duke, "For the Rich It's Richer: Print Experiences and Environments Offered to Children in Very Low- and Very High-Socioeconomic Status First-Grade Classrooms," *American Educational Research Journal* 37, no. 2 (2000): 441–78.

14. Personal e-mail correspondence.
15. Moore, "On the Same Page."
16. Patricia Greenfield and Jessica Beagles-Roos, "Radio vs. Television: Their Cognitive Impact on Children of Different Socioeconomic and Ethnic Groups," *Journal of Communication* 38, no. 2 (1988): 71–92.
17. Robertson Davies, *One Half of Robertson Davies* (New York: Viking, 1977), p. 1.
18. Nancy Pearl, *Book Lust: Recommended Reading for Every Mood, Moment, and Reason* (Seattle: Sasquatch Books, 2003); and Nancy Pearl, *More Book Lust: Recommended Reading for Every Mood, Moment, and Reason* (Seattle: Sasquatch Books, 2005).
19. Personal interview.
20. Personal e-mail correspondence.
21. Ibid.
22. David McCullough, "The Course of Human Events," Jefferson Lecture, May 15, 2003, http://www.neh.gov/whoweare/mccullough/lecture.html.

Chapter 5: Sustained Silent Reading: Reading Aloud's Natural Partner

1. Report of the National Reading Panel: *Teaching Children to Read: An Evidence-Based Assessment of the Scientific Research Literature on Reading and Its Implications for Reading Instruction—the Summary Report* (Washington, DC: National Institute of Child Health and Human Development, NIH, Publication 00-4754, 2000), p. 13. Available online at http://www.nichd.nih.gov/publications/nrp/upload/smallbook_pdf.pdf.
2. The NRP's own scientific standards have come under severe attack since the report was issued, the most notable being Steven L. Strauss, "Challenging the NICHD Reading Research Agenda," *Phi Delta Kappan*, February 2003, pp. 438–42. See also Joanne Yatvin, "Babes in the Woods: The Wanderings of the National Reading Panel," *Phi Delta Kappan*, January 2002, pp. 364–69; and James Cunningham, "The National Reading Panel Report," *Reading Research Quarterly* 36, no. 3 (2001): 326–35.
3. Stephen Krashen, "More Smoke and Mirrors: A Critique of the National Reading Panel Report on Fluency," *Phi Delta Kappan*, October 2001, pp. 119–23. See also Stephen Krashen, "Is In-School Free Reading Good for Children? Why the National Reading Panel Report Is (Still) Wrong," *Phi Delta Kappan*, February 2005, pp. 444–47; Cunningham, "The National Reading Panel Report"; Elaine M. Garan, *Resisting Mandates: How to Triumph with the Truth* (Portsmouth, NH: Heinemann, 2002), pp. 22–24; and Stephen Krashen, *Free Voluntary Reading* (Santa Barbara, CA: Libraries Unlimited, 2011).
4. Stanovich, "Matthew Effects in Reading." See also Richard L. Allington, "Oral Reading," in *Handbook of Reading Research*, P. David Pearson, ed. (New York: Longman, 1984), pp. 829–64; Elley and Mangubhai, "The Impact of Reading on Second Language Learning"; and Foertsch, *Reading In and Out of School*.

5. Kirsch et al., *Reading for Change.*

6. Elley, *How in the World Do Students Read?*

7. P. L. Donahue, K. E. Voelki, J. R. Campbell, and J. Mazzeo, *NAEP 1998 Reading Report Card for the Nation and States* (Washington, DC: U.S. Department of Education, Office of Educational Research and Improvement, National Center for Education Statistics, 1999). See also Ina V. S. Mullis et al., *NAEP 1992 Trends in Academic Progress*, ETS/Office of Educational Research and Improvement, http://www.eric.ed.gov/PDFS/ED378237.pdf; also found in *America's Smallest School: The Family*, Educational Testing Service, http://www.ets.org/Media/Education_Topics/pdf/5678_PER CReport_School.pdf.

8. Wilbur Schramm, *The Process and Effects of Mass Communication* (Urbana: University of Illinois Press, 1954). See also Wilbur Schramm, "How Communication Works," in *The Process and Effects of Mass Communication*, 6th ed., Wilbur Schramm, ed. (Urbana: University of Illinois Press, 1965), pp. 3–26; more online at http://web.archive.org/web/20030505143554 and http://www.ciadvertising.org/studies/student/99_fall/theory/lazarski/Paper%20Leck%20htm.htm.

9. Alan Neuharth, "Why Newspapers Are More Popular in Asia," *USA Today*, June 3, 2005. See also Alan Neuharth, "Why Are Newspapers So Popular in Japan?" *USA Today*, November 26, 2004.

10. Jason Singer, "Lonesome Highways: In Japan, Big Tolls Drive Cars Away," *Wall Street Journal*, September 15, 2003.

11. Howard W. French, "The Rising Sun Sets on Japanese Publishing," *New York Times Book Review*, December 10, 2000.

12. S. Jay Samuels, "Decoding and Automaticity: Helping Poor Readers Become Automatic at Word Recognition," *Reading Teacher* 41, no. 8 (1988): 756–60. See also Anderson, Fielding, and Wilson, "Growth in Reading."

13. Anderson et al., *Becoming a Nation of Readers*, p. 119.

14. Mark Sadoski, "An Attitude Survey for Sustained Silent Reading Programs," *Journal of Reading* 23, no. 8 (1980): 721–26.

15. Richard Allington is the author of *Big Brother and the National Reading Curriculum: How Ideology Trumped Evidence* (Portsmouth, NH: Heinemann, 2002) and *What Really Matters for Struggling Readers: Designing Research-Based Programs* (Boston: Allyn & Bacon, 2012).

16. Richard Allington, "If They Don't Read Much, How They Gonna Get Good," *Journal of Reading* 21 (1977): 57–61.

17. Anderson, Fielding, and Wilson, "Growth in Reading," p. 152.

18. Edward Fry and Elizabeth Sakiey, "Common Words Not Taught in Basal Reading Series," *Reading Teacher* 39, no. 5 (1986): 395–98.

19. Timothy A. Keller and Marcel Just, "Altering Cortical Connectivity: Remediation-Induced Changes in the White Matter of Poor Readers," *Neuron* 64, no. 5 (2009): 624–31. See also Jon Hamilton, "Reading Practice Can Strengthen Brain 'Highways,'" *All Things Considered*, National Public Radio, December 9, 2009, http://www.npr.org/templates/story/story.php?storyId=121253104.

20. Personal correspondence.

21. Robert A. McCracken and Marlene J. McCracken, "Modeling Is the Key to Sustained Silent Reading," *Reading Teacher* 31, no. 4 (1978): 406–8. See also Linda B. Gambrell, "Getting Started with Sustained Silent Reading and Keeping It Going," *Reading Teacher* 32, no. 3 (1978): 328–31.

22. Barbara Heyns, *Summer Learning and the Effects of Schooling* (New York: Academic Press, 1978). See also Doris R. Entwistle and Karl L. Alexander, "Summer Setback: Race, Poverty, School Composition, and Mathematics Achievement in the First Two Years of School," *American Sociological Review* 57, no. 1 (1992): 72–84; Barbara Heynes, "Schooling and Cognitive Development: Is There a Season for Learning?" *Child Development* 58, no. 5 (1987): 1151–60; Larry J. Mikulecky, "Stopping Summer Learning Loss Among At-Risk Youth," *Journal of Reading* 33, no. 7 (1990): 516–21; Harris Cooper, Barbara Nye, Kelly Charlton, James Lindsay, and Scott Greathouse, "The Effects of Summer Vacation on Achievement Test Scores: A Narrative and Meta-Analytic Review," *Review of Educational Research* 66, no. 3 (1996): 227–68; Richard L. Allington and Anne McGill-Franzen, "The Impact of Summer Setback on the Reading Achievement Gap," *Phi Delta Kappan*, September 2003, pp. 68–75; Richard L. Allington, Anne McGill-Franzen, Gregory Camilli, Lunetta Williams et al., "Addressing Summer Reading Setback Among Economically Disadvantaged Elementary Students," *Reading Psychology* 31, no. 5 (2010): 1–17; Richard Allington and Anne McGill-Franzen, "Got Books?" *Educational Leadership*, April 2008, pp. 20–23; James S. Kim and Thomas G. White, "Teacher and Parent Scaffolding of Voluntary Summer Reading," *Reading Teacher* 62, no. 2 (2008): 116–25. The "summer gap" was explored by American RadioWorks (American Public Media) in its podcast of May 27, 2011, http://download.publicradio.org/podcast/ameri canradioworks/podcast/arw_4_48_summerslide.mp3.

23. Jimmy Kim, "Summer Reading and the Ethnic Achievement Gap," *Journal of Education for Students Placed at Risk* (JESPAR) 9, no. 2 (2004): 169–88. See also Debra Viadero, "Reading Books Is Found to Ward Off 'Summer Slump,'" *Education Week,* May 5, 2004.

24. Paul E. Barton, *Parsing the Achievement Gap*, http://www.ets.org/Media/ Research/pdf/PICPARSINGII.pdf.

25. Greg Toppo, "Poor, Minority Kids Face Long Odds in Education," *USA Today*, November 24, 2003.

26. Jay R. Campbell, Catherine M. Hombo, and John Mazzeo, *NAEP 1999 Trends in Academic Progress: Three Decades of Student Performance*, U.S. Department of Education (Washington, DC: National Center for Education Statistics, 2000), http://nces.ed.gov/nationsreportcard/pubs/main1999/ 2000469.asp. For international comparison, see Kirsch et al., *Reading for Change*.

27. Stephen Krashen, "Does Accelerated Reader Work?" *Journal of Children's Literature* 29, no. 2 (2003): 16–30, http://www.sdkrashen.com/articles/ does_accelerated_reader_work/. See also Krashen, *Free Voluntary Reading*, pp. 45–52; and Steven Ross, John Nunnery, and Elizabeth Goldfeder, "A Randomized Experiment on the Effects of Accelerated Reader/Reading Renaissance in an Urban School District: Preliminary Evaluation Report,"

University of Memphis (Memphis, TN: Center for Research in Educational Policy, 2004), http://research.renlearn.com/research/pdfs/322.pdf; and John Nunnery and Steven Ross, "The Effects of the School Renaissance Program on Student Achievement in Reading and Mathematics," *Research in the Schools* 14, no. 1 (2007): 40–59, http://www.memphis.edu/crep/pdfs/Effects_of_School_Renaissance-JournalArticle.pdf.

28. Linda M. Pavonctti, Kathryn M. Brimmer, and James F. Cipielewski, "Accelerated Reader: What Are the Lasting Effects on the Reading Habits of Middle School Students Exposed to Accelerated Reader in Elementary Grades?" *Journal of Adolescent and Adult Literacy* 46, no. 4 (2002). See also Jean M. Stevenson and Jenny Webb Camarata, "Imposters in Whole Language Clothing: Undressing the Accelerated Reader Program," *Talking Points* 11, no. 2 (2000): 8–11. I don't agree with everything in this article, but there are some points that are very valid.

29. Susan Straight, "Reading by the Numbers," *New York Times Book Review*, August 30, 2009.

30. John T. Guthrie, "Contexts for Engagement and Motivation in Reading," in M. L. Kamil, P. B. Mosenthal, P. D. Pearson, and R. Barr, eds., *Handbook of Reading Research: Volume III* (New York: Erlbaum, 2000), pp. 403–22, http://www.readingonline.org/articles/handbook/guthrie/. See also M. Csikszentmihalyi, "Literacy and Intrinsic Motivation," *Daedalus* 119, no. 2 (1990): 115–40.

31. Kirsch et al., *Reading for Change*.

32. "The Man with Two Brains," *New York Times*, October 9, 1989.

33. Stephen D. Krashen and Kyung-Sook Cho, "Acquisition of Vocabulary from the Sweet Valley Kids Series: Adult ESL Acquisition," *Journal of Reading* 37, no. 8 (1994): 662–67. Similar results were accomplished in the Sponce English Language Program at the University of Southern California, using Harlequin romances. See also Rebecca Constantino, "Pleasure Reading Helps, Even If Readers Don't Believe It," *Journal of Reading* 37, no. 6 (1994): 504–5.

34. Carlsen and Sherrill, *Voices of Readers*; and Krashen, *The Power of Reading*, pp. 91–110.

35. Viking Brunell and Pirjo Linnakylä, "Swedish Speakers' Literacy in the Finnish Society," *Journal of Reading* 37, no. 5 (1994): 368–75.

36. Leslie Campbell and Kathleen Hayes, "Desmond Tutu," interview from *The Other Side's Faces of Faith*, pp. 23–26.

37. Arthur Schlesinger Jr., "Advice from a Reader-Aloud-to-Children," *New York Times Book Review*, November 25, 1979. For the most up-to-date summary of the Tintin experience, see Charles McGrath, "An Innocent in America," *New York Times*, January 3, 2012.

38. Sid T. Womack and B. J. Chandler, "Encouraging Reading for Professional Development," *Journal of Reading* 35, no. 5 (1992): 390–94.

39. Stanley I. Mour, "Do Teachers Read?" *Reading Teacher* 30, no. 4 (1977): 397–401. This study was somewhat skewed in favor of teachers because the subjects were more motivated professionally as graduate students. If anything, the results would be worse with teachers not as professionally involved. Included in the numbers were 202 females and 22 males, 6 counselors,

6 principals, 5 supervisors; most of the teachers (145) were elementary level. See also Kathleen Stumpf Jongsma, "Just Say Know!" *Reading Teacher* 45, no. 7 (1992): 546–48.

40. Tom Bradshaw, Bonnie Nichols, Kelly Hill, and Mark Bauerlein, *Reading at Risk: A Survey of Literary Reading in America*, National Endowment for the Arts (Washington, DC: NEA, Research Division, Report no. 46, 2004), http://www.nea.gov/pub/readingatrisk.pdf; Nicholas Zill and Marianne Winglee, *Who Reads Literature?* (Cabin John, MD: Seven Locks Press, 1990). This item is now available as a free PDF download from ERIC (Education Resources Information Center) using the ERIC search ED302812, http://www.eric.ed.gov/.

41. Cheryl B. Littman and Susan S. Stodolsky, "The Professional Reading of High School Academic Teachers," *Journal of Educational Research* 92, no. 2, November 1998, p. 75. The 51 percent who did professional reading regularly were also more apt to belong to professional associations linked to their teaching area. The survey group averaged fifteen years of teaching, with 63 percent holding graduate degrees. Science teachers led all disciplines, with 61.8 percent reading at least one journal, while social studies trailed the faculty at 36.4 percent.

42. I borrowed the "date" analogy from the novelist Kurt Vonnegut Jr., who when asked if you could actually teach a person how to write replied indignantly that such teaching is the job of an editor, the person who teaches the writer how to behave on "a blind date with a total stranger," the reader. See Kurt Vonnegut Jr., "Despite Tough Guys, Life Is Not the Only School for Real Novelists," *New York Times*, May 24, 1999.

43. D. T. Max, "The Oprah Effect," *New York Times Magazine*, December 26, 199.

44. From personal correspondence and interview.

Chapter 6: The Print Climate in the Home, School, and Library

1. Lesley Mandel Morrow, "Home and School Correlates of Early Interest in Literature," *Journal of Educational Research* 76, no. 4 (1983): 221–30.

2. David E. Sanger, "The Price of Lost Chances" *New York Times Special Section* "The Reckoning," September 11, 2011.

3. Susan B. Neuman and Donna Celano, "Access to Print in Low-Income and Middle-Income Communities: An Ecological Study of Four Neighborhoods," *Reading Research Quarterly* 36, no. 1 (2001): 8–26; and Susan B. Neuman, Donna C. Celano, Albert N. Greco, and Pamela Shue, *Access for All: Closing the Book Gap for Children in Early Education* (Newark, DE: International Reading Association, 2001).

4. Nell K. Duke, "For the Rich It's Richer: Print Experiences and Environments Offered to Children in Very Low- and Very High-Socioeconomic Status First-Grade," *American Educational Research Journal* 37, no. 2 (2000): 441–78.

5. Krashen, *The Power of Reading.* See also Stephen Krashen, "Our Schools Are Not Broken: The Problem Is Poverty," Commencement Address, Graduate School of Education and Counseling, Lewis and Clark College, Portland,

OR, June 5, 2011, http://www.sdkrashen.com/articles/Our_schools_are_not_broken.pdf; video for the speech, http://graduate.lclark.edu/live/news/12363-commencement-speaker-stephen-krashen-questions.

6. Jeff McQuillan, *The Literary Crisis: False Claims, Real Solutions* (Portsmouth, NH: Heinemann, 1998).

7. Richard Allington, Sherry Guice, Kim Baker, Nancy Michaelson, and Shouming Li, "Access to Books: Variations in Schools and Classrooms," *Language and Literacy Spectrum*, Spring 1995, pp. 23–25. Also Richard L. Allington and Sherry Guice, "Something to Read: Putting Books in Their Desks, Backpacks, and Bedrooms," in Phillip Dreyer, ed., *Vision and Realities in Literacy: Sixtieth Yearbook of the Claremont Reading Conference* (Claremont, CA: Claremont Reading Conference, 1996), p. 5.

8. Keith Curry Lance, Marcia J. Rodney, and Christine Hamilton-Pennell, *How School Librarians Help Kids Achieve Standards: The Second Colorado Study*, Colorado State Library, Colorado Department of Education; Keith Curry Lance, Lynda Welborn, and Christine Hamilton-Pennell, *The Impact of School Media Centers on Academic Achievement*, Colorado Department of Education. See also Christine Hamilton-Pennell, Keith Curry Lance, Marcia J. Rodney, and Eugene Hainer, "Dick and Jane Go to the Head of the Class," *School Library Journal* 46, no. 4 (2000): 44–47.

9. Sarah Sullivan, Bonnie Nichols, Tom Bradshaw, and Kelli Rogowski, *To Read or Not To Read: A Question of National Consequence*, Research Report no. 47 (Washington. DC: National Endowment for the Arts, 2007), pp. 72–74, http://www.nea.gov/research/toread.pdf. See also Campbell, Hombo, and Mazzeo, *NAEP 1999 Trends in Academic Progress*.

10. Mullis et al., *PIRLS 2001 International Report*. See also Evans et al., "Family Scholarly Culture."

11. Elley, *How in the World Do Students Read?* See also Patricia Koskinen, Irene Blum, Stephanie Bisson et al., "Book Access, Shared Reading, and Audio Models: The Effects of Supporting the Literacy Learning of Linguistically Diverse Students in School and at Home," *Journal of Educational Psychology* 92, no. 1 (2000): 23–36.

12. James C. Baughman, "School Libraries and MCAS Scores," paper presented at library symposium, Graduate School of Library and Information Science, Simmons College, Boston, MA, October 26, 2000, http://web.simmons.edu/~baughman/mcas-school-libraries/. Another study found "access to books in school and public libraries was a significant predictor of 2007 fourth-grade NAEP reading scores, as well as the difference between grade 4 and grade 8 2007 NAEP reading scores"; Stephen Krashen, Syying Lee, and Jeff McQuillan, "Is the Library Important? Multivariate Studies at the National and International Level," *Journal of Language and Literacy Education* 8, no. 1 (2012): 26–38, http://jolle.coe.uga.edu/wp-content/uploads/2012/06/Is-the-Library-Important.pdf.

13. R. Constantino and Stephen Krashen, "Differences in Print Environment for Children in Beverly Hills, Compton, and Watts," *Emergency Librarian* 24, no. 4 (1997): 8–9. See also Stephen Krashen, "Bridging Inequity with Books," *Educational Leadership*, January 1998.

14. Many of Krashen's findings and recommendations can be found in Stephen Krashen, *Every Person a Reader: An Alternative to the California Task Force Report on Reading*, distributed by ALTA Book Center, 14 Adrian Ct., Burlingame, CA 94010, telephone (800) ALTA-ESL, online at www.languagebooks.com/books/every_person_a_reader.html. See also Krashen, *The Power of Reading*.

15. Kathleen Kennedy Manzo, "California Continues Phaseout of Whole Language Era," *Education Week*, July 9, 1997.

16. "Statistics About California School Libraries," California Department of Education, http://www.cde.ca.gov/ci/cr/lb/schoollibrstats08.asp.

17. James Ricci, "A Saving Grace in the Face of Our School Library Scandal," *Los Angeles Times Magazine*, November 12, 2000. See also Douglas L. Achterman, "Haves, Halves, and Have-Nots: School Libraries and Student Achievement in California," University of North Texas UNT Digital Library, http://digital.library.unt.edu/ark:/67531/metadc9800/.

18. Duke, "For the Rich It's Richer."

19. Greg Toppo, "Poor, Minority Kids Face Long Odds in Education," *USA Today*, November 24, 2003.

20. See Chapter 5, page 89.

21. Allington et al., "Addressing Summer Reading Setback." See also Allington and McGill-Franzen, "Got Books?" pp. 20–23; Cooper et al., "The Effects of Summer Vacation on Achievement Test Scores"; and Kim and White, "Teacher and Parent Scaffolding of Voluntary Summer Reading." The "summer gap" was explored by American RadioWorks in its podcast of May 27, 2011, http://download.publicradio.org/podcast/americanradioworks/podcast/arw_4_48_summerslide.mp3.

22. Ted Widmer, "Lincoln's Other Mother," *Opinionator* (blog), *New York Times*, January 29, 2011, http://opinionator.blogs.nytimes.com/2011/01/29/lincolns-other-mother/. Widmer is a former speechwriter for President Bill Clinton and director of the John Carter Brown Library at Brown University. His essay details Lincoln's eighteen-hour journey to say good-bye to his stepmother before departing for Washington to begin his first term as president. Four years after his assassination, she was buried in an unmarked grave in the black dress he brought her on that farewell visit. Fifty-five years later a local Lions Club put a marker on the grave, something Widmer noted was more than due—"for if Lincoln saved the Union, she saved him, and for that alone she's entitled to a decent respect. Measured by the usual yardsticks of wealth and distinction, her own life may not have made much of a dent in the historical record. But at just the right moment, she encountered a small motherless boy, and helped him to become Abraham Lincoln."

23. Evans et al., "Family Scholarly Culture." See also http://www.rodneytrice.com/sfbb/articles/home.pdf.

24. Allington et al., "Addressing Summer Reading Setback."

25. Vin Crosbie, "What Newspapers and Their Web Sites Must Do to Survive," *USC Annenberg Online Journalism Review*, 2004, http://www.ojr.org/ojr/business/1078349998.php.

26. "Americans Spending More Time Following the News," Pew Research Center for the People and the Press, September 2010, http://people

-press.org/2010/09/12/americans-spending-more-time-following-the-news/.

27. Noam Cohen, "The Final Bell Rings for *Weekly Reader*, a Classroom Staple," *Media Decoder* (blog), *New York Times*, July 24, 2012, http://media decoder.blogs.nytimes.com/2012/07/24/the-final-bell-rings-for-weekly-reader-a-classroom-staple/.

28. David Carr, "The Lonely Newspaper Reader," *New York Times*, January 1, 2007, http://www.nytimes.com/2007/01/01/business/media/01carr.html.

29. Leo Burnett Worldwide, "Save the Troy Library: Adventures in Reverse Psychology," YouTube video, 2:53, November 15, 2011, http://www.youtube.com/watch?v=nw3zNNO5gX0. See also "Leo Burnett Worldwide Takes Home 23 Awards on the First Day of Cannes," PR Newswire, http://www.prnewswire.com/news-releases/leo-burnett-worldwide-takes-home-23-awards-on-the-first-day-of-cannes-159605035.html.

30. Figures for Enfield Public Library, Enfield, Connecticut, Henry Dutcher, director, 2011.

31. Hector Tobar, "The Disgraceful Interrogation of L.A. School Librarians," *Los Angeles Times*, May 13, 2011, http://articles.latimes.com/2011/may/13/local/la-me-0513-tobar-20110513.

32. Anna Jane Grossman, "Is Junie B. Jones Talking Trash?" *New York Times*, July 26, 2007, http://www.nytimes.com/2007/07/26/fashion/26junie.html.

33. Jack Hitt, "The Theory of Supermarkets," *New York Times Magazine*, March 10, 1996.

34. Robin Fields and Melinda Fulmer, "Markets' Shelf Fees Put Squeeze on Small Firms," *Los Angeles Times*, January 29, 2000.

35. Jann Sorrell Fractor et al., "Let's Not Miss Opportunities to Promote Voluntary Reading: Classroom Libraries in the Elementary School," *Reading Teacher* 46, no. 6 (1993): 476–84.

36. Mary B. W. Tabor, "In Bookstore Chains, Display Space Is for Sale," *New York Times*, January 15, 1996.

37. Julie Bosman, "To Lure 'Twilight' Teenagers, Classic Books Get Bold Looks," *New York Times*, June 28, 2012.

38. Jonathan Yardley, *Our Kind of People: The Story of an American Family* (New York: Weidenfeld & Nicholson, 1989), p. 288.

39. Catherine Sheldrick Ross, "If They Read Nancy Drew, So What? Series Book Readers Talk Back," *Library and Information Science Research* 17, no. 3 (1995): 201–36. This research won the American Library Association's research award in 1995. A shortened version appears in *School Library Media Quarterly*, Spring 1996, pp. 165–71. See also Suzanne M. Stauffer, "Developing Children's Interest in Reading." *Library Trends* 56, no. 2 (2007): 402–42.

40. Roger Kimball, "Closing Time? Jacques Barzun on Western Culture," New Criterion, June 2000; www.newcriterion.com/articles.cfm/jacques-barzun-at-100-3697.

41. Ross, "If They Read Nancy Drew, So What?"

Notes 319

42. Carlsen and Sherrill, *Voices of Readers: How We Come to Love Books.*
43. David A. Bell, "The Bookless Library," August 2, 2012, *The New Republic*, www.tnr.com/article/books-and-arts/magazine/david-bell-future -bookless-library.
44. Seth Godin, "The Future of the Library," *Seth Godin's Blog*, May 16, 2011, http://sethgodin.typepad.com/seths_blog/2011/05/the-future-of-the -library.html.
45. Jason Boog, "eBook Revenues Top Hardcover," *Galleycat* (blog), Mediabistro, June 15, 2012, http://www.mediabistro.com/galleycat/ebooks-top -hardcover-revenues-in-q1_b53090.
46. Matt Richtel and Julie Bosman, "For Their Children, Many E-Book Fans Insist on Paper," *New York Times*, November 20, 2011.
47. Julie Bosman, "A Children's Story Series: Will a Game Help Books?" *New York Times*, December 20, 2011.
48. Audrey Watters, "School Libraries Struggle with E-Book Loans," *Mind/Shift* (blog), KQED Public Radio, September 15, 2011, http://mindshift .kqed.org/2011/09/school-libraries-struggle-with-e-book-loans/.
49. The original spoof page is at http://zapatopi.net/treeoctopus/.
50. Donald Leu, David Reinking, Julie Coiro et al., "Defining Online Reading Comprehension: Using Think Aloud Verbal Protocols to Refine a Preliminary Model of Internet Reading Comprehension Processes," presented at the Annual Meeting of the American Educational Research Conference, Chicago, April 9, 2007, http://docs.google.com/Doc?id=dcbjhrtq _10djqrhz; and Beth Krane, "Researchers Find Kids Need Better Online Academic Skills," *UConn Advance*, November 13, 2006, http://advance .uconn.edu/2006/061113/06111308.htm. See also "Pacific Northwest Tree Octopus," Wikipedia, http://en.wikipedia.org/wiki/Pacific_Northwest _tree_octopus.
51. Steve Kolowich, "What Students Don't Know," *Inside Higher Ed* (blog), August 22, 2011, http://www.insidehighered.com/news/2011/08/22/ erial_study_of_student_research_habits_at_illinois_university_libraries _reveals_alarmingly_poor_information_literacy_and_skills. See also Lynda M. Duke and Andrew D. Asher, eds., *College Libraries and Student Culture: What We Now Know* (Chicago: ALA Editions, 2011).
52. A built-in "detector" would be deep background knowledge, usually achieved through extensive reading, something largely lacking in today's youth.
53. Julie Bosman, "After 244 Years, Encyclopaedia Britannica Stops the Presses," *Media Decoder* (blog), *New York Times*, March 13, 2012, http://me diadecoder.blogs.nytimes.com/2012/03/13/after-244-years -encyclopaedia-britannica-stops-the-presses/.
54. Jim Giles, "Special Report Internet Encyclopaedias Go Head to Head," *Nature* 438 (December 15, 2005), http://www.nature.com/nature/journal/ v438/n7070/full/438900a.html. See also Dan Goodin, "'Nature': Wikipedia Is Accurate," Associated Press, December 14, 2005, http://www.usa today.com/tech/news/2005-12-14-nature-wiki_x.htm; and Rebecca J. Rosen, "Does Wikipedia Have an Accuracy Problem?" *The Atlantic*,

February 16, 2012, http://www.theatlantic.com/technology/archive/2012/02/does-wikipedia-have-an-accuracy-problem/253216/.

55. Bill Keller, "Steal This Column," *New York Times*, February 6, 2012.

Chapter 7: Digital Learning:
Good News and Bad

1. Dalton Conley, "Wired for Distraction: Kids and Social Media," *Time*, March 19, 2011.

2. "Textbook Weight in California: Analysis and Recommendations," California State Board of Education (2004), http://www2.cde.ca.gov/be/ag/ag/may04item21.pdf.

3. "Download Free Books from Gutenberg.org to Kindle on iPad," YouTube video, 2:02, January 21, 2011, http://www.youtube.com/watch?v=NHon EWPN2x8.

4. http://www.pbs.og/wgbh/americanexperience/films/memphis/.

5. Khan Academy is an extremely popular online free turtoring service consisting of more than 3,300 math, science, and history tutorials. See Clive Thompson, "How Khan Academy Is Changing the Rules of Education," *Wired*, August 2011. See also Steve Kolowich, "The Problem Solvers," *Inside Higher Ed* (blog), December 7, 2011, http://www.insidehighered.com/news/2011/12/07/khan-academy-ponders-what-it-can-teach-higher-education-establishment; Erin Klein, "New iPad App Lets Any Teacher Be Like Sal Khan," *Edudemic* (blog), December 21, 2011, http://edudemic.com/2011/12/educreations/; "Khan Academy: The Future of Education?" *60 Minutes* video, 13:27, March 11, 2012, http://www.cbsnews.com/video/watch/?id=7401696n; and "Salman Khan of Khanacademy.org," *Charlie Rose* video, 22:00, May 4, 2011, http://www.clicker.com/tv/charlie-rose/salman-khan-of-khanacademy-org-1740074/.

6. Jim Sadwith, "Meeting Salinger," interview by Dick Gordon, *The Story*, American Public Media, July 9, 2009, http://thestory.org/archive/the_story_812_Meeting_Salinger.mp3/view.

7. Kara Yorio, "Author Signings Are Going Digital," *The Record*, June 3, 2012, http://www.northjersey.com/arts_entertainment/156881955_Author_signings_are_going_digital.html.

8. Noam Cohen, "A Digital Critique of a Famous Autobiography," *New York Times*, May 9, 2011.

9. Jan M. Noyes and Kate J. Garland, "Computer- vs. Paper-Based Tasks: Are They Equivalent?" *Ergonomics* 51, no. 9 (2008): 1352–75, http://www.princeton.edu/~sswang/Noyes_Garland_computer_vs_paper.pdf.

10. Mark Changizi, "The Problem with the Web and E-Books Is That There's No Space for Them," *Nature, Brain, and Culture* (blog), *Psychology Today*, February 7, 2011, http://www.psychologytoday.com/blog/nature-brain-and-culture/201102/the-problem-the-web-and-e-books-is-there-s-no-space-them. See also Maia Szalavitz, "Do E-Books Make It Harder to Remember What You Just Read?" *Time Healthland*, March 14, 2012, http://healthland.time.com/2012/03/14/do-e-books-impair-memory/; Lorien Crow, "Are E-Books Bad for Your Memory?" *Mobiledia*, March 15,

2012, http://www.mobiledia.com/news/133298.html; and Kate Garland and Jan Noyes, "Attitudes and Confidence Towards Computers and Books as Learning Tools: A Cross-Sectional Study of Student Cohorts," *British Journal of Educational Technology* 36, no. 1 (2005): 85–91.

11. In a 2009 study for Britain's Royal Mail, an MRI study was done to see if there were differences in how the brain processed paper images versus digital images (normal and scrambled images). Among the findings were that paper images stimulated more response in brain areas that processed visual and spatial information, as well as areas involving emotional responses. Both brain areas enhance later recall of information. Conclusion: "Physical material is more 'real' to the brain. It has a meaning, and a place. . . . Tangible materials leave a deeper footprint in the brain" than do the virtual. "Using Neuroscience to Understand the Role of Direct Mail," Millward Brown and Bangor University, 2009, http://www.millward brown.com/Libraries/MB_Case_Studies_Downloads/MillwardBrown _CaseStudy_Neuroscience.sflb.ashx.

12. Tamar Lewin, "For Many Public Universities, Fight at Virginia Is All Too Familiar," *New York Times*, June 26, 2012. See also Tamar Lewin, "Universities Reshaping Education on the Web," *New York Times*, July 17, 2012.

13. Cathy N. Davidson, *Now You See it: How the Brain Science of Attention Will Transform the Way We Live, Work, and Learn* (New York: Viking, 2011). For a short video presentation by Davidson, see "Shifting Attention," YouTube video, 2:49, August 16, 2011, http://www.youtube.com/watch?v=eG3HpEN9Y8E. See also "Cathy N. Davidson on Evolving Education," *Spark* (blog), CBC Radio, September 2, 2011, www.cbc.ca/spark/2011/09/full-interview-cathy-n-davidson-on-evolving-education/.

14. Nate Stulman, "The Great Campus Goof-off Machine," *New York Times*, March 15, 1999.

15. Winnie Hu, "Seeing No Progress, Some Schools Drop Laptops," *New York Times*, May 4, 2007. See also Matt Richtel, "Wasting Time Is New Divide in Digital Era," *New York Times*, May 30, 2012.

16. Stephanie Reitz, "Many Schools Adding iPads, Trimming Textbooks," Associated Press, *Springfield Republican*, September 4, 2011.

17. Matt Richtel, "In Classroom of Future, Stagnant Scores," *New York Times*, September 3, 2011.

18. Mark Dynarski, Roberto Agodini et al., *Effectiveness of Reading and Mathematics Software Products: Findings from the First Student Cohort*, Washington, DC: U.S. Department of Education, Institute of Education Sciences (2007), http://ies.ed.gov/ncee/pdf/20074006.pdf; Daniel Sheehan, Catherine Maloney, and Fanny Caranikas-Walker, "Evaluation of the Texas Technology Immersion Pilot: Final Outcomes for a Four-Year Study (2004–08)," Austin, Texas: Texas Center for Educational Research (2009), www.tcer.org/research/etxtip/documents/y4_etxtip_final.pdf; What Works Clearinghouse, "Effectiveness of Reading and Mathematics Software Products: Findings for Two Student Cohorts," U.S. Department of Education, Institute of Education Sciences, http://ies.ed.gov/ncee/wwc/pdf/quick_reviews/rms_032310.pdf; and Barbara Means, Yukie Toyama, Robert Murphy, Marianne Bakia, and

Karla Jones, "Evaluation of Evidence-Based Practices in Online Learning: A Meta-Analysis and Review of Online Learning Studies," Washington, DC: U.S. Department of Education, Office of Planning, Evaluation, and Policy Development (2010), http://www2.ed.gov/rschstat/eval/tech/evidence-based-practices/finalreport.pdf.

19. Trip Gabriel and Matt Richtel, "Inflating the Software Report Card," *New York Times*, October 9, 2011.

20. Center for Research on Education Outcomes (CREDO), "Charter School Performance in Pennsylvania," Stanford University (2011), http://credo.stanford.edu/. See also John Tulenko, "Online Public Schools Gain Popularity, but Quality Questions Persist," PBS Newshour video, 13:21, February 23, 2012, http://www.pbs.org/newshour/bb/education/jan-june12/cyberschools_02-23.html.

21. Valerie Strauss, "Whose Children Have Been Left Behind? Framing the 2012 Ed Debate," *Answer Sheet* (blog), *Washington Post*, January 3, 2012, quoting Dr. Diane Ravitch, education historian, speaking at a December 2011 national education conference in Washington, http://www.washingtonpost.com/blogs/answer-sheet/post/whose-children-have-been-left-behind-framing-the-2012-ed-debate/2012/01/02/gIQAz3nDXP_blog.html.

22. Walter Isaacson, *Steve Jobs* (New York: Simon & Schuster, 2010), pp. 553–54.

23. Matt Richtel, "A Silicon Valley School That Doesn't Compute," *New York Times*, October 23, 2011. Richtel's article came almost a year after a lengthier piece ran in *San Francisco* Magazine with more details of Silicon Valley familes' philosophy on education, including genuine concerns that some of the gadgets are plain bad for children; see Dan Fost, "Tech Gets a Time-out," *San Francisco*, March 2010, http://www.modernluxury.com/san-francisco/story/tech-gets-time-out; and Rehema Ellis, "The Waldorf Way: Silicon Valley School Eschews Technology over iPads," *NBC News*, November 30, 2011, http://dailynightly.msnbc.msn.com/_news/2011/11/30/9118340-the-waldorf-way-silicon-valley-school-eschews-technology.

24. "U.S. Teen Mobile Report: Calling Yesterday, Texting Today, Using Apps Tomorrow," *NielsenWire* (blog), October 14, 2010, http://blog.nielsen.com/nielsenwire/online_mobile/u-s-teen-mobile-report-calling-yesterday-texting-today-using-apps-tomorrow/. See also Katie Hafner, "Texting May Be Taking a Toll," *New York Times*, May 25, 2009; and Amanda Lenhart, "Teens, Cell Phones and Texting," Pew Research Center's Internet and American Life Project, April 20, 2010, http://www.pewinternet.org/~/media//Files/Reports/2010/PIP-Teens-and-Mobile-2010-with-topline.pdf.

25. Rideout, Foehr, and Roberts, *Generation M2*.

26. Eyal Ophir, Clifford Nass, and Anthony D. Wagner, "Cognitive Control in Media Multitaskers," Depts. of Communication and Psychology and Neurosciences, Stanford University, Stanford, CA, July 20, 2009, http://www.pnas.org/content/early/2009/08/21/0903620106.full.pdf+html.

27. Marcel Adam Just, Timothy A. Keller, and Jacquelyn Cynkar, "A Decrease in Brain Activation Associated with Driving When Listening to Someone

Speak," *Brain Research* 1205 (2008): 70–80, http://www.distraction.gov/research/PDF-Files/carnegie-mellon.pdf.

28. William Deresiewicz, "The End of Solitude," *Chronicle of Higher Education,* January 30, 2009, http://chronicle.com/article/The-End-of-Solitude/3708.

29. M. Csikszentmihalyi and K. Sawyer, "Creative Insight: The Social Dimension of a Solitary Moment," in R. Sternberg and J. Davidson, eds., *The Nature of Insight* (Cambridge, MA: MIT Press, 1996), pp. 329–61.

30. Jonah Lehrer, "The Virtues of Daydreaming," *Frontal Cortex* (blog), *The New Yorker,* June 5, 2012, http://www.newyorker.com/online/blogs/frontal-cortex/2012/06/the-virtues-of-daydreaming.html.

31. Marc Berman, Stephen Kaplan, and John Jonides, "The Cognitive Benefits of Interacting with Nature," *Psychological Science* 19, no. 12 (2008): 1207–12. See also Eric Jaffe, "This Side of Paradise: Discovering Why the Human Mind Needs Nature," *Observer,* May/June 2010, http://www.psychologicalscience.org/observer/getArticle.cfm?id=2679.

32. Matt Richtel, "Digital Devices Deprive Brain of Needed Downtime," *New York Times,* August 24, 2010, http://www.nytimes.com/2010/08/25/technology/25brain.html. See also Loren Frank, one of the neuroscientists doing research on downtime and learning among rats, can be heard in an interview on WNYC at http://www.wnyc.org/shows/bl/2010/aug/26/open-phones-mental-down-time/.

33. Hafner, "Texting May Be Taking a Toll."

34. Nicholas Carr, *The Shallows: What the Internet Is Doing to Our Brains,* (New York: W. W. Norton, 2010), pp. 122, 127-30. If true, this doesn't bode well for districts like Munster, Indiana, which converted all of its grade 5–12 curriculum to laptop-accessible versions; see Alan Schwarz, "Out with Textbooks, In with Laptops for an Indiana School District," *New York Times,* October 19, 2011.

35. Torkel Klingberg, *The Overflowing Brain: Information Overload and the Limits of Working Memory,* trans. Neil Betteridge (Oxford: Oxford University Press, 2009), pp. 72–75. See also Julie Bosman and Matt Richtel, "Finding Your Book Interrupted . . . By the Tablet You Read It On," *New York Times,* March 5, 2012.

36. Klingberg, *The Overflowing Brain,* pp. 129–31.

37. Ibid., pp. 133–35.

38. Martin Langeveld, "Print Is Still King: Only 3 Percent of Newspaper Reading Actually Happens Online," *Nieman Journalism Lab* (blog), April 13, 2009, http://www.niemanlab.org/2009/04/print-is-still-king-only-3-percent-of-newspaper-reading-actually-happens-online/. See also Ryan Chittum, "Print Newspapers Still Dominate Readers' Attention," *The Audit* (blog), *Columbia Journalism Review,* July 30, 2009, http://www.cjr.org/the_audit/newspapers_time_spent.php; and Hal Varian, "Newspaper Economics: Online and Offline," *Google Public Policy Blog,* Google, March 9, 2010, http://googlepublicpolicy.blogspot.com/2010/03/newspaper-economics-online-and-offline.html.

39. Bob Sutton, "Larry Page, My Wife's Lament, and Reading on Books vs. Screens," *Work Matters* (blog), comment by Karole Sutherland, February

23, 2012, http://bobsutton.typepad.com/my_weblog/2012/02/larry-page-my-wifes-lament-and-reading-on-books-vs-screens.html.

Chapter 8: Television and Audio: Hurting or Helping Literacy?

1. Jim Trelease offers a free single-page brochure for parents at his Web site that tells the story of Ben Carson, along with the story of Pulitzer Prize–winning journalist Leonard Pitts Jr. and his mother. Despite the ravages of American poverty, Mrs. Pitts did enough of the right things (as did Mrs. Carson) to raise a son who became one of the nation's top newspaper columnists. The brochure highlights the efforts of these two parents and what other parents can learn from them. Titled "Two Families Every Parent Should Meet," it is available at http://www.trelease-on-reading.com/brochures.html.
2. Rideout, Foehr, and Roberts, *Generation M2*.
3. Alan L. Mendelsohn, Samantha B. Berkule, Suzy Tomopoulos et al., "Infant Television and Video Exposure Associated with Limited Parent-Child Verbal Interactions in Low Socioeconomic Status Households," *Archives of Pediatrics and Adolescent Medicine* 162, no. 5 (2008): 411–17.
4. Dimitri A. Christakis, Frederick J. Zimmerman, David L. DiGiuseppe, and Carolyn A. McCarty, "Early Television Exposure and Subsequent Attentional Problems in Children," *Pediatrics* 113, no. 4 (2004): 708–13, http://www.aap.org/advocacy/releases/tvapril.pdf. See also Joseph Shapiro, "Study Links TV, Attention Disorders in Kids," *Morning Edition*, National Public Radio, April 5, 2004, http://www.npr.org/templates/story/story.php?storyId=1812501.
5. Linda Carroll, "The Problem with Some 'Smart Toys': (Hint) Use Your Imagination," *New York Times*, October 26, 2004. See also Tamar Lewin, "See Baby Touch Screen. But Does Baby Get It?" *New York Times*, December 15, 2005, p. 1.
6. Tamar Lewin, "No Einstein in Your Crib? Get a Refund," *New York Times*, October 24, 2009.
7. Dina L. G. Borzekowski and Thomas N. Robinson, "The Remote, the House, and the No. 2 Pencil," *Archives of Pediatrics and Adolescent Medicine* 159 (2005): 607–13.
8. Rideout, Foehr, and Roberts, *Generation M2*, pp. 15–16.
9. Ibid.
10. Ibid., p. 4.
11. Judith Owens et al., "Television-Viewing Habits and Sleep Disturbance in School Children," *Pediatrics* 104, no. 3 (1999): 552.
12. Pam Belluck, "Reason Is Sought for Lag by Blacks in School Effort," *New York Times*, July 4, 1999. See also Debra Viadero, "Even in Well-off Suburbs, Minority Achievement Lags," *Education Week*, March 15, 2000; Debra Viadero and Robert C. Johnston, "Lifting Minority Achievement: Complex Answers," *Education Week*, April 5, 2005; Debra Viadero, "Lags in Minority Achievement Defy Traditional Explanations," *Education Week*, March 22, 2000; and Abigail Thernstrom and Stephan Thernstrom,

No Excuses: Closing the Racial Gap in Learning (New York: Simon & Schuster, 2004).

13. Rideout, Foehr, and Roberts, *Generation M2*, p. 5. See also Donald Roberts, Ulla G. Foehr, Victoria Rideout, and Mollyann Brodie, *Kids and Media @ the New Millennium* (Menlo Park, CA: The Henry J. Kaiser Family Foundation, 1999).

14. Robert J. Hancox, Barry J. Milne, and Richie Poulton, "Association of Television Viewing During Childhood with Poor Educational Achievement," *Archives of Pediatrics and Adolescent Medicine* 159, no. 7 (2005): 614–18.

15. Tom Shachtman, *The Inarticulate Society: Eloquence and Culture in America* (New York: Free Press, 1995), pp. 115–35.

16. Stuart Webb and Michael P. H. Rodgers, "Vocabulary Demands of Television Programs," *Language Learning* 59, no. 2 (2009): 335–66.

17. Patricia A. Williams, Edward H. Haertel, Geneva D. Haertel, and Herbert J. Walberg, "The Impact of Leisure-Time Television on School Learning: A Research Synthesis," *American Educational Research Journal* 19, no. 1 (1982): 19–50.

18. Rideout, Foehr, and Roberts, *Generation M2*.

19. The brochure can be found in the list available at http://www.trelease -on-reading.com/brochures.html.

20. Rideout, Foehr, and Roberts, *Generation M2*, p. 39.

21. Ibid., p. 2.

22. Arthur M. Schlesinger Jr., *A Life in the Twentieth Century* (Boston: Houghton Mifflin, 2000).

23. Kirsch et al., *Reading for Change*. See also "OECD Pisa 2003 Results: Young Finns Still at the OECD Top," Finland's Ministry of Education (2003), http://www.oecd.org/dataoccd/1/60/34002216.pdf.

24. Hancock, "Why Are Finland's Schools Successful?" See also "The Finland Phenomenon"; Anderson, "From Finland, a Story of Educational Success"; Alvarez, "Suutarila Journal: Educators Flocking to Finland"; Coughlan, "Education Key to Economic Survival."

25. Elley, *How in the World Do Students Read?*

26. Susan B. Neuman and Patricia Koskinen, "Captioned Television as 'Comprehensible Input': Effects of Incidental Word Learning from Context for Language Minority Students," *Reading Research Quarterly* 27, no. 1 (1992): 95–106; P. S. Koskinen, R. M. Wilson, C. J. Jensema, "Using Closed-captioned Television in the Teaching of Reading to Deaf Students," *American Annals of the Deaf* 131 (1986): 43–46; Patricia S. Koskinen, Robert M. Wilson, Linda B. Gambrell, and Susan B. Neuman, "Captioned Video and Vocabulary Learning: An Innovative Practice in Literacy Instruction," *Reading Teacher* 47, no. 1 (1993) 36–43; Robert J. Rickelman, William A. Henk, and Kent Layton, "Closed-captioned Television: A Viable Technology for the Reading Teacher," *Reading Teacher* 44, no. 8 (1996): 598–99.

27. Anderson, "From Finland, a Story of Educational Success."

28. Helen Aron, "Bookworms Become Tapeworms: A Profile of Listeners to Books on Audiocassette," *Journal of Reading* 36, no. 3 (1992): 208–12.

29. Peter Osnos, "The Coming Audio Books Boom," *The Atlantic*, September 27, 2011, http://www.theatlantic.com/entertainment/archive/2011/09/the-coming-audiobooks-boom/245729/.

Chapter 9: Dad—What's the Score?

1. Jack Jennings, *Can Boys Succeed in Later Life If They Can't Read as Well as Girls?* (Washington, DC: Center on Education Policy, 2011).
2. Naomi Chudowsky and Victor Chudowsky, *Are There Differences in Achievement Between Boys and Girls?* (Washington, DC: Center on Education Policy, 2010), p. 6.
3. David Kohn, "The Gender Gap: Boys Lagging," *60 Minutes*, February 11, 2009, http://www.cbsnews.com/stories/2002/10/31/60minutes/main527678.shtml. See also Kevin Wack and Beth Quimby, "Boys in Jeopardy at School," *Portland Press Herald*, March 18, 2010, http://www.pressherald.com/archive/boys-in-jeopardy-at-school_2008-02-07.html.
4. U.S. Census Bureau, *Educational Attainment in the United States: 2009*, http://www.census.gov/hhes/socdemo/education/. See also Hanna Rosin, "The End of Men," *The Atlantic*, July/August, 2010, http://www.theatlantic.com/magazine/archive/2010/07/the-end-of-men/8135/.
5. Tom Chiarella, "The Problem with Boys . . . Is Actually a Problem with Men," *Esquire*, July 1, 2006, http://www.esquire.com/features/ESQ0706SOTAMBOYS_94.
6. Jay Mathews, "Are Boys Really in Trouble?" *Washington Post*, June 27, 2006, http://www.washingtonpost.com/wp-dyn/content/article/2006/06/27/AR2006062700638.html.
7. Wack and Quimby, "Boys in Jeopardy at School."
8. There is a whole cottage industry helping affluent families organize their disorganized boys; see Alan Finder, "Giving Disorganized Boys the Tools for Success," *New York Times*, January 1, 2008.
9. Thomas L. Friedman, *The World Is Flat* (New York: Farrar, Straus & Giroux, 2005); Thomas L. Friedman, "It's a Flat World, After All," *New York Times Magazine*, April 3, 2005. See also "For Workers, 'The World Is Flat,'" an interview with Friedman on *Fresh Air*, National Public Radio, April 14, 2005, http://www.npr.org/templates/story/story.php?storyId=4600258.
10. Rosin, "The End of Men." See also Thomas L. Friedman, "Average Is Over," *New York Times*, January 25, 2012.
11. Thomas L. Friedman, "Pass the Books, Hold the Oil," *New York Times*, March 11, 2012.
12. Doug Lederman, "Winning Football, Falling Grades," *Inside Higher Ed* (blog), December 20, 2011, http://www.insidehighered.com/news/2011/12/20/football-teams-win-male-students-grades-lose. See also Jason Lindo, Isaac Swensen, and Glen Waddell, "Are Big-time Sports a Threat to Student Achievement?" Working Paper No. 17677, National Bureau of Economic Research, December 2011, http://www.nber.org/papers/w17677.
13. See http://www.trelease-on-reading.com/wilt.html.

14. Clyde C. Robinson, Jean M. Larsen, and Julia H. Haupt, "Picture Book Reading at Home: A Comparison of Head Start and Middle-class Pre-schoolers," *Early Education and Development* 6, no. 3 (1995): 241–52.
15. Janelle M. Gray, "Reading Achievement and Autonomy as a Function of Father-to-Son Reading" (Master's thesis, California State University, Stanislaus, CA, 1991). See also the study of thirty men from blue-collar families. Half stayed blue-collar when they grew up and the other half became college professors; fathering made the difference: Olga Emery and Mihaly Csikszentmihalyi, "The Socialization Effects of Cultural Role Models in Ontogenetic Development and Upward Mobility," *Child Psychiatry and Development and Human Development* 12, no. 1 (1981): 3–18.
16. David Lubar, "Kid Appeal," quoted from Jon Scieszka, ed., *Guys Read: Funny Business* (New York: Walden Pond Press, 2010).

Chapter 10: A Hyper Kid's Road to Reading

1. Robert Lipsyte, "Boys and Reading: Is There Any Hope?" *New York Times Book Review*, August 19, 2011.
2. Johnson, "Confessions of a 'Bad' Teacher." See also Winerip, "Hard-Working Teachers."

Bibliography

Adams, Marilyn Jager. *Beginning to Read: Thinking and Learning About Print— A Summary.* Champaign-Urbana: University of Illinois, Center for the Study of Reading, 1990.

Allington, Richard. *Big Brother and the National Reading Curriculum: How Ideology Trumped Evidence.* Portsmouth, NH: Heinemann, 2002.

Anderson, Richard C., Elfrieda H. Hiebert, Judith A. Scott, and Ian A. G. Wilkinson. *Becoming a Nation of Readers: The Report of the Commission on Reading.* Champaign-Urbana: University of Illinois, Center for the Study of Reading, 1985.

Applebee, Arthur N., Judith A. Langer, Ina V. S. Mullis, Andrew S. Latham, and Claudia A. Gentile. *NAEP 1992 Writing Report Card.* Educational Testing Service. Washington, DC: U.S. Department of Education, 1994. http://www.eric.ed.gov/ERICWebPortal/contentdelivery/servlet/ERIC-Servlet?accno=ED370119.

Bae, Yupin, Susan Choy, Claire Geddes, Jennifer Sable, and Thomas Snyder. *Trends in Educational Equity of Girls and Women.* Washington, DC: U.S. Government Printing Office, 2000.

Barton, Paul E. *Parsing the Achievement Gap: Baselines for Tracking Progress.* Princeton, NJ: Educational Testing Service, 2003.

Barton, Paul E., and Richard J. Coley. *America's Smallest School: The Family.* Princeton, NJ: Educational Testing Service, 1992. http://www.ets.org/Media/Education_Topics/pdf/5678_PERCReport_School.pdf.

———. *Captive Students: Education and Training in America's Prisons.* Princeton, NJ: Educational Testing Service, Policy Information Center, 1996.

Barzun, Jacques. *Begin Here.* Chicago: University of Chicago Press, 1991.

Beatty, Alexandra S., Clyde M. Reese, Hilary R. Persky, and Peggy Carr. *NAEP 1994 U.S. History Report Card.* Washington, DC: U.S. Department of Education, Office of Educational Research and Improvement, 1994.

Berliner, David C., and Bruce J. Biddle. *The Manufactured Crisis.* Reading, MA: Addison-Wesley, 1996.

Bradshaw, Tom, Bonnie Nichols, Kelly Hill, and Mark Bauerlein. *Reading at Risk: A Survey of Literary Reading in America.* Washington, DC: National Endowment for the Arts, Research Division, Report No. 46, 2004.

Bruer, John T. *The Myth of the First Three Years.* New York: Free Press/Simon & Schuster, 1999.

Bruner, Jerome S., Allison Jolly, and Kathy Sylva, eds. *Play—Its Role in Development and Evolution.* New York: Penguin, 1976.

Butler, Dorothy. *Cushla and Her Books.* Boston: Horn Book, 1980.

Cain, Susan. *Quiet: The Power of Introverts in a World That Can't Stop Talking.* New York: Crown, 2012.

Campbell, Jay R., Catherine M. Hombo, and John Mazzeo. *NAEP 1999 Trends in Academic Progress: Three Decades of Student Performance.* U.S. Department of Education. Washington, DC: National Center for Education Statistics, 2000. Also available at http://nces.ed.gov/nationsreportcard.

Carlsen, G. Robert, and Anne Sherrill. *Voices of Readers: How We Come to Love Books.* Urbana, IL: National Council of Teachers of English, 1988. http://www.eric.ed.gov/PDFS/ED295136.pdf.

Carr, Nicholas. *The Shallows: What the Internet Is Doing to Our Brains.* New York: W. W. Norton, 2010.

Carson, Ben. *Gifted Hands: The Ben Carson Story.* Grand Rapids, MI: Zondervan, 1990.

Cazden, Courtney B. *Child Language and Education.* New York: Holt, Rinehart and Winston, 1972.

Children's Defense Fund, *The State of America's Children 2011 Report.* Washington, DC, 2011. http://www.childrensdefense.org/child-research-data -publications/state-of-americas-children-2011/.

Clark, Margaret M. *Young Fluent Readers.* London: Heinemann, 1976.

Coley, Richard J. *An Uneven Start: Indicators of Inequality in School Readiness.* Princeton, NJ: ETS, Policy Information Center, 2002.

Davidson, Cathy N. *Now You See it: How the Brain Science of Attention Will Transform the Way We Live, Work, and Learn.* New York: Viking, 2011.

Davies, Robertson. *One Half of Robertson Davies.* New York: Viking, 1977.

Davis, Sampson, George Jenkins, Rameck Hunt, and Lisa Frazier Page. *The Pact: Three Young Men Make a Promise and Fulfill a Dream.* New York: Riverhead, 2003.

Denton, Kristen, and Jerry West. *Children's Reading and Mathematics Achievement in Kindergarten and First Grade.* Washington, DC: U.S. Department of Education, NCES, 2002. http://nces.ed.gov/pubsearch/pubsinfo.asp?pubid= 2002125.

Donahue, Patricia L., Kristin E. Voelki, Jay R. Campbell, and John Mazzeo. *NAEP 1998 Reading Report Card for the Nation and the States.* Washington, DC: U.S. Department of Education, NCES, 1999.

Dreyer, Phillip, ed. *Vision and Realities in Literacy: Sixtieth Yearbook of the Claremont Reading Conference.* Claremont, CA: Claremont Reading Conference, 1996.

Durkin, Dolores. *Children Who Read Early.* New York: Teachers College, 1966.

Dynarski, Mark, Roberto Agodini et al. *Effectiveness of Reading and Mathematics Software Products: Findings from the First Student Cohort.* Washington, DC: U.S. Department of Education, Institute of Education Sciences, 2007.

Elkind, David. *The Hurried Child: Growing Up Too Fast Too Soon.* 3rd ed. Cambridge, MA: Perseus/DaCapo, 2001.

Elley, Warwick B. *How in the World Do Students Read?* Hamburg: International Association for the Evaluation of Educational Achievement, 1992. Available from ERIC at http://www.eric.ed.gov/. Use ERIC search # ED360613.

Ferguson, Ronald F. *What Doesn't Meet the Eye: Understanding and Addressing Racial Disparities in High-Achieving Suburban Schools.* Northern Central Regional Educational Laboratory, 2002.

Foertsch, Mary A. *Reading In and Out of School.* Educational Testing Service/Education Information Office. Washington, DC: U.S. Department of Education, 1992.

Friedman, Howard S., and Leslie R. Martin. *The Longevity Project: Surprising Discoveries for Health and Long Life from the Landmark Eight-Decade Study.* New York: Hudson Street Press, 2011.

Friedman, Thomas L. *The World Is Flat.* New York: Farrar, Straus & Giroux, 2005.

Garan, Elaine M. *In Defense of Our Children: When Politics, Profit, and Education Collide.* Portsmouth, NH: Heinemann, 2004.

———. *Resisting Mandates.* Portsmouth, NH: Heinemann, 2002.

Gawande, Atul. *The Checklist Manifesto: How to Get Things Right.* New York: Metropolitan Books, 2009.

Goleman, Daniel. *Emotional Intelligence: Why It Can Matter More Than IQ.* New York: Bantam, 1995.

Goodman, Kenneth, Patrick Shannon, Yvonne Freeman, and S. Murphy. *Report Card on Basal Readers.* New York: Richard Owen, 1988.

Gopnik, Alison, Andrew N. Meltzoff, and Patricia K. Kuhl. *The Scientist in the Crib.* New York: Morrow, 1999.

Graff, Harvey. *The Literacy Myth.* San Diego, CA: Academic, 1979.

Hart, Betty, and Todd Risley. *Meaningful Differences in the Everyday Experience of Young American Children.* Baltimore, MD: Brookes Publishing, 1996.

Heyns, Barbara. *Summer Learning and the Effects of Schooling.* New York: Academic Press, 1978.

Hodgkinson, Harold L. *The Same Client: The Demographics of Education and Service Delivery Systems.* Washington, DC: Institute of Educational Leadership, 1989.

Hout, Michael, and Stuart W. Elliott. *Incentives and Test-Based Accountability in Education.* National Research Council. Washington, DC: National Academies Press, 2011.

Institute of Education Sciences, U.S. Department of Education. *The Nation's Report Card: Reading 2011* (NCES 2012–457). Washington, DC: National Center for Education Statistics, 2011.

Isaacson, Walter. *Steve Jobs*. New York: Simon & Schuster, 2010.

Kamil, M. L., P. B. Mosenthal, P. David Pearson, and R. Barr, eds. *Handbook of Reading Research*. Vol. 3. New York: Erlbaum, 2000.

Kandel, Eric R., James H. Schwartz, and Thomas M. Jessell, eds. *Principles of Neural Science*. 3rd ed. Center for Neurobiology and Behavior, College of Physicians and Surgeons of Columbia University and the Howard Hughes Medical Institute. Norwalk, CT: Appleton & Lange, 1991.

Kirsch, Irwin, John de Jong, Dominique LaFontaine, Joy McQueen, Juliette Mendelovits, and Christian Monseur. *Reading for Change: Performance and Engagement Across Countries—Results from Pisa 2000*. Organisation for Economic Co-operation and Development (OECD). http://www.oecd .org/dataoecd/43/54/33690904.pdf.

Klingberg, Torkel. *The Overflowing Brain: Information Overload and the Limits of Working Memory*. Oxford: Oxford University Press, 2009.

Kohn, Alfie. *Punished by Rewards: The Trouble with Gold Stars, Incentive Plans, A's, Praise, and Other Bribes*. Boston: Houghton Mifflin, 1993.

Krashen, Stephen. *Free Voluntary Reading*. Santa Barbara, CA: Libraries Unlimited, 2011.

———. *The Power of Reading*. 2nd ed. Portsmouth, NH: Libraries Unlimited and Heinemann, 2004.

———. *Writing: Research: Theory and Applications*. Torrance, CA: Laredo Publishing Company, 1984.

Kubey, Robert, and Mihaly Csikszentmihalyi. *Television and the Quality of Life*. Hillsdale, NJ: Erlbaum, 1990.

Lance, Keith Curry, Lynda Welborn, and Christine Hamilton-Pennell. *The Impact of School Media Centers on Academic Achievement*. Englewood, CO: Libraries Unlimited, 1993.

Lance, Keith Curry, Marcia J. Rodney, and Christine Hamilton-Pennell. *How School Librarians Help Kids Achieve Standards: The Second Colorado Study*. Denver: Colorado State Library, 2000.

Lee, E., and David T. Burkam. *Inequality at the Starting Gate: Social Background Differences in Achievement as Children Begin School*. Washington, DC: Economic Policy Institute, 2002.

Marmot, Michael. *The Status Syndrome: How Social Standing Affects Our Health and Longevity*. New York: Times Books, 2004.

McQuillan, Jeff. *The Literary Crisis: False Claims, Real Solutions*. Portsmouth, NH: Heinemann, 1998.

Mogel, Wendy. *The Blessings of a B Minus: Using Jewish Teachings to Raise Resilient Teenagers*. New York: Scribner, 2010.

Mormino, Gary R., and George E. Pozzetta. *The Immigrant World of Ybor City: Italians and Their Latin Neighbors in Tampa, 1885–1985*. Gainesville: Florida Sand Dollar Books/University Press of Florida, 1998.

Mullis, Ina V. S., J. R. Campbell, and A. E. Farstrup. *NAEP 1992 Reading Report Card for the Nation and States*. Washington, DC: National Center for Education Statistics, U.S. Government Printing Office, 1993. http://timss .bc.edu/pirls2001i/PIRLS2001_Pubs_TrR.html.

Mullis, Ina, John A. Dossey, Jay R. Campbell, Claudia A. Gentile, Christine O'Sullivan, and Andrew Latham. *NAEP 1992 Trends in Aca-*

demic Progress. Washington, DC: Office of Educational Research and Improvement, U.S. Department of Education, 1994.

Mullis, Ina, Michael O. Martin, Eugene J. Gonzalez, and Ann M. Kennedy. *PIRLS 2001 International Report: IEA's Study of Reading Literacy Achievement in Primary School in 35 Countries.* Chestnut Hill, MA: International Association for the Evaluation of Educational/International Study Center, Boston College, 2003. http://pirls.bc.edu/isc/publications.html.

National Assessment of Educational Progress. *Literacy: Profiles of America's Young Adults.* Princeton, NJ: Educational Testing Service, 1987.

National Center for Education Statistics. *National Household Education Survey.* Washington, DC: U.S. Government Printing Office, 1999.

National Commission on Excellence in Education, Superintendent of Documents. *A Nation at Risk: The Imperative for Educational Reform.* Washington, DC: U.S. Government Printing Office, 1983. http://www2.ed.gov/pubs/NatAtRisk/index.html.

National Reading Panel. *Report of the National Reading Panel: Teaching Children to Read: An Evidence-Based Assessment of the Scientific Research Literature on Reading and Its Implications for Reading Instruction; Reports of the Subgroups.* Washington, D.C.: National Institute of Child Health and Human Development, NIH, Publication 00-4754, 2000.

National Survey of Student Engagement. *Fostering Student Engagement Campuswide—Annual Results 2011.* Bloomington: Indiana University Center for Postsecondary Research, 2011. http://nsse.iub.edu/NSSE_2011_Results/pdf/NSSE_2011_AnnualResults.pdf.

Neuman, Susan B., Donna C. Celano, Albert N. Greco, and Pamela Shue. *Access for All: Closing the Book Gap for Children in Early Education.* Newark, DE: International Reading Association, 2001.

Nichols, S. L., ed. *Educational Policy and the Socialization of Youth for the 21st Century.* New York: Teachers College Press, 2013.

Nielsen Media Research. *2000 Report on Television: The First 50 Years.* New York: Nielsen Media Research, 2000.

Niles, J. A., and L. A. Harris. *New Inquiries in Reading Research and Instruction.* Rochester, NY: National Reading Conference, 1982.

OECD. *PISA 2009 Results: Overcoming Social Background, Equity in Learning Opportunities and Outcomes (Volume II).* PISA, OECD Publishing, 2010. http://dx.doi.org/10.1787/9789264091504-en.

Ogbu, John U. *Black American Students in an Affluent Suburb: A Study of Academic Disengagement.* Mahwah, NJ: Erlbaum, 2003.

Ozma, Alice. *The Reading Promise: My Father and the Books We Shared.* New York: Grand Central, 2011.

Pamuk, E., D. Makuc, K. Heck, C. Reuben, and K. Lockner. *Health, United States, 1998: Socioeconomic Status and Health Chartbook.* Washington, DC: U.S. Government Printing Office, 1998.

Pearl, Nancy. *Book Lust: Recommended Reading for Every Mood, Moment, and Reason.* Seattle: Sasquatch Books, 2003.

———. *More Book Lust.* Seattle: Sasquatch Books, 2005.

Pearson, P. David, ed. *Handbook of Reading Research.* New York: Longman, 1984.

Perie, M., R. Moran, and A. D. Lutkus. *NAEP 2004 Trends in Academic Progress: Three Decades of Student Performance in Reading and Mathematics.* U.S. Department of Education, Institute of Education Sciences, National Center for Education Statistics. Washington, DC: U.S. Government Printing Office, 2005.

Pratt, Rebecca et al. *The Condition of Education 2000.* Washington, DC: U.S. Department of Education, NCES, 2000.

Rampey, B. D., G. S. Dion, and P. L. Donahue. *NAEP 2008 Trends in Academic Progress* (NCES 2009–479). U.S. Department of Education, Institute of Education Sciences, National Center for Education Statistics. Washington, DC: U.S. Government Printing Office, 2009.

Ravitch, Diane. *The Death and Life of the Great American School System: How Testing and Choice Are Undermining Education.* New York: Basic Books, 2010.

Rideout, Victoria J., Elizabeth A. Vandewater, and Ellen A. Wartella. *Zero to Six: Electronic Media in the Lives of Infants, Toddlers, and Preschoolers.* Menlo Park, CA: The Henry J. Kaiser Family Foundation, 2003. http://www.kff.org.

Rideout, Victoria J., Ulla G. Foehr, and Donald F. Roberts. *Generation M2: Media in the Lives of 8- to 18-Year-Olds.* Menlo Park, CA: The Henry J. Kaiser Family Foundation, 2010. http://www.kff.org.

Roberts, Donald F., Ulla G. Foehr, and Victoria Rideout. *Generation M: Media in the Lives of 8–18-Year-Olds.* Menlo Park, CA: The Henry J. Kaiser Family Foundation, 2005.

Roberts, Donald F., Ulla G. Foehr, Victoria Rideout, and Mollyann Brodie. *Kids and Media @ the New Millennium.* Menlo Park, CA: The Henry J. Kaiser Family Foundation, 1999.

Schlesinger, Arthur M. Jr. *A Life in the Twentieth Century.* Boston: Houghton Mifflin, 2000.

Schramm, Wilbur. *The Process and Effects of Mass Communication.* Urbana: University of Illinois Press, 1954.

Schramm, Wilbur, ed. *The Process and Effects of Mass Communication,* 6th ed. Urbana: University of Illinois Press, 1965.

Shachtman, Tom. *The Inarticulate Society: Eloquence and Culture in America.* New York: Free Press, 1995.

Snow, Catherine E., M. Susan Burns, and Peg Griffin, eds. *Preventing Reading Difficulties in Young Children.* Washington, DC: National Academy Press, 1998.

Snowdon, David. *Aging with Grace: What the Nun Study Teaches Us About Leading Longer, Healthier, and More Meaningful Lives.* New York: Bantam, 2001.

Stoll, Clifford. *Silicon Snake Oil.* New York: Doubleday, 1995.

Sum, Andrew et al. *Getting to the Finish Line: College Enrollment and Graduation, A Seven Year Longitudinal Study of the Boston Public Schools Class of 2000.* Center for Labor Market Studies. Boston: Northeastern University Press, 2008.

Susskind, Ron. *A Hope in the Unseen: An American Odyssey from the Inner City to the Ivy League.* New York: Random House, 1999.

Taylor, Gordon Rattray. *The Natural History of the Brain.* New York: Dutton, 1979.

Thernstrom, Abigail, and Stephan Thernstrom. *No Excuses: Closing the Racial Gap in Learning.* New York: Simon & Schuster, 2004.

Underhill, Paco. *Why We Buy: The Science of Shopping.* New York: Simon & Schuster, 1999.

U.S. Department of Education. *Trends in Educational Equity of Girls and Women.* Washington, DC: National Center for Education Statistics, 2000.

Vernez, Georges, Richard Krop, and C. Peter Ryde. *Closing the Education Gap: Benefits and Costs.* Santa Monica, CA: Rand Corporation, 1999.

West, Jerry, Kristin Denton, and Elvira Germino-Hausken. *America's Kindergartners: Findings from the Early Childhood Longitudinal Study, Kindergarten Class of 1998–99, Fall 1998.* Washington, DC: U.S. Department of Education, NCES, 2000.

Yardley, Jonathan. *Our Kind of People: The Story of an American Family.* New York: Weidenfeld & Nicholson, 1989.

Zill, Nicholas, and Marianne Winglee. *Who Reads Literature?* Cabin John, MD: Seven Locks Press, 1990. This is now available online from ERIC (Education Resources Information Center) using the ERIC search # ED302812, at http://www.eric.ed.gov/.

Subject Index
for the Text

Page numbers in bold indicate section devoted to a subject.
For books listed in the Treasury, see the Author-Illustrator Index, pp. 345–50.

Author-Illustrator Index
for the Treasury

Italics are for illustrator only; ★ after page number gives location of a group of books by an author or illustrator.

Photograph credits

Unless otherwise indicated, photographs are by Jim Trelease.

9: Cigar makers, used by permission of Tampa Hillsborough County Public Library System

49: Sterling A. Leonard and Harold Y. Moffett Junior Literature: Book Two (New York: The Macmillan Company, 1930)

50: Donald Powell Wilson, *My Six Convicts: A Psychologist's Three Years in Fort Leavenworth* (New York: Rinehart & Company, 1951).

Charts

3: Based on "NAEP 2008 Trends in Academic Progress," (NCES 2009–479), online at:http://nces .ed.gov/nationsreportcard/pdf/main2008/2009479.pdf

Kindergarten Children's Home/Behavior Inventory, by the author, "Based on "Home and School Correlates of Early Interest in Literature," *Journal of Educational Research*, April 1983

7: Based on "Where Is the Best Place to Invest $102,000—In Stocks, Bonds, or a College Degree?" The Hamilton Project/Brookings Institution, November 9, 2011, online at: http//www.brookings .edu/papers/2011/0625_education_greenstone_looney.aspx

8: Based on Richard J. Coley, *An Uneven Start: Indicators of Inequality in School Readiness* (Princeton, N.J. : Policy Information Center, ETS, 2002)
American Children (Baltim...

14: Based on Donald P. Hayes and Margaret G. Ahrens, "Vocabulary Simplification for Children: A Special Case for 'Motherese,'" *Journal of Child Language*, vol. 15, 1988, pp. 395–410

26: Based on findings by Center for Summer Learning, Johns Hopkins University

28: Based on the report *Reading for Change: Performance and Engagement Across Countries, Results from Pisa 2000*, Organisation for Economic Co-Operation and Development (OECD)

41: Based on the study "The Remote, the House, and the No.2 Pencil," *Archives of Pediatrics & Adolescent Medicine*, July 2005 (vol. 159)

42: Based on the study "Association of Television Viewing During Childhood with Poor Educational Achievement," *Archives of Pediatrics & Adolescent Medicine*, July 2005 (vol. 159)

AVAILABLE FROM PENGUIN

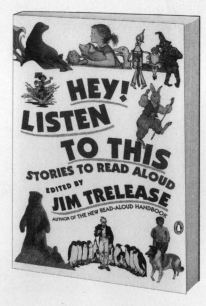

Hey! Listen to This
Edited by Jim Trelease

This beguiling anthology contains 48 read-aloud selections organized by subject and level of difficulty. An ideal resource for parents and teachers to share with children ages five through nine.

ISBN 978-0-14-014653-0

Great Stories, Poems, and Newspaper Pieces for Reading Aloud
Edited by Jim Trelease

From *Narrative of the Life of Frederick Douglass* to *Maniac Magee*, sci-fi to op-ed, this diverse collection of excerpts from newspapers, magazines, and books will turn young people on to the many pleasures of reading. With selections representing many different cultures, genres, writing styles, and interests, *Read All About It!* is a wonderful introduction to the riches of literature and to a lifetime of reading.

ISBN 978-0-14-014655-4

PENGUIN BOOKS